Frederick Douglass and Scotland, 1846

I am trying to preach and practice a genuine antislavery life, turning neither to the right or left, and I think not without success.

Frederick Douglass, Kilmarnock, 29 March, 1846

Frederick Douglass and Scotland, 1846

Living an Antislavery Life

Alasdair Pettinger

EDINBURGH
University Press

Edinburgh University Press is one of the leading university presses in the UK. We publish academic books and journals in our selected subject areas across the humanities and social sciences, combining cutting-edge scholarship with high editorial and production values to produce academic works of lasting importance. For more information visit our website: edinburghuniversitypress.com

Edinburgh University Press Ltd
The Tun – Holyrood Road
12(2f) Jackson's Entry
Edinburgh EH8 8PJ

First published in hardback by Edinburgh University Press 2019

Typeset in 11/14 Adobe Sabon by
IDSUK (DataConnection) Ltd, and
printed and bound by CPI Group (UK) Ltd,
Croydon, CR0 4YY

A CIP record for this book is available from the British Library

ISBN 978 1 4744 4425 5 (hardback)
ISBN 978 1 4744 4426 2 (paperback)
ISBN 978 1 4744 4427 9 (webready PDF)
ISBN 978 1 4744 4428 6 (epub)

Contents

for Jack

List of Figures and Maps

Figures

Maps

Acknowledgements

This book has been long in the making, longer even than David Octavius Hill's large painting of the first General Assembly of the Free Church of Scotland, and I have accumulated many debts along the way.

The initial spark came from a passing reference to Douglass's visit to Scotland in Paul Gilroy's *Black Atlantic* (1993), a book bristling with ideas which has shaped my thinking on slavery and abolitionism over the years since. A footnote sent me to George Shepperson, who, I discovered to my astonishment, wrote about Douglass and Scotland in the 1950s, foundations that C. Duncan Rice and Richard Blackett built on thirty years later. I soon became obsessed.

The first fruits of my research were presented at A Liberating Sojourn (1995), a conference at Keele University marking the 150th anniversary of Douglass's first visit to Britain and Ireland. And then at Frederick Douglass: At Home and Abroad (Washington, DC, 1999), which included a memorable visit to the Wye Plantation; and at Frederick Douglass and Herman Melville (New Bedford, Massachusetts, 2005), a few blocks from Nathan and Mary Johnson's house on Seventh Street. I have also tried out some of my thoughts on Douglass before audiences at the following universities: Liverpool Hope (Textports, 2000), Greifswald (Sea Changes, 2000), Aberdeen (Travel, Missions, Empire, 2001), Edinburgh (Across the Great Divide, 2003), Swansea (Transatlantic Exchange, 2007), Glasgow (8th Symbiosis Conference, 2011), Rostock (Agents of Transculturation, 2011) and York (African Intellectual Mobilities, 2015).

I am grateful to the organisers of these events and for the comments of participants, with special thanks to Gesa Mackenthun, Janet Remmington, Daniel Williams and especially Frank Farragasso, who organised the conference in DC and introduced me to the treasures of Cedar Hill, Douglass's home from 1877 until his death in 1895.

These occasions have allowed me to make the acquaintance of some brilliant Douglass scholars, who have transformed my understanding of his life and times, in particular Celeste-Marie Bernier and Fionnghuala Sweeney.

Visiting research fellowships at the University of Central Lancashire (2000), Nottingham Trent University (2004–7) and the University of Liverpool (2010–13) gave me access to academic resources otherwise out of reach of the general public. For that, thanks are due to Alan Rice, Tim Youngs and Charles Forsdick, who have given me many opportunities to speak and publish over the years. Alan deserves special mention for his unstinting support of this project, with words of wisdom and encouragement ever since we first crossed paths in Edinburgh in 1991. His engagement with researchers, artists and curators has helped to sustain a thriving informal network which continues to shed fresh light on Douglass's transatlantic connections. Another precious friend, Lisa Merrill, generously shared her work in progress and helped me appreciate the theatrical aspect of abolitionist activism.

I have learnt a great deal about slavery's place in Scottish history and literature from Stephen Mullen (whose suggestions and tip-offs were always spot-on) and Michael Morris (who kindly read and commented on a draft of Part III). Vicky Davidson was there from the start, and early on saw the potential for telling Douglass's story through the medium of radio, while Jim Muotune showed me the possibilities of historical re-enactment. The bold initiatives of the DRB Scottish Women's History Group and Hannah Murray's Frederick Douglass Map have also been an inspiration.

The staff of various libraries have been most helpful and patient with my requests and enquiries: Glasgow University Library, the National Library of Scotland, the Mitchell Library in Glasgow, Edinburgh University Library, University of Liverpool Library, the Carnegie Library in Ayr, Dundee Central Library, the Heritage Hub in Hawick and Paisley Central Library. I am grateful to Ka'mal McClarin at the Frederick Douglass National Historic Site at Cedar Hill for sending me scans of the edition of Burns presented to Douglass in 1846.

My many colleagues, past and present, at the Scottish Music Centre have kept me afloat with their unfailing support and irreverent humour. Little did I know when I started working there that it would later relocate to Glasgow's City Halls, where Douglass spoke to packed audiences nearly 200 years ago. I like to think that the proximity in space, if not in time, helped to keep me on track.

The Harding family have been generous in their encouragement and hospitality. I am especially grateful to Frances for her comments on early drafts and, above all, to Martha, who read every word more than once, and patiently helped me to better organise my thoughts and express myself more clearly, making connections I would never have made myself. She is my ideal reader and much else besides.

Finally, I dedicate this book to Jack, a most stimulating companion, whose interruptions joyfully rescued me from the discipline of the desk when it was time for other things to matter.

Abbreviations

People

FD	Frederick Douglass
GT	George Thompson
HCW	Henry Clarke Wright
JB	James Buffum
MWC	Maria Weston Chapman
RW	Richard Webb
WLG	William Lloyd Garrison

Organisations

AASS	American Anti-Slavery Society
AFASS	American and Foreign Anti-Slavery Society
ASL	Anti-Slavery League
BFASS	British and Foreign Anti-Slavery Society
FCS	Free Church of Scotland
GES	Glasgow Emancipation Society

Dramatis Personae

Key individuals whom Douglass encountered or corresponded with, 1845–7. Those marked with an asterisk did not travel to Britain or Ireland during this period.

Frederick DOUGLASS

James BUFFUM, *his companion*

The HUTCHINSON SINGERS, *singing group from New Hampshire*

Captain Charles H. E. JUDKINS *of the British and North American Steam-Packet Company*

Charles MacIVER, *Liverpool Agent of the British and North American Steam-Packet Company*

American Abolitionists

Henry Clarke WRIGHT, *abolitionist and peace campaigner of Massachusetts*

William Lloyd GARRISON, *editor of the* Liberator, *abolitionist of Boston*

*Maria Weston CHAPMAN
*Edmund QUINCY } *abolitionists of Boston*

*Francis JACKSON

*Anna DOUGLASS, *wife of Frederick DOUGLASS*

*Ruth COX, *their adopted daughter ('Harriet')*

*Abigail MOTT, *family friend in Albany, tutor to the Douglasses' eldest daughter Rosetta*

American Slaveholders

*Thomas AULD *of Talbot County, Maryland; owner of Frederick DOUGLASS from 1827–45*

*Hugh AULD, *his brother, of Fells Point, Baltimore, owner of Frederick DOUGLASS from 1845–6*

*Sophia AULD, *wife of Hugh AULD*

*A. C. C. THOMPSON *of Wilmington, Delaware*

British and Irish Abolitionists

George THOMPSON, *abolitionist of London*

John MURRAY
William SMEAL } *abolitionists of Glasgow*

Jane WIGHAM, *his sister*
Eliza WIGHAM, *her daughter-in-law* } *abolitionists of Edinburgh*

Richard WEBB
William HAUGHTON } *abolitionists of Dublin*

Elizabeth PEASE, *abolitionist of Darlington*

Anna RICHARDSON, *abolitionist of Newcastle*

Henry RICHARDSON, *her husband*

Ellen RICHARDSON, *his sister*

John B. ESTLIN, *abolitionist of Bristol*

Joseph STURGE, *Secretary of the British and Foreign Anti-Slavery Society*

George GILFILLAN, *United Secession Church, School Wynd, Dundee*

Patrick BREWSTER, *Church of Scotland, Abbey Church, Paisley*

Free Church of Scotland and its Supporters

Thomas CHALMERS, *Principal of New College, Free Church of Scotland*

Robert CANDLISH, *Free Church Minister, St George's Church, Edinburgh*

William CUNNINGHAM, *Chair of Church History, New College; Leader of Free Church Delegation to the United States*

George LEWIS, *St David's Church, Dundee* ⎫ *Members of the Free*
Robert BURNS, *Laigh Kirk, Paisley* ⎬ *Church Delegation to*
⎭ *the United States*

Michael WILLIS, *Renfield Church, Glasgow* ⎫ *Members of the*
James MACBETH, *Lauriston Church, Glasgow* ⎬ *Free Church Anti-*
⎭ *Slavery Society*

John M'NAUGHTAN, *Free Church Minister, High Church, Paisley*

Hugh MILLER, *editor of the* Witness

Thomas SMYTH, *Second Presbyterian Church, Charleston, South Carolina*

Others

George COMBE, *phrenologist*

Daniel O'CONNELL, *Irish political leader*

Isabella BURNS BEGG, *sister of the poet Robert Burns*

Elihu BURRITT, *social reformer of Connecticut, founder of the League of Brotherhood (1846)*

Molliston Madison CLARK, *African Methodist Episcopal Church delegate to the Evangelical Alliance*

Part I

The Voyage

People who have never gone to sea [. . .] can not imagine how puzzling and confounding it is. It must be like going into a barbarous country, where they speak a strange dialect, and dress in strange clothes, and live in strange houses.

Herman Melville, Redburn

Chapter 1

'Throw Him Overboard'

'That's a lie,' called out Mr Hazzard from Connecticut.

As was the custom on the last evening of the eleven-day voyage, the meal-hour was extended, wine was served at table and spirits ran high, prompting several extra courses of congratulatory speeches. Holyhead Mountain appeared faintly on the horizon, and diners went outdoors to cool their heads, heated with champagne and verbosity. One of the stewards rang a hand-bell, summoning them to the promenade deck. At the invitation of Captain Judkins, a passenger who had till then kept largely to himself prepared to address them. Copies of his newly published autobiography had been passed around the ship during the past ten days. No doubt many of those who had perused the *Narrative of the Life of Frederick Douglass, An American Slave, Written by Himself* were looking forward to hearing eloquent and moving testimony from the author in person.

Douglass barely had time to speak before the man stepped forward. 'That's a lie.' And each time Douglass tried to resume, Hazzard repeated his objection. It was impossible for Douglass to proceed. But, encouraged by his supporters, the lecturer came out from under the awning to stand by the main mast.

'Well, ladies and gentlemen,' he said. 'Since what I have said has been pronounced lies, I will read, not what I have written, but what the southern legislators themselves have written – I mean the law.' He took up the book he was holding and began:

'If more than seven slaves are found together in any road, without a white person, twenty lashes a piece; for visiting a plantation without a written pass, ten lashes; for letting loose a boat from where it is made fast, thirty-nine lashes for the first offence, and for the second, shall have cut from off his head one ear; for keeping or carrying a club, thirty-nine lashes; for having any article for sale without a ticket from his master, ten lashes; for travelling in any other than the most usual and accustomed roads, when going alone to any place, forty lashes; for being found in another person's negro quarters, forty lashes; for hunting with dogs in the woods, thirty lashes; for being on horseback without the written permission of his master, twenty-five lashes; for riding or going abroad in the night, or riding horses in the day time, without leave, a slave may be whipped, cropped, or branded on the cheek with the letter R, or otherwise punished, not extending to life, or so as to render him unfit for labor.'

But this tactic only provoked his opponents more. 'Down with the nigger,' said one. 'He shan't speak,' said another. They closed in on him, raised their fists and swore to silence him. Other passengers rushed to Douglass's defence, but the threats only grew more menacing. 'Oh, I wish I had you in Cuba,' bawled a slaveholder used to getting his own way, and a little the worse for drink. 'Ah,' said a man beside him, 'I wish I had him in Savannah! We would use him up!' A third onlooker announced flatly, 'I will be one of a number to throw him overboard.'

Standing nearby was Captain Thomas Bunbury Gough of the 33rd Regiment of Foot – one of several off-duty army officers on board. He was a very tall, imposing Irishman: in telling the story later, Douglass compared him to a giraffe. Gough laughed and, holding a glass to his eye, peered down at the short, plump antagonist. 'Have you ever thought, my friend, that two can play at that game?'

The audience found itself divided into two angry opposing camps. And, amid the jeering and the jostling, the deck of the *Cambria* suddenly felt very dangerous indeed.[1]

The voyage had begun smoothly enough. On Saturday, 16 August 1845, the wooden paddle steamer pulled away from Boston harbour. The Hutchinson Family, a singing group on their first trip to Europe, sang a tuneful farewell to friends who had gathered at the dockside. They swung their hats and handkerchiefs and gave out a great cheer, returned by passengers on the rail. Many of them no doubt prayed for good weather, an uneventful voyage and safe arrival in Liverpool before the end of the month. They would not have forgotten the shocking disappearance, four years earlier, of the *President* in a gale crossing the Atlantic with 136 on board. Douglass himself had

Figure 1.1 The *Cambria*.

known one of those who had perished.[2] And it was not uncommon for ships to run aground in fog.

The vessel followed the coast north and called in at Halifax, Nova Scotia, where a party went ashore, observing a large regiment drilling as they entered the town. Resuming their voyage, they headed out into the open sea. Those used to the noise of ropes and the rushing of sailors on sailing ships or to the din of the engines on other steamers must have been pleasantly surprised at how quiet the ship was, its vast machinery – and the infernal work of the stokers and engineers – insulated from their eyes and ears below deck.

The passengers sought to ease the monotonous rhythm of the days, knitting, sewing, reading, singing, walking. Some of them amused themselves with shuffleboard, checkers or a rubber of whist. Religious services were held on Sundays. Those not afflicted with sea-sickness ate hearty meals in the saloon, where joints were carved at the table. Wine glasses and tumblers hung overhead in a swinging rack, and a few passengers succumbed to the temptations of strong drink, freely available from six in the morning till eleven at night.

They encountered – and overtook – other ships, the captains engaging in silent conversations with flags. Early one morning, the steward woke the passengers to tell them they were passing between icebergs and they gathered on deck in heavy coats to gaze upon a dozen or so specimens towering over them, like huge sphinxes or enormous cathedrals. One of these collapsed as they watched, its bulk falling into the calm sea with a sound like the roar of a thousand cannon, sending spray high into the air, then dispersing to reveal a low island of rough snow.

'Splendid boat, the *Cambria*', wrote one passenger in his diary. It 'rides over the waves with as much ease as the wild sea gull.' Although it never broke the record set two years later by the *Hibernia*, which made the crossing in just over nine days, its reputation for punctuality was formidable. True to its nickname, the 'Flying *Cambria*' made excellent time.

Notes

1. FD gave a number of accounts of the voyage. See FD, Dublin, 9 September 1845 (*Dublin Evening Packet*, 11 September 1845; *Freeman's Journal*, 13 September 1845); FD, Cork, 27 October 1845 (FDP 1.1, pp. 62–6); FD, Belfast, 5 December 1845 (*Belfast News-Letter*, 9 December 1845); FD, Glasgow, 15 January 1846 (FDP 1.1, pp. 139–42); FD to WLG, Dublin, 1 September 1845 (FDP 3.1, pp. 47–50); FD to Thurlow Weed, Dublin, 1 December 1845 (FDP 3.1, pp. 67–8); and the retrospective account in BF, pp. 365–8 (A, pp. 370–2; FDP 2.2, pp. 209–11). I draw freely on these and also Alexander, *L'Acadie*, vol. 2, pp. 258–62; Cockrell, *Excelsior*, pp. 315–23; Hutchinson, *Story of the Hutchinsons*, vol. 2, pp. 142–7; Gac, *Singing for Freedom*, pp. 208–10; Warburton, *Hochelaga*, vol. 2, pp. 54–63. See also *Liberator*, 3 October 1845, 10 October 1845; *National Anti-Slavery Standard*, 18 December 1845.

2. The man FD knew was Rev. George Cookman, an exception among the clergymen he knew at St Michael's in Maryland, who genuinely 'took an interest in our temporal and spiritual welfare', and for that was loved and venerated by the slaves: BF, pp. 198–9 (A, p. 253; FDP 2.2, pp. 113–14).

Chapter 2

The Making of a Fugitive

Frederick Douglass was born Frederick Bailey in February 1818, a slave belonging to Aaron Anthony, an overseer employed by Colonel Edward Lloyd in Talbot County, Maryland, on the eastern shore of the Chesapeake Bay. The boy scarcely knew his mother, who was expected back at work on Anthony's own farm soon after the birth, and he was raised by his grandmother in a cabin in the backwoods where her husband, a free man, earned a precarious living as a wood-cutter. At the age of six Frederick was considered ready to take up duties at the big house of Lloyd's Wye Plantation, twelve miles distant, rejoining his three older siblings. Here he first witnessed the cruelties of overseers, which haunted him for the rest of his life. And then, two years later, he was wrenched away once more. Anthony's son-in-law, Thomas Auld, sent the young boy to live with his brother Hugh and his wife Sophia in Baltimore, the second largest city in the United States at the time, and the best part of a day's sail from the plantation.

There was no question of the boy receiving any formal education, but Sophia began to teach him how to read, before her husband stopped her, declaring that it was against the law, and even she now became cold towards him. But Frederick was tenacious and thereafter he sought every opportunity to continue his education in secret: he got hold of a copy of the *Columbian Orator*, a popular textbook with extracts from famous speeches, copying letters and enlisting the (sometimes unwitting) help of white boys he encountered in the shipyards.

When he was fifteen, Thomas Auld, now his owner, called him back to Talbot County and hired him out to various farms. This would have been Frederick's first real taste of demanding manual labour in the open air, and hard to take after the relatively light duties he had enjoyed in Baltimore. Auld, determined to take him down a peg or two, probably relished his discomfort. Indeed, after discovering that the enterprising youth had set up a clandestine Sabbath school, he resolved to teach him a lesson. In January 1834 he hired him out for a year to Edward Covey, a man with a reputation for disciplining hard-to-manage slaves. The work was tough, and Covey whipped his slaves for every imagined infraction. Frederick admitted he felt broken, and his only solace was in dreaming of freedom as he watched sailing ships in the Chesapeake Bay make their way to the ocean.

One time Covey assaulted him, Frederick decided he had had enough and fought back. According to the account he later gave of it in his *Narrative*, the struggle lasted several hours, but in the end, Frederick prevailed, and Covey never laid a finger on him again. This was, he wrote, 'the turning-point in my career as a slave', introducing the episode by announcing, 'You have seen how a man was made a slave; you shall see how a slave was made a man.'[1] Proclaiming his adulthood and his maleness as well as his humanity, henceforth all his efforts were geared to securing his freedom in body as well as in spirit.

His first attempt was a failure. Plans he had made to escape with five close friends were uncovered, and Auld had to get him out of jail. But when he sent him back to his brother in Baltimore, new opportunities presented themselves. Frederick bided his time; he wanted to be sure of success. He was sent to work in the shipyards, and later persuaded Hugh Auld to let him choose his own jobs and live in his own lodgings, on the condition that he passed on an agreed portion of his wages to him. Many of his fellow workers were free men, and he no doubt began to enlarge his knowledge of the world at this time. He attended services of the African Methodist Episcopal Church and formed a secret debating society. It was through one or the other that he met Anna Murray, a free woman from the Eastern Shore who had found work in the city as a domestic servant. They became engaged, and with her help and careful planning, he boarded a train north disguised as a sailor. He was just twenty years old.[2]

As soon as she heard he had reached New York City safely, Anna joined him, and they married at once. The couple moved to New Bedford, the whaling port in Massachusetts, where, after several changes of surname designed to confuse any pursuers, he settled on Douglass, which was how he was known for the rest of his life. He took what manual jobs he could get on the wharves and preached for while in a black church. Douglass subscribed to the abolitionist newspaper the *Liberator* and attended, and then began to speak at, antislavery meetings. Within three years, he was engaged as a lecturer by the Massachusetts Anti-Slavery Society and faced hostile, sometimes violent crowds as he toured New England, New York, Pennsylvania, Ohio and Indiana, alongside more experienced campaigners.

Northern states had largely abolished slavery by 1800 (although small pockets remained until the 1830s). Even so, the abolitionist message was not widely welcomed there, with many whites expressing their insecurities in racial terms, and welcoming measures that limited the rights and opportunities of former slaves and their descendants living in their midst. It was not just the abolitionists' denunciations of slavery, or the assistance they gave to fugitives, that provoked their opponents, but their struggle for the equality of free black people.[3]

Douglass, for instance, took part in the campaign to persuade Rhode Island to repeal the legislation it had introduced in 1822 that allowed only white males to vote – a success that was not, however, repeated elsewhere. He also joined protests against the Massachusetts railroads when they introduced a separate car to which black passengers were assigned. Douglass and other activists would sit in the first-class car and refuse to move when asked, prompting them to be forcibly dragged from the train. The railroad companies eventually backed down, but 'Jim Crow', the nickname for the separate car, came to refer to the whole range of formal and informal codes by which black people were kept in their place, with an arbitrariness and unpredictability that brought an element of anxiety to every public encounter.[4]

In 1842 Douglass moved the family to Lynn, a shoe-manufacturing town and abolitionist stronghold ten miles north of Boston. Anna had given birth to three children already – Rosetta, Lewis, and Frederick – and a fourth, Charles Remond, would soon follow. With Douglass spending long periods away on the road, Anna must have relied on the support of friends, especially Ruth Cox, a fugitive slave from Maryland Douglass met at an abolitionist meeting and whom he invited to join the household.[5]

He may not have risen to such prominence so quickly had he not been championed by William Lloyd Garrison, founder of the *Liberator* in 1831. Garrison, who began his working life as a printer's apprentice, soon made a name for himself as a journalist and editor. An uncompromising Christian moralist with strong views on temperance and Sabbath observance, at first he showed little interest in slavery, deferring to the dominant gradualist philosophy of the American Colonization Society, which encouraged freed slaves to emigrate to Liberia in West Africa rather than standing up for their equal rights in the United States. But in the late 1820s he began to heed the criticisms of black abolitionists, denounced the colonisationists and espoused the cause of immediate and unconditional emancipation. Three years after it launched, Garrison noted that only a quarter of the subscribers to his newspaper were white. 'The paper, then, belongs emphatically to the people of color,' he declared. 'It is their organ.'[6] They remained its core readership as he steered the white abolitionist movement in a radically new direction. Garrison became the leading spokesman for what by the late 1830s had become a mass movement, embracing over a thousand local societies with 140,000 members, co-ordinated by the national American Anti-Slavery Society of which he was the Corresponding Secretary.[7]

The young Douglass certainly admired Garrison, a father figure to him in some ways, though only twelve years his senior. And Douglass stuck by him even though a significant number had seceded from the national society to form a rival organisation. Garrison saw how useful Douglass was for the cause, but sometimes introduced him to audiences as if he were a circus act: 'It is recorded in holy writ, that a beast once spoke,' he announced on one occasion, alluding to the Old Testament story of Balaam's Ass. 'A greater miracle be here tonight.'[8] Douglass certainly saw himself as more than a talking mule.

At first Douglass's speeches focused on his own experiences in Maryland, but before long he found, as he expressed it later, 'it did not entirely satisfy me to narrate wrongs; I felt like denouncing them'.[9] In the juridical language used by abolitionists, his role as a witness soon augmented into that of a prosecutor.[10] Even so it was Douglass's life story that captured the imagination of a wider public, and he began to write it down. Published in Boston in May 1845, his *Narrative* was instant success. The initial run of 5,000 copies sold out in a few months, and by 1853 it had sold over 30,000 copies in over twenty editions in Britain and the United States and had been translated into Dutch and French.[11] It was one of the best known of the hundred or more slave narratives published in the thirty years before the Civil War.[12] Their testimony was of vital importance to the radical abolitionist movement, not just because their authors exposed the horrors of slavery, but because they had escaped from its grip and wrote about it themselves.

The book was written partly to answer those who heard Douglass's accomplished speeches and doubted he ever was a slave. But by providing the details of his experience in slavery, 'giving names of persons, places, and dates', as he put it, he placed himself in grave danger. The story of his escape

> soon became known in Maryland, and I had reason to believe that an effort would be made to recapture me [. . .] [A]nd while [. . .] there was little probability of successful recapture, if attempted openly, I was constantly in danger of being spirited away, at a moment when my friends could render me no assistance. In traveling about from place to place – often alone – I was much exposed to this sort of attack. Any one cherishing the design to betray me, could easily do so, by simply tracing my whereabouts through the anti-slavery journals, for my meetings and movements were promptly made known in advance.[13]

The Fugitive Slave Law of 1793 permitted slaveholders and their agents to track down fugitive slaves who had sought refuge in the 'free' states of the North and force them to return. Hence Douglass's precaution of changing his name. In 1842 the slave George Latimer, who had escaped from Virginia with his wife, arrived in Boston, only to be immediately recognised by someone who knew him and had him arrested. Abolitionists – including Douglass – rallied and considered how to spring him from jail if the courts did not rule in their favour. In the end Latimer was released, but only on a technicality, and despite the efforts of states such as Massachusetts to find ways round the federal law, fugitive slaves like Douglass remained highly vulnerable. (In 1846 a stowaway, Joe, made it to Boston only to be recaptured and sent to New Orleans before activists were alerted.) And, as abolitionists suspected, it would only get worse. In 1850 a new Fugitive Slave Law closed the loopholes and a fresh nightmare began.[14]

The danger of recapture was a real one. What was Douglass to do? One option was to leave the country for a while. To British Canada perhaps, where slavery barely survived the 1790s and thousands of fugitives had already resettled, although they faced similar hostility and discrimination to those who didn't slip across the border. In Britain itself Douglass could expect a warmer welcome, and if he could rouse audiences there he had a chance of furthering the abolitionist agenda at home, to the extent that British public opinion still commanded some respect in the United States. And so, in August 1845, he decided to sail to Liverpool. He must have thought long and hard about his decision to leave his wife and four young children. Only a few years earlier both he and Anna had, in moving North, made the choice to leave behind their closest relatives in Maryland, with whom they had no way of communicating directly. That they renamed Ruth Cox 'Harriet Bailey' after Douglass's younger sister, who died in infancy, suggests the trauma of that separation did not recede quickly. Could they now endure a separation from each other? They must have calculated that even to be parted by an ocean for a year would be nothing compared to the permanent rupture they would face if Douglass was handcuffed and returned to Thomas Auld, and, in all likelihood, sold on. And his long absences on lecture tours may have prepared them both for a more protracted time apart.

His book exposed Douglass to danger, especially as he was a public figure who could be easily located. But it also offered a great opportunity. In Britain and Ireland, he could promote the *Narrative* to a whole new market. He could join forces with the abolitionists there who, having helped to bring about the emancipation of slaves in the West Indies, had now turned their attention to the United States. There he would find a different kind of audience: perhaps less hostile than he was used to, but still demanding patience and resourcefulness if he was to rouse them to a keen passion. It was a challenge he was more than ready for. An ambitious man, aware of his talents as an orator and a writer, he must have felt limited as a hired hand, paraded as a professional fugitive, for the Massachusetts Anti-Slavery Society. Here was a chance to step on stage as an intellectual in his own right and to enjoy a freedom that was denied him, even in the Northern states.

He did not travel alone, but as the only person of colour, he was the only member of the party for whom that taste of freedom would be transformative. Significantly, perhaps, it was not Garrison who accompanied him, or another leading spokesman for the Society, but the gentle, lesser-known James Needham Buffum. Douglass had known him since at least the summer of 1841 and they had crossed paths many times on the campaign trail, including the protests on the railroads in which Buffum had also taken part. But Buffum was not one to seek the spotlight. He was considered an excellent speaker, if not an electrifying one, and was happy to play a supporting role, providing the statistics while Douglass held audiences with the drama of his delivery. One abolitionist called him a 'walking magazine of facts'.[15]

The entertainment at the farewell meeting held at Lynn's Lyceum Hall was provided by the Hutchinson Family. A singing group from New Hampshire consisting of three brothers and a sister, also about to embark on their first trip to Europe, they were much loved in abolitionist circles for their moving and inspirational anthems. The next morning, on the deck of the *Cambria* as it lay off in the stream, Jesse Hutchinson gathered the well-wishers in a circle and the family sang 'Home Sweet Home'. As the last strains died away, the bell sounded, and, with final handshakes, they bade each other adieu. The last sight his friends had of Douglass as they were ferried back to the wharf was him waving his hat in the distance.[16]

As he did so, he may have reflected that although he was following in the footsteps of Garrison, who had visited Britain in 1833 and 1840, Douglass's path was also prepared by several black Americans who had crossed the Atlantic during the previous decade or so, some of them staying for several years. They travelled for a variety of reasons: Nathaniel Paul to raise money for the Wilberforce Colony of free blacks in Ontario; James McCune Smith to study medicine; Robert Purvis to visit his father's family in Fife; Moses Roper to secure an education and train as a missionary; Charles Lenox Remond to attend the World Anti-Slavery Convention in London; Moses Grandy to raise funds to purchase the freedom of relatives; and James W. C. Pennington to attend the second World Anti-Slavery Convention. But all of them attended or addressed antislavery meetings, and those who had grown up enslaved (Roper and Grandy) recounted their experiences both on the lecture platform and in autobiographies published in Britain and Ireland, which (like Douglass) they sold on speaking tours.

Some of them subsequently returned to Britain, including Pennington (three times before the Civil War), while Roper, after two years in Canada, came back in 1846 to arrange a new edition of his *Narrative of the Adventures and Escape of Moses Roper from*

American Slavery and lectured, mostly in Scotland and Ireland, at the same time as Douglass, although there is no evidence they met. Molliston Madison Clark was also in Britain over the same period, as a delegate of the African Methodist Episcopal Church to the Evangelical Alliance conference in London.[17]

Douglass clearly benefited from their example. Some of them he was close to: Douglass had campaigned alongside Remond in Massachusetts, and named his third child after him, Pennington was the church minister who had married him and Anna in New York, while Smith later became the New York correspondent for *Frederick Douglass' Paper*. He was not the first black abolitionist to visit the British Isles, but he was to become by far the best known, creating a stir even before his arrival in Liverpool – news of which soon spread far and wide once the first reports of the eventful voyage appeared in US and British newspapers.[18]

Notes

1. N, pp. 113, 107 (A, pp. 65, 60; FDP 2.1, pp. 54, 50).
2. On FD's childhood (up to 1838) see Preston, *Young Frederick Douglass*, pp. 3–156; also Quarles, *Frederick Douglass*, pp. 1–8; Foner, *Frederick Douglass*, pp. 15–22; Huggins, *Slave and Citizen*, pp. 1–14; McFeeley, *Frederick Douglass*, pp. 4–73; Barnes, *Frederick Douglass*, pp. 11–22; Fought, *Women in the World of Frederick Douglass*, pp. 9–51.
3. On his time in New Bedford see Quarles, *Frederick Douglass*, pp. 8–27; Huggins, *Slave and Citizen*, pp. 15–17; Foner, *Frederick Douglass*, pp. 23–7, 45–52; McFeely, *Frederick Douglass*, pp. 75–90; Barnes, *Frederick Douglass*, pp. 25–36; Fought, *Women in the World of Frederick Douglass*, pp. 52–7.
4. On the campaign in Rhode Island see Quarles, *Frederick Douglass*, pp. 21–2; Sinha, *The Slave's Cause*, p. 322. On the protests against the 'Jim Crow' railroad car see Pryor, *Colored Travelers*, pp. 76–102; and on desegregation struggles more generally, Sinha, *The Slave's Cause*, pp. 325–30.
5. On FD's time in Lynn see Quarles, *Frederick Douglass*, pp. 27–34; Foner, *Frederick Douglass*, pp. 52–9; McFeely, *Frederick Douglass*, pp. 91–114; Barnes, *Frederick Douglass*, pp. 36–44; Fought, *Women in the World of Frederick Douglass*, pp. 58–67. McFeely states that FD moved there in the fall of 1841 (p. 92), but Fought cites evidence that the date was more likely to be fall 1842 (p. 329 n.).

6. WLG, 'To the Friends of the *Liberator*', printed circular enclosed in a letter to Ebenezer Dole, Boston, 15 April 1834 (BPL Ms. A.1.1 v. 1, p. 37), available at <https://archive.org/details/lettertomydearsi00garr4> (last accessed 7 May 2018), quoted courtesy of the Trustees of the Boston Public Library/Rare Books.

7. On the emergence of 'Garrisonianism' see Sinha, *The Slave's Cause*, pp. 214–27; Goodman, *Of One Blood*, pp. 36–44. The figures on the number of societies and members are from Goodman, *Of One Blood*, p. 66.

8. WLG, Boston, 28 January 1842 (*Liberator*, 4 February 1842).

9. BF, p. 362 (A, p. 367, FDP 2.2, p. 208).

10. See DeLombard, *Slavery on Trial*, pp. 101–49.

11. Andrews, 'Introduction' to Andrews, *Critical Essays*, p. 2; FDP 2.1, p. xxxii.

12. Note, however, that it was superseded by his second autobiography, *My Bondage and My Freedom* (1855), and then a third, *The Life and Times of Frederick Douglass* (1881, revised 1892), which overshadowed it for more than a century; the *Narrative*, though pre-eminent today, was out of print for over a century and was not republished until 1960. See Levine, *The Lives of Frederick Douglass*, esp. pp. 11–12.

13. BF, pp. 363–4 (A, p, 368; FDP 2.2, p. 209).

14. On the operation of the Fugitive Slave Law of 1793 see Campbell, *The Slave Catchers*, pp. 3–15; and Nogee, 'The Prigg Case', pp. 185–205. FD and Charles Lenox Remond lectured in support of Latimer in New Bedford (*Liberator*, 18 November 1842) and Latimer subsequently shared the platform at meetings with FD and other abolitionists (*Liberator*, 9 December 1842). FD mentions the Latimer case in Paisley, 17 April 1846 (FDP 1.1, pp. 230–1). On kidnappings in the 1830s and 1840s and the impact of the 1850 law see Sinha, *The Slave's Cause*, pp. 381–93, 500–9.

15. RW, 'From Our Dublin Correspondent', *National Anti-Slavery Standard*, 30 July 1846. For comparisons between JB's and FD's speaking styles see *Dundee Courier*, 3 February 1846; and *Arbroath Guide*, 14 February 1846 (repr. *Liberator*, 27 March 1846).

16. 'Departure of Frederick Douglass, James N. Buffum, and the Hutchinson Family', *Liberator*, 22 August 1845.

17. The best sources for black abolitionist visitors to Britain and Ireland during this period are Blackett, *Building an Antislavery Wall*, and the valuable documents and editorial apparatus of BAP1. Also in Britain at the same time as FD was Harriet Jacobs, later to become well known for her own autobiography, *Incidents in the Life of a Slave Girl* (1861), but not yet a public figure. She was travelling with the widower Nathaniel Parker Willis as the nursemaid for his daughter Imogen, and

spent most of her time at the home of Imogen's aunt and uncle in Berkshire. See Yellin, *Harriet Jacobs*, pp. 83–7.

18. The first accounts of the confrontation appeared in the *Dublin Evening Packet*, 11 September 1845, reporting FD's speech in Dublin on 9 September 1845 (repr. *Belfast Commercial Chronicle*, 13 September 1845); and FD's letter to WLG, Dublin, 1 September 1845, in which he described the voyage, appeared in the *Liberator*, 26 September 1845. And on 3 October 1845 the *Liberator* reprinted comments on the incident (both highly abusive of FD) from the *New York Herald* and *Boston Times* – the latter a letter to the editor from a 'pro-slavery American, in London' – suggesting how far the news had spread.

Chapter 3

'Put Them in Irons'

Trouble on the *Cambria* began long before Douglass was invited to address the passengers on the promenade deck on the last evening of the voyage. In a number of speeches he gave in Ireland and Scotland that autumn and winter, he explained that even before he boarded the vessel he was told by the agent at Boston that he was not allowed to take first-class cabin passage because of the colour of his skin.

Douglass was no stranger to discrimination. He faced it every day in Massachusetts and had campaigned vigorously against the practice on the state's railroads. He did not, however, expect to face this kind of prejudice at the hands of a British company.[1] The *Cambria* was one of the fleet of four ships operated by the British and North American Steam Packet Company, which began services between Liverpool, Halifax and Boston in 1840 after securing the government mail contract. The contract even stipulated that an officer of the Royal Navy had to be on board every vessel to ensure the safety of its precious cargo. A cat was also required to catch the rats which would otherwise have gnawed into the mailbags, as well as a cow and chickens so the passengers could enjoy fresh milk and eggs. One can sense Douglass's bitter disappointment in discovering – as he told an audience in Glasgow – that 'the corrupting influence of American customs and manners extended [to] the deck of a British steamer, under the British flag'. And all because

a few pro-slavery, cadaverous, lantern-jawed Americans were on board. (Cheers and laughter.) There were a few pale-faced Americans on board, whose olfactory nerves would have been most offended if he had come anywhere in the neighbourhood of them. He was ready to take a cabin passage, and to pay for it, and to behave himself as other men did, but he was refused on the ground that he was a coloured man. (Shame.) Yes, it was a shame for England so far to lower its dignity as to adopt the prejudices of the slaveholders on board any of her vessels, and to violate the British cross, merely to please the slaveholding, woman-stripping, cradle-plundering Americans.[2]

Careful to acknowledge the kindness of the captain and other members of the crew who, it seemed, were disinclined to prevent him from mingling with other passengers, Douglass portrays himself as one who, at least initially, intended to keep a low profile, confident in the knowledge that the power of those who sought to restrict him would evaporate once he reached Britain's shores. The report continued:

Well, when he got on board he took his position before the mast, and spent his days in the forecastle, feeling quite happy, and what gave him the greatest consolation was, that every revolution of the ponderous wheels of their noble ship bore him farther from the land of those proscriptions which he had then escaped.[3]

The driving force behind the British and North American Steam Packet Company was Samuel Cunard in partnership with the two Glasgow ship-owners, and the company was more commonly referred to as 'Cunard's line' from the start. The steamers took cabin passengers only, with fares out of the range of most people: $120 for first cabin and $70 for second.[4] Some commentators, including Douglass himself, refer to his being forced to travel 'steerage' – a term normally reserved for the crowded communal area on a lower deck with minimal facilities, at fares of around $12 for an eastward passage – but this option was available only on sailing ships at the time.[5] In fact, it seems clear that Douglass (or rather Buffum, on his behalf) was obliged to purchase a second-cabin ticket.[6] Nevertheless, conditions were spartan compared to their competitors, and furthermore the company seemed to treat complaints rather dismissively. Charles MacIver, who ran operations at Liverpool, told a disappointed traveller: 'Going to sea was a hardship. The Company did not undertake to make anything else out of it.'[7]

Furthermore, the mix of passengers could be an explosive one. Douglass observed:

[O]ur passengers were made up of nearly all sorts of people, from different countries, of the most opposite modes of thinking on all subjects. We had nearly all sorts or parties in morals, religion, and politics, as well as trades and callings, and professions. The doctor and the lawyer, the soldier and the sailor, were there. The scheming Connecticut wooden clock-maker, the large, surly, New-York lion tamer, the solemn Roman Catholic Bishop, and the Orthodox Quaker were there. A minister of the Free Church of Scotland, and a minister of the Church of England – the established Christian and the wandering Jew, the Whig and the Democrat, the white and the black – were there. There was the dark-visaged Spaniard, and the light-visaged Englishman – the man from Montreal, and the man from Mexico.[8]

But the deepest fault line that divided the passengers – as events were to dramatically show – was the matter of slavery, Douglass neatly evoking the clash of ideologies by contrasting his own book and the recently published *Two Letters on Slavery in the United States* by the governor of South Carolina, James Henry Hammond, which claimed to offer a defence of slavery on both biblical and scientific grounds.[9]

There were slaveholders from Cuba, and slaveholders from Georgia. We had anti-slavery songs and pro-slavery grumbling; and at the same time that Governor Hammond's Letters were being read, my Narrative was being circulated.[10]

Confined together for nearly two weeks on a small ship, where the conventional division of spheres between men and women and between adults and children was harder to maintain, passengers had to find ways of getting along and modifying their conduct accordingly. The Hutchinsons, who regularly entertained the passengers, realised that their '[s]ongs must be all kinds in order to fit any of the many kinds of human minds on board the Cambria' and they drew on a wide repertoire, including 'God Save the Queen', 'Yankee Doodle', 'America' and 'Life on the Ocean Wave' in a diplomatic nod to different national allegiances, as well as, perhaps, to deflect any hostility that might have greeted their own compositions extolling temperance, women's rights and the abolition of slavery.[11]

That order was generally maintained on such vessels – at least as far as the passengers were concerned – shows how well people had learned to govern themselves. To some extent this was down to the organisation of space and time on board. Cunard ships were subject to strict regulations drawn up by MacIver, which covered not only matters such as navigation, fire safety and the consumption of coal, but also the cleaning of staterooms, the opening hours of the bar and the timing of 'lights-out'.[12]

With only first-class ticket holders entitled to dine in the saloon – the others had to take their meals in their cabins – large public gatherings were discouraged, and with no steerage passengers, all were spared contact with emigrants of the lower classes. The often uneventful days – barring storms, or the sight of icebergs, whales or other ships – were punctuated with regular mealtimes and the sound of the half-hour bells, to which routines were added the customary forms of amusement encouraged on board.

The success of these unobtrusive forms of management is indicated by the relative infrequency by which rules and regulations on board are referred to in travellers' accounts, for it is usually only when they seem arbitrary and imposing that they merit attention.

One subject of controversy was MacIver's insistence (which Samuel Cunard tried to persuade him to relax) that captains were expected, on Sundays, to 'read the Church of England Service to your crew and Passengers in the Saloon at a fixed hour, as nearly as you can'.[13] When the showman P. T. Barnum sailed back to the United States in February 1847, he became involved in an argument with the same Captain Judkins for not allowing the Presbyterian clergyman, the Rev. Dr Robert Baird (most definitely not an Anglican), to preach to passengers in the forward cabin, as this was – Judkins declared flatly – 'against the rules of the ship'. Barnum protested forcefully, until Judkins threatened him: 'If you repeat such language, I will put you in irons.' Barnum suggested that if he arrived in New York in such a condition, it might stretch the credulity of those upholding 'Yankee ideas of religious intolerance'. Baird himself, on being apprised of the situation, quietly conceded, saying, 'if the rules of this ship are so stringent I suppose we must submit'. Afterwards, Judkins apologised to Barnum for his manner and the two washed down their differences with a bottle of champagne.[14]

The arbitrary nature of the rules was also evident in the practices of the company relating to the treatment of black passengers.

Scottish newspapers in particular had had a keen eye on this ever since James McCune Smith was refused passage on a ship return-ing from Glasgow to New York in 1837.[15] They also reported the ill-treatment of Charles Remond on his outward voyage in 1840.[16] Neither of these cases involved Cunard vessels and according to Remond, on his return journey on the Cunard ship *Columbia*, cap-tained by Judkins, 'every politeness was shown me by the officers, and every kindness and attention by the stewards'.[17] But Judkins was not always so fair-minded.

The year before Douglass's outward voyage, George Lewis, a minis-ter with the Free Church of Scotland, returning from the United States on the *Acadia*, noted in his journal that

[t]he only disagreeable circumstance that occurred in the home-ward voyage was the exclusion of a young gentleman, a passenger from Hayti, who had paid a cabin passage, and yet was not permitted to enter the saloon and dine at the common table. About one-third of the passengers joined in a request to the captain that he should be invited to join us in the saloon. The remonstrance was unheeded. The Captain at one moment saying that it was contrary to orders, and at another time declaring that he had no authority on the sub-ject, but that the American passengers would not tolerate it. Finding no redress from Captain Judkins, we drew up a remonstrance to the owners at Glasgow and Liverpool, against this ungenerous outrage on the feelings of a coloured gentleman in a British vessel carrying her Majesty's mail. Most of the British and colonial passengers, and several of the New Englanders, signed the remonstrance; but the Southerns contemptuously refused, and one young Southern, from New Orleans, who spent most of the voyage at the card-table, got up a counter petition that the cow should be admitted to the saloon. The jest only showed the breeding of the slaveholder, and was not relished by the [other] passengers.[18]

The remonstrance may have had some effect, for a year later Jud-kins appears to have taken a relaxed attitude to Douglass, who – despite the prohibition imposed on him at Boston – found that he could move freely about the ship. It would appear that the captain was permitted some discretion in deciding whether to enforce the discriminatory conditions set by the agents on shore and was guided by an assessment of the consequences of allowing such racial mixing on board. In the earlier voyage, it seems that Judkins risked the anger of a substantial proportion of the passengers, but this anger found a relatively safe outlet in the form of the remonstrance, subsequently published in the *Glasgow Argus*.[19] In the later voyage, it is possible that Judkins's easy-going attitude was rewarded by Douglass's own circumspection in choosing to remain in his cabin for much of the voyage.

The decks of a transatlantic steamer were negotiated spaces, in which custom and routine made it relatively easy to impose racial segregation, but the response would have been hard to predict. Every voyage would have been different, and the captain would have been required to read the characters and moods of the passengers in order to weigh the risk of granting – or withholding – black travellers the right to associate with whites. Assailed by conflicting requests, he would have to be fairly certain that any decision he made would not lead to anything more serious than grumbles or – at worst – formal complaints. It was rare that situations got out of hand to the point that passenger safety was in peril.[20]

The confrontation on the *Cambria* drew in other members of the party. Voices and fists were raised. According to the army officer Captain Warburton, who included an account of the voyage in a book of his travels published the following year, the ugly scene lasted 'for at least an hour', though 'in the mean time, this demon of discord had vanished, and we saw or heard no more of him or his lectures'.[21] John Hutchinson puts it rather differently, describing how the speaker was 'so disturbed [. . .] that he was forced to suspend, and with a sentence half-finished, he retreated under the awning and thence down the stairs to the steerage, his only hiding place, where he was sheltered from the wrath of those blood-thirsty Americans whose "chivalry" was so much shocked'.[22]

Judkins, who, after introducing Douglass, had retired to partake of a luxurious banquet given to him by friends, was eventually roused by the disturbances. Calling Douglass to his side, he admonished those who had prevented him from speaking. 'You have acted derogatory to the character of gentlemen and Christians,' he told them. 'Those who are not desirous to hear him, let them go to another part of the vessel.' And he invited the speaker to continue. 'Mr. Douglass,' he said, 'Go on, pitch into them like bricks!'[23]

At this moment, a passenger from Philadelphia stepped up and indicated his dissent. The captain took him aside, and the man made to pull something from under his coat. Judkins drew back a little, expecting a knife of some sort, but it turned out to be a business card. 'Meet me in Liverpool,' he challenged. 'Very well', replied the captain, 'I will be there.'[24]

But the tumult went on and threats continued to rent the evening air. Judkins called the boatswain and ordered him to bring the irons, to prevent, as Douglass put it, 'a fatal exhibition of their wicked feelings'.[25] The ironic reversal of roles was a gift to the orator. 'You see,' he said later in Belfast, 'he was about to play the slaveholder over them.' To his listeners in Glasgow, he explained: 'They had been accustomed to put irons upon black people, but the idea of putting irons upon democratic republicans they could not under-stand.'[26] And to cap the story with a theatrical flourish, on at least two occasions the narrative concluded with Douglass or Buffum holding up the instruments of torture and restraint they had brought with them: an iron collar, manacles and a whip, rattling them before the audience.[27]

It seems that Warburton has a point when he claims that 'but for the certainty of being immediately amenable to English law, it would have been the occasion of great violence, if not loss of life'.[28] If Judkins encouraged Douglass to give his lecture, he was taking a considerable gamble. While he risked a petition through antagonis-ing the defenders of the rights of man by excluding a Haitian pas-senger from the saloon in 1844, he risked even more by allowing drunken slaveholders to express their outrage in 1845. After all, the 'mobs' associated with antislavery activity in the North were the abolitionists' opponents. The abolitionists themselves, while often accused of inciting violence, rarely perpetrated it. That angry sup-porters of slavery were more of a liability than angry abolitionists would surely have been an important consideration for the captain of a ship responsible for maintaining the safety of his passengers and crew and punctual delivery of cargo and mail.

As Samuel Ringgold Ward argued in relation to his own experi-ences on a ship several years later: 'if any one made a disturbance on board [. . .] that was the person to be deprived of his rights, and not an innocent person'.[29] But Captain Judkins's principled stand could so easily have gone awry. On land, the threat of disorder in a public hall, or on a branch railroad – exaggerated or not – may have been something worth risking, given the greater resources available to contain it. The authorities could disperse crowds and bring in reinforcements from elsewhere. At sea, however, even with Wales on the horizon, the danger of losing a passenger overboard was real indeed, as the barely disguised glee at the prospect of a 'negro tossed to the sharks' voiced in some American newspapers makes chillingly clear.[30]

At any rate, Douglass must have arrived in Liverpool with more than the usual sense of relief at the end of an ocean voyage. Once ashore, he was free to move and speak unmolested. He often figured his journey as his own transformation from 'chattel' to 'man'.[31] In Britain and Ireland he frequently alluded to the pleasures he could take in occupying public spaces, perhaps never more so than in this public letter to Garrison he wrote on New Year's Day, 1846:

> The second day after my arrival at Liverpool, in company with my friend Buffum, and several other friends, I went to Eaton Hall, the residence of the Marquis of Westminster, one of the most splendid buildings in England. On approaching the door, I found several of our American passengers, who came out with us in the Cambria, waiting for admission, as but one party was allowed in the house at a time. We all had to wait till the company within came out. And of all the faces, expressive of chagrin, those of the Americans were pre-eminent. They looked as sour as vinegar, and as bitter as gall, when they found I was to be admitted on equal terms with themselves. When the door was opened, I walked in, I could see, I had as much attention paid me by the servants that showed us through the building, the statuary did not fall down, the pictures did not leap from their places, the doors did not refuse to open, and the servants did not say, '*We don't allow niggers in here!*'[32]

In the young republic he has left behind he was faced with proscription at every turn. In the old monarchy across the sea, even the abusive Americans who travelled with him must hold their tongues. '[H]ere, how different!' said Douglass at the end of his trip. 'Why, sir, the very dogs of old England know that I am a man!'[33]

The contrast is overdrawn, as we shall see, but there is no doubt that the next twenty-one months in the British Isles would transform Douglass almost beyond recognition. In this book we follow his movements in Scotland, watching him gaining the confidence, mastering the skills and fashioning the distinctive voice and public image that transformed him as a campaigner. He arrived as a subordinate envoy of white abolitionists, technically still a fugitive slave. He returned as a free man ready to embark on a new stage of his career, as editor and proprietor of his own newspaper and a leader in his own right. Scotland was of course not the only crucible of Douglass's development, but circumstances there did offer him opportunities to experiment and assert himself in ways he had not done previously.

Although the main body of this book is framed by accounts of Douglass's outward and return sea voyages in Parts I and V, it does not offer a chronological narrative of his speaking engagements in Scotland. Instead, each of the three main intervening Parts focuses on a different set of encounters with notable Scots in order to suggest the vital role they played in transforming Douglass. In particular, they prompted far-reaching changes in his styles of speaking and writing, in his choice of heroes and how he identified with them, and in the new fervour with which he attempted to control the way he was represented verbally and pictorially.

Part II re-examines Douglass's role in the 'Send Back the Money' campaign that castigated the Free Church of Scotland for accepting donations from pro-slavery churches in the United States. I discuss the arguments of Douglass and Free Church leaders such as Thomas Chalmers and William Cunningham in relation to the abolitionist movement's own strategies of fund-raising, its anxieties about the corrupting power of money, and uncertainty over whether it was right to buy Douglass's freedom. Faced with the intransigence of his opponents in public and snide criticisms from his supporters in private, Douglass learnt quickly to respond by refining his rhetorical skills both on the lecture platform and in his personal correspondence.

The different ways in which Douglass engaged with the work of Walter Scott and Robert Burns are explored in Part III. That Douglass took his surname from *The Lady of the Lake* is relatively well known, but the significance of his choice, how he exploited it in Scotland and his later deployment of a recognisably Scott-ish idiom in his second autobiography are subjected to scrutiny for the first time here. Likewise, Douglass's admiration for Burns has received notice in recent years, but the ambivalence of his remarks about the poet and their relation to Burns's own conflicting remarks about slavery have not before been pursued at length. If in Ireland he had signalled his bond with his audiences by aligning himself with the living, and somewhat controversial, reformer Daniel O'Connell, in Scotland Douglass chooses for the first time to more shrewdly identify with canonical authors and historical figures who enjoyed near-universal veneration.

Part IV takes off from his meeting with the phrenologist George Combe in order to investigate Douglass's attitudes towards early Victorian visual culture. Douglass's own suspicion of the prevailing assumption that heads and faces offered a reliable guide to character was intensified by the awareness that the novelty of his appearance was drawing audiences already familiar with the performances of blackface minstrel troupes, which were touring Scotland at the same time. It also helps to explain the bad-tempered correspondence with his Irish publisher over which portrait to use for the frontispiece of a new edition of his *Narrative*, when he arrived in Glasgow with only a few copies left. It is in Scotland that Douglass shows himself taking bold steps to take control of his image, sharply criticising those who describe him reductively as a 'runaway' or 'fugitive', and alert to the differences between the effect of one engraving of a black man in a suit and another.

An afterword considers the significance of Douglass today: in the context of the growing academic study and public awareness of Scotland's slavery and antislavery past, and in the context of the changing image of 'Scotland' in the United States. Douglass remains one of the few prominent African Americans who have chosen to identify (however rhetorically) as Scottish, despite the large numbers of black people who are descended from Scots. What does this mean for his twenty-first-century counterparts, those fleeing persecution and seeking protection in Scotland today? Would one invoke Douglass in order to celebrate the freedom they enjoy or to steel them for the struggles that lie ahead?

Notes

1. For discussions of the treatment of FD and other black passengers on transatlantic crossings see Pettinger, '"At Sea – Coloured Passenger"', pp. 149–66; McDaniel, 'Saltwater Anti-Slavery', pp. 141–63; Pryor, *Colored Travelers*, pp. 126–48. For the early history of the Cunard line see esp. Hyde, *Cunard and the North Atlantic*; and Fox, *The Ocean Railway*.
2. FD, Glasgow, 15 January 1846 (FDP 1.1, p. 139).
3. FD, Glasgow, 15 January 1846 (FDP 1.1, pp. 139–40).

4. In an agreement between the Cunard and Collins steamship lines, maximum first and second cabin fares were set at $120 and $70 eastward (and £35 and £20 westward) in 1850: see Hyde, *Cunard and the North Atlantic*, p. 40. In 1845 it seems that FD's second cabin ticket was $70; and in 1847 his first cabin ticket was £40 19s.

5. Bowen, *A Century of Atlantic Travel*, p. 37. FD himself refers to his being forced to travel 'steerage', e.g. FD, Cork, 23 October 1845 (FDP 1.1, p. 63); FD, Paisley, 17 April 1846 (FDP 1.1, p. 215). For steerage fares see Killick, 'Transatlantic Steerage Fares'.

6. That JB purchased a second-cabin ticket is indicated in a letter from FD referring to Buffum, who, 'aware of my poverty stepped forward with his characteristic liberality and kindly offered to collect a sufficient sum to pay my passage to this land. He tried and succeeded in getting 68 dollars just 2 dollars short of my expenses in the steerage': FD to MWC, Kilmarnock, 29 March 1846 (FDP 3.1, p. 99; BAA, p. 258). It is not clear from this whether Buffum's fund-raising target was originally $70 or was reduced to this once he was told that a first-cabin passage was not available.

7. Hyde, *Cunard and the North Atlantic*, p. 75.

8. FD to WLG, Dublin, 1 September 1845 (FDP 3.1, p. 48).

9. Hammond, *Two Letters*. Although addressed to the English abolitionist, ostensibly in reply to Clarkson, *Letter to Such Professing Christians*, Hammond's letters were primarily aimed at readers in the United States.

10. FD to WLG, Dublin, 1 September 1845 (FDP 3.1, p. 48).

11. Cockrell, *Excelsior*, p. 319; Hutchinson, *Story of the Hutchinsons*, vol. 1, p. 146.

12. D. and C. MacIver, *Captain's Memoranda*, 25 March 1848 (MacIver Papers, D138/2/4).

13. 'I am under the impression that you would do well to reconsider the regulation respecting the religious observance of the Sabbath': Samuel Cunard to Charles MacIver, London, 1 May 1847 (MacIver Papers, D138/4/1).

14. Barnum, *Struggles and Triumphs*, pp. 242–3. Henry Ward Beecher voiced a similar complaint regarding the rules on religious observances in 'Church and Steamboat – Cunard's Line', unidentified news clipping (MacIver Papers, D138/8/).

15. See John Murray's letter to Captain Bigley of the *Canonicus*, and other documents, published in the Glasgow Chartist newspaper *New Liberator*, 20 May 1837, repr. in GES, *Third Annual Report*, pp. 121–5 and in *Colored American*, 17 February 1838.

16. On Remond's outward voyage on the *Columbus* see N. P. Rogers, Edinburgh, 24 July 1840 (*Liberator*, 21 August 1840); WLG, Glasgow,

27 July 1840 (*Glasgow Argus*, 30 July 1840, repr. *Liberator*, 28 August 1840).

17. Remond's remarks were made in the course of his testimony before a committee of the Massachusetts legislature gathering evidence on the segregation of the railroads: 'Remarks of Charles Lenox Remond', *Liberator*, 25 February 1842.

18. Lewis, *Impressions of America*, pp. 390–1.

19. 'Exclusion of a Gentleman of Colour from the Saloon of the Acadia Steamer', *Glasgow Argus*, 5 August 1844. This letter is reproduced in GES, *Tenth Annual Report*, pp. 40–1, and the incident discussed on pp. 21–2. A subcommittee of the GES looked into the policies of the company and in their report quoted an unnamed partner, who admitted that 'coloured persons' had on more than one occasion been excluded from the saloon, arguing that while 'prejudice against colour was wrong', the policy had been adopted for 'practical' reasons and was designed 'for the comfort of the coloured persons themselves & the other passengers': Minutes of GES committee meeting, 17 October 1844 (Smeal Collection, Reel 1). For further details regarding the (unnamed) 'Haytien gentleman' and the discrimination he faced in the city of Boston, as well as at the hands of the Cunard line, with reference to Remond's outward passage in 1840, see 'The Cunard Steam Packets – Prejudice Against Color', *National Anti-Slavery Standard*, 4 August 1844 (repr. *Glasgow Argus*, 4 September 1844).

20. Babcock asserts that it was 'the last such disturbance to occur on a Cunard ship', without referring to any previous disturbance: Babcock, *Spanning the Atlantic*, p. 126. The incident on the *Cambria* in 1845 is the only case I have come across.

21. Warburton, *Hochelaga*, vol. 2, p. 360.

22. Hutchinson, *Story of the Hutchinsons*, vol. 1, p. 146.

23. FD, Cork, 23 October 1845 (FDP 1.1, p. 65).

24. FD, Belfast, 5 December 1845 (*Belfast News-Letter*, 9 December 1845). The report noted the 'sepulchral tone of voice' with which Douglass delivered the line, and the 'considerable merriment among the audience' it occasioned.

25. FD, Dublin, 9 September 1845 (*Freeman's Journal*, 13 September 1845).

26. FD, Belfast, 5 December 1845 (*Belfast News-Letter*, 9 December 1845); FD, Glasgow, 15 January 1846 (FDP 1.1, p. 142).

27. FD, Dublin, 9 September 1845 (*Dublin Evening Packet*, 11 September 1845; *Freeman's Journal*, 13 September 1845); FD, Cork, 23 October 1845 (FDP 1.1, p. 66).

28. Warburton, *Hochelaga*, vol. 2, p. 361.

29. Ward, *Autobiography of a Fugitive Negro*, p. 232.

30. 'Abolition Riot on the Atlantic', *Liberator*, 3 October 1845 (reprinting comments from the *New York Herald*).
31. FD to WLG, Belfast, 1 January 1846 (FDP 3.1, p. 74); FD, Belfast, 6 January 1846 (FDP 1.1, p. 128).
32. FD to WLG, Belfast, 1 January 1846 (FDP 3.1, p. 76).
33. FD, London, 30 March 1847 (FDP 1.2, p. 50).

Part II

Dark, Polluted Gold

It is dangerous to trace the genealogy of money, if we hold that it may be cast by a flaw in its lineage.

Hugh Miller

Send back the Money! send it back!
'Tis dark polluted gold;
'Twas wrung from human flesh and bones,
By agonies untold.

Anti-Slavery Songs

Chapter 4

Electric Speed

Soon after his arrival in Liverpool, Douglass was on the move again, crossing the Irish Sea to rendezvous with abolitionists in Dublin. After a four-month speaking tour that took him to Wexford, Waterford, Cork, Limerick and finally Belfast, he prepared to depart for Scotland. Having paid twelve shillings each for a first-class cabin on the paddle steamer *Firefly* or *Glow-Worm*, he and Buffum sailed from Donegal Quay at 10 o'clock on the morning of Saturday 10 January 1846, across the North Channel and up the Firth of Clyde to dock at the fashionable resort of Ardrossan on the Ayrshire coast.[1]

Here they would have transferred to a connecting train to Glasgow, which followed the arc of the bay before heading inland, passing weavers' cottages, country houses and castle ruins, through fertile fields, verdant meadows and neat plantations, halting at small towns with their church spires, mill chimneys, collieries and iron foundries. Douglass would pass through these towns again in the coming months, addressing eager audiences in some of them. Looking north, they may have caught a glimpse in the fading afternoon light of a snow-capped Ben Lomond in the distance. Fellow passengers may have proudly drawn their attention to Elderslie House, the ancient seat of William Wallace, and told them about the famous oak in which Wallace often hid from English troops. Leaving the dense industrial concentration of Paisley, where many factories still lay idle after the town was badly hit by a depression in trade in 1837 and again in the early 1840s, they would have had their first sight of ships' masts on the Clyde, and the dim outline of the Strathblane and Kilpatrick Hills beyond.

Whether Douglass was enjoying a period of quiet contemplation, or eavesdropping on his fellow passengers, attuning himself to their unfamiliar cadences and turns of phrase (some of which he would adapt in the speeches he would give in the coming days), that time was nearly over. There was work to be done, and there were new faces to greet. Perhaps he took out the 'golden gift' he had been presented at his farewell breakfast in Belfast, a small, elegantly bound Bible, and drew strength from its inscription, which expressed admiration for the 'eloquent lectures' he had recently delivered there. 'When far separated,' it read, 'they trust that the possession of this Bible will remind him that in Belfast there are many who sympathise with those who are in bonds, and who are also the personal friends and well-wishers of Mr Frederick Douglass.'[2]

Approaching Glasgow, an embankment afforded closer views of ranked tenements and a dense proliferation of manufactories, thin fingers of smoke, the horizon dominated by the giant stack of the St Rollox chemical works, the tallest in the world at the time. Finally, curving left, the line proceeded along a forty-arch viaduct overlooking the vast Tradeston Cotton Works of the Lancefield Spinning Company, to arrive at its terminus on the south bank of the river.[3]

Emerging into the crowded upper floor of the two-storey station, with its grand portico on Bridge Street, they were likely met by William Smeal and John Murray, the men who had invited them. Smeal was a tea merchant, Murray a customs official; together, they steered the Glasgow Emancipation Society, of which they were the secretaries. It was one of the first antislavery organisations to be formed in Britain after the passage of the Slavery Abolition Act in 1833.[4] Smeal and Murray had no doubt been impressed by the English activist George Thompson, at that time beginning to acquire a formidable reputation as an orator, dispatched to Scotland by the Agency Committee of the London-based Anti-Slavery Society to debate a representative of the West India Association at public meetings earlier that year. And the two secretaries were inspired by Garrison, who made his first journey across the Atlantic that summer, particularly his *Appeal to the Friends of Negro Emancipation throughout Great Britain*, which they reprinted in the Society's first annual report.

While other abolitionist groups (including the Emancipation Society's predecessor, the Glasgow Anti-Slavery Society) dissolved and wondered how next to proceed, Smeal and Murray were not satisfied with self-congratulation. Emancipation in the West Indies involved a sickening compromise: it insisted on a transitional period of so-called 'apprenticeship' (which conferred some rights on the former

Figure 4.1 William Lloyd Garrison (left), George Thompson (right)

slaves, but still obliged them to work for their former owners over a specified period) and provided for the compensation of slave-owners to the tune of £20 million.[5]

The Society played a leading role in the campaign against the Apprenticeship System and demanded that compensation payments be suspended until its abuses were curtailed (the system was eventually abandoned by the colonial assemblies themselves, just ahead of legislation by Westminster in 1838).[6] But it also set its sights on those parts of the world where slavery still prevailed, particularly the United States. One of its first acts was to finance George Thompson's speaking tour there (1834–5), marking the beginning of an association with 'our gifted and devoted, and approved Missionary' that lasted many years.[7] Virtually every black abolitionist to visit Scotland before Douglass was welcomed by Murray and Smeal. A member of the committee of the Glasgow Emancipation Society while a medical student at Glasgow University in the 1830s, James McCune Smith had attended its first annual meeting alongside Nathaniel Paul, with whom he shared a platform at the Trades' Hall; after they returned to

America they were made honorary members. Robert Purvis addressed a public meeting organised by the Society in 1834, 'much to the satisfaction of the audience', while Charles Remond was fêted in Glasgow after attending the World Anti-Slavery Convention in London in 1840, the first major attempt to bring British and American abolitionists together in one place and co-ordinate their activities.[8]

Scottish abolitionists had been anticipating Douglass's arrival for several months. Already, in October, the committee of the Glasgow Emancipation Society had taken note of the report in the *Liberator* of the eventful crossing on the *Cambria*, and resolved to convey its gratitude to Captain Judkins for 'his firm and noble conduct' and have a notice to that effect published in the *Glasgow Argus*, a paper that, as we have seen, had for some years demonstrated a keen interest in the treatment of black passengers on transatlantic vessels. The Committee also made plans for a public meeting at which Douglass would lecture on American Slavery.[9] 'We hope to have Frederick Douglass in Scotland shortly,' wrote Smeal's sister, Jane Wigham, of the Edinburgh Ladies' Emancipation Society, in November.[10] But they would have to wait.

In Dublin, Douglass stayed at the home of Richard Davis Webb, a Quaker printer and secretary of the Hibernian Anti-Slavery Society in the city, who had been an ally and close friend of Garrison ever since they met in London in 1840. It was Webb who set up Douglass's speaking tour of Ireland but his plans had to adapt to changing circumstances. Buffum, who had accompanied him to Dublin, left him in Cork in October to attend an Anti-Corn-Law League meeting in Manchester, and Douglass expected to meet him again in Belfast a few weeks later.[11] Then, in Limerick, Douglass announced his intention to go direct to Scotland once Buffum linked up with him in Dublin towards the end of November.[12] But his friend remained in England, and Douglass proceeded alone to Belfast, where, fired by his enthusiastic reception, he determined to stay for a few weeks. Pressed by Smeal, he considered cancelling a brief trip to Birmingham in December but felt he could not break the engagement, even though, as he confided to Webb, 'I ought to go to Glasgow as early as I possibly can. They are certainly anxious to see me and hear me. They ought to be gratified. They have taken every pains to secure me. Thus far to no purpose. I fear they'll grow impatient.'[13] In the end, he went to Birmingham and returned to Belfast to deliver more lectures, and did not leave until Buffum joined him there in the new year.

The men donned their hats and buttoned up their coats against the cold evening air. Exiting the station, Smeal and Murray would have escorted the two men across Telford's fine, wide granite bridge, observing on the left, on both sides of the river, forests of masts, quays crowded with vessels, sometimes nine deep, loading and discharging their cargoes in the twilight. They continued to Jamaica Street, crowded by carts, waggons, noddies and omnibuses negotiating their way to and from the harbour. And then, turning right, they navigated the busy pavements of the broad gas-lit thoroughfare of Argyle Street and the Trongate, past its fashionable arcades, behind which lurked vast warehouses and open and covered markets. The hosts no doubt drew their visitors' attention to some notable landmarks: the Theatre Royal, rebuilt a few years earlier; the new City Hall, where Douglass and Buffum would speak the following week; and the Tontine Hotel, with its fine piazza and large reading room, for a long time the commercial hub of the metropolis until the Royal Exchange on Queen Street opened in 1829. Here, at Glasgow Cross, they would have passed into a poorer district, indicated by its humbler dwellings and a profusion of spirit-houses and whisky cellars. The Americans may have been struck by the 'squalid, stolid misery and degradation' described by Margaret Fuller in her dispatches that year for the *New York Tribune*, in which Glasgow 'more resembles an *Inferno* than any other [city] we have yet visited'.[14] A few hundred yards further on was Smeal's residence, situated above his grocer's shop at 161 Gallowgate, a few blocks short of the infantry barracks.[15]

After a day of rest, which may well have been disturbed by a riot in which a large crowd looted a cotton mill ravaged by fire half a mile away in Bridgeton, Smeal introduced his guests to the Glasgow Emancipation Society committee on Monday evening, to finalise the arrangements for the long-awaited meeting at City Hall on Thursday 15 January.[16] Here Douglass made his first public appearance in Scotland, topping the bill, which announced that 'Frederick Douglass, a self-liberated American slave, will deliver a lecture on American slavery.'[17] This was to be the occasion of a reunion with the peace campaigner Henry Clarke Wright, an old associate of Garrison with whom Douglass had shared antislavery platforms from his earliest days as an abolitionist speaker in Massachusetts. Wright had been in Europe for over three years, lecturing intensively, at some danger to his health. He was eventually persuaded to take several months

Figure 4.2 Henry Clarke Wright.

off at a water-cure establishment in the Alps, returning to the fray in the spring of 1845, addressing audiences across Scotland; Douglass would have followed his progress in the regular reports Wright sent to the *Liberator*. In the event, Wright did not speak at City Hall that night but had a letter read out on his behalf, explaining that he could not attend due to previous engagements.[18] He and Douglass would not meet until the following week, in Perth.[19]

For Douglass, the City Hall meeting was the first of over a hundred and fifty speaking engagements during the year – more than half of them in Scotland, where he was based for the first five months, apart from one brief unscheduled trip to London. He passed through again at the end of July, and after joining Garrison soon after his arrival in England, they looped around Scotland twice on their rapid tour of the provinces in the autumn. He spoke everywhere, from chapels in small towns to concert halls in big cities, sometimes alone, sometimes supported by Buffum, and sometimes alongside other campaigners, including temperance advocates and political campaigners, but nearly always stole the show.[20]

Mr. Douglass especially enchained the attention of his audience, by the narration of a number of anecdotes relating to himself and other slaves, who had escaped from bondage. This gentleman exercises a wonderful power over the sympathies of his audience. He is alternatively humorous and grave – argumentative and declamatory – lively and pathetic. While there is an entire absence of any effort after effect, there is the most perfect identity of the speaker with the subject on which he is dwelling, and an extraordinary power of rousing corresponding feelings in the minds of those whom he addresses. This power was singularly manifested on this occasion, and none, we think, who heard him, will ever forget the impression produced upon themselves, or the effect produced upon others. The entertainment evidently afforded the highest and purest satisfaction to all present.[21]

While his mission was to brandish the horrors of slavery before the wider world, it was also vitally important to let Americans know he was doing so. In Britain and Ireland, he was not only addressing those sympathisers who came to hear him speak, but also those slaveholders in Baltimore, Charleston or New Orleans who would, within a few weeks, read, as he explained in London, 'that some negro of theirs has broken loose from his chains [. . .] and is now exposing their deeds of deep damnation to the gaze of the Christian people of England'.[22] As he reminded his listeners several times, 'the extraordinary [. . .] rapidity with which intelligence is transmitted from one country to another' was made possible by what he called the 'magic power of steam', which had revolutionised the newspaper and book publishing industries and modes of communication in the preceding decade, bringing more words to more readers in less time.[23] In 1840 the completion of the Glasgow–Ayr railway, the introduction of a regular steamer service from Ardrossan to Liverpool, and Cunard's new steam-packet service from there to Boston had nearly halved the time it took for a speech reported in the Scottish press to be reprinted in the *Liberator*, reducing it from seven to four weeks.[24] No wonder that it was around this time that travellers began to refer to the Atlantic as no more than a 'big pond'.[25]

Douglass shared with many of his contemporaries a sense of awe at the changes taking place around him. As he put it a few years later:

Walled cities and empires have become unfashionable. The arm of commerce has borne away the gates of the strong city. Intelligence is penetrating the darkest corners of the globe. It makes its pathway over and under the sea, as well as on the earth. Wind, steam, and lightning are its chartered agents. Oceans no longer divide, but link nations together. From Boston to London is now a holiday excursion. Space is comparatively annihilated. – Thoughts expressed on one side of the Atlantic are distinctly heard on the other.[26]

Here Douglass, following many of his contemporaries, was repurposing a 'modest request' that Alexander Pope had ridiculed a century before as a bad use of hyperbole ('Ye Gods! Annihilate but space and time / And make two lovers happy'), which seemed less absurd in the new industrial age.[27]

Reflecting on his dizzy itinerary near the end of his tour, Douglass declared, 'I have journeyed upon highways, byways, railways, and steamboats. I have myself gone, I might say, with almost electric speed,' adding humorously, to indicate that all did not always go according to plan, 'but at all events my trunk has been overtaken by electric speed.'[28] Douglass here uses a striking expression that was gaining currency at the time – two years earlier Disraeli, in his novel *Sybil*, had described how, by singing, striking workers could spread 'by an almost electrical agency' news of a labour leader's arrival in town – due in large part to the rapid expansion of the electric telegraph.[29] An article describing the new connection between Glasgow and Edinburgh in January 1846 explained that it allowed messages to be exchanged between the cities along a single continuous 46-mile-long galvanised iron wire in the course of two minutes. But in applying 'electric speed' to his own movement, it is almost as if Douglass is not only harnessing these communication technologies, but actually embodies them.[30]

A sense of the historical moment – and the possibilities for change welling within it – that Douglass shared with his fellow campaigners is wonderfully captured in a letter Henry Clarke Wright sent to Garrison from Dunsinane in Perthshire shortly before Douglass's arrival. He was writing at the end of a week that saw the resignation of the Conservative prime minister Robert Peel, the failure of the Whig opposition to form a new government, and Peel's resumption of office – a turmoil provoked by his declared intention to repeal the corn laws, which blocked cheap grain imports and kept the price of bread high. This disturbed many in Peel's own party, which traditionally represented the aristocratic landowners. Radical reformers such as Wright believed the end of protective tariffs would usher in a new era of world peace and democratic, republican governments:[31]

This kingdom boils like a cauldron. All eyes turn to London. Peel goes out – the Queen sends for Russell – all men come to a stand – wonder what next. Russell give up – Peel is re-called. The Anti-Corn Law League, under its plebeian leaders, hated by aristocracy, has the public ear, and controls the nation. A power is rising in Britain, that will sweep away the Corn Laws – the State Church – restricted Suffrage – Primogeniture – the National Debt – Aristocracy and Royalty – all but the *name*; and that without bloodshed. Revolution – bloodless revolution, must be the watchword of Britain for the next half century. It is impossible to enter into and understand the nature and bearings of the present crisis, except by those who are constituents parts of the community. May the God of nations speed the car of revolution!'[32]

As Douglass caught up with local news in the *Herald* and *Argus* – perhaps perusing them beneath the elaborate chandeliers of the Tontine Hotel reading room, which was supported by subscribers paying £1 12s a year but open to strangers free of charge for a limited time[33] – he would have been plunged into screeds of tiny print documenting Scotland's breathless contribution to the debates, not only of Peel's bill about to be presented to the parliament in Westminster (Peel outlined his plans on 27 January), but the manic expansion of the railway network soon to connect Glasgow and Edinburgh to the South, the desecration of the Sabbath, the spoiling of the potato crop and the prospect of war with the United States. And amid the news items recording fatal accidents, mill fires, bankruptcies and sentences of transportation for petty crimes, advertisements for Bibles and pianofortes, cheap gloves and draining slates, table beer and genuine foreign cigars, perhaps he paused to note the appearance of the latest Christmas book from Charles Dickens, *The Cricket on the Hearth*, and an announcement of the discovery of a new planet, Astraea.

And yet, for all his self-conscious modernity, Douglass's rousing speeches – in Glasgow, Edinburgh, Paisley, Dundee and a host of smaller towns – often reached their climax with a single curious, almost biblical, slogan that seems to hark back to an earlier age. At the very least, it suggests that the expanding network of international commerce was not always a force for good.

I want to have all the people saying, 'Send back the money;' and in order to rivet these words in the minds of the audience, I propose that they give three cheers, not hurrahs, but say 'Send back the money.'

(The vast assembly spontaneously complied with Mr. Douglass's request. The effect produced was indescribable. Mr. Douglass then sat down amid reiterated rounds of applause.)[34]

'Let this be the theme in every town in Scotland,' he urged.[35] And his wish was granted. As far away as Aberdeen it was remarked:

'Send back the money,' 'Why don't you send the money back?' are cries as common in the southern towns of Scotland, as 'All round my hat,' or 'Does your mother know you're out?' used to be in this great metropolis. Nay, we understand that, in Glasgow and Paisley, the old plan of advertising blacking has been resorted to, and on every wall and public place there is chalked up the significant phrase, 'Send back the money.' Eminent saints and pious divines have been mobbed on the streets and had their houses surrounded by crowds of little urchins bawling at the top of their voices, 'Send back the money!' 'Send back the money!'[36]

In broadsheets published in Edinburgh, popular songs were given new words. In 'My Boy Tammy' the question was changed from 'War hae ye been a' the day?' to 'Whaur got ye a' the bawbees?' while the refrain of the old Jacobite song 'There'll never be peace till Jamie comes hame' became 'till the siller's sent hame'.[37] 'The very boys in the street are singing *Send back that money*,' Douglass wrote.[38]

In Arbroath there was painted in blood red capitals, SEND BACK THE MONEY. A woman was sent to wash it, but the letters still remained visible, SEND BACK THE MONEY. (Great applause.) A mason was afterwards got to chisel it out, but there still was left in indelible characters, SEND BACK THE MONEY. (Cheers.) I want men, women, and children to send forth this cry, wherever they go. Let it be the talk around the fireside, in the street, and at the market-place – indeed, everywhere. It is a fitting subject even on the Sabbath day.[39]

According to one report, Douglass went so far as to carve the slogan with a spade on the grassy slopes of Arthur's Seat in Edinburgh, with 'two fair Quakeresses as his companions' – presumably Jane Wigham and her stepdaughter Eliza, also active in the Edinburgh Ladies' Society.[40]

How so? What was this money, where did it come from, and why was Douglass so keen that it was returned? In answering these questions, we must step back a few years to consider the religious upheavals that had shaken Scotland to the core.

Notes

1. 'Friend Douglass and myself left Belfast, Ireland, on the [Saturday] morning of the 10th of January, and arrived in the city of Glasgow the same evening': JB to WLG, Bowling Bay, 14 April 1846 (*Liberator*, 15 May 1846). Ferries crossed from Belfast to Ardrossan every Tuesday, Thursday and Saturday; the first-class cabin fare was 12s (*Glasgow Herald*, 5 January 1846).
2. FD, Belfast, 6 January 1846 (FDP 1.1, pp. 126–8). For the inscription see *Belfast News-Letter*, 9 January 1846.
3. My account draws freely from the *Guide to the Glasgow & Ayrshire Railway* and *The Topographical Gazetteer of Scotland*, vol. 1, pp. 667–8.
4. Jezierski, 'The Glasgow Emancipation Society', p. 23.
5. For useful overviews of the directions taken by the British abolitionists after 1833 see Temperley, *British Antislavery*, pp. 19–92; and Huzzey, *Freedom Burning*, pp. 5–20.
6. Jezierski, 'Glasgow Emancipation Society', pp. 117–18.
7. Ibid. pp. 100–3. The quotation is from GES, *Second Annual Report*, p. 11.
8. On Smith see John Stauffer, 'Introduction' to Smith, *Works*, pp. xxi–xxii; BAP1, pp. 68–70. On Paul see BAP1, pp. 53–9; 'George Thompson in England', *Liberator* 4 June 1836; GES, *First Annual Report*. On Purvis see Bacon, *But One Race*, p. 46; Jezierski, 'Glasgow Emancipation Society', p. 118; 'Letter from the Glasgow Female Anti-Slavery Society', Glasgow, 3 September 1834 (GES, *First Annual Report*, p. 45; *Liberator*, 7 March 1835). Remond addressed a 'Great Public Meeting of the Glasgow Emancipation Society: Reception of the American Delegates' on 27 July 1840 (*Glasgow Argus*, 30 July 1840, repr. *Liberator*, 28 August 1840) and the Annual Meeting of the GES on 8 August 1840: GES, *Report of the Annual Meeting*, pp. 16–19.
9. GES, Minutes of Committee Meetings, 17 October, 21 October and 5 November 1845 (Smeal Collection, Reel 1).
10. Jane Wigham to MWC, Edinburgh, 23 November 1845 (BAA, p. 244). 'I hear oft from James and Frederick in Dublin. Expect to meet them in Glasgow soon,' wrote HCW to WLG, Abroath, 27 September 1845 (*Liberator*, 24 October 1845).

11. FD to WLG, Cork, 28 October 1845 (FDP 3.1, p. 62).
12. FD to RW, Limerick, 10 November 1845 (FDP 3.1, p. 64).
13. FD to RW, Belfast, 7 December 1845 (LWRD5, p. 15). Rice suggests that FD delayed because of his reservations concerning HCW: Rice, *The Scots Abolitionists*, p. 133.
14. Fuller, *At Home and Abroad*, p. 159.
15. I draw freely here from *Black's Economical Guide through Glasgow* and *The Topographical Gazetteer of Scotland*, vol. 1, pp. 643–4, 647, 662–3.
16. Minutes of GES committee meeting, 12 January 1846 (Smeal Collection, Reel 1). FDP 1.1, p. xcvii has this as 10 January; and while discrepancies of dates do occur in the the GES minute books, this is unlikely as committee meetings did not take place on Saturdays. On the Bridgeton fire see *Glasgow Herald*, 12 and 19 January 1846. JB later wrote to WLG of the drunkenness that characterised Sundays in Glasgow: JB to WLG, Bowling Bay, 14 April 1846 (*Liberator*, 15 May 1846).
17. *Glasgow Argus*, 12 January 1846.
18. *Glasgow Argus*, 22 January 1846.
19. HCW to WLG, Perth, 26 January 1846 (*Liberator*, 27 February 1846). This letter indicates that the meeting on 26 January was the fourth; we may assume that they met on 23 January, FD having lectured in Glasgow on 22 January, according to the *Witness*, 24 January 1846.
20. See Appendix 1, 'List of Speaking Engagements'. I have found evidence for eighty-four speaking engagements in Scotland; it is likely there were at least 100. FDP 1.1 lists seventy, of which eight certainly did not take place. FDP 1.1 lists 135 for 1846 as a whole (fifty-eight in England, six in Ireland and one in Wales) (FDP 1.1, pp. xcvii–cii).
21. FD, Edinburgh, 1 May 1846 (*Manstealers*, p. 56).
22. FD, London, 22 May 1846 (FDP 1.1, p. 274).
23. For 'extraordinary [. . .] rapidity' see FD, London, 30 March 1847 (FDP 1.2, pp. 44–5); for 'magic power of steam' see FD, Leeds, 23 December 1846 (FDP 1.1, p. 477). On the revolutionary impact of steam power on early Victorian communications and printing technology see Secord, *Victorian Sensation*, esp. pp. 25–32.
24. For example, O'Connell's speech in Glasgow on 23 September 1835 did not appear in the *Liberator* until 14 November 1835 (over seven weeks later), while the speeches of WLG, Remond and others in Edinburgh on 24 July 1840 were reported in the *Liberator* on 21 August (just four weeks later).
25. For example, WLG to Francis Jackson, London, 29 August 1846 (GL3, p. 392).
26. FD, Rochester, NY, 5 July 1852 ('What to the Slave is the Fourth of July?') (FDP 1.2, p. 387).

27. Pope, 'Peri Bathous', p. 219.
28. FD, London, 30 March 1847 (FDP 1.2, p. 49).
29. Disraeli, *Sybil*, p. 338.
30. 'Electric Telegraph on the Edinburgh and Glasgow Railway', *Glasgow Herald*, 19 January 1846.
31. For the political vicissitudes in London of late December 1845 see Bates, *Penny Loaves*, pp. 9–28.
32. HCW to WLG, Dunsinane, 26 December 1845 (*Liberator*, 6 February 1846).
33. '[T]he room, which is amply supplied with Scotch, English, and Irish newspapers, and periodical publications of every kind, is lighted by richly-cut glass chandeliers [. . .] The reading-room is supported by an annual subscription of £1.12., but is open to strangers gratuitously for a limited time': Lewis, *Topographical Dictionary*, vol. 1, p. 490.
34. FD, London, 22 May 1846 (FDP 1.1, p. 299).
35. FD, Paisley, 25 April 1846 (FDP 1.1, p. 242).
36. *Aberdeen Herald*, 16 May 1846.
37. *Anti-Slavery Songs. Bawbees*: money; *siller*: silver.
38. FD to RW, Dundee, 10 February 1846 (FDP 3.1, p. 92).
39. FD, Paisley, 25 April 1846 (FDP 1.1, pp. 242–3). On the Arbroath graffito see also HCW to WLG, Arbroath, 11 February 1846 (*Liberator*, 3 April 1846).
40. *American Slavery*, p. 20. This from a speech by Dr Campbell citing 'one of the Scotch papers', probably the *Witness* of 20 May 1846, but reprinted in other newspapers, including the *Fife Herald*, 21 May 1846.

Chapter 5

That Ticklish Possession

During the 1830s the Church of Scotland was in crisis. The Evangelical party, led by Thomas Chalmers, replaced the Moderates as the dominant force in the Church. Their vision of a much more active and crusading future was disappointed, however, by the insufficiency of financial support from the State, coupled with a series of legal decisions in the House of Lords that seriously limited the Church's control over its own internal affairs, most notably the appointment of ministers. Finding themselves at an impasse, on 18 May 1843 Chalmers and his Evangelical supporters walked out of the General Assembly to establish a new Church of their own, which they called the Free Church of Scotland.

In what is known as the Disruption of the Church of Scotland, over a third of its ministers and roughly half of its lay members declared allegiance to the new body. Deprived of state support, it was not an Established Church, but Chalmers and his colleagues had high hopes that it would fulfil the same role – a truly national Church that would care for the spiritual and educational needs of the whole population. They sharply distinguished themselves from other Presbyterian churches, known as 'Voluntaries', including those which had seceded in the eighteenth century, which had been campaigning for the complete separation of church and state, allowing all sects to compete on an equal footing. Chalmers insisted that the Free Church adhered to the Establishment principle. But in doing so it faced a huge challenge. While other Churches could support themselves from the contributions of its congregations, they were only viable in the wealthier areas of the towns. In working-class districts and in the country, a Church required additional sources of income. Not only that, of course, but the Free Church initially did not have

Figure 5.1 Thomas Chalmers.

any church or school buildings to call its own, and in some places, services were conducted in the open air.[1]

A huge fund-raising programme was set in motion, at home and abroad. Representatives were dispatched to England and Ireland the same summer, and at the end of the year a five-man deputation set sail for the United States, where they reaped the benefit of long-standing links with the Presbyterians.[2] (That these American churches did not adhere to the Establishment principle was an irony not lost on the Free Church's opponents.) Reporting back on the visit to the General Assembly of 1844, Dr Cunningham, the leader of the delegation, estimated that £3,000 had been raised in America before the deputation left, and £6,000 since, with a few thousand perhaps still to come.[3] He singled out the generosity of Mr James Lenox of New York for special mention,[4] but it would appear that the bulk of the money was raised in the South, due mainly to the efforts of Cunningham's colleague, Rev. George Lewis of St David's Church, Dundee, whose travels took him to Charleston, Mobile, New Orleans and other cities. On his return, Lewis published his *Impressions of America and*

Figure 5.2 George Lewis.

the American Churches (1845), a book-length account of his experiences, including the incident involving the passenger from Haiti on his return voyage, referred to in Chapter 3.[5]

At this time, the abolitionist movement in the United States was divided. In a disruption of its own, a minority left the American Anti-Slavery Society to form the breakaway American and Foreign Anti-Slavery Society in 1840. The new body, led by Arthur and Lewis Tappan, believed the way forward was to engage in electoral politics and soon began working closely with the Liberty Party, formed the same year, which put forward candidates for several US presidential contests. The 'old organisation', under the charismatic leadership of William Lloyd Garrison, kept its distance from these new developments, convinced that the Constitution was an intrinsically pro-slavery document which did not authorise the federal government to interfere with the internal affairs of the slave states. Appealing to individual conscience, the Garrisonians hoped to agitate public opinion through the speeches of travelling lecturers and a range of publications.[6] In practice, however, this approach – often misleadingly called 'moral suasion' – did not stop them contesting cases in the courts, campaigning and voting in elections, and engaging in various forms of direct action.[7]

In Britain and Ireland, most local societies were affiliated to the British and Foreign Anti-Slavery Society in London, a body established in 1839 by Joseph Sturge, which maintained close ties with the Tappans' 'new organization'. But in a few towns, notably Dublin, Glasgow and Edinburgh, abolitionists tended to be defiantly Garrisonian in sympathy, as was the freelance lecturer George Thompson, whose services they frequently hired.[8] Divisions within the American movement crossed the Atlantic in dramatic fashion when delegates from both factions attended the World Anti-Slavery Convention in London in 1840, organised by Sturge, exposing another issue which had led to the rift: women's rights.

Garrison used his position to support the work of women abolitionists, including black women such as Maria Stewart and Sojourner Truth, whose books he published. But his attempt to push for the full participation of women in the American Anti-Slavery Society faced stiff opposition. When Abby Kelley, one of its leading lecturers, was elected to the business committee, the resignations began. In a provocative move, seven of the London delegates representing the 'old organization' loyal to Garrison were women.

Although the invitation had not specified that the delegates be men, it was not entirely unexpected when the women – in accordance with what was deemed British 'customs and usages' – were allowed only to observe proceedings from the gallery. Four American male delegates, including Garrison and Remond, sat with them in protest.[9] The ramifications spread far and wide. The presence of these men at a Glasgow Emancipation Society meeting welcoming them to Scotland after the Convention caused some discomfort among more conservative members and the issue was the catalyst for resignations from the Society the following year, strengthening its Garrisonian stance, if not to the extent of admitting women as members.[10]

There were religious differences between the two wings of the movement too. Garrison and his supporters tended to belong to non-evangelical denominations such as the Unitarians or the Society of Friends, or even shunned organised religion altogether in an anti-clericalism that troubled their mainstream evangelical rivals. This would have influenced the resignations in Glasgow too. Nevertheless, they were agreed on one thing at least: the need to expose the pro-slavery character of the American churches, especially those in the South.[11] The careful documentation of James Gillespie Birney's booklet *American Churches the Bulwarks of American Slavery* (1840) was to become an influential reference work for all antislavery campaigners over the next decade.[12] And so it was only a matter of time before the Free Church's fund-raising mission would provoke outrage among abolitionists of all shades of opinion.[13]

The first move was made by the Glasgow Emancipation Society at a public meeting on 14 March 1844. Its members included several ministers of the Free Church. One of them was Rev. Michael Willis of Renfield Church, who served on the committee (and was subsequently elected a vice-president of the Society). Another was Dr Robert Burns of the Laigh Kirk in Paisley, who, as one of the five-man deputation, was still travelling in the United States.[14] Nevertheless, the Society condemned the Free Church's solicitation of the contributions from the Southern churches and Willis was among those who spoke in favour of the motion that called on its leaders to

> refuse and send them back to the donors, accompanied with a faithful & plain dealing testimony to the American churches against slavery, universally allowed and practiced by ministers and members of churches in the Southern states, by which 2½ millions of our fellow men are bought & sold, bred & forced to live like cattle, & shut out from all access to moral & religious knowledge.[15]

The Glasgow society, as we have noted, was aligned with Garrison. But, as if to underline the consensus across the movement, on 2 April Garrison's rivals in the American and Foreign Anti-Slavery Society, in an initiative of their own, wrote an open letter to the Free Church condemning its actions, a letter which would be distributed outside the Free Church's General Assembly the following month.[16] Their stance was probably inspired, or at least emboldened, by the example of Daniel O'Connell, who led the campaign to repeal the 1800 Acts of Union of Great Britain and Ireland. In a notorious speech at a meeting of the Repeal Association in Dublin on 11 May 1843, he declared his intention to refuse 'blood-stained money' from pro-slavery Repeal groups in the United States.[17] The American letter concludes, naming the Free Church leader and two members of the deputation: 'What O'Connell refused to touch, when brought to his hand, Dr. Chalmers sent, and Drs. Cunningham and Burns went 4000 miles to solicit!'[18]

By the time Douglass and Buffum arrived in Glasgow, the protest had gathered pace considerably. The American abolitionist and peace campaigner Henry Clarke Wright, who probably came up with the powerful 'Send Back the Money' slogan, had been lecturing exhaustively across Scotland on the matter without a break since March 1845.[19] Joining forces, the three of them intensified the campaign. 'We went to Perth, Dundee, Arbroath, Montrose, Aberdeen, Paisley, Kelso, Ayr, Greenock, Helensburgh and Dumbarton, in succession,' reported Douglass, 'making the people acquainted with the true position of the Free Church of Scotland in regard to slaveholding.'[20] In April 1846 George Thompson travelled from London to support them in a burst of a dozen meetings in Edinburgh through the month leading up to the Free Church's General Assembly at the end of May, at which the abolitionists hoped to secure victory.[21]

Douglass set the campaign alight. It was only after he added his voice that the controversy attracted sustained interest in the Scottish press.[22] Less than three weeks after his arrival, he could feel it. 'Under these rallying cries, old Scotland boils like a pot,' he wrote. 'The agitation goes nobly on – all this region is in a ferment.'[23] He did not invent the slogan 'Send Back the Money', but he did use it more effectively in his speeches, repeating it as his orations reached their climax, urging his audiences to chant it back to him. And if the abolitionists had already settled on the round figure of £3,000 as the amount of the contested contribution to the Free Church, Douglass sophisticated rhetoric endowed the number with an almost numerological significance, donated on behalf of thirty thousand slaveholders who held three million human beings in bondage three thousand miles across the sea.[24]

Notices advertising Douglass's forthcoming appearances often promised a 'lecture on American slavery', as if he would be delivering a dispassionate, educational discourse on astronomy, literature or practical midwifery. Abolitionist meetings were usually more intense and emotional than that, with speakers denouncing slavery, exhorting audiences to act and sometimes rebuking them for their passivity. To convey their message, they drew not only on the oratorical traditions of the early lyceum, but also the more flamboyant elocutionary conventions of the church pulpit and the theatrical stage.[25]

Douglass was a master of both. From his earliest days as an anti-slavery speaker in Massachusetts, Douglass had stood out for the way he recognised that in order to win over an audience, he needed to entertain them. He was well equipped to do so, steeped as he was in the vernacular traditions of the black preacher, singer and story-teller, and also quick to absorb the techniques of popular theatre. He was a talented mimic. A parody of a pro-slavery sermon was a set piece of his from at least 1842 and went down well, but it was never fully integrated into his speeches, which largely consisted of personal testimony of his experiences as a slave, followed by direct exhortations to his listeners.[26]

In Scotland, the Free Church issue forced Douglass to expand his repertoire. Although he was boasting about the effect of the campaign quite early on, he admitted later that he initially 'found the people for the most part cold and indifferent'.[27] In Glasgow, he said, 'I was besought not to agitate the question there, and for a time, I confess my hands hung down – I felt almost incapable of prosecuting my work.'[28] He may well have been misled by Henry Clarke Wright's glowing reports of his activities the previous year. When Douglass headed north to meet up with Wright in Perth he found that his colleague had not broken in audiences as much as he had been led to believe. Wright's confrontational style as well as his controversial views on other matters – an atheist and anarchist in the eyes of some – may partly account for that. Newspaper reports suggest that in Douglass's four speeches there, and the three following in Dundee, while he did issue strong condemnations of the Free Church for accepting money from slaveholders, he did so only in passing, and even then, there were murmurs of dissent among his listeners.[29]

Douglass may well have reflected on this in conversations with George Gilfillan, the United Secession minister who hosted his first lectures in Dundee at the School Wynd Church, and probably invited him and Buffum to the manse on Paradise Road. Gilfillan was widely read and relatively secular in outlook. His first *Gallery of Literary Portraits* had been published the previous year, and he counted Thomas de Quincey and Thomas Carlyle among his friends. He had embraced the abolitionist cause after hearing George Thompson speak in Glasgow in 1836 and was close to two ministers on the committee of the Glasgow Emancipation Society.[30] On their way between the manse and the chapel, they would have passed close by the flax-spinning mills that would produce the thread that would be woven into Osnaburg linen and exported to the plantations to be worn by slaves such as Douglass, who, as a child, 'was kept almost naked' except for 'a coarse tow linen shirt, reaching only to my knees'.[31]

Figure 5.3 George Gilfillan.

Perhaps Gilfillan told Douglass of the recent protests when six young women at Baxter's mill were sentenced to ten days' imprisonment with hard labour for taking the afternoon off after their request for a modest pay rise in line with other operatives was refused.[32]

But Gilfillan was also an admirer of Thomas Chalmers.[33] At a meeting a few weeks later he represented him as an enemy of slavery, and was reluctant to condemn the Free Church, unsure who to blame for its conduct.[34] We can only imagine the private discussions between Gilfillan and Douglass and guess what impact they had on their views. For his part, Gilfillan subsequently adopted a firmer stance regarding the donations from the Southern clergy, if worded somewhat more timidly than most of the abolitionists' campaign slogans: 'Well, that money is rather a ticklish possession, perhaps the best plan after all is to send it back?'[35] And his guest may have been led to reconsider his approach too.

Douglass began to realise that it wasn't enough for him to describe the horrors of slavery, and then denounce the Free Church. He had to find a way of conveying how its actions directly affected the lives of the enslaved. He had to persuade audiences to imagine the fund-raising mission from the point of view of those who ultimately created the wealth that made the donations possible in the first place. Douglass began to experiment, and in his fourth speech in Dundee on 30 January at the more spacious Bell Street Chapel he changes his tactics considerably, introducing telling empirical details, deploying carefully chosen quotations and inserting a dramatic interlude.[36]

From the start he announces that his subject will be 'the connection of the Free Church of Scotland with the Churches in America', but he makes it clear that his argument is not with the Free Church as such.[37] He is there to speak not on behalf of 'opposing religious denominations' but rather 'the cause of the slave'.[38] And he takes care to emphasise how unchristian slavery is – forbidding slaves to marry or to read the word of God, with Douglass powerfully breaking this last injunction by reading several verses from *Isaiah* which castigate the sinful people of Sodom and Gomorrah, whose 'hands are full of blood', in order to lend biblical authority to his argument that the American churches deserve to be condemned likewise.[39] For their hands too are 'full of blood', a phrase Douglass justifies by explaining that 'the coats, the boots, the watches, the houses, and all they possess, are the result of the unpaid toil of the poor, fettered, stricken and branded slave'.[40]

In shaking these hands in 'good Christian fellowship', Douglass continues, the Free Church has this blood on its hands too. But, not satisfied that he has won over the doubters, he anticipates the objection that the American churches do in fact provide religious instruction to the slaves by treating the audience to his set piece, his parody of a Southern preacher, whose mission is to instil worldly obedience among his enslaved flock, not spiritual enlightenment.[41] And then, to press home his point further, he reads a passage from the New Orleans *Picayune* eulogising Thomas Chalmers, followed by some of the advertisements for runaway slaves printed in the same newspaper.[42] Only then does he feel confident enough to bring his speech to a climax by appealing to 'the people of Scotland' to let the Free Church know what they feel and demand that it 'send back the blood-stained dollars'. Douglass's closing words are met with '[g]reat cheering'.[43]

The *Dundee Courier* added a note to its report of the speech that after the meeting several devoted adherents to the Free Church were heard to 'declare that they will not contribute one additional sixpence towards her support till the "blood-stained money is sent back"'.[44] Nonetheless, despite the radical overhaul of his approach, Douglass's argument remains disjointed. The 'connection' between the Free Church and its allies in the United States – and why it was wrong – was a difficult idea to express memorably and succinctly, and Douglass probably felt that this speech did not accomplish its purpose. He needed a way of distilling his argument into a single compelling narrative.

Following ten days' rest, he spoke in Dundee again on 9 February, but by this time he and his companions were on the back foot, forced to respond to an offensive report of the earlier meeting in the Free Church newspaper the *Northern Warder*, which referred to the speakers' 'irrational abuse' and their 'abundant want of justice and good sense'.[45] On this occasion Douglass and Buffum chose to read descriptions of slavery by one of the Free Church delegates themselves – from George Lewis's *Impressions of America* – in order to rebut their critics.[46] When the two of them arrived the next day in Arbroath, twenty miles up the coast, Douglass must have reflected once more on how to reshape the campaign. They discovered that despite – or perhaps because of – Wright's earlier efforts, which had resulted in the 'Send Back the Money' slogan being daubed in large red letters on the wall of a building – they could secure no church for their meetings in the town, and they had to use the unsatisfactory Trades' Hall, until the 'more commodious' Abbey Church was made available.[47] In the meetings there, and in Aberdeen and Montrose in early March, Douglass's speeches were dominated by argumentation which, however sparkling, remained somewhat defensive.[48]

But by the time he returned to Dundee on 10 March, Douglass had hit on a solution. George Gilfillan welcomed back the abolitionists to his church for an 'Anti-Slavery Soirée' in honour of Douglass, Buffum and Wright. The special guests could not afford to be complacent. Although he had secured permission from the managers to hold the meeting, the decision had been far from unanimous, a fact to which Gilfillan alluded in his opening remarks.[49] Nonetheless an expectant crowd of 1,200 were gathered to hear Douglass speak, and he was not to disappoint them.

Douglass began by mocking the attacks on him and his colleagues by the *Northern Warder* and expressing his gratitude to the *Dundee Courier* for its support. And then, adopting the voice of a prosecutor, he spells out ten charges of which the Free Church is accused. The charge-sheet is a new addition to his armoury – and that there are 'as many [. . .] as there are laws in the decalogue' is a pleasing flourish. But thus far he remains within the argumentative and denunciatory mode he has practised over the previous six weeks.

In what comes next Douglass tries out something new. He tells the audience that slaves often talked of freedom in code – using the word 'pig's foot' instead. So, when they heard that members of a 'Free' Church were coming, 'many a slave would be saying, "Well, pig's foot come at last."'[50] His listeners might have suspected Douglass was pulling their leg here, contriving an excuse to indirectly insult the Church, but the laughter that follows suggests they enjoyed it. But the more serious point is that the slaves' expectations were about to be dashed to pieces.

Douglass goes on to explain why by means of a stunningly conceived dramatisation of a single hypothetical episode in which the Free Church delegate, Dundee's own Rev. George Lewis, visits his master Thomas Auld in Maryland. And in a brilliant twist, Douglass projects himself into the scene, as the boy who becomes the centre of it. In reading the newspaper report of this theatrical masterpiece, which is worth quoting at length, we can imagine Douglass expertly adopting the voices and mannerisms of its four protagonists: Lewis, Auld, a slave auctioneer, and his younger self.

Sir, I see brother Lewis calling on the slaveholder. I can almost go down south, and see him, when I was a slave, calling on my old master, Mr Thomas Auld (who would be a very likely party to call on), with his subscription paper. When brother Lewis knocks at the door, I answer, and he asks, 'Well, my lad, is your master in?' (Laughter.) 'Yes, Sir.' Well, he walks into the house, sees my master, and introduces himself thus (for my ear would be at the keyhole immediately on the door being shut) – 'My object in making this call this morning is to see if you would do something for the cause of religious freedom in Scotland. We have been labouring some time back, and have undergone severe struggles, for Gospel freedom in Scotland, and we have thought it right to call upon you, as a benevolent man and as having means to bestow, to see what you can do for us.' My master would reply, 'Brother Lewis, I deeply sympathize with your efforts; and as I see the cause recommended by Deacon such-a-one, I would like to have my name down with his. I'll tell you what I will do. I have a fine young negro who is to be sold, and I will sell him to-morrow and give you a contribution to the cause of freedom. (Applause and laughter.) If you will call, brother Lewis, and take your breakfast with me, I will then see what I can do; and as the slave is to be sold at Easton, I will feel happy if you also take a ride so far with me, as you may not have seen the capital of the county. Come about nine o'clock, brother, and I will see what I can do for the cause of freedom in Scotland.' (Laughter and cheering.)

The morning comes, and the breakfast hour, and brother Lewis also. (I have a son called Lewis, but I think I'll change his name.) (Applause.) The Bible is given to brother Lewis, and he reads, 'Blessed are the poor in spirit – Blessed are they that give to the poor,' and so on. All goes on delightfully. Brother L. prays, and after prayer sits down and partakes of the bounties produced by the blood of the slave, watered by the sweat and enriched by the blood of the half-famished negro. (Applause.) Brother Auld orders the carriage to be brought round to the door – I am tied behind the carriage and taken away, as I have seen often done: I am on the auction block, and the auctioneer is crying 'Who bids for this comely stout young negro? He is accustomed to his work, and has an excellent trade on his hands.' Well, 500 dollars are bid. Oh, how brother Lewis' eyes twinkle! (Laughter.) The auctioneer continues – 'This is not half the value of the negro; he is not sold for any bad quality. His master has no desire to get rid of him, but only wants to get a little money to aid the cause of religious freedom in Scotland.' Once, twice, thrice, is said by the auctioneer, and I am sold for 600 dollars.[51]

As the speech rises to its climax, its rhythms and repetitions lead to the inevitable conclusion:

When the Free Church says – Did not Abraham hold slaves? the reply should be, Send back that money! (Cheers). When they ask did not Paul send back Onesimus? I answer, Send you back that money! (Great cheering). That is the only answer which should be given to their sophistical arguments, and it is one which they cannot get over. (Great cheering). In order to justify their conduct, they endeavour to forget that they are a Church, and speak as if they were a manu-facturing corporation. They forget that a Church is not for making money, but for spreading the Gospel. We are guilty, say they, but these merchants are guilty, and some other parties are guilty also. I say, send back that money! (Cheering). There is music in that sound. (Continued cheering). There is poetry in it.[52]

What we see in this speech in Dundee is what made Douglass's inter-vention in Scotland so explosive: his new-found ability to seamlessly combine different registers. But the 'Send Back the Money' campaign prompted more striking innovations in his oratory. Here he presents a mini-drama, which makes use of the techniques of the 'monopolylogue', a form of entertainment popularised by the English actor Charles Mathews in which a solo performer takes the parts of several characters.[53] It is spellbinding as a performance in itself: the laughter that follows the first lines Douglass speaks as Lewis suggests he does so in a Scots (perhaps even a Dundonian) accent, and the different ways in which he conveys the minister's naivety are clearly much appreciated. But at the same time it allows Douglass to dramatise a conspiratorial relationship between American slaveholders (represented by 'brother Auld') and the Free Church ('brother Lewis'), artfully juxtaposing their sumptuous breakfast and the cause of 'freedom' (and carefully chosen verses from the Sermon on the Mount) with the back-breaking toil of enslaved labourers and their casual sale in order to meet unanticipated expenses.

Something of this scenario is captured in an illustration printed in Glasgow which may have been inspired by Douglass's dramatisation in Dundee (which he reprised in Perth, Paisley and Glasgow later that month).[54] On the left we see the transaction between a Free Church minister, taking a bag marked '£3,000' from the cigar-smoking, whip-carrying slaveholder. And on the right, the abolitionists in Scotland look on. George Thompson is pointing an accusing finger ('Mark those *brethren*!', echoing perhaps Douglass's pairing of 'brother Lewis' and 'brother Auld'), while James Buffum and Henry Clarke Wright share a few words ('There will be a noise about that yet, I guess Henry.' 'They shall send that money back.') Between them, a somewhat minstrelised Douglass is portrayed expressing his outrage – 'Is that the *Free* Church?' – the artist possibly alluding to his impersonation of the response of his fellow slaves who were expecting the visit to herald their emancipation.

Douglass was not exaggerating the consequences such a visit might have for him. As a boy he lived with the threat of being sold to traders on the Eastern Shore, especially after the death of his master in 1826, at which time a healthy young male slave could be bought for $400 in Talbot County and shipped to New Orleans where he would fetch twice as much. Colonel Lloyd was one of many Maryland planters who did business with the notorious Austin Woolfolk in the 1820s. Douglass certainly would have known slaves purchased and taken away by 'Woldfolk', as he calls him in his autobiography.[55]

Figure 5.4 'Send back the money!!'

The repetition of 'brother Lewis', some seven times, prepares the audience for the shift from anecdote to the rousing close, where Douglass alludes, more learnedly, to biblical defences of slavery within an exhortatory appeal to the Free Church to 'send back that money', also repeated, and each time to great cheers. It is clear from the report that Douglass has captured his listeners, confident enough to slip into the carefully paced rhythms of the preacher's sermon, calling out and surely finding his words echoed back by an energised assembly whose participation may have even surprised themselves. 'There is music in that sound,' he declares. We can imagine his deep, loud voice raised above the tumult, inviting it to subside, before he completes the perfect cadence. 'There is poetry in it.'

Notes

1. See Brown, 'The Ten Years' Conflict'; Brown, *Thomas Chalmers*, pp. 282–349; and Honeycutt, 'William Cunningham', pp. 77–210.
2. See FCS, *Proceedings 1843*, pp. 69–82, 39–45 and 170; Whyte, '*Send Back the Money!*', pp. 13–24. William Cunningham and Henry Ferguson sailed in December; the other three (George Lewis, Robert Burns and William Chalmers) followed early in the new year.
3. FCS, *Proceedings 1844*, p. 71. For further discussion of the amount raised see Shepperson, 'Thomas Chalmers', pp. 519–20.
4. FCS, *Proceedings 1844*, p. 72.
5. Lewis, *Impressions of America*. For other accounts see the biography of another member of the deputation, which includes extracts from his journal: Burns, *The Life and Times of the Rev. Robert Burns*, pp. 176–200.
6. The approach was powerfully articulated in what was known as the 'Declaration of Sentiments' (probably written by WLG): 'Declaration of the National Anti-Slavery Convention', *Liberator*, 14 December 1833.
7. On the relationship between Garrisonian and Liberty Party politics see Sinha, *The Slave's Cause*, pp. 461–99.
8. The geographical distribution of Garrisonian sympathies is evident in the lists of 'ladies' who 'have consented to receive donations for the American Anti-Slavery Society' published in the Irish and English editions of Douglass's *Narrative*: very few in London and the South-East compared to the South-West, Midlands and North, with Scotland, Wales and Ireland well represented (D1, pp. 123–4; D2, pp. cxxxiii–cxxxv).

9. See Sklar, '"Women Who Speak for an Entire Nation"'; Maynard, 'The World's Anti-Slavery Convention of 1840'; Billington and Billington, 'A Burning Zeal for Righteousness'; and Tyrrell, '"Women's Mission"'. The reference to British 'customs and usages' is in Mott, *Three Months in Great Britain*, p. 18.

10. Jezierski, 'Glasgow Emancipation Society', pp. 134–52.

11. The Presbyterian Churches had split on North–South lines in 1837 and the Baptist and Methodist Churches followed in 1844–5, but the Northern Churches were not exempt from censure from abolitionists. See Smith, *In His Image, But . . .*, pp. 74–128; Sernett, *Black Religion*, pp. 36–58; and McKivigan, *The War against Proslavery Religion*.

12. This was one of the main topics of discussion at the Annual Meeting of the BFASS in 1840, at which Thomas Clarkson made his last public appearance. His address (Clarkson, *A Letter to the Clergy*) and Birney's pamphlet *American Churches the Bulwarks of American Slavery* were to be influential texts in the movement during the following decade. See for example Fladeland, *Men and Brothers*, pp. 270–2.

13. In fact, the leader of the deputation, William Cunningham, almost anticipated this. He had not intended to visit the Southern states, and discouraged his colleagues from doing so, especially Rev. Robert Burns, who showed signs of being the least likely to keep his abolitionist sympathies in check (Honeycutt, 'William Cunningham', p. 167). And soon after his return, Cunningham seemed resigned to 'being branded by the Abolitionists as having been corrupted by the money and hospitality of slave-holders' (quoted ibid. p. 173).

14. On 14 March, Burns was in Alexandria, Virginia: see Burns, *The Life and Times of the Rev. Robert Burns*, p. 192.

15. Minutes of meeting of GES, 14 March 1844 (Smeal Collection, Reel 1); *Glasgow Argus*, 18 March 1844 (repr. *Liberator*, 26 April 1844).

16. AFASS, *Letter from the Executive Committee*. The letter was reprinted in the *Liberator*, 26 April 1844. On its distribution at the General Assembly see Honeycutt, 'William Cunningham', p. 169 n.

17. O'Connell's remark about 'blood-stained money' was reported in the *Liberator*, 9 and 30 June 1843, and the *British and Foreign Anti-Slavery Reporter*, 9 August 1843. O'Connell had previously accepted donations but had been encouraged to rethink his position by James Haughton. His 11 May speech (and his condemnation of slavery more generally) damaged his support in the United States, not only in the South. See Kinealy, *Daniel O'Connell*, pp. 113–19; and Riach, 'Daniel O'Connell'. According to Laurence Fenton, the refusal was rhetorical and only one donation was ever returned, and even that probably not because of the pro-slavery position of the New Orleans Repeal Society: Fenton, *Frederick Douglass in Ireland*, p. 94. FD himself refers his audiences

to O'Connell's example in Ayr on 24 March 1846 (*Ayr Observer*, 31 March 1846) and in Newcastle on 7 August 1846 (FDP 1.1, pp. 337–8), as does JB in Glasgow, 21 April 1846 (*Manstealers*, p. 27).

18. AFASS, *Letter from the Executive Committee*, p. 8.

19. Gerald Fulkerson claims that the campaign was 'virtually dead' and 'moribund' by the time FD arrived in Scotland ('Exile as Emergence', pp. 74, 77), but HCW had been lecturing extensively on the subject without a break since March 1845 (as reported in the *Liberator* from 9 May 1845 onwards). As far as I can tell, Wright first uses the phrase 'send back the money' (without special emphasis) at a public meeting of the GES on 18 November 1844 (*Glasgow Argus*, 21 November 1844; repr. *Liberator*, 24 January 1845), but it acquired a more incantatory flavour in an open letter to William Cunningham, Glasgow, 15 March 1845 (*Glasgow Argus*, 24 March 1845, repr. *Liberator*, 9 May 1845).

20. FD, Belfast, 16 June 1846 (*Belfast News-Letter*, 19 June 1846). See Appendix 1, but note that FD may not have visited all these places, as duties were shared with JB and HCW.

21. The most comprehensive account of the campaign is Whyte, '*Send Back the Money!*'. Whyte builds on the work of Shepperson, 'The Free Church and American Slavery'; Shepperson, 'Thomas Chalmers'; Shepperson, 'Frederick Douglass and Scotland'; and Rice, *The Scots Abolitionists*, pp. 124–46.

22. There are very few references to the 'Send Back the Money' campaign in the Scottish press before January 1846. Newspapers in Dundee led the way in February, both the *Dundee Courier* (supportive of FD) and the *Northern Warder* (a Free Church organ).

23. FD to Francis Jackson, Dundee, 29 January 1846 (FDP 3.1, p. 90); FD to RW, Dundee, 10 February 1846 (FDP 3.1, p. 92). HCW claimed 'Scotland is in a blaze' in Glasgow, 21 April 1846 (*Manstealers*, p. 8).

24. If the abolitionists refer to a figure at all it is usually £3,000. See, for example, HCW, 'A Letter from Henry C. Wright to Ministers and Members of the Free Church of Scotland', Edinburgh, 20 May 1846, published in *The Free Church and her Accusers*, pp. 6, 7, 10, 11; Dr Campbell, London, 22 May 1846, where the £3,000 is stated to be 'a paltry sum' out of a total of £750,000 or £760,000: *American Slavery*, p. 27; GT, Edinburgh 28 April 1846, where he states that slaveholders 'purchased the Free Church for the sum of £3000' (*Manstealers*, p. 49); FD, Paisley, 1 May 1846 (FDP 1.1, p. 242); FD, Newcastle, 3 August 1846 (FDP 1.1, p. 331). For references to 300,000 slaveholders, three million slaves and 300 years of slavery, see, for example, FD, London, 22 May 1846 (FDP 1.1, pp. 272, 292).

25. For an excellent study which places FD's oratory in the broader context of Anglo-American lecture traditions see Wright, *Lecturing the*

Atlantic, esp. pp. 49–80. See also Baxter, *Frederick Douglass's Curious Audiences*.

26. For a parody of a slave sermon in FD's early speeches see FD, Boston, 28 January 1842 (FDP 1.1, pp. 15–17).
27. FD, Dublin, 16 June 1846 (*Belfast Commercial Chronicle*, 17 June 1846).
28. FD, Dublin, 16 June 1846 (*Belfast News-Letter*, 19 June 1846).
29. *Perthshire Constitutional*, 28 January 1846 (repr. *Liberator*, 27 February 1846); *Perthshire Advertiser*, 29 January 1846; *Northern Warder*, 29 January 1846.
30. See Black, *Gilfillan of Dundee*; and Watson and Watson, *George Gilfillan*.
31. N, p. 71 (A, p. 33; FDP 2.1, p. 28). On the Dundee linen industry see Lewis, *Topographical Dictionary of Scotland*, vol. 1, p. 317; Miskell and Whatley, '"Juteopolis" in the Making'.
32. Dodd, *The Laboring Classes of England*, pp. 92–3. A petition, organised by 'several respectable inhabitants of Dundee', condemning their harsh treatment was submitted to Parliament in February 1846: *Dundee Courier*, 3 March 1846.
33. On Gilfillan's admiration of Chalmers see Watson and Watson, *George Gilfillan*, p. 120.
34. George Gilfillan, Dundee, 10 March 1846 (*Dundee Courier*, 17 March 1846).
35. Gilfillan, *The Debasing and Demoralizing Influence of Slavery*, p. 15.
36. The *Northern Warder* remarked that this lecture was different from the preceding lectures in Dundee, how its subject 'changed from an exposition of the slave system of America to a discussion of the conduct of the Free Church', *Northern Warder*, 5 February 1846.
37. FD, Dundee, 30 January 1846 (FDP 1.1, p. 144).
38. FD, Dundee, 30 January 1846 (FDP 1.1, p. 145).
39. FD, Dundee, 30 January 1846 (FDP 1.1, pp. 146–7).
40. FD, Dundee, 30 January 1846 (FDP 1.1, p. 149).
41. FD, Dundee, 30 January 1846 (FDP 1.1, pp. 151–4).
42. FD, Dundee, 30 January 1846 (FDP 1.1, pp. 154–5).
43. FD, Dundee, 30 January 1846 (FDP 1.1, pp. 155–6).
44. *Dundee Courier*, 3 February 1846.
45. *Northern Warder*, 5 February 1846.
46. FD, Dundee, 9 February 1846 (*Dundee Courier*, 10 February 1846; *Dundee Advertiser*, 10 February 1846).
47. FD, Arbroath, 10 February 1846 (*Arbroath Guide*, 14 February 1846, repr. *Liberator*, 27 March 1846; *Northern Warder*, 12 February 1846).
48. FD, Arbroath, 12 February (FDP 1.1, pp. 156–64); FD, Aberdeen, early March 1846 (*Aberdeen Journal*, 11 March 1846); FD, Montrose, 9 March (*Montrose Standard*, 13 March 1846, repr. *Liberator*, 24 April 1846).

49. See Black, *Gilfillan of Dundee*, pp. 49–53. The use of the church for the 10 March Anti-Slavery meeting ultimately led to the resignations of several committee members the following year. For Gilfillan's opening remarks see *Dundee Courier*, 17 March 1846.

50. FD, Dundee, 10 March 1846 (FDP 1.1, p. 178).

51. FD, Dundee 10 March 1846 (FDP 1.1, pp. 179–80).

52. FD, Dundee 10 March 1846 (FDP 1.1, pp. 181–2).

53. On Mathews see Waters, *Racism on the Victorian Stage*, pp. 91–4; Davis, 'Acting Black, 1824'; Lindfors, *Ira Aldridge: The Early Years*, pp. 47–60.

54. FD, Perth, 12 March 1846 (*Perthshire Advertiser*, 19 March 1846); FD, Paisley, 20 March 1846 (FDP 1.1, pp. 193–4); and FD, Glasgow, 21 April 1846 (FDP 1.1, pp. 236). FD's performance was not always appreciated: reporting his lecture in Perth, the local paper wrote: 'Mr. Douglass's mimicry of the Rev. Mr Lewis, Dundee, was in very bad taste' (*Perthshire Advertiser*, 19 March 1846).

55. Preston, *Young Frederick Douglass*, pp. 79–80.

Chapter 6

The Free Church Responds

The distinction Douglass makes in his speech in Dundee between moral principles ('spreading the Gospel') and material self-interest ('making money') is a common one. But the dispute between the abolitionists and the Free Church was not quite so simple.

For one thing, the Free Church was not unanimous. As we have seen, some of its own members had reservations about the propriety of accepting funds from the Southern Churches, and, perhaps emboldened by the Glasgow Emancipation Society's intervention, they forced the matter to be debated at the General Assembly of the Free Church in May 1844, following the submission of 'overtures' from two Synods. They may have expected a sympathetic response from Rev. Robert Candlish. Only a month before, he had spoken at a public meeting at the Edinburgh Music Hall called to protest the death sentence imposed on John L. Brown in South Carolina for assisting a slave to escape. In the course of his speech he expressed his 'private personal opinion' that other Churches should withdraw fellowship from the American churches if they continued to admit slaveholders to their communion.[1] But on this occasion, he was diplomatically cautious and insisted that the Assembly should seek clarification of the American Presbyterians' position. The matter was referred to a committee, which submitted an interim report in September, and a copy was sent to the United States.[2]

The report sets out what seems to be an uncompromising position. 'In its own nature,' it states, 'slavery in all its forms is to be regarded as a system of oppression which cannot be defended.'[3] Moreover, '[t]he committee cannot but consider it the duty of Christian churches, as such, to set themselves against its manifold abuses, and to aim decidedly at its abolition.'[4] But in practice, how those churches choose to attain those ends is up to them. '[I]t is not for

Figure 6.1 Robert Candlish.

this church to decide peremptorily what ought to be regarded as the particular course of duty to be immediately and universally adopted,' it reassured its American readers, not least because, it argued, it was not sufficiently aware of the circumstances in which the Southern churches operated.[5]

The report did not go anything like far enough in addressing the demands of the Glasgow Emancipation Society, which convened a public meeting in November 1844 to respond.[6] But it was already going too far for others. The fact that the Free Church had felt the need to discuss the matter at all incurred the displeasure of Southern churchmen, notably Dr Thomas Smyth of Charleston, whom the Scottish deputation had visited in March.[7] In May, Smyth had written to Chalmers, enclosing a bill for some of the money he had helped to raise, but taking care to indicate the distress caused him by Candlish's recent remarks, which meant he faced 'the possibility of having our gifts reciprocated by anathema and abuse'.[8] Not receiving a satisfactory reply, he wrote again in August, urging Chalmers to publish a clear statement of his position.[9]

Chalmers replied on 25 September. He reassured Smyth

how little I sympathize with those who – because slavery happens to prevail in the Southern States of America – would unchristianize that whole region; and who even carry their extravagance so far as to affirm that, so long as it subsists, no fellowship or interchange of good offices should take place with its churches, or its ministers.[10]

Evidently Smyth had shared Chalmers' letter widely among his contacts. This may have been with the agreement of Chalmers: the two men had met in Edinburgh during Smyth's visit to Britain that year.[11] The secretaries of the Edinburgh Emancipation Society, Edward Cruickshank and John Dunlop, secured a copy of the letter and persuaded Hugh Miller to publish it in the *Witness*, the newspaper sympathetic to the Free Church, along with their correspondence with Chalmers, which urged him to review his opinions. Miller, author of an important contribution to geology, *The Old Red Sandstone* (1841), brought an athletic masculinity to his editorial duties, writing confrontational prose at a breakneck pace. Not surprisingly, he sided with Chalmers, who, he insisted, belonged to a long-established, noble British Christian antislavery tradition, and railed against the newly imported, irreligious ideas of the 'Transatlantic abolitionists' who 'set, by their extremeness, a fool's cap on a good cause'.[12] A week later Miller, his blood up, renewed his assault on the Garrisonians by mocking their support for women's rights, confident his readers would be amused when he invited them to imagine

armed regiments of equalized women charging in petticoat breeches some male anti-equal-right enemy, who had come to invade their country from without; and squadrons of female dragoons emancipated from matrimonial thrall and the side-saddle, trampling all horrid into dust, broken cohorts of imperative husbands and despotic lovers, who had assailed them in unnatural rebellion from within.[13]

Chalmers, in a more considered response, assured Cruikshank and Dunlop that he would give the matter due consideration, other commitments permitting. In fact they had to wait until the following May before he published a fuller statement of his views. In this

Figure 6.2 Hugh Miller.

letter, he insists that a 'distinction ought to be made between the character of a system and the character of the persons whom circumstances have implicated therewith'. He admits that slavery is a fertile breeding ground of vice and that therefore 'there will [. . .] be a more frequent call for ecclesiastical discipline in the slaveholding congregations' – but only if the individuals concerned do succumb to such vices. Being a slaveholder in itself is no sin, and so no one should be excluded from church membership on that ground alone.[14]

Douglass referred to this letter several times in his speeches. Here he is in Arbroath in February 1846, in a response which uses Chalmers's words as an ironic refrain:

'DISTINCTION *ought to be made between the character of the system and the character of the person whom* CIRCUMSTANCES *have implicated therewith*.' The Doctor would denounce slaveholding, robbery, and murder as sin, but would not denounce the slaveholder, robber, and murderer as a sinner: he would make a DISTINCTION between sins and the persons whom CIRCUMSTANCES have implicated therewith; he would denounce the dice, but spare the sharper; he would denounce the adultery, but spare the adulterer; for, says the Doctor, 'distinction ought to be made between the character of the system and the character of the person whom circumstances have implicated therewith.' Oh! The artful Dodger.

This earns appreciative laughter each time Douglass makes the comparison, but as if comparing the great man to a fictional pickpocket is not enough, he goes on to align Chalmers with the determinist philosophy of the socialist Robert Owen:

He says that distinction should be made between the character of a system, and the character of the persons whom circumstances have implicated therewith. Yes, circumstances – the doctrine of circumstances. Who proclaims it? Dr. Chalmers. Yes, this doctrine, which has justly brought down upon the head of infidel, Robert Owen, the execrations of Christendom, is now proclaimed by the eloquent Scotch divine. The Doctor has been driven to this hateful dilemma by taking a false step, in fellowshipping slaveholders as Christians. This doctrine carried out does away with moral responsibility. All that a thief has to do in justification of his theft is to plead that circumstances have implied him in theft, and he has Dr. Chalmers to apologise for him, and recognize him as a Christian.[15]

The American response to the interim report was not received until May 1845 – too late to be debated at the General Assembly that year. But it was discussed at the General Assembly the following year, after overtures on the subject of slavery were presented by the Synods of Sutherland and Caithness and of Angus and Mearns, as well as a petition from elders and other members of the church in Dundee. The debates of May–June 1846 marked perhaps the height of the 'Send Back the Money' campaign.[16]

Chalmers's younger colleagues, Robert Candlish and William Cunningham, made it clear that they believed there were definite shortcomings in the attitude of the American Presbyterian Churches. They were not so serious as to warrant the Free Church severing any connection with them: this should only be considered as a last resort. But it was important that the Assembly made it clear that their willingness to admit slaveholders was problematic to say the least.

Figure 6.3 William Cunningham.

Although, like Chalmers, Candlish and Cunningham did not go so far as to make slaveholding as a practice sinful, they insisted that it carried with it a whole range of moral obligations. Even if the law placed restrictions on emancipation, on slave marriages, on teaching slaves to read and write, slaveholders must convince the Church they are doing all they can despite such restrictions – treating the slaves humanely, looking after their moral and religious improvement. The American Presbyterians, they argue, are too easily convinced, and must be persuaded to take a more forceful stand – including a vigorous attempt to repeal the relevant laws.

At the same time, it was recognised that the particular circumstances in which the Churches found themselves meant it was not always a good idea that they

> should expel every slaveholder from communion, or should carry on a constant and open war against slavery, when the effect would, to all appearances, be that of losing their existing opportunities of Christian usefulness, and of increasing rather than diminishing the oppression.[17]

Douglass – who attended the Assembly – was severely disappointed. At a meeting at Edinburgh's Music Hall a few days later, he patiently laboured to show how deluded the Free Church was about the Southern Churches by reading out resolutions adopted by their governing bodies. They show, he says, 'that so far from being averse to slavery, they are its most strenuous advocates'.[18]

But if Cunningham's position was not consistent with a moral denunciation of slavery in general, nor was it merely a cynical attempt to mask primarily materialistic motives. Rather it arose from an attempt to honestly weigh the various consequences of excluding slaveholders from church membership.

Cunningham puts this point rather well:

[T]here is somehow or other a class of cases intermediate between those, on the one hand, which are characterised by eternal and immutable morality, and those, on the other, which are merely expedient, proper, and becoming, or the reverse – a class of cases in regard to which there are some moral considerations bearing on their general character and affecting the general duty of men regarding them, but respecting which you are not at liberty to look upon them as involving in every instance direct and immediate obligation.[19]

Such 'intermediate' cases were the province of much nineteenth-century social philanthropy which aimed at ameliorating the condition of women, children, the poor, the imprisoned and the sick. Chalmers himself had, over thirty years, placed his faith in a series of model schemes in some of the most deprived parishes in Glasgow and Edinburgh which were designed to show that a cheaper and more efficient alternative to the Poor Laws was possible. Rather than statutory handouts from the public authorities, the Church would set up an intensive campaign of door-to-door visiting, closely acquainting its officers with detailed knowledge of the circumstances of each household. Its primary focus would be religious and moral education, and in providing assistance in finding work for the unemployed, funded by voluntary contributions from the wealthy. The longer-term campaigns to improve working conditions, housing or public health were not Chalmers's concern. He wanted to see what could be done within the 'circumstances' which currently prevailed.[20]

The schemes were not a great success. But Chalmers may have fancied a similarity between the goals of his inner-city projects and those of the missionary work of Southern Churches. He was probably aware of the writings of Charles Colcock Jones, one of the best-known promoters of plantation missions, who drew on the example of his own efforts in Liberty County, Georgia in his book *The Religious Instruction of the Negroes in the United States* (1842).[21] And, in any case, by the time George Lewis returned with the account of his travels in the South, the Free Church would have had at its disposal a finely detailed picture of the procedures and effects of this religious instruction, for it includes descriptions of church services and sabbath schools of various denominations attended by black worshippers.[22] At the African Methodist Church he visits in Mobile, Alabama, 'there were not fewer than a thousand blacks present'. Even if Lewis did not have the resources or vocabulary to understand it, his account provides a glimpse of a distinctly black American form of worship, with its characteristic call-and-response pattern and echoes of spirit possession, whose emotional physicality underpins the entire service and which finally moves him to tears.[23]

Douglass consistently derided religious slaveholders – routinely describing them as the worst kind. In Dundee, after taunting Lewis for not having the courage to face his accusers, he mimicked a preacher at great length, fashioning a sermon that exposed its cynical purpose in securing the docile obedience of slaves.[24] And yet Lewis's account is not one to be casually dismissed. Indeed, it has been cited as a credible and illuminating source by several modern historians of the antebellum South, who have emphasised that plantation missions did not so much impose an ideology as provide the symbolic frame of reference in which slaves fashioned a distinctively black Christianity, which would eventually flourish in the independent black Churches, which remain, to this day, crucial institutions in African American life. Furthermore, Sunday schools, church services and camp meetings placed some slaves and free blacks in positions of considerable trust and responsibility, effectively making them training grounds for the first generation of black leaders to emerge during Reconstruction after the Civil War.[25]

Douglass was not impressed by the fine distinctions made by Cunningham at the General Assembly in 1846. For him, the reasons for his refusal to break fellowship with the American Presbyterians were very simple. 'I tell you why he does it,' he told an audience in Paisley to 'loud and long-continued cheering': 'He's got the bawbees.'[26] If the Free Church leaders could not benefit from the hindsight of twentieth-century historians, their instinctive appreciation of the work of Southern clergy in contributing to the moral and religious education of slaves in circumstances that required them to suppress abolitionist sentiment ought to be acknowledged, even if they failed to recognise the slaves' own role in their self-transformation. At any rate, the Free Church position was certainly prompted by considerations other than material self-interest.

Towards the end of the year, the *Herald* reported that a messenger from one of Glasgow's banks had left behind a parcel containing £3,000 in notes when he alighted from the train at Falkirk.[27] The money sent from the United States for the Free Church was neither lost nor sent back, but in any case formed a very small proportion of the total raised for the sustenation fund, which stood at £334,000 by the end of the first financial year.[28] Its absence would not have caused anything like the 'vast uneasiness' felt in Glasgow during the night once news of the missing parcel arrived there, and had fortunes changed, no one would have lamented, as the *Herald* did on this occasion, that the electric telegraph had not been used to notify the parties sooner that the parcel had been safely retrieved from the carriage on arrival in Edinburgh.

Notes

1. Robert Candlish, Edinburgh, 29 March 1844 ('Public Meeting – Sentence of Death for Aiding the Escape of a Slave', *Witness*, 30 March 1844).
2. FCS, *Proceedings 1844*, pp. 163–4; Whyte, *'Send Back the Money!'*, pp. 36–40.
3. FCS, *Proceedings 1846*, p. 4. The Report was read out at the 1845 General Assembly (FCS, *Proceedings 1845*, pp. 256–7) and printed in full in FCS, *Proceedings 1846*, itself an appendix to the proceedings of the 1846 General Assembly. The Report was also reprinted in *The Free Church of Scotland and American Slavery*, pp. 87–9.
4. FCS, *Proceedings 1846*, p. 5.
5. Ibid. p. 5. For a more detailed discussion of the Report see Whyte, *'Send Back the Money!'*, pp. 40–2.
6. Minutes of public meeting of GES, City Hall, 18 November 1844 (Smeal Collection, Reel 1); *Glasgow Argus*, 21 November 1844 (repr. *Liberator*, 17 Dec 1844, misdating the meeting as 18 October).
7. Lewis, *Impressions of America*, pp. 108–9, 120.

8. Thomas Smyth to Thomas Chalmers, Charleston, 24 May 1844, repr. in Shepperson, 'Chalmers', p. 524.

9. Thomas Smyth to Thomas Chalmers, [Edinburgh?], 29 August 1844, repr. in Shepperson, 'Chalmers', p. 525. See also Whyte, *'Send Back the Money!'*, pp. 43–6.

10. Thomas Chalmers to Thomas Smyth, Edinburgh, 25 September 1844 (*Witness*, 18 December 1844, repr. in Hanna, *Memoirs*, vol. 4, pp. 566–7 and in Smyth, *Autobiographical Notes*, pp. 351–2.

11. Whyte, *'Send Back the Money!'*, p. 50. On meeting Chalmers in Edinburgh in 1844 see Smyth, *Autobiographical Notes*, pp. 217–19.

12. [Hugh Miller], 'The Slavery Question', *Witness*, 18 December 1844.

13. [Hugh Miller], 'The Slavery Question Again', *Witness*, 25 December 1844.

14. Thomas Chalmers to editor, Edinburgh, 12 May 1845 (*Witness*, 14 May 1845, repr. in Hanna, *Memoirs*, vol. 4, pp. 568, 569.

15. FD, Arbroath, 12 February 1846 (FDP 1.1, pp. 162–4); see also FD, Paisley, 20 March 1846 (FDP 1.1, pp. 192–3); and FD, Glasgow, 21 April 1846 (FDP 1.1, pp. 236–7). Several other contemporaries compared Chalmers's ideas to those of Robert Owen, and the two men corresponded. See Brown, *Thomas Chalmers*, pp. 122, 149–51, 247.

16. Whyte, *'Send Back the Money!'*, pp. 88–94.

17. FCS, *Proceedings 1846*, p. 42.

18. FD, Edinburgh, 4 June 1846 (FDP 1.1, p. 301). On the weaknesses of the arguments of the FCS leaders see Blackett, *Building an Anti-Slavery Wall*, pp. 91–3.

19. FCS, *Proceedings 1846*, p. 40.

20. Brown, *Chalmers*, pp. 122–44, 239–41, 355–63; and on social work see pp. 376 and 416 n. 68. See also Rice, *Scots Abolitionists*, p. 125. For an appraisal of nineteenth-century philanthropy see Prochaska, *The Voluntary Impulse*. Honeycutt draws attention to Cunningham's casuistical reasoning here: 'William Cunningham', p. 188.

21. Jones, *The Religious Instruction of the Negroes*. See Mathews, 'Charles Colcock Jones'.

22. Lewis, *Impressions of America*, pp. 66–7, 129–30, 167–70, 194.

23. Ibid. pp. 167–9. For a fuller discussion see Pettinger, 'George Lewis and the American Churches'.

24. FD, Dundee, 30 January 1846 (FDP 1.1, pp. 151–4).

25. See Blassingame, *The Slave Community*; Cornelius, *Slave Missions and the Black Church*; Genovese, *Roll, Jordan, Roll*; Levine, *Black Culture and Black Consciousness*; Loveland, *Southern Evangelicals and the Social Order*; Mathews, *Religion in the Old South*; Raboteau, *Slave Religion*; Touchstone, 'Planters and Slave Religion'. For citations of Lewis see Blassingame, *Slave Community*, pp. 380; Loveland, *Southern*

Evangelicals, p. 274; Touchstone, 'Planters', p. 255; Cornelius, *Slave Missions*, p. 268; and Bailey, 'Protestantism and Afro-Americans', pp. 455, 456, 469, 470.

26. FD, Paisley, 23 September 1846 (FDP 1.1, p. 430). 'Money! money! was the entire actuating motive of their hearts': FD, Dundee, 10 March 1846 (FDP 1.1, p. 178).

27. 'Three Thousand Pounds Supposed Lost, and Found', Glasgow *Herald*, 20 November 1846.

28. Brown, *Thomas Chalmers*, p. 344.

Chapter 7

The Price of Freedom

The donations of Southern US Presbyterians were not the only financial transactions that preoccupied abolitionists when Douglass was in Scotland in 1846.

They were also committed to raising funds for their own cause. Members of local societies in Britain and Ireland, mainly women, solicited contributions for boxes they would send to the annual fair or bazaar organised by Maria Weston Chapman of the Boston Female Anti-Slavery Society. The contributions, which included clothes, shoes, handkerchiefs, non-perishable foods, children's toys, drawings, paintings, books and pamphlets, were sold to raise money for the American Anti-Slavery Society, and indeed were its chief source of income.[1] Starting off in private homes, the bazaar became a major public event, taking place in Boston's Faneuil Hall, raising $4,000 annually.[2] To be sure, from a purely economic point of view it would have been more efficient if supporters had simply donated money.[3] But, as a notice in the *Liberator* pointed out, the 'pecuniary benefit derived from these sales' was 'but one of several reasons in their favor'.[4] The fair was a remarkable space, run by women, where men and women both black and white and of different classes could mingle safely without censure.[5] In addition, it was a celebration of international co-operation. Not only were the various items for sale visibly cosmopolitan in origin (a feature reinforced by the inventories published in the *Liberator*), they were often prized because they bore the tactile traces of their donors across the Atlantic (locks of hair, autographs, daguerreotypes and goods which were either home-made or bearing personalised mottoes).[6] All this helped to define the antislavery movement as one that crossed borders, with the bazaar, as Chapman's own striking simile had it, a world in miniature:

The world is like the sea-anemone: any part of it, however small, has the capacity of becoming a complete model of the whole; and truly and well does this little world in Faneuil Hall show forth a larger one, affording a perfect illustration of the whole anti-slavery cause, that in its turn typifies the great moral movement of this age, of which it is the van-guard.[7]

Nevertheless, the pecuniary element grew in importance, as British women wrote to Chapman, wanting to know which items sold well and what prices to put on them. Although Chapman expressed concern about the increasingly depersonalised character of donations, she herself could be shrewdly businesslike, sending crochet bags from Paris she had bought for $20 with instructions to sell them for $100. Eventually she gave up the fair and replaced it with a monetary subscription.[8]

But some abolitionists also expressed concerns about each other's economic circumstances, their own attitude to money, and how it might detract them from higher moral purpose.[9] While Bristol's John

Figure 7.1 Maria Weston Chapman.

Estlin believed that Douglass 'had been well advised in not making his tour a money getting one', he did not know how he was managing to support himself.[10] We know that Buffum had rallied supporters to pay for his passage on the *Cambria*, and Douglass had left Boston with $350 he had saved from sales of his *Narrative* in the United States.[11] On tour, he could often rely on the hospitality of friends and supporters; sometimes they might pay his hotel bills, but he would have had to take care of his travel and other out-of-pocket expenses himself. According to Garrison he received a 'small stipend from the Edinburgh friends', but he was 'chiefly dependent upon the sale of his *Narrative*', issued in two new editions in runs of 2,000 copies each by Richard Webb in Dublin.[12] Douglass bought copies to sell at his lectures at two-and-sixpence and in February 1846 Webb estimated that, 'if he go on as he begun [. . .] he will pocket 2500 dollars in twelve months' time.'[13] A few weeks later Webb remarked that Douglass's earnings far exceeded those of his fellow campaigner Henry Clarke Wright, who, he waspishly added, 'has no combination of interesting circumstances to recommend him' – as if Douglass's status as a fugitive slave were his only asset, reduced to a cynical marketing stunt.[14]

In Boston, Chapman had long nursed doubts about Douglass's loyalty to the Garrisonian cause, and in a letter to Webb, with whom she kept up a regular correspondence, asked him to maintain a close watch on Douglass who, she believed, would be easily led astray by temptations offered by rival abolitionist organisations, specifically the British and Foreign Anti-Slavery Society in London.[15]

Webb clearly shared these concerns – he repeatedly enumerated what he saw as defects in Douglass's character – describing the man who stayed in his house as proud, easily offended and susceptible to flattery, or 'petting', a word he uses several times and which hints that these temptations are not just financial but might also involve a certain sexual waywardness. In one letter to Chapman, for example, he wonders how Douglass 'will be able to bear the sight of his wife – after all the petting he gets from beautiful, elegant, and accomplished women in a country where prejudice against colour is looked upon as a thing only to be laughed at'.[16] Similar sentiments are voiced by John Estlin, who – throwing in a phrase made popular by Byron that alludes to the pursuit of heightened sensual experience – remarked:

You should hardly imagine how he is noticed – *petted* I may say by *ladies*. Some of them really a little exceed the bounds of propriety, or delicacy, as far as appearances are concerned [. . .] My fear is that often associating so much with white women of education & refined taste & manners, he will feel a 'craving void' when he returns to his own family.[17]

Not surprisingly, remarks about 'petting' could easily escalate into more insulting accusations. In the summer of 1846, clerical opponents of Douglass started a rumour that he had 'been seen coming out of a Brothel in Manchester' – a rumour repeated by the minister from Charleston Thomas Smyth on a visit to his native Belfast in 1846, until Douglass's lawyers forced a retraction.[18]

With an astonishing lack of sensitivity, Webb read out portions of the letter in which Chapman expressed her fears that he may 'yield to temptation' before a private gathering of fellow abolitionists at which Douglass was present, shortly after his initial arrival in Dublin. Webb thought her concerns were justified and its target would appreciate her frankness. But Douglass must have felt a little like Jane Eyre at Lowood, perched on a stool, forced to listen while Brocklehurst demolished her character in front of the whole school.[19] Douglass was livid – though Webb considered his reaction was just another sign of his tendency to exaggerate the slightest hurt.[20] From Kilmarnock six months later Douglass, still smarting from the insult, wrote to Chapman, much aggrieved that she should think that he 'might be bought up by the London committee', referring to the rival British and Foreign Anti-Slavery Society. 'I am trying to preach and practice a genuine antislavery life,' he urges, 'turning neither to the right or left, and I think not without success.' He insists that his motives are not 'sordid' and that he has received no 'pecuniary aid' from his public appearances; she is wrong to assume that 'either the love of money – or the hate of poverty, will drive me from the ranks of the old organized antislavery society'.

His letter as a whole, however, is a masterpiece of diplomacy. Douglass prefaces his remarks by telling Chapman that he has agreed to include an appeal on behalf of her bazaar in the new edition of his *Narrative* currently in preparation, perhaps subtly reminding her of her own immersion in commercial networks. And he ends by sharing news of the recent efforts of Wright, Buffum and himself in their campaign against the Free Church – its final words (like many of his speeches at this time), 'send back the money', as if to draw attention to economic matters of rather greater import than those that appear to preoccupy her.[21]

The matter did not end there. When Douglass spoke at the annual meeting of the British and Foreign Anti-Slavery Society in London on 18 May, Chapman could not resist communicating her displeasure, even though he had shared the platform with George Thompson, whose loyalty she never doubted. In response, Douglass made it very clear that he was not interested in sectarian rivalries. 'I will speak in any meeting when freedom of speech is allowed and where I may do anything towards exposing the bloody system of slavery.'[22]

He goes on to reassure her that 'I was not carried there by what you term "money temptations" – no such was offered and I may say (though you may think it an evidence of my self sufficiency) no such temptation would have been availing.' Indeed, he had used the opportunity to strike 'an important blow in behalf of "sending back the money".'[23] And concludes:

> I recently got a little circle to work for the Bazaar at Boston consisting a few influential young ladies in 'Carlile' (Eng.) They will send a box this autumn. Mr. J. D. Carr of the same place will send a valuable contribution to the refreshment table of a large box of fancy biscuits. I am sorry I cant say more. The lad is waiting to take this to the office.[24]

Despite his haste, Douglass makes time for a final paragraph about 'fancy biscuits', as if to remind his correspondent that far from being motivated by personal material gain, he has been industrious in persuading others to help raise funds for her project, not his.

The fears of Chapman and Webb that Douglass would abandon the cause did not materialise. They were no doubt reassured when Garrison himself landed in England at the beginning of August 1846, and, working closely with Douglass and Thompson in London, pursued plans to launch what they called the Anti-Slavery League, a network (modelled on the Anti-Corn-Law League) they hoped would displace their rivals in the British and Foreign Anti-Slavery Society.

But the question of money would rear its head again towards the end of the year, when it became known that some supporters were preparing to purchase Douglass's freedom.

Over the summer, Douglass had spent some time in Newcastle-upon-Tyne, a guest of Anna and Henry Richardson. They were abolitionists more sympathetic to (but not uncritical of) the British and Foreign Anti-Slavery Society than the Garrisonians.[25] Many years later, another visiting American – the civil rights campaigner Ida B. Wells – invited Anna's sister-in-law Ellen to recall the occasion.

> She said that Mr. Douglass, her brother and herself were at the seaside; that while sitting on the sand listening to the fugitive slave's talk and observing his sadness, she suddenly asked him, 'Frederick, would you like to go back to America?' Of course his reply was in the affirmative and like a flash the inspiration came to her. 'Why not buy his freedom?'[26]

She didn't tell Douglass at first, suspecting that he would not agree to it on principle, but, discreetly, Ellen Richardson wrote letters to 'different influential persons' in Britain asking for support. A contribution of £50 from John Bright, the Radical MP for Durham, encouraged her, and only then did she confide in Anna. Communicating through lawyers in Boston and Baltimore, they persuaded Hugh Auld (ownership having passed from his brother Thomas) to agree to a price of £150. The formalities were completed in December and Douglass was now a free man.[27]

Very few people knew about the plan. Those involved were presumably sworn to secrecy. We do not know when the sisters told Douglass what they were up to, and he may well have read the signs before they did so. But by the middle of November, the news was out. The reactions of some of Douglass's supporters were muted to say the least. In Glasgow, Catherine Paton wrote, 'I could not aid nor approve of the buying of Frederick as I thought it compromising of principle, & a recognition of the right of property in man; I could not see how Garrison could approve of it.'[28] The same day, Mary Welsh of the Glasgow Female Anti-Slavery Society told Chapman: 'Some of us have been very much grieved at Anna Richardson getting that money to purchase Frederick Douglass's ransome.'[29]

The most forthright response came from Henry Clarke Wright, who addressed Douglass directly. 'This is the first letter of advice I ever wrote to you —,' he began. 'It is the last.'[30] He went on to express his revulsion at the transaction, which he 'cannot think of [. . .] without vexation'.[31] 'That certificate of your freedom, that Bill of Sale of your body and soul [. . .] I wish you would not touch it.'[32] By acquiescing in the arrangement, Douglass had conceded the validity of Auld's claim on him, and if he returned to the United States a free man rather than a fugitive slave, he would lose the moral authority and rhetorical power that comes from provocative defiance. 'It is worth running some risk,' he wrote, as someone who would never have to run such a risk himself, 'for the sake of the conflict, and the certain result.'[33]

Douglass's reply was considered. He was not only happy that the transaction had been effected, but happy to publicly acknowledge it. He saw no violation of the principle that no one has the right to own another. In receiving the manumission papers, he concedes nothing. He simply wishes to return to the United States without the risk of being legally recaptured. It does not imply a recognition of the legality of slavery any more than eating bread is an endorsement of the unjust duty on corn. Indeed, it is no different from Wright's own willingness to carry a passport on his international speaking tours even though he utterly condemns the 'system' that restricts the freedom of movement by requiring it.[34]

What of Garrison? When he published the exchange between Wright and Douglass in the *Liberator*, he remarked: 'We think the reply of Mr. Douglass is not only entirely satisfactory and conclusive, but remarkably pertinent and forcible. The "passport" illustration is a very good bit, as our dear friend H. C. W. will readily acknowledge, we think.'[35] Previously he had kept his feelings to himself when Chapman, Webb and others had taken it on themselves to monitor Douglass's behaviour in the name of the cause. This time, Garrison openly defied the Garrisonians and unequivocally backed Douglass, taking a much more pragmatic line than his own supporters. In a more expansive comment on the affair a few weeks later, Garrison admitted that the sale breached a general principle – he would never have countenanced negotiating the purchase of the entire slave population (as the British government had effectively done in 1834) – but insisted it was 'expedient' and 'sound policy' to do so in individual cases. 'Human liberty,' he declares, 'is of incomparably greater value than money.' And he indicates his disinclination to enter into a prolonged discussion of the matter.[36]

Even before Douglass joined in the campaign against the Free Church to 'send back the money' it had unscrupulously solicited from unprincipled counterparts, fellow Garrisonians were expressing doubts about Douglass's dedication to the noble cause, concerned about his susceptibility to the pecuniary temptations offered by their rivals. The parallels are striking. Did Douglass take on the arguments of Chalmers, Cunningham and Candlish with such enthusiasm in order to show his sceptical supporters what 'blood-stained money' really meant, a pact with evil in comparison with which their own – exaggerated – sectarian misgivings about the 'London Committee' were trivial indeed? Or did Douglass find in the campaign a convenient way of channelling anxieties of his own: his own financial insecurity, his impatience with the patronising way his allies and supporters often treated him, his willingness to breach sectarian etiquette, the plans to buy his freedom?

But perhaps the most noteworthy configuration here is the way Douglass's defence of his manumission makes a distinction, not only shared by his scathing critic Wright, but also at the heart of the arguments of the Free Church: the distinction between the all-or-nothing posture of moral condemnation of a system (such as slavery) and the gradations of ethical judgement that often require compromises with that system in order to work effectively within it. And of course the British abolition of slavery that became effective on 1 August 1834 involved a compromise of towering proportions: not just the transitional 'apprenticeship' system in the West Indies, but the monetary compensation of slaveholders. The American abolitionists had no intention of supporting any such qualifications, but even so, it did not stop them, even Garrisonians, from celebrating the anniversary of 1 August for many years.[37]

Notes

1. Bennett, *Democratic Discourses*, pp. 18–44. Income from the 1853 Bazaar – over $3,000 – accounted for roughly half of the AASS annual budget (p. 20).
2. MWC, 'The Twelfth National Anti-Slavery Bazaar', *Liberator*, 23 January 1846.
3. Huzzey, *Freedom Burning*, p. 37.
4. 'The Ladies' Fair', *Liberator*, 2 January 1837.
5. Bennett, *Democratic Discourses*, pp. 37–9.
6. See McDaniel, *The Problem of Democracy in the Age of Slavery*, pp. 83–5; and Morgan, 'The Politics as Personal', pp. 78–96.
7. MWC, 'The Twelfth National Anti-Slavery Bazaar', *Liberator*, 23 Jan 1846.

8. Chambers-Schiller, '"Good Work"', pp. 268–70. Bennett also remarks that the fairs did, to some extent, commodify slave labour and images of slaves: *Democratic Discourses*, p. 40.

9. In what follows, I have benefited greatly from the discussion of 'the economics of the text' in Sweeney, *Frederick Douglass and the Atlantic World*, pp. 37–51.

10. John B. Estlin to [RW?], Bristol, 5 November 1846 (BAA, p. 240).

11. FD to MWC, Kilmarnock, 29 March 1846 (FDP 3.1, p. 99; BAA, p. 258).

12. WLG to John B. Estlin, London, 8 September 1846 (GL3, p. 400).

13. RW to Edmund Quincy, Dublin, 2 February 1846 (BAA, p. 249). RW's calculation is of the gross income FD would receive from the sale of 4,000 copies of his *Narrative* at half a crown or 2s 6d each (roughly equivalent to US 60¢), but out of this he would have had to reimburse RW's costs for printing, binding and shipping, retaining about 60% if RW's calculation of £150 net income from 2,000 copies in the same letter is reliable. According to the Limerick *Reporter*, 11 November 1845, copies of the *Narrative* were available for purchase at a meeting for half a crown; and 2s 6d is mentioned as price of the *Narrative* in advertisements in e.g. *Bristol Mercury*, 29 August 1846 and *Cork Examiner*, 22 October 1845.

14. RW to MWC, Dublin, 26 February 1846 (BAA, p. 254).

15. This letter does not appear to have been preserved, but we know of it from RW's and FD's responses to it. See below. RW quotes from it in a letter back to her: RW to MWC, Dublin 16 May 1846 (BAA, pp. 259–60).

16. RW to MWC, Dublin, 31 October 1846 (BPL Ms. A.9.2 v. 22, p. 109), available at <https://archive.org/details/lettertomydearfr00webb31> (last accessed 7 May 2018), quoted courtesy of the Trustees of the Boston Public Library/Rare Books. For other examples of 'petting' see RW to MWC, Dublin, 16 November 1845 (BAA, p. 243); RW to MWC, Dublin, 26 Feb 1846 (BAA, p. 254); and RW to MWC, Dublin, 26 March 1846 (BAA, p. 254). See also RW to Edmund Quincy, Dublin, 2 February 1846 (BAA, p. 250); RW to MWC, Dublin, 16 May 1846 (BAA, p. 259). There is a good discussion of the 'petting' motif in Rice, *Radical Narratives of the Black Atlantic*, pp. 179–87; see also Fought, *Women in the World of Frederick Douglass*, pp. 86–7. RW was also not sparing in his personal attacks on rival abolitionists, describing Joseph Sturge of the BFASS as 'snuffling, secretive, bigotted, and destitute of magnanimity': RW to MWC, Dublin, 16 July 1846 (BAA, p. 272).

17. John B. Estlin to Samuel May, Bristol, 12 January 1847 (BAA, 248). The phrase is from a letter from Byron to Annabella Milbanke, 6 September

1813: 'The great object of life is sensation – to feel that we exist, even though in pain. It is this "craving void" which drives us to gaming – to battle, to travel – to intemperate, but keenly felt, pursuits of any description, whose principal attraction is the agitation inseparable from their accomplishment': Byron, *Works*, vol. 3, p. 401.

18. Smyth, *Autobiographical Notes*, pp. 362–78. The rumour itself is specified in a letter from Douglass's lawyers in Belfast dated 16 July 1846 (p. 372). See Whyte, '*Send Back the Money!*', 113–16. The affair is summarised in the *Edinburgh Evening Post*, 19 August 1846; see also FD, Edinburgh, 24 September 1846 (*Edinburgh Evening Post*, 30 September 1846) for his own account.

19. Brontë, *Jane Eyre*, p. 98. It has been argued that Brontë's novel owes much to the form and substance of the American slave narrative, with which its author was almost certainly familiar. See Lee, *The American Slave Narrative*, pp. 25–52.

20. RW to MWC, Dublin, 16 May 1846 (BAA, p. 259).

21. FD to MWC, Kilmarnock, 29 March 1846 (FDP 3.1, pp. 98–100; BAA, pp. 258–9).

22. FD to MWC, London, 18 August 1846 (BAA, p. 277).

23. FD to MWC, London, 18 August 1846 (BAA, p. 277). FD's willingness to speak at the BFASS meeting was perhaps a strategic non-partisan gesture, as was the invitation, though the BFASS no doubt also calculated to benefit from FD's popularity: Blackett, *Building an Anti-Slavery Wall*, p. 111.

24. FD to MWC, London, 18 August 1846 (BAA, p. 278).

25. Anna Richardson to [S. May], undated (BAA, p. 301).

26. Wells, 'Newcastle Notes', p. 162.

27. See McFeely, *Frederick Douglass*, pp. 137–8, 143–4; Fought, *Women in the World of Frederick Douglass*, pp. 90–1.

28. Catherine Paton to unidentified recipient, Glasgow, 17 November 1846 (BAA, p. 299).

29. Mary Welsh to MWC, Edinburgh, 17 November 1846 (BAA, p. 300).

30. HCW to FD, Doncaster, 12 December 1846 (FDP 3.1, p. 179).

31. HCW to FD, Doncaster, 12 December 1846 (FDP 3.1, p. 181).

32. HCW to FD, Doncaster, 12 December 1846 (FDP 3.1, p. 180).

33. HCW to FD, Doncaster, 12 December 1846 (FDP 3.1, p. 181).

34. FD to HCW, Manchester, 22 December 1846 (FDP 3.1, pp. 183–9.) The following day HCW and FD shared a platform in Leeds (FDP 1.1, p. 482). FD repeated his defence of the sale in a letter to the *Durham Chronicle*, which was widely reprinted in the British press: FD to editor, Coventry, 22 January 1847 (FDP 3.1, pp. 196–200).

35. WLG, 'The Ransom', *Liberator*, 29 January 1847.

36. WLG, 'The Ransom of Douglass's, *Liberator*, 5 March 1847. RW, however, continued to voice his disapproval: 'Letter from our Dublin Correspondent', *National Anti-Slavery Standard*, 6 May 1847; 'From our Dublin Correspondent', *National Anti-Slavery Standard*, 24 June 1847.
37. See Kerr-Ritchie, *Rites of August.*

Chapter 8

The Genealogy of Money

It is often said that the 'Send Back the Money' campaign was a fail-ure.[1] Certainly Candlish and Cunningham managed the concerns of most of the Free Church members very skilfully. Considering the 'American letter' at the General Assembly of 1846, Candlish noted that while it 'contains a clear and unequivocal disapproval of the system of slavery, your committee find several points upon which they are not prepared to agree with what seem to be the sentiments entertained by their brethren'.[2]

At the end of the debate, the wording of the reply – which gently rebukes the American churches for their lack of vigour in chal-lenging the 'circumstances' in which its ministers find themselves – is approved and adopted. But it is prefaced with the following remark:

> It is not with a view to a prolonged discussion between you and us, far less with any thing like a desire to bring about ultimate severance, that we again return in a few sentences, to a subject which has already forced itself into our communications with one another.[3]

Frustrated at not getting their voice heard, Michael Willis and James MacBeth formed the Free Church Anti-Slavery Society that summer. They published a number of pamphlets, one of them authored by George Gilfillan, but without making much impact. At the General Assembly in 1847, two petitions were quickly dismissed, and with the loud abolitionists now out of the country, the issue was reduced to a humorous remark as Cunningham was greeted by laughter and cheers after characterising their campaign as a 'device of Satan'. Like characters in a Victorian novel, Willis soon gave up the

fight and accepted a position in Toronto, while MacBeth, plagued by
allegations of sexual misconduct – eventually withdrawn or declared
unproven by the church authorities but (together with the scurrilous
rumours about Douglass spread by Smyth when he visited Belfast
from Charleston) indicative perhaps of the lengths to which some
supporters of the Free Church would go – also left for Canada. And
the matter was not raised by the General Assembly again.[4]

There was little likelihood of any other outcome. Did Douglass
and the Glasgow Emancipation Society miscalculate by making
'Send Back the Money!' the focus of their activity? The tone of the
campaign was perhaps ill-chosen: such an uncompromising burst of
self-righteous anger did not make it easy for the Free Church leadership to make a dignified retreat.[5] Henry Clarke Wright's tendency to
complicate the issue with his controversial views on other matters,
which for some verged on anarchism and atheism, did not help, and
Douglass had been wary of working with him from the start.[6] It is
not surprising that a Free Church paper like the *Northern Warder*
unfavourably contrasted the 'grossly abusive style of declamation'
of Douglass and his colleagues with the strictly autobiographical
lectures of Moses Roper, praised for the way in which, focusing on
'his own sufferings under slavery', he 'exercises rather more discretion in his vocation'. The paper regretted that the expectation that
Roper would be 'one of the same cast' (in other words, a declamatory Garrisonian) resulted in smaller audiences, because he actually
displays 'a very different spirit'.[7] Committee resolutions were usually
more diplomatically worded than campaign speeches, but even private overtures to Chalmers from more neutral parties did not appear
to have any effect.[8]

More significantly, they probably underestimated the extent to
which their campaign could be turned into a vehicle for religious
sectarianism. Many of those who gleefully took up the slogans were
venting their hostility to the Free Church for entirely different reasons. That the campaign attracted the support of prominent Voluntaries like George Gilfillan and Church of Scotland ministers like
Patrick Brewster (and held meetings in United Secession and Relief
churches) did not help.[9] If the abolitionists themselves scrupulously
avoided criticising Chalmers, Cunningham and Candlish on any
other grounds than their refusal to break fellowship with American
Churches, this did not stop Free Church members feeling that they
had been unfairly singled out for criticism.

Through the summer of 1846, Hugh Miller published letters in the *Witness* that pointed out that other Churches had accepted 'slave-holders' money' too, including the Rose Street Secession Church in Edinburgh (a venue used by abolitionists for meetings in April and May), which in 1839 had benefited from a donation of £500 to its Mission Building Fund from the proprietors of the Goshen estate in St Ann's, Jamaica, assumed to have been drawn from their share of the £20 million set aside by the government to compensate slave-owners after Emancipation.[10] The profits of slavery were everywhere, insisted Miller, and it was ludicrous to hold organisations to impossible standards of moral purity, essentially adding weight to his argument two years earlier, when he defended Chalmers in these terms:

> With regard to the [. . .] principle [. . .] that at issue with the receiving of money which slave-labour has contributed to earn [. . .] we are afraid it involves difficulties and embarrassments of which no man, – not even an American Abolitionist, – can see the end. That which a Church ought not to receive, a Church member ought not to receive. Churches consist of members, and what is wrong in the aggregate cannot be right in the individual. And yet Church members in this country receive many indirect benefits from slavery; and Churches, Voluntary and Established, derive, in turn, many direct benefits from them. It is dangerous to trace the genealogy of money, if we hold that it may be cast by a flaw in its lineage. There is still not a little of West Indian wealth in Britain, which tasked, in its earning, the thews and sinews of the slave. Nay, in our cotton manufactories in the west, slave-grown cotton is almost exclusively employed; and in the exact degree in which our manufacturers find its use more profitable than that of cotton reared by free labour, do they benefit indirectly by slavery. But do they perpetrate a moral wrong in purchasing or making money by it? Or do the Churches which they support share any degree of guilt in benefiting by it at second hand?[11]

Miller had a point and he knew it. Abolitionists themselves regularly emphasised how deep and far the slave economy extended, well beyond the fields and auction blocks of the Southern United States, Brazil and Cuba. It seeped into every corner of daily life: clothes, food and drink, even the paper used to print banknotes. The week Douglass made his first acquaintance with Glasgow, among the ships arriving in the Clyde with cargoes of molasses and rum from Demerara, mahogany from Honduras, herrings from New Brunswick and oranges from Lisbon, were the *Unicorn* and *Nestor* from New Orleans laden with bales of raw, slave-grown cotton.[12] Waiting to spin them into yarn and weave it into fabrics were over 150 factories in the city and surrounding area, employing some 30,000 workers: a textile industry small in comparison to Lancashire but the second-largest in Britain.[13]

When Garrison spoke in Glasgow in 1840 he couldn't help pointing out that British import tariffs kept out free-grown corn from the United States, while its ports were open to its 'blood-stained cotton'.[14] The following year, George Thompson, lecturing at the Relief Church, John Street, elaborated with some precise statistics:

> Upwards of 50 millions of capital are embarked in the cotton manufactures of this country. Nearly 20 millions sterling are paid for the *raw material* landed on your wharfs. A million and a half of the hardy and industrious people of this country are employed in the trade [. . .] Yet I cannot forget that our supply of this article is both precarious and polluted. It comes from America. I cannot forget that of the 500 millions of pounds weight of cotton wool imported into this country 4-5ths are the produce of slaves in America.[15]

Thompson himself was at the time closely involved with the British India Society, which was pushing for land reforms and an end to the legal recognition of slavery in order that the Subcontinent would become a viable alternative source to slave-labour produce.[16] This was one of the strands of the transatlantic free produce movement that emerged in the late eighteenth century and revived after West Indian Emancipation. Thompson, like many other abolitionists, believed that slavery could be peacefully undermined if manufacturers began to buy free-labour produce instead:

> There is a silent power at work, which, with sure and resistless energy, would destroy their system, without a sermon, a remonstrance, an anti-slavery tract, or a solitary newspaper article. Free labour is at work. [. . .] It is being discovered that the sugar of Bengal is as bright and as sweet as that of Louisiana, or Brazil, or Cuba; that the cotton of Tinnevelly and Guzerat will spin as well as that of New Orleans. That the tobacco of Java will sell as well at Amsterdam as the tobacco of Maryland or Virginia. That the rice of Patna makes as good puddings as that of Carolina.[17]

Certainly the Glasgow Emancipation Society saw such initiatives as part of the arsenal of abolitionism and it supported Thompson in this as it did in many other of his endeavours, voting to become an auxiliary of the British India Society in 1839, and conferring honorary membership on the manufacturer and indigo planter Dwarkanath Tagore of Calcutta.[18]

The Free Produce movement faced considerable challenges. The supply of alternatives was far less than was needed to make a difference; few manufacturers were persuaded to switch and even fewer consumers willing to pay the higher prices. It proved almost impossible to separate free-labour from slave-labour produce through all the stages of the manufacturing and distribution process, despite the introduction of a special mark designed to make it easier to detect fraud by retailers.[19] Garrison's enthusiasm for Free Produce waned in the late 1830s, although his reservations mainly related to those advocates who placed special emphasis on the personal abstention from consuming slave-labour produce, making it a veritable 'test' of whether one was a true abolitionist or not.[20]

Of course, as Thompson admitted, had everyone immediately abstained from consuming such produce, a 'national calamity' would have ensued, as the British economy collapsed.[21] Not that there was any danger of this happening, as even on an individual level, let alone that of a manufacturer importing large quantities of raw materials, abstention confronted insuperable difficulties: one could 'not live twenty-four hours without touching such products', as one contributor to the debate on the issue at the 1840 World Anti-Slavery Convention pointed out.[22] In practice even the most zealous abstainers had to make practical, rather than principled, choices between which products to avoid and which not.

While the Glasgow Emancipation Society encouraged the development of free-labour produce, it never, any more than the American Anti-Slavery Society, required its members to personally abstain from using the produce of slave-labour. From 1841, two of its vice-presidents were James Oswald and John Dennistoun, Glasgow's two Members of Parliament, and, more to the point, mill-owners who had made their fortunes from cotton.[23] And while they did not play an active role in the Society, Oswald and Dennistoun probably did not see a conflict between their business interests and their abolitionism. In due course cotton manufacturers like them would have found their economic self-interest increasingly aligning with antislavery in the following decade as the sectional crisis in the United States – and then the Civil War itself – made the need to switch to alternative sources more compelling.

Douglass and his fellow campaigners targeted churches for a reason. If there was one thing the two broad factions of abolitionists could agree upon, it was that, as the title of the influential pamphlet had it, American Churches were the 'bulwarks of slavery', institutions which had spectacularly failed to condemn the system of bondage and to expel members who owned other human beings. When Douglass spoke of wanting to surround the United States with a 'wall of anti-slavery fire', he was expressing the desire to isolate and shame those who were perpetrating the system, actively or passively, to let them know they would find no sympathy in other countries.[24]

If the least that churches in Britain could do was to refuse fellowship with their counterparts across the Atlantic, the Free Church of Scotland – having strengthened the hand of friendship by accepting financial assistance from Presbyterians in South Carolina – had set a very poor example indeed. The fact that other churches in Scotland (and elsewhere in the kingdom) had no doubt benefited from the profits of slavery and the compensations paid out to the owners of West Indian slaves after 1834 was irrelevant. It was not the *origin* of their wealth that mattered, but the ongoing *relationship* between their leaders and their counterparts in the United States, where slavery continued to prevail. As the title of one inflammatory pamphlet had it, it was the Free Church's '*alliance* with man-stealers' which was fundamentally at issue, not the 'bloody gold' which was its most rhetorically convenient symptom.

In fact, the abolitionists did not reserve their antislavery ire for the Free Church alone. On his first visit to Belfast Douglass had lent his support to Rev. Isaac Nelson, who was hoping to persuade the Presbyterian Church of Ireland to sever ties with its counterparts in the United States. Douglass returned in July to attend its General Assembly. While Nelson's motion was watered down, the Assembly was much more forthright in its criticisms of the American churches than the Free Church ever was.[25] Another delegate was Chalmers's friend Smyth from South Carolina, who had spread the rumour about Douglass visiting a brothel. While letters flew back and forth between their lawyers, Douglass was pleased to note that Smyth was asked to exclude himself from the proceedings.[26]

Another strand to the abolitionists' 'no fellowship' campaign – one which consumed much energy and drew in Garrison and Thompson as well as Douglass – was the pressure that they brought to bear on the Evangelical Alliance, a new association that aspired to forge closer relations between the mainstream Protestant churches on both sides of the Atlantic. At a preliminary meeting in Birmingham in March, even the Free Church's Robert Candlish added his voice to those calling for invitations to slaveholding ministers to be withheld.[27] The proposal to exclude slaveholders from membership of the Alliance was hotly debated in London in August and, with no prospect of agreement between the two sides, a decision was postponed. Douglass chastised the weakness of the British delegates in accepting the compromise, and mocked the arguments of the Americans, including Thomas Smyth, fresh from his humiliation in Belfast, although he saved his bitterest invective for the delegate of the African Methodist Episcopal Church, Dr Molliston Madison Clark, whom he branded 'a recreant black man' and a 'traitor to his race'.[28]

If neither the intervention in Belfast nor in London brought unqualified success, it did show that the Free Church was not alone in facing the wrath of the agitators, as some of its supporters seemed to imply. And the cumulative effect of the campaign against religious fellowship with slaveholders did yield results. While Douglass was in Scotland, both the Secession and the Relief Churches passed resolutions at their general assemblies advocating no fellowship, and, following the meeting of the Evangelical Alliance, more than fifty British members resigned.[29] By the 1850s, most British churches had abandoned any form of fellowship with American Churches.[30]

Still, the fact that Douglass's anger was not generally pointed at other British institutions merits further scrutiny. At the Evangelical Alliance conference, one American delegate, Dr William Patton, invoking the title of Birney's pamphlet, 'pointed out that the bulwark of slavery was not the American church but the price paid for cotton in Liverpool'.[31] We have already noted that abolitionists frequently made reference to the way the products of American slave-labour made their way into every British home – and made many industrialists very rich. A year after returning to the United States, Douglass printed in his newspaper excerpts from a free produce pamphlet that included the subhead 'No Commercial Union with Slaveholders'.[32] In the circumstances, it seems strange that Douglass devoted so much of his energy in Scotland to deriding religious fellowship.

At the end of his virtuoso speech in Dundee, where he acted out the imaginary encounter between George Lewis and Thomas Auld, he accused the Free Church of acting 'as if they were a manufacturing corporation' and forgetting that their objective should not be 'making money' but 'spreading the Gospel'.[33] This might suggest that Douglass thought that churches should be held to a higher moral standard than capitalist enterprises. But there is more to it than that. Political expediency required that 'making money' was something generally best left to itself.

He could have tried to rouse audiences by calling on businesses to stop importing slave-grown sugar, and while some abolitionists did just this, the strategy was not widely pursued, not least because of the practical problems the Free Produce movement faced. At this point at least, for Douglass as it was for Garrison, a boycott would have been a distraction. At a speech in Edinburgh he did express his disapproval of Parliament's decision to abolish the sugar tariffs – increased after Emancipation to help fund the compensation promised to slaveholders, but with lower rates applied to colonial sugar in an effort to encourage the West Indian economy. The new measure would reduce the price of sugar but would boost imports of slave-grown produce from the United States, Cuba and Brazil. Said Douglass, 'The people of England, who were so anxious to sweeten their palates, should bear in mind that they were about to do so at the expense of bones and blood of their fellow creatures.'[34] While the British and Foreign Anti-Slavery Society had fought hard to ensure the duties were retained (in a modified form), the issue had fallen by the wayside, and the legislation passed without significant protest. For many abolitionists, moral concerns tended to lose out when they clashed with their commitment to free trade.[35]

He might have also taken to the platform to denounce the Anti-Corn Law League for its cosy relationship with American pro-slavery ideologues John C. Calhoun and George McDuffie, and for accepting financial support from them. James Haughton, for one, remonstrated, as he had over the donations to the Irish Repeal Association, but his was a lone voice, and here again the economic arguments of free trade trumped the moral claims of abolitionism.[36] In neither case would Douglass have drawn crowds had he tried to make it a *cause célèbre*.

The reason Douglass stayed clear of these other concerns was that 'no fellowship with American churches' *worked* – not because it achieved its stated, immediate goal, but because it offered a plausible objective that could command widespread support and give rise to public meetings that – most importantly of all – would be reported and read in the United States as evidence of strong antislavery feeling in Britain. The strategy of the Garrisonians required them to formulate demands that could mobilise a constituency big and vocal enough to make it into the papers. Only then could it stand a chance of stirring the conscience of those complicit in terrible wrongdoing. No other issue would have come close to creating the impact the 'Send Back the Money' campaign had.

Notes

1. Whyte, *'Send Back the Money!'*, p. 146; Rice, *Scots Abolitionists*, p. 137; Blackett, *Building an Anti-Slavery Wall*, p. 96; McFeely, *Frederick Douglass*, p. 133.
2. FCS, *Proceedings 1846*, p. 14.
3. Ibid. p. 50.
4. For a detailed account see Whyte, *'Send Back the Money!'*, pp. 129–45. For the 1847 General Assembly see FCS, *Proceedings 1847*, pp. 262–78, esp. p. 272; and Rice, *Scots Abolitionists*, pp. 142–3.
5. See Blackett, *Building an Anti-Slavery Wall*, p. 94; McFeely, *Frederick Douglass*, p. 133.
6. For FD's reservations concerning HCW see FD to RW, Limerick, 10 November 1845 (FDP 3.1, p. 64).
7. There are reports of lectures by Moses Roper in Perth (*Northern Warder*, 11 June 1846), Crieff and Methven (*Northern Warder*, 25 June 1846). Roper's appearances in 1846 were mostly in towns and villages in Fife, Perthshire, Angus and Aberdeenshire. In Edinburgh on 25 May 1846, GT (who helped Roper when he first arrived in England in 1835) refers to him simply as 'another slave [who] has come from America to plead the cause', without naming him, and while not promising 'that he will be quite so eloquent and effective as Mr Douglass, still his *plain* and *simple* story will no doubt produce its effects' (*Edinburgh Evening Post*, 30 May 1846). I have found no other reference to Roper by any of the other Garrisonian lecturers that year.
8. See for example Thomas Chalmers to Adam Black, 15 May 1846 (Chalmers Papers, CHA 4.321) and Chalmers's reply, 23 May 1846 (Chalmers Papers, CHA 3.17); and A. Ross to Thomas Chalmers, 10 November 1846 (Chalmers Papers, CHA 4.326).

9. See Rice, *Scots Abolitionists*, pp. 137–9; Blackett, *Building an Anti-Slavery Wall*, pp. 94–5; and McFeeley, *Frederick Douglass*, p. 135.

10. In May 1846, the *Witness* published letters on this issue (notably 2 May, 6 May, 9 May and 13 May). Miller's editorial contributions include 'The Free Church and Her Accusers' (13 May), 'The Beam and the Mote' (16 May), 'The Established Church Petitioning Slaveholders to Send Them Money' (28 May), 'The Free Church and American Slavery' (10 June), 'More New Morality' (24 June) and 'How Did the Christians of Scotland Act Towards Our Own Slaveholders' (27 June). The claims made regarding Rose Street Church were first made by 'Spectator' in a letter to the editor, 9 May 1846, drawing on some remarks made (in a note added to the third and subsequent printings) in Cameron, *The Free Church and Her Accusers*, pp. 35–6.

11. [Hugh Miller], 'The Slavery Question', *Witness*, 18 December 1844. See also 'D'., 'American Slavery', *Dumfries and Galloway Standard*, 13 May 1846.

12. 'Ship News', *Glasgow Herald*, 9 and 12 January 1846. In 1820 another ship named *Unicorn* was searched by customs officials in Baltimore on suspicion of carrying kidnapped or smuggled slaves for sale in New Orleans, one of them a two-year-old boy, the same age as Douglass: see Schermerhorn, *The Business of Slavery*, pp. 42–3; and Schermerhorn, 'The Coastwise Slave Trade', pp. 210–16. In the early 1820s Douglass would have been well aware of the threat posed by the thriving business of Austin Woolfolk and other traders, who acquired slaves on the Eastern Shore, and then shipped them, via Baltimore, to New Orleans: see Preston, *Young Frederick Douglass*, pp. 76–80.

13. Scottish figures extrapolated from Bremner, *The Industries of Scotland*, pp. 286–7. According to Edward Baines, about three times as many were employed in the industry in Lancashire as in Lanarkshire and Renfrewshire (combined): Baines, *History of the Cotton Manufacture*, p. 421.

14. WLG, Glasgow, 27 July 1840 (*Glasgow Argus*, 30 July 1840, repr. *Liberator*, 28 August 1840).

15. GT, Glasgow, 1 November 1841 (*Christianity versus Slavery*, pp. 30–1). GT may have taken the figure of 1.5 million from Baines in his 1833 estimate of the numbers employed in the industry and in trades that depended on it: Baines, *History of the Cotton Manufacture*, pp. 396–7, 402, 413. The figures for the amount of capital invested, the volume of raw cotton imports and the price paid for them are close to those given for 1840 in Mann, *The Cotton Trade of Great Britain*, pp. 91, 94, 112. Most sources agree that the proportion of raw cotton imported from the United States represented around 80% of the total in the period between 1830 and 1860: see Baines, *History of the*

Cotton Manufacture, pp. 309–10; Mann, *The Cotton Trade of Great Britain*, pp. 42, 112; and Ellison, *The Cotton Trade of Great Britain*, p. 86. All these figures relate to Britain as a whole.

16. For Thompson's interest in India see Temperley, *British Antislavery*, pp. 101–2; Laidlaw, '"Justice to India"', pp. 309–24; Fisher, *Counterflows to Colonialism*, pp. 285–8; Kling, *Partner in Empire*, pp. 167–78.

17. GT, Glasgow, 1 November 1841 (*Christianity versus Slavery*, p. 29).

18. Minutes of GES Committee meeting, 1 August 1839 (Smeal Collection, Reel 1); GES, *Eighth Annual Report*. Tagore travelled to Britain in 1841 and returned the following year to Bengal with Thompson, who secured a lucrative position working for the Raja of Satara.

19. For a survey see Holcomb, *Moral Commerce*. See also Billington, 'British Humanitarians and American Cotton'; and Faulkner, 'The Root of the Evil'.

20. WLG, 'Tests', *Liberator*, 2 August 1844; WLG, 'Products of Slave Labor', *Liberator*, 5 March 1847.

21. GT, Glasgow, 1 November 1841 (*Christianity versus Slavery*, p. 30).

22. *Proceedings of the General Anti-Slavery Convention*, vol. 1, p. 444. The speaker was George Bradburn.

23. According to the Factory Inspectorate, in 1833 there were 74 cotton mills in Lanarkshire employing a total of 17,949 people, an average of 243 employees each. Oswald & Co. (with 453 employees) and J. Dennistoun (with 330) were clearly two of the larger enterprises. See Butt, 'The Industries of Glasgow', p. 102. See also Cooke, 'The Scottish Cotton Masters'.

24. FD, London, 22 May 1846 (FDP 1.1, p. 295).

25. Whyte, *'Send Back the Money!'*, pp. 108–19; Blackett, *Building an Anti-Slavery Wall*, pp. 83–6; Maclear, 'Thomas Smyth, Frederick Douglass's, pp. 286–97.

26. FD, Edinburgh, 31 July 1846 (*Edinburgh Evening Post*, 5 August 1846). Another blow to Smyth was the abrupt curtailment of plans to confer on him an honorary degree at Glasgow University around 1850, a rejection he blamed on the legacy of the abolitionist agitation of 1846: see Smyth, *Autobiographical Notes*, pp. 227–8, 257–62.

27. Whyte, *'Send Back the Money!'*, p. 120; Blackett, *Building an Anti-Slavery Wall*, p. 97.

28. Blackett, *Building an Anti-Slavery Wall*, pp. 98–100; FD, Glasgow, 5 October 1846 (FDP 1.1, pp. 447–8). Clark subsequently reviewed his support for the Alliance: 'M. M. Clark on American Slavery', *National Anti-Slavery Standard*, 26 November 1846, citing a letter from Clark, dated Brighton, 9 October 1846, published in the *London Patriot*.

29. Blackett, *Building an Anti-Slavery Wall*, p. 90; Jezierski, 'Glasgow Emancipation Society', p. 171.

30. 'The approach can be said to have been broadly successful, and after the middle of the century Britons could congratulate themselves that their churches refused communion with slaveholders': Huzzey, *Freedom Burning*, p. 77.

31. Blackett, *Building an Anti-Slavery Wall*, p. 99, paraphrasing Patton here: the exact quotation, which is not quite so neat, is to be found in Evangelical Alliance, *Report of the Proceedings*, p. 316.

32. H.R. [Henry Richardson], 'Revolution of the Spindles', *North Star*, 23 June 1848.

33. FD, Dundee, 10 March 1846 (FDP 1.1, p. 182).

34. FD, Edinburgh, 31 July 1846 (*Edinburgh Evening Post*, 5 August 1846).

35. For background see Temperley, *British Antislavery*, pp. 137–67; Harling, 'Sugar Wars'.

36. See Morgan, 'The Anti-Corn Law League', pp. 87–107, esp. 103.

Chapter 9

Gilded Cages

We know that on many occasions, Douglass drew large crowds. In March 1846, nearly 1,200 people filled George's Chapel in Dundee; a month later, two meetings on the same night in Paisley attracted similar numbers to each; and on 1 May he addressed an audience of 2,000 people paying sixpence a head at Edinburgh's Music Hall.[1] Newspaper reports tell us how his words elicited cheers, applause, laughter, sharp intakes of breath and sometimes hisses of disapproval. Many of these meetings were great social occasions, and 'soirées', 'tea parties' and 'public breakfasts' offered refreshments and musical entertainment. If the presence of women at political meetings was still occasionally frowned upon in the press, antislavery gatherings open to the public were usually mixed and the men and women sometimes sat together.[2] 'The immense room was filled to overflowing,' wrote a reporter at the Music Hall. 'The orchestra was crammed from top to bottom, and hung with a galaxy of ladies and gentlemen, like a drop scene of a theatre. The room itself, and all the passages, were crowded – hundreds could not get seats.'[3]

But it is harder to tell how his campaign speeches in Scotland *transformed* his listeners – emotionally, intellectually. The speeches denouncing the Free Church are distinctive in their repeated use of the same slogan – the rhythmic 'send back the money' that was often chanted by his audience, providing – as such formulae often do – a sense of shared feeling that temporarily binds disparate people together. Douglass and his fellow speakers rarely analyse what these emotions might be, beyond congratulating themselves on the ferment of antislavery sentiment they have induced.

Some measure of their impact may be indicated by the 'ladies of Kirkcaldy' who, according to the *Fife Herald*, inspired by Douglass's visit in June, 'recently formed themselves into an Anti-Slavery Society, to co-operate with other institutions of the same kind in this country, for the purpose of collecting money or articles of some value to be sent to the American Anti-Slavery Bazaar'.[4] In doing so, they were following the example of nearly thirty women across Britain and Ireland whose names appeared in a list of those credited with supporting the cause in the second Irish edition of Douglass's *Narrative*, published a few months before.[5]

We may glimpse a more personal response to Douglass's speeches in the letters of two women who had attended his speeches condemning the Free Church, which they addressed to two men at the heart of the controversy. One is written to Thomas Chalmers by a woman not known to him, and choosing not to identify herself, who had recently seen Douglass in Dundee. The other was sent to Thomas Smyth in Charleston by Mary Cunningham in Belfast. They had been close friends as teenagers (before he emigrated with his family as a young man fifteen years earlier), and had met in 1844 on his first return to his home town.

Both writers are keenly aware of the argument that the American churches have been insufficiently critical of slavery and accepted slaveholders into their congregations without question, and that because of their actions their addressees have a case to answer. The women regard them as men of great influence and call on them to respond to their critics and to prove them wrong, daring them to challenge the scriptural authority that, they insist, has no place for slavery. In doing so, they defy the colourful stereotypes of women employed by both sides of the 'Send Back the Money' controversy. The authors of these letters hardly correspond to the 'squadrons of female dragoons' in 'petticoat breeches' imagined by Hugh Miller. Nor do they resemble the victims of the Free Church that would, in the words of an establishment minister, 'rob servant girls of the hard-won money that ought to have gone for ribbons and gum-flowers, and washerwomen of their savings-banks accumulations'.[6]

The woman from Dundee imagines the 'strangers' (Douglass and Buffum) were sent by God not only to show the error of the ways of Chalmers and the Free Church but to persuade her to examine her own conduct.

> To me also were there [sic] words reproofs. I was shewing a little of the slaveholder my own conscience tell me so. I was also beginning to murmur for more liberty I thought that I could not well get alone.

But it was the *Grand Intruder* that was ever following me with his suggestions. God in mercy sent these men to shew me my transgressions, by telling me what my sisters are suffering pent up in chains, bloodhounds their guardians *Iron Collars* their necklaces, *Whips* instead of the strong arm of Man to lean on or ward off ill. And are we content to leave it *so*.[7]

Her own circumstances – represented here by 'necklaces' and the supportive 'strong arm of man' – hardly approach those of her enslaved sisters whose freedom is constrained by iron collars and bloodhounds. And yet in her confined domesticity she too has begun 'to murmur for more liberty I thought that I could not well get alone'. If Douglass's speeches made her feel a little ashamed of the limited horizons of her feminism (in which she now glimpses 'a little of the slaveholder' in herself), they also provide an opportunity to overcome them, if only in the act of writing and posting a letter to Chalmers.

But this soul-searching co-exists with humour, which she somewhat incautiously shares with her addressee. She tells him how the abolitionists quoted his words before dramatically inviting the audience to imagine a rather improper scene:

When the Collar and whip were produced it was remarked would the application of these to *you* or your daughters make you *change* your views on slavery. This caused *laughter*. . . Oh it is too serious a matter to make sport of – Fre. Douglass did make me laugh when he preached the boys in Dundee send *back* the money –

We know that, on occasion, Douglass (like other antislavery orators) displayed instruments of slave restraint and torture, to vividly bring home to his audiences the horrors of slavery, sometimes claiming that they were the very ones used in the events he is recalling.[8] Here, we are told, in a more unusual performative flourish, that he invited his audience to imagine them being applied to Chalmers and his daughters – a rather risqué move (especially if it was Douglass who was holding them) that partly accounts for the (presumably) somewhat embarrassed laughter at the meeting. But if the letter-writer dutifully steps back a moment to condemn the frivolity, she can't help mischievously admitting to Chalmers that she herself was amused. If she expects the leader of the Free Church

to imagine her in stitches as she pictures him being whipped by a
fugitive slave, then she has unravelled the declared pious intent of
her epistle.[9]

Mary Cunningham tells Smyth of 'the eloquent, and affecting
lectures' she has attended, lectures which she says opened her eyes
to 'the heart sickening horrors of this dreadful system'.[10] She is
most vexed by the revelation that so-called Christians participate in
this system, in flagrant disregard of the Great Commandment and
Golden Rule. She riffs on the ironies of 'the land of liberty' holding
millions in bondage, which was one of Douglass's favourite rhetorical tactics.

> You reside in the land, called falsely, (it is now represented,) 'The
> Land of Liberty,' the place of freedom, the picture now before us, is
> dark indeed, all the false coloring, has been wiped away, and nothing
> left for the eye, to gaze upon, but the gloomy, ghastly, features of this
> hideous monster.

'Hideous monster' is a term Douglass uses to describe slavery in
his famous 'What to the Slave is the Fourth of July?' speech in 1852
and he may have used it earlier, though this has not been documented.
But she certainly did not take from Douglass the image which she
chooses to close the letter:

> Oh! the thought of 'liberty,' the birds, that wing their joyous flight,
> above the clouds of Heaven, afford, ample proof, of the wise, benefi-
> cent, and glorious intention of our Heavenly Father, contrasted with
> the drooping, and imprisoned tenant, of a gilded cage, though that
> cage, be living in the palace of an Emperor.

The caged bird is an ancient symbol of imprisonment. The 'gilded
cage' more specifically (as a space of confinement so comfortable or
luxurious that it may appear otherwise) is at least as old as Chaucer
(where it appears in the 'The Manciple's Tale') and was a perva-
sive Victorian metaphor for the limited opportunities of middle-class
women. There is nothing 'gilded' about the slave plantation whose
brutal violence is repeatedly described by Douglass, who identified
not with a caged bird but other, more roughly handled creatures such
as the 'bridled horse and muzzled ox', as he did in one of his Belfast

speeches.[11] The cage Mary Cunningham had in mind was more likely to have been her own.

Both letters draw on the arguments and capture the gestures that Douglass evidently made in his speeches in Belfast and Dundee (we have newspaper reports of them), repeating them to the people whom he accused but who were not there to hear them. But they also reinterpret them, transposing their largely secular message into a more Christian key that was more agreeable to themselves as well as their addressees, and hint that the 'Send Back the Money' campaign aroused more private feelings of shame and guilt as well as emboldening them to assert themselves, taking up their pens to call influential men to account.

Perhaps it is not just a coincidence that the repeated injunction to resist the temptation of filthy lucre in the context of a fight against slavery should make these women call up images of 'necklaces' and other trappings of the 'gilded cage' in which they are confined. If we multiply these letters by the thousands of individuals who were moved by Douglass's speeches, who knows how many lives they touched, realigned and transformed?

Notes

1. FDP 1.1, pp. 171, 240, 244.
2. On the changing attitudes to women attending and taking part in political meetings see Pickering and Tyrrell, *The People's Bread*, pp. 116–25.
3. 'Free Church and American Slavery', *Edinburgh Evening Post*, 30 May 1846.
4. *Fife Herald*, 24 September 1846. The paper says FD visited Kirkcaldy in May. He was to have spoken there on 19 May but his appearance was postponed until 1 June. (See Appendix I.)
5. 'To the Friends of the Slave', D2, p. cxxxv.
6. Quoted by Rice, 'Controversies over Slavery', p. 46.
7. Anon to Thomas Chalmers, 2 April 1846 (Thomas Chalmers papers CHA.4.321).
8. FD, Dublin, 4 October 1845 (FDP 1.1, p. 35); FD, Cork, 23 October 1845 (FDP 1.1, p. 66); FD, Limerick, 10 November 1845 (FDP 1.1, pp. 85–6); FD, Dundee, 30 January 1846 (*Dundee Courier*, 3 February 1846). On other occasions it is JB rather than FD who is reported as

exhibiting instruments of torture (*Ayrshire Advertiser*, 26 March 1846; *Manstealers*, p. 52; *Freeman's Journal*, 13 September 1845).

9. I can find no reference to such an episode in newspaper reports of FD's speeches, in Dundee or anywhere else. In Dundee on 30 January 1846 FD is reported as saying, 'Do you think Dr Chalmers would ever have said this, if, like me, he had four sisters and one brother in bondage?' (FDP 1.1, p. 155). Perhaps these hypothetical sisters were misremembered as a daughter, with the theatrical application of the whip a fanciful addition?

10. Mary Cunningham to Thomas Smyth, Glenwood, 14 January 1846 (Smyth, *Autobiographical Notes*, p. 365).

11. FD, Belfast, 5 December 1845 (FDP 1.1, p. 93).

Part III

Douglass, Scott and Burns

In Scotland, too, renowned in her struggles for liberty by the heroic deeds of Wallace and Bruce, and his own great prototype Douglass, a land illustrious in poetic associations of Burns the ploughman poet, and Walter Scott of Abbotsford – there from the elite of Edinburgh and Glasgow, as also the peasantry of Loch Katrine, 'O'er hill and dale, / By the bonnie highland heather,' in contrast with the awards of Republican America, Frederick Douglass was honored, as the language of Scotia's own bard proclaimed, 'A man for a' that.'

From William Cooper Nell's introduction to FD, 'Reception of Frederick Douglass at the Belknap-Street Church, Boston, 3 May 1847', as reported in the Liberator, *21 May 1847*

Chapter 10

'One of Scotland's Many Famous Names'

'My father was a white man,' wrote Douglass. 'He was admitted to be such by all I ever heard speak of my parentage.'[1] It was rumoured that his master was his father, but he had no way of telling. In any case, he was not named after Captain Aaron Anthony, Colonel Lloyd's chief overseer at the Great House Farm and a slaveholder himself, but after his mother, Harriet Bailey, though he barely knew her. Her duties on Anthony's own farm took her away from her children, and Frederick was brought up by his grandmother Betsy Bailey and her husband Isaac in their cabin not far away, but at the age of six the boy was sent to the Lloyd plantation twelve miles distant.[2]

Frederick Augustus Washington Bailey – 'Washington' was a common patriotic flourish, while 'Augustus' may have honoured an uncle who died shortly before he was born – dispensed with his two middle names early in life.[3] When he escaped North, he adopted several other surnames, including Stanley, designed to throw any pursuers off the track, and arrived in New Bedford, Massachusetts as Johnson.[4] But the name Johnson was very common in that town, and was even the name of the family who took him in. It was time for another change. Recalling the occasion in his *Narrative* seven years later, Douglass wrote:

> I gave Mr. Johnson the privilege of choosing me a name, but told him he must not take from me the name of 'Frederick.' I must hold on to that, to preserve a sense of my identity. Mr. Johnson had just been reading the 'Lady of the Lake,' and at once suggested that my name be 'Douglass.' From that time until now I have been called 'Frederick Douglass;' and as I am more widely known by that name than by either of the others, I shall continue to use it as my own.[5]

We don't know for sure why the surname of Walter Scott's James Douglas acquired an extra 's'. Douglass's biographer William McFeely has suggested that this was the way 'prominent black families in Baltimore and Philadelphia spelled it', and so he was merely conforming to a standard practice.[6] But it was not just peculiar to those cities. The Federal Census of 1840 shows that 'Douglass's was three times more common a surname in the United States than 'Douglas'.[7]

In this, his first account of his renaming, Douglass gives all the credit to Nathan Johnson, although this does not necessarily mean that he wasn't familiar with Scott's famous poem himself. At the time, Douglass probably never dreamed that his escape would eventually take him to Scotland. But when it did, he made full use of the historical and literary associations of his new name, as he suggests (twice emphasising its Scottishness) when he writes about his arrival in New Bedford in his second autobiography of 1855. His host

> had been reading the 'Lady of the Lake,' and was pleased to regard me as a suitable person to wear this, one of Scotland's many famous names. Considering the noble hospitality and manly character of Nathan Johnson, I have felt that he, better than I, illustrated the virtues of the great Scottish chief. Sure I am, that had any slave-catcher entered his domicile, with a view to molest any one of his household, he would have shown himself like him of the 'stalwart hand.'[8]

He generously compares Johnson to the main protagonist, but he must have seen parallels with himself too. The couplet quoted in part here more fully reads: 'Douglas of the stalwart hand/Was exiled from his native land'.[9] Like the fugitive slave, James Douglas is an outlaw and an exile. At one point in the poem, he is compared to a 'hunted stag'.[10] This must have had some resonance for the author of the 1845 *Narrative* who recounted his escape from 'the hunters of men'.[11]

Douglass recognised that the character in *The Lady of the Lake* was not the only famous Scot to bear his name. There was another, who may have appealed to him more. In Perth in January 1846, he composed a reply to the charges of a Mr A. C. C. Thompson, who had claimed in a letter to the *Delaware Republican* that the recently published *Narrative* had been written by someone else. Thompson cannot make the connection between the 'unlearned and rather ordinary Negro' he used to know and the book he has just read. But

Douglass reminds him of the huge difference between the boy he once was and the adult he now is:

> The change wrought in me is truly amazing. If you should meet me now, you would scarcely know me. You know when I used to meet you near Covey's wood-gate, I hardly dared to look up at you. If I should meet you where I now am, amid the free hills of Old Scotland, where the ancient 'Black Douglass' [sic] once met his foes, I presume I might summon sufficient fortitude to look you full in the face. It may be that, wearing the brave name which I have assumed, might lead me to deeds which would render our meeting not the most agreeable. Especially might this be the case, if you should attempt to enslave me. You would see a wonderful difference in me.[12]

The historical existence of a 'black Douglass' no doubt confirms his choice of name as serendipitous. The original Black Douglas was the Good Sir James Douglas, Robert the Bruce's leading military commander in the campaign to secure the freedom of Scotland from forces loyal to Edward II of England. He was knighted by Bruce on the eve of the Battle of Bannockburn (1314). Legend has it that after his death, Douglas preserved Bruce's heart in a silver case and wore it round his neck, and later, when fighting the Moors in Spain, he threw it among the enemy and was slain where it lay, the 'bludy hert' thereafter incorporated in the family seal and coat of arms.[13]

Douglass placed much importance on his reply to Thompson, which was published in Garrison's *Liberator* in Boston and also included – heavily revised – as an Appendix to both the second Irish and subsequent English editions of his *Narrative*, despite his publisher's reservations.[14] He echoed some of its phraseology in a speech he gave in Dundee a few days later, referring to his presence in a 'land whose every hill has been made classic by heroic deeds performed by her noble sons – a land whose every brook and river carry the songs of freedom as they pass to the ocean – a land whose hills have nearly all been watered with blood in behalf of freedom'.[15]

Many of his listeners and readers (on both sides of the Atlantic) would have been familiar with these 'heroic deeds' of the leading figures of the Scottish wars of independence. They would have learnt about them from traditional ballads and Jane Porter's widely read novel about William Wallace, *Scottish Chiefs* (1810). But above all, it was the writings of Walter Scott who would have fixed them in their imagination, especially his popular *Tales of a Grandfather* (1828–30), dashing stories from history designed to entertain his sick grandson.[16]

In his *Tales*, Scott suggests that the Black Douglas was so-called because of his 'swarthy complexion' and 'dark hair'.[17] But for his enemies, the epithet was less likely to refer to his appearance than to his ruthless cruelty (or 'deeds [. . .] not the most agreeable', as Douglass delicately puts it). 'You must know', writes Scott, 'that the name of Douglas had become so terrible to the English, that the women used to frighten their children with it, and say to them when they behaved ill, that they "would make the Black Douglas take them".'[18] No doubt this reputation gave special force to the cry of 'Douglas, Douglas!', which Scott, drawing on ancient sources, explained 'was the shout with which that family always began battle'.[19] A fictionalised Sir James features in Scott's last novel, *Castle Dangerous* (1832), lurking threateningly off-stage, for the most part, before recapturing his fortress from the English garrison occupying it.

Scott's poetry and fiction did much to reinvent Scottish history and landscape in the first half of the nineteenth century, in the wake of the reconstruction of the Highlands that followed the defeat of the Jacobite rebellion at Culloden in 1746. 'Not a year passes without seeing numbers flocking from England and other countries to Scotland, to visit scenes which they would probably never have heard of but for Scott,' observed a guidebook in 1846.[20] Emblems of the outlawed culture were duly transformed, so that instead of signs of resistance to the Hanoverian state, or of the poverty, famine and migration that ensued, they became, in the hands of an emerging English-speaking elite, tokens of a picturesque wilderness haunted by poetic ghosts safely sealed in an ancient past. By the time of Douglass's visit, sightseers travelled there on military roads, some of them enjoying recreation on the new sporting estates. 'Highlandism' had rapidly developed into a romantic image of Scotland as a whole, officially endorsed at the highest level by George IV wearing a kilt on his official visit to Edinburgh in 1822 (which Scott orchestrated), and by Victoria and Albert, who embraced tartan with a vengeance after they began taking holidays north of the Tay from 1842.[21]

One unmistakeable indication of Scott's importance was the 200-foot monument erected to his memory on Princes Street in Edinburgh. Completed in 1844, twelve years after his death, it was officially opened in August 1846, shortly after Douglass's third visit to the city.

Figure 10.1 Scott Monument, Edinburgh.

And the new railway station in the cutting below (ushering in those tourists eager for their first sight of the lochs, glens and mountains) would soon bear the name *Waverley*, the title of Scott's first novel that came to be applied collectively to its successors.

When Douglass alludes to the Scottishness of his name and, albeit playfully, identifies with the 'Black Douglass', he is also inviting his audiences to associate him not only with Sir James but with the whole mediaeval dynasty of Douglases. While Douglass does not refer to them individually, many of them appear in Scott's poetry and fiction. For devotees of Scott, as many of Douglass's British and American readers and listeners were, their exploits were proverbial. As these historical and literary figures are less familiar today, it is worth specifying them in some detail, so we can better appreciate the resonances of Douglass's chosen name for those who were drawn to his lectures and writings.

The whole line of Sir James's descendants were known collectively as the Black Douglases, starting with William, the first earl of Douglas, the subject, according to Scott's notes, of 'The Tragedy of Douglas', a ballad he included in *Minstrelsy of the Scottish Border* (1802–3).[22] Other ballads – 'The Battle of Otterburn' and 'Chevy Chase' – record the death in combat of William's son James, the second earl, fighting English forces commanded by Sir Henry 'Hotspur' Percy.[23] Archibald the Grim (or 'Blak' Archibald), the third earl, also fell foul of Percy, who took him prisoner at the Battle of Homildon Hill; he makes an appearance as 'that dark baron on whose eye was death' in Scott's *The Fair Maid of Perth* (1828), furious at the brazen infidelities of his son-in-law the Duke of Rothsay, but also merciless in his vengeance on those who turned against him and allowed him to die in captivity.

By the middle of the fifteenth century the Douglas family was at the height of its power, rivalling the Crown in wealth and military strength, a situation deemed intolerable by King James II and his advisors, who arranged first the murder of William, the sixth earl (the so-called 'Black Dinner') and then, a few years later, his uncle, the eighth earl, also William. Securing the support of other nobles fearing the strength of the earls of Douglas (including a branch of the same family, the earls of Angus), James saw off the allies of William, the ninth earl, at the Battle of Arkinholme in 1455, and confiscated their estates – giving rise, Scott tells us, to 'the saying that "the Red Douglas (such was the complexion of the Angus family) had put down the Black".'[24]

The earls of Angus were rewarded for their loyalty, but before long they too were in rebellion. Archibald Douglas, the fifth earl, known as 'Bell-the-Cat', earns a mention in *Marmion* (1808), to which Scott later added a historical note that dwells on his brutal murder of the king's counsellor Cochran, hung from the bridge in the town of Lauder.[25] It was the sixth earl, also Archibald, who, entrusted with the guardianship of his stepson, the young James V, effectively imprisoned him in 1525. The king escaped in 1528 and managed to win back his authority, and subsequently passed sentence of forfeiture against the earls of Angus, '[a]nd thus,' comments Scott, 'the Red Douglasses [. . .] shared almost the same fate with the Black Douglasses, of the elder branch of that mighty house'.[26] *The Lady of the Lake* (1810) bears only an oblique relationship to historical events and personages, but Scott identified the outlaw of his poem with James Douglas, a nephew of Archibald, also known as the fourth earl of Morton, who, during the period of his family's banishment, lived in the north of Scotland under an assumed name.[27]

How much Frederick Douglass had read of Scott, beyond *The Lady of Lake*, by the time he proudly referred, in Perth in 1846, to the 'brave name' he had adopted, we have no way of knowing. But if he didn't study the books till later, he would have known the legends at second hand. Abolitionists who toured Scotland before him had written of the thrill of visiting places rich in historical associations, largely filtered through Scott's retellings.[28] It is also likely that the people introduced to Douglass on his travels would have felt compelled to tell him stories about his illustrious namesakes, perhaps starting with his fellow passengers as his train stopped at Elderslie on the way to Glasgow. Moreover, his acquaintances could hardly have avoided referring to a famous play not written by Scott, but much admired by him.

John Home's *Douglas: A Tragedy* caused controversy when it opened in 1756 (the author, a church minister, was forced to resign by a scandalised presbytery) but it was a huge success, regularly staged well into the nineteenth century, attracting many leading actors of the day. The drama took its inspiration from the traditional Scots ballad 'Child Maurice' (or 'Gil Morice'), which tells of a jealous nobleman who murders a young man, mistaking him for his wife's lover, only to discover that he was her long-lost son. In the ballad, the boy is the son of an anonymous 'earl'; for much of the play, he is known as Norval, after the shepherd who raised him. But Home chose his title after the birth name he bestows on him, 'a name through all the world renown'd, / A name that rouses like the trumpet's sound', as the Prologue reminded its Edinburgh audience, drawn to the performance, as the playwright no doubt intended, by its rich, heroic and patriotic associations.[29]

The play does not identify the character with a specific historical figure, and indeed confuses matters by setting it during not an English but a Danish invasion of Scotland, a prudent choice only a decade after Culloden. But it does draw on more generic elements of the family story, such as its military prowess, the heart motif (which provides the first clue to the boy's identity), and the notorious rallying call of 'Douglas, Douglas!', which, uttered on three separate occasions by Lady Randolph, is converted from a war cry into an expression of private emotion, marking her transitions through grief (for her long-departed son at the beginning of Act I), joy (when he unexpectedly reappears in Act II) and finally distress (as she witnesses his death at the hand of her husband near the end of Act V).[30]

Eight years after his return to the United States, Douglass published in his newspaper a poem from a contributor that referred to the mediaeval confrontations between 'Percy' and 'Douglass' [sic], and added a footnote that quotes first Westmoreland from Shakespeare's *I Henry IV* ('Young Harry Percy and brave Archibald, / That ever valiant and approved Scott, / At Holmedon met, / Where they did spend a sad and bloody hour') and then Home's young protagonist ('the blood of Douglass [sic] can protect itself') before remarking that it 'was not always true, nor in good taste for *real* tragedy'– a wry allusion not only to the dramatic necessity of the hero's demise at the end of the play, but also, perhaps, to the editor's own real-life tribulations.[31]

That *Frederick Douglass' Paper* can so effortlessly couple the two citations (without needing to give the source of either) is testimony to the popularity *Douglas* also enjoyed in North America from its first production there in 1758. The great Shakespearean actor Edwin Forrest made his stage debut in the title role at the Walnut Street Theatre, Philadelphia in 1820, and the play featured in the repertoire of the first African Theatre, established by William Alexander Brown in Greenwich Village the following year.[32] A Scottish visitor attending one of Brown's productions, featuring the African American performer James Hewlett, remarked that 'a black Douglas, with a kilt, makes a most preposterous appearance'.[33] Preposterous or not, it did not stop another 'black Douglas', two decades later, eagerly exploiting the resonance of his adopted Scottish name that could signify both his status as an outlaw and hunted fugitive on the one hand, and his dream of leading his oppressed compatriots to victory over their enemies on the other.

Notes

1. N, p. 48 (A, p. 15; FDP 2.1, p. 13). See also BF, pp. 51–2 (A, p. 151; FDP 2.2, pp. 30–1).
2. See Preston, *Young Frederick Douglass*, pp. 34–8.
3. On the provenance of 'Augustus' see Preston, *Young Frederick Douglass*, p. 6.
4. N, pp. 146–7 (A, p. 92; FDP 2.1, p. 77).
5. N, p. 147 (A, p. 92–3; FDP 2.1, p. 77).
6. McFeely, *Frederick Douglass*, p. 78.

7. 1,198 instances as against 388. 'Douglass' declined in popularity but remained more common than 'Douglas' as a surname until the 1880s: searches of US Federal Census data conducted at <http://ancestry.com> (last accessed 6 November 2014). A search of 1840 census data at <https://familysearch.org> (last accessed 27 October 2016) returned 1,133 entries for 'Douglass' against 339 for 'Douglas'.

8. BF, p. 343 (A, p. 354; FDP 2.2, p. 197).

9. Scott, *The Lady of the Lake* [1810], V, xxiv, in Scott, *Poetical Works*, p. 259.

10. Scott, *The Lady of the Lake* [1810], II, xxxvii, in Scott, *Poetical Works*, p. 229.

11. N, p. 49 (A, p. 94; FDP 2.1, p. 78).

12. D2, p. cxxvii.

13. Scott, *Tales of a Grandfather*, vol. 1, pp. 172–5.

14. FD's letter to WLG (Perth, 27 January 1846) was first published in the *Liberator*, 27 February 1846 (FDP 3.1, pp. 81–8), but substantially revised when it was included in the appendix of D2, pp. cxxv–cxxviii (and subsequent English editions of the *Narrative*). He later reproduced the original version in his newspaper *The North Star*, 13 October 1848. FD spells the Scottish name 'Douglass' in all three versions. Webb felt the refutation 'clever but swaggering': RW to Edmund Quincy, Dublin, 2 February 1846 (BAA, p. 250).

15. FD, Dundee, 30 January 1846 (FDP 1.1, p. 148).

16. Scott's principal sources were Barbour, *The Bruce*; Holland, *The Buke of the Howlat*; Hume, *The History of the House of Douglas*; and Hume, *The History of the House of Angus*.

17. Scott, *Tales of a Grandfather*, vol. 1, p. 174.

18. Ibid. vol. 1, p. 142.

19. Ibid. vol. 1, p. 146. See also vol. 1, pp. 197, 239; Scott, *History of Scotland*, vol. 1, p. 105; and Scott, 'Halidon Hill', II, i, in *Poetical Works*, p. 857. The slogan figures repeatedly in the earliest historical sources: e.g. Barbour, *The Bruce*, pp. 207, 385, 601.

20. *The Land We Live In*, vol. 2, p. 75.

21. Jarvie, *Highland Games*, pp. 43–70.

22. Scott, *Minstrelsy of the Scottish Border*, vol. 3, pp. 243–50. Douglas is referred to as 'the Black Douglas' in this ballad.

23. Child, *The English and Scottish Popular Ballads*, vol. 3, pp. 289–315. The ballads are numbered 162 and 163.

24. Scott, *Tales of a Grandfather*, vol. 1, p. 296. The best modern history of the family during this period is Brown, *The Black Douglases*.

25. Scott, *Marmion* [1808], 'Note LXIX', in *Poetical Works*, p. 196.

26. Scott, *Tales of a Grandfather*, vol. 2, p. 12.

27. Scott, *The Lady of the Lake*, 'Note XVI' in *Poetical Works*, pp. 282–3. Scott refers to the historical James Douglas as 'the son of the banished Earl of Angus', although his source, Godscroft, makes it clear he was his nephew. (His father was also banished, but his father was not the earl of Angus).

28. Nathaniel Rogers, for example, wrote of his excitement at being at Melrose Abbey, 'where the Bruces, the Wallaces and the Douglasses had *tramped* in the days of Scottish story': Nathaniel P. Rogers, 'Ride into Edinburgh', *Herald of Freedom*, 30 October 1840 (repr. in Rogers, *Newspaper Writings*, pp. 113–15). HCW's letters from Scotland in 1845 and 1846 are replete with such references.

29. Home, *Douglas*, p. 21. Scott quotes these lines from the Prologue in *Tales of a Grandfather*, vol. 1, p. 240. A different Prologue was written for the London performances; less confident of the audience's familiarity with the fame of Douglas, he is introduced via his English counterpart, Sir Henry Percy ('Hotspur'), who faced James Douglas at Otterburn and Archibald Douglas, the fourth earl, at Homildon Hill (implicitly ranking Home's play as the equal of the history plays of Shakespeare that feature the English hero, a tactic that seemed to work for at least one Scots enthusiast at the first London performance, who famously (but apocryphally?) cried out 'Whaur's yer Wully Shakespeare noo?'). Jane Porter, also mindful of her English readers, pairs Douglas with Percy in the Preface to her *Scottish Chiefs*, p. 22.

30. Home, *Douglas*, pp. 25, 38, 71. FD may also have known of the play from Robert Burns's poem 'Scots Prologue for Mr Sutherland's Benefit Night, Dumfries', which also underlines the wider resonance of his adopted surname: 'One Douglas lives in Home's immortal page, / But Douglases were heroes every age . . .': Currie, *Works* (1841), vol. 1, p. 134. As elaborated below, this is an edition of Currie's *Works* which FD is known to have owned at the time of his 1845–7 tour of Britain and Ireland. It does not appear in the other edition, presented to him in Scotland in January 1846: Currie, *Complete Works* (1844). For the standard modern edition see Burns, *Poems and Songs*, vol. 3, p. 544.

31. Luke Lichen, 'A Lady's Tear', *Frederick Douglass' Paper*, 6 April 1855. The lines from Shakespeare refer to the encounter between Percy and Archibald, the fourth earl of Douglas in 1402. I develop the theme of 'blood' in FD's writings and speeches in Chapter 26.

32. Thompson, *A Documentary History of the African Theatre*, p. 113; McAllister, *Whiting Up*, pp. 65–7.

33. Neilson, *Recollections*, p. 20.

Chapter 11

A Wild Proposition

Frederick Douglass would have been known by some other name had Walter Scott not been so widely read in the United States. The Waverley novels were among the first bestsellers in North America, and almost single-handedly transformed the book publishing and distribution business there.[1] We have seen how his choice of 'Douglass' allowed him to exploit the aspirations and values associated with his mediaeval Scottish namesakes. But that he chose a name immortalised by Scott and not some other author endows that choice with an additional significance which derives from the particular distribution of Scott's popularity. 'While the rest of America read Scott with enthusiasm,' writes one historian, 'the South assimilated his works into its very being.'[2] If it is true that 'the South' – in other words, the members of slaveholding families who bought or borrowed his poetry and novels – especially prized Walter Scott, then what does that say about a fugitive slave's willingness to follow suit?

The contours of Scott's appeal are open to dispute. Another scholar replied, 'There is no hard evidence that Scott was read in Charleston or New Orleans with any significantly greater enthusiasm than in Boston or New York.'[3] But the idea that his popularity took a different form – or that his writing was popular for different reasons – in the South, has exercised several generations of critics. Certainly, the nature of Scott's specific influence in the slave states has long been a subject of some controversy, since Mark Twain – in *Life on the Mississippi* (1883) – railed against 'the debilitating influence of his books'.[4] According to Twain, the author of mediaeval romances single-handedly set the world in love with dreams and phantoms; with decayed and swinish forms of religion; with decayed and degraded systems of government; with the sillinesses and emptinesses, sham grandeurs, sham gauds, and sham chivalries of a brainless and worthless long-vanished society. He did measureless harm; more real and lasting harm, perhaps, than any other individual that ever wrote.[5]

And he famously concluded that

Sir Walter had so large a hand in making Southern character as it existed before the war, that he is in great measure responsible for the war.[6]

Twain's avowedly 'wild proposition'[7] is echoed elsewhere in his work in ways that suggest that the comic exaggeration hid a deeply felt wound.[8] It was solemnly elaborated a few decades later by Hamilton James Eckenrode and William Dodd.[9] They argued that Scott's mediaevalism was a key contributory factor to the antidemocratic backlash to Jeffersonian ideas in the second and third decades of the nineteenth century. When Eckenrode suggested that 'the South of 1860 might be not inaptly nicknamed Sir Walter Scottland',[10] his thought was not a kind one:

The evil of his influence lies in the fact that he did so much to put the South out of harmony with the world by which it was surrounded. The South had stood in the full stream of eighteenth century life; it stood wholly aside from the nineteenth century. The chivalric ideal served to check the South's industrial development and industrial progress.[11]

Planters commonly referred to themselves as 'The Chivalry' and embraced 'Southron', an old Scots word used in *Waverley* and *Rob Roy*. The form 'aristocratical' (which appears in *Old Mortality*) was preferred by Southerners as more elegant than 'aristocratic' and persists to the present day. They also used the term 'Saxons' (found in *The Lady of the Lake* and used by clansmen in the Waverley novels to scorn English enemies) to contemptuously refer to Northerners and identified themselves as 'Normans', adopting the names of the contending forces in *Ivanhoe*.[12] The alignment was perhaps most vividly captured in a tournament at Fauquier White Sulphur Springs,

Virginia in 1845 which featured contesting knights named Brian de Bois-Guilbert and Wilfred of Ivanhoe, after Scott's 1820 novel.[13] The tournament was inspired by a similar event organised by Lord Eglinton on his Ayrshire estate in Scotland in 1839, which attracted some 100,000 spectators – although the heavy rain on that occasion allowed the press to mock the sight of knights in umbrellas.[14]

Events like this were based on a highly selective reading of Scott, whose attitude to Norman chivalry in *Ivanhoe* was rather more critical than Twain and his supporters gave him credit for.[15] Furthermore, only a small part of his output was set in the Middle Ages, and Scott was only one of many influences that would have formed a planter's character.[16] Still, the fact remains that for some in the planter class in the antebellum South, Walter Scott did stand for a kind of mediaeval lordship which they admired and perhaps sought to emulate, if only in play. Perhaps this was why it was *Scott*'s novels that the sisters Angelina and Sarah Grimké chose to destroy in 1828 as one of the rituals marking their transformation from dutiful daughters of a South Carolina slaveholding family to committed abolitionists.[17]

However, the association of those novels – and especially *Ivanhoe* – with all that was backward and barbaric about the antebellum South did not become widely established until *after* the Civil War. The recruitment of motifs from Scott to furnish the undisguised white supremacism of Thomas F. Dixon's novel and play *The Clansman* (1905) and *The Birth of the Nation* (1915), the film that D. W. Griffith made of it, suggests Twain's 'proposition' has more value as a prophecy than as a historical claim.[18]

One reason for thinking so is that American abolitionists rarely condemned Scott's novels. During his speaking tour of the Scottish Borders in Spring 1846, Douglass's fellow campaigner Henry Clarke Wright visited Abbotsford, the baronial mansion that Scott had built on the banks of the Tweed. In the letters reporting his activities that Garrison printed in the *Liberator* Wright was sharply dismissive of what he called 'the Tory novelist, the despiser of the people' whose grandiose 'castle' suggested to him a 'low and contemptible' show of vanity for which posterity will judge him 'a fool or a madman'.[19] Yet these were assessments of the man rather than his writings, which evidently Wright knew well. He does not even take the opportunity, as he might have done, to compare Abbotsford to the slaveholder's 'big house'. Far from identifying Scott as an ally of the plantocracy, the most enduring image Wright leaves the reader is of the 'glorious motto' over the entrance to Dryburgh Abbey, where Scott was buried: 'No American to be allowed to enter here, if he is a slaveholder.'[20]

In general, antislavery campaigners spoke of Scott with reverence and respect. The *Liberator* reported his final illness and death with due solemnity in several pieces in 1832. Garrison and other North American delegates to the World Anti-Slavery Convention in London in 1840 (including Nathaniel P. Rogers and Lucretia Mott) made the trip to Abbotsford, as did William Wells Brown in 1851 and Harriet Beecher Stowe in 1853.[21] Scottish donations to fund-raising antislavery fairs in the United States were made knowing full well that their recipients would swoon on receiving 'relics from places consecrated by the presence of genius and virtue, or their hallowing associations. Abbotsford and Dryburgh, the residence and burial-place of Scott, Melrose and Loch Katrine, immortalized by his pen.'[22] And when Scott's work was quoted within articles in the abolitionist press, it was for the same purpose it usually quoted other literary giants: to borrow a well-turned or memorable phrase in order to lend weight to an argument condemning slavery and racial discrimination, not to subject them to a withering critique.[23] Even the dramatic gestures of the Grimké sisters may have symbolised less a disgust with Scott in particular than a suspicion of all imaginative literature which they, as converted Quakers, would have shared with many others in the Society of Friends.[24]

We should therefore be cautious in following Twain in crudely aligning Scott with truculent pro-slavery attitudes in the South. But there is one undisputed – if apparently trivial – way in which Scott left his mark across the region well before the Civil War, and this acquires special importance when assessing the significance of Douglass's choice of name. For white Southerners also adopted proper names from Scott's poetry and novels, a practice that extended well beyond the *noms de guerres* of knights in shining armour at mock tournaments. Travelling in the West and South-west in 1829, the US politician Edward Everett took a steamer north from New Orleans and, finding several Waverley novels in the boat's library, read them all, 'noticing with interest that Scott's characters supplied the names for steamboats, canal barges, and even stage-coaches in the South – Rob Roy being the particular favourite'.[25] Scott's work inspired the names of plantations, towns and even children, if the numbers of Walter Scotts, Rowenas, Ellen Douglases, Flora MacIvors and Ivanhoes are any indication.[26] If this was not a uniquely Southern phenomenon, the decision of Frederick Douglass to follow suit, just a few months after escaping from Maryland, must be understood as the action of one who was claiming a right to name normally exclusively reserved for the class to which his former masters belonged. A slave who did so would surely be deemed 'guilty of impudence, one of the greatest crimes in the social catalogue of southern society'.[27]

Once he escaped from Baltimore and resettled in Massachusetts, Douglass's new life as an abolitionist campaigner meant that his writings and speeches were largely aimed at Northern audiences, for which purpose he refashioned himself as one of them. But, as he sometimes reminded them, he was 'not a Yankee'.[28] Not only did he acquire a deep affection for the landscape of his youth – evident in the many returns he made to Maryland after Emancipation[29] – he absorbed the values of a culture that nurtured, in the words of one critic, a 'white manhood [. . .] shaped not by competitive capitalist emphasis on individualism, but by an honor-driven need to perform one's worthiness in the eyes of other men [. . .]. His primary gender identifications were not as an idealized Northern bourgeois but as a white Southern master.'[30]

If there is some truth in this assessment, then his choice of name must have been rooted in this primary identification that persisted long into Douglass's maturity. But identifications are rarely straightforward affairs. For an action or a statement by a master may signify differently when repeated by slaves, generating the kind of 'double meaning' Douglass distinguished in their singing of 'Sweet Canaan': 'In the lips of some, it meant the expectation of a speedy summons to a world of spirits; but, in the lips of *our* company, it simply meant, a speedy pilgrimage towards a free state, and deliverance from all the evils and dangers of slavery.'[31] Similarly, the phrase 'Give me liberty or give me death' meant one thing when it came from the mouth of the revolutionary patriot Patrick Henry, but something 'incomparably more sublime [. . .] when *practically* asserted by men accustomed to the lash and chain'.[32]

In naming himself after a character in *The Lady of the Lake*, was Douglass acting out his fantasies of becoming a Southern gentleman? Or can we detect a 'double meaning' in which he surreptitiously mocked the slaveholder's aristocratic pretensions? Perhaps there was a mixture of the two. It would be unwise to rule out either. In any case, neither impulse is likely to have been a fully conscious one.

Notes

1. Todd, 'Establishing Routes for Fiction', pp. 100–28; Rezek, *London and the Making of Provincial Literature*, pp. 40–61.
2. Osterweis, *Romanticism and Nationalism*, p. 41.
3. Hook, *From Goosecreek to Gandercleugh*, p. 105. See also Landrum, 'Sir Walter Scott', p. 258.
4. Twain, *Life on the Mississippi*, p. 416.
5. Ibid. p. 467.
6. Ibid. p. 469.
7. Ibid. p. 469.
8. See Manning, 'Mark Twain', pp. 9–13.
9. Eckenrode, 'Sir Walter Scott and the South'; Dodd, 'The Social Philosophy of the Old South'.
10. Eckenrode, 'Sir Walter Scott and the South', p. 601.
11. Ibid., p. 602.
12. Osterweis, *Romanticism and Nationalism*, pp. 46–8. See also Watson, *Normans and Saxons*.
13. Osterweis, *Romanticism and Nationalism*, pp. 3–5, drawing on an account in the *Richmond Enquirer*, 2 September 1845.
14. For accounts of the Ayrshire tournament see Anstruther, *The Knight and the Umbrella*; and Girouard, *The Return to Camelot*, pp. 88–110.
15. Watson, *Normans and Saxons*, p. 61; Manning, 'Mark Twain', esp. pp. 19–21; O'Brien, *Rethinking the South*, pp. 52–4.
16. Orians, 'Walter Scott'; Landrum, 'Sir Walter Scott'.
17. Lumpkin, *The Emancipation of Angelina Grimké*, p. 31.
18. See Rigney, *The Afterlives of Walter Scott*, pp. 119–26.
19. HCW to WLG, Melrose, 28 March 1846 (*Liberator*, 1 May 1846); HCW to WLG, Melrose, 10 April 1846 (*Liberator*, 8 May 1846).
20. HCW to WLG, Melrose, 28 March 1846 (*Liberator*, 1 May 1846). See also 'A Prohibition to Slaveholders', *Illustrated London News*, 18 January 1845, p. 43; and G. A. S., *Notes of Travel at Home*, p. 30.
21. Rogers gives a vivid account of exploring Melrose Abbey with Garrison in Nathaniel P. Rogers, 'Ride into Edinburgh' (in *Newspaper Writings*, pp. 113–15). See also Mott, *Three Months in Great Britain*, p. 73; Mott, *Slavery and 'The Woman Question'*, pp. 72–3; Brown, *Three Years in Europe*, pp. 186–93; Stowe, *Sunny Memories*, vol. 1, pp. 128–68.
22. 'Philadelphia Fair', *Liberator*, 25 December 1840.
23. For example, in January 1848 the *Liberator* printed a letter from William Cooper Nell, publisher of the *North Star*, revealing how he and Douglass were initially refused entry to an event marking the anniversary of the birth of Benjamin Franklin on the grounds that it was 'a violation of the rules of society for colored people to associate with whites'.

Eventually, after forcing a vote, they were admitted, the vice-president doing his best to dispel any ill-feeling, and Douglass was invited to speak. For Nell, the enthusiastic reception that followed his speech was evidence of the great progress made by Garrison's movement over the previous two decades, but the episode also illustrated the formidable forces they were up against, which he conveys by means of two literary references. Firstly, Tacitus' dictum about 'hating those whom we have injured', and secondly, the passage in *Waverley* in which Fergus MacIvor remarks: 'You see the compliment they pay to our Highland strength and courage. Here we have lain until our limbs are cramped into palsey, and now they send six soldiers with loaded muskets to prevent our taking the castle by storm.' Unpacking his own 'analogy', Nell explains that he is referring to 'the omnipotent, omnipresent influence of American pro-slavery in crushing every noble and praiseworthy aspiration of the persecuted colored man'. William C. Nell to WLG, Rochester, 23 January 1848 (*Liberator*, 11 February 1848).

24. Although even strict parents, such as those of Harriet Beecher Stowe, often made an exception of Scott, and praised his moral seriousness: Todd, 'The Transatlantic Context', pp. 140–1.

25. Frothingham, *Edward Everett*, p. 118. Rigney confirms the existence of at least one Mississippi steamboat called (like the wreck in *The Adventures of Huckleberry Finn*) *Walter Scott*: Rigney, *Afterlives*, p. 117.

26. Landrum, 'Sir Walter Scott', p. 262; Rigney, *Afterlives*, p. 120.

27. BF, p. 260 (A, p. 295; FDP 2.2, p. 148).

28. FD, Boston, 8 June 1849 (LWFD1, p. 388).

29. See Preston, *Young Frederick Douglass*, pp. 159–97.

30. Jones, 'Engendered in the South', pp. 101–5.

31. BF, p. 278–9 (A, p. 308; FDP 1.2, pp. 158–9).

32. BF, p. 284 (A, p. 312; FDP 1.2, p. 162).

Chapter 12

New Relations and Duties

But something is missing here, because these blunt alternatives – was Douglass essentially a Northerner or a Southerner? – do not allow that slave society itself was changing during the antebellum period. And it is by attending to these changes that we can perhaps begin to offer a more plausible, modest alternative to Twain's 'wild proposition'. Scott may have provided a tempting array of set pieces that helped wealthy Southerners to cling onto the antiquated rituals of a distant past, but he also embedded them in narratives that allowed those readers to imagine ways of adapting to the future – and to embrace changes that even Douglass, to some extent, recognised as improvements.

These narratives are often driven by the need to resolve conflicts represented by pairs of opposing characters who are (to varying degrees) either coarse, impetuous, vengeful and superstitious, on the one hand, or refined, disciplined, conciliatory and rational on the other. Universal human types they may be, but as Scott explains at the beginning of *Waverley*, our passions are necessarily mediated by 'the state of manners and laws' that prevail in a given society. The same impulse that once might have been personified by 'the baron who wrapped the castle of his competitor in flames, and knocked him on the head as he endeavoured to escape from the conflagration' is in more recent times likely to be associated with 'the proud peer who can now only ruin his neighbour according to law, by protracted suits'.[1]

The confrontations between Scott's protagonists often take place against a background of economic and political upheavals in which one ethical culture is giving way to another, described in terms that echo those used by philosophers of the Scottish Enlightenment like Adam Ferguson who mapped the contrasting moral contours of 'rude' and 'polished' nations.[2] In other words, Scott – and this is what makes him one of the first truly *historical* novelists – anchors his characters in emergent or declining social forces, in a way that, say, Porter's *Scottish Chiefs*, in which we find similar moral pairings, does not. And while Scott was clear about the benefits of progress, he was not unsympathetic to the values and traditions that it was sweeping aside. Furthermore, there is nothing inevitable about these changes, and the tensions are sometimes tellingly embodied in a single individual who hovers – like *Waverley*'s aptly named eponymous protagonist – between the old and the new, the ancient and the modern. In his narratives a backward-looking romantic impulse struggles with a more pragmatic, realistic one, and the outcomes are neither predictable nor straightforward.[3]

The historical transformations charted by the earlier Waverley novels (set in Scotland during the long eighteenth century) were experienced, unevenly, across the rest of Europe and in the Americas too, and to a greater or lesser extent these narratives would have dramatised social conflicts lived by many of their first readers. In 1820 Scott's fiction turned to more distant times and places for inspiration, but continued to wrestle with the same ethical concerns, if presenting them more anachronistically. The relationship between the barbaric and enlightened modes of feudal lordship represented by Ivanhoe and Bois-Guilbert attempts to make sense of the Age of Revolution as much as the contrasting values of the Highland rebel Rob Roy MacGregor and the Glasgow merchant Bailie Nicol Jarvie. This is somewhat obscured by the way Scott, across all his work, revives the antiquated language of mediaeval chivalry: even the changes in 'manners' he summarises in that passage from *Waverley* is expressed by way of a heraldic metaphor. But one place where that language was still spoken was the American South, and this may explain why Scott's sophisticated understanding of different codes of honour, and how they changed over time, had particular appeal there.[4]

Since the 1980s, a growing number of studies have examined the distinctive ethical culture of the antebellum South. If the Puritan ideal of dignity became dominant in the North, it was the aristocratic notion of honour that held sway in the South, where the values of physical courage, display, and family obligations and allegiances counted for more than of those of hard work, private introspection and individual rights. As Bertram Wyatt-Brown put it: 'Honor, not conscience, shame, not guilt, were the psychological and social underpinnings of Southern culture.'[5] However, as he goes on to show, from the beginning of the nineteenth century, the evangelical revival ushered in a religious and feminine sensibility that undermined the violent warrior ethos, and 'primal honor' began to give way to a more sociable and restrained form he calls 'gentility'.[6]

How far these changes reflect changes in social relations and material practices rather than simply modulations of the self-image of the dominant elite, it is hard to gauge. But the rhetoric certainly made it into plantation management manuals, which urged slave-owners to develop more humane ways of controlling and motivating their workforce and to cultivate the virtues of patience, self-restraint, consistency. The ideal master was a firm but gentle patriarch who studied the habits, character and disposition of each slave with an eye to their physical and spiritual well-being, rather than a tyrannical brute whose constant and only resort was the lash. The benefits of a mild temper – and a low tone of voice – were repeatedly emphasised.[7] One planter from Mississippi wrote in 1856:

> [T]reat your negro *well* and he will respond to it with fidelity and honesty: kind words, humane consideration, justness in discipline, unhesitating authority when required, forbearance towards venal offenses, arousing pride of character, recognizing the *personality* of each one, not only in the week's rations but in the week's work.[8]

'Do not kill the goose to obtain the golden egg,' advised a committee in Alabama, suggesting that those practising such enlightened methods of management would reap economic as well as moral rewards.[9]

Scholars are beginning to understand the reading habits of Southerners before the Civil War.[10] It is now possible to get a sense of how popular Walter Scott was through the analysis of sales of his books and the records of public libraries: the evidence is that readers often rapidly worked their way through entire sets of Waverley novels, some novels more than once.[11] We have noted that names, phrases and occasionally activities made their way from his printed pages to leave their mark on the Southern landscape and social calendar, suggesting that certain images bewitched the largely slaveholding class that enjoyed Scott's fiction. How they understood and emotionally engaged with them is much harder to ascertain.

But perhaps we also need to consider that the ethical transformations he narrated struck them forcefully too. In his study of the rise of what he calls 'the domestication of slavery' in South Carolina and Georgia, Jeffrey Robert Young emphasises the role of recreational reading: 'Tantalized by the possibilities lurking within the realm of fiction, the slaveholders began to frame their own experiences with language and style that was taken straight off the pages of their favourite books.'[12] Drawing on a South Carolina planter family's privately recorded responses to Porter's *Scottish Chiefs*, he suggests that it appealed to them because it 'presented ideal models for mastery in a domestic setting' and suggested that 'universal love for subordinate members of society would be rewarded by the positive impact of these individuals who, encouraged by their leader's mercy and confidence, conducted themselves with propriety and courage.'[13]

Likewise, we might conclude that Scott's fictions provided an interpretive framework that allowed them – in identifying with Ivanhoe rather than Bois-Guilbert – to be more open to the changes afoot in the management of slaves, while reassuring them (in a way Porter's novel, because it isn't a historical novel, could not) that the changes were organic, gradual and not destructive of their traditional way of life. Furthermore, since the interest in Scott extended beyond his *oeuvre* to the man himself, a demand that led to numerous accounts of his domestic life in the periodical press, the plantocracy may well have felt more kinship with the improving laird of Abbotsford than readers elsewhere.[14] Without more conclusive evidence, it seems plausible at least to suggest that the distinctive appeal of Scott in the South was that he provided – both in the stories he told, and in his own example as the owner of a landed estate – imaginative resources well suited to those readers adapting to a culture in which primal honour was mutating into gentility.

How far the advice in the plantation manuals was heeded is not easy to assess. The debate over whether conditions were 'improving' for slaves in the period before the Civil War will go on and on. The romanticised image of the harmonious plantation promulgated in novels such as John Pendleton Kennedy's *Swallow Barn* (1832), itself influenced by Scott, should not be dismissed as mere propaganda, cynically contrived to answer abolitionist critics and reassure slaveholders. As we saw in Chapter 6, historians are now more likely to take seriously the kind of changes documented by travel accounts of the South like that of the Free Church minister George Lewis. Studies of antebellum medicine and missions to the slaves suggest a genuine interest in, if not certain improvements to, their material and spiritual welfare. Visiting doctors and clergymen, who feature in many slave narratives, were often agents of moderating influence; and many slaves acquired valuable leadership and communication skills in being allowed positions of responsibility for healthcare and Christian worship.[15]

Nevertheless, slaves were not invited to contribute to the debates over plantation management and they had very little influence over the conduct of masters and overseers. It is no wonder, therefore, that Douglass – in common with other abolitionists – did not place a great deal of significance in the changes recommended by the plantation manuals, whether they were followed or not. His campaign speeches are characterised by sweeping denunciations of the South as a whole: his targets are *all* slaveholders, *all* Southern churchmen and so on. The differences between them are of very little account. For him, his one reference to 'southern chivalry' is represented not by an act of kind generosity but, sarcastically, by Hugh Auld's impatience with a 'crippled servant'.[16]

And yet when Douglass comes to recount his experiences in any detail, it becomes clear that masters were not all the same, and that the differences between plantations were not insignificant. Douglass alludes to the differences between the border states and those further south, or between rural and urban slavery, or between the zones of tobacco, rice and cotton cultivation. But he also – as do other authors of slave autobiographies – highlights the differences between the characters and management styles of the individuals who owned them, typically by presenting, in a manner reminiscent of Scott, an antithesis between a severe despotic master and a kinder and more humane one.

Douglass's first autobiography, the 1845 *Narrative*, was perhaps too short and polemical to make no more than passing reference to these differences (although even here they mark turning points that give his boyhood experiences twists and turns that engage the reader's narrative curiosity). But by the time he came to write his second, the much longer and more novelistic *My Bondage and My Freedom* (1855), the crude distinction between a slave South and a free North had come to be complicated by a recognition of the many and varied forms that discrimination and oppression could take, in Maryland as much as in Massachusetts.

Just as advice to slaveholders emphasised the need to get to know the personality of each slave in order to be able to manage them effectively, so each slave had to be able to 'read' every gesture of their master – as a matter of survival. On numerous occasions in *My Bondage and My Freedom*, Douglass shows how important it is to know the individual character of slaveholders. In the case of Captain Anthony, for instance, Douglass distinguishes between his apparently gentle, affectionate nature, and what is revealed in his private 'mutterings, attitudes and gestures'. Such 'vocal crevices' betray 'the very secrets of his heart' to the slaves whose presence means no more to him than the presence of 'ducks and geese'.[17] And Douglass stresses the necessity of slaves acquainting themselves with the finer points of a master's personality if they are to be able to predict his behaviour – while at the same time ensuring that they appear not to know these things.[18]

As we learned in Chapter 2, in 1833 Douglass was hired out to Edward Covey, a man who whipped him severely for the slightest offence, until one day in August, Douglass fought back, in a scene which he later identified as a pivotal one in his life as a slave. When his service ended on Christmas Day, Douglass had gained a reputation for being intransigent and he had little expectation that his next master would make his life any easier. However, in a chapter entitled 'New Relations and Duties', he tells us:

> I was not long in finding Mr. Freeland to be a very different man from Mr. Covey. Though not rich, Mr. Freeland was what may be called a well-bred southern gentleman, as different from Covey, as a well-trained and hardened negro breaker is from the best specimen of the first families of the south. Though Freeland was a slaveholder, and shared many of the vices of his class, he seemed alive to the sentiment of honor. He had some sense of justice, and some feelings of humanity. He was fretful, impulsive and passionate, but I must do him the justice to say, he was free from the mean and selfish characteristics which distinguished the creature from which I had now, happily, escaped. He was open, frank, imperative, and practiced no concealments, disdaining to play the spy. In all this, he was the opposite of the crafty Covey.[19]

Douglass suggests that this difference may have something to do with the fact that Freeland, unlike Covey, made no profession of religion, for 'religious slaveholders are the worst'.[20] And he goes on to describe two neighbouring slaveholders (Rev. Weeden and Rev. Hopkins) in order to illustrate his point, before returning to his characterisation of Freeland:

> At Mr Freeland's, my condition was every way improved. [. . .] It is quite usual to make one slave the object of especial abuse, and to beat him often, with a view to its effect upon others, rather than with any expectations that the slave whipped will be improved by it, but the man with whom I now was, could descend to no such meanness and wickedness. Every man here was held individually responsible for his own conduct.[21]

Religion cannot fully account for this. Class is a factor, as Douglass's casting Freeland as a 'well-bred [. . .] gentleman' as against a 'well-trained [. . .] negro breaker' might suggest. But above all, what makes Freeland 'alive to the sentiment of honor' – and we may assume that Douglass means the kinder, gentler form of honour rather than the older, more primal kind it was beginning to displace – is that broader shift in the ethical culture of the South which encouraged new kinds of relationships between masters and slaves, refashioning selves on both sides. Douglass uses the word 'improvement' and its cognates five times in two pages here, referring both to his own 'condition', a slave's conduct, the rules of the farm, and the 'implements of husbandry'.[22]

The moral contrasts of the 'New Relations and Duties' chapter would be familiar to readers of Scott's novels. The way Freeland is set against Weeden and Hopkins recalls the relation between the moderate Morton and the fanatics Burley and Claverhouse in *Old Mortality*. It even begins, like that novel, with a discussion of the way holidays can serve as a form of social control.[23] And Douglass allows himself a moment to share the enjoyment he takes as a writer in naming and exposing these unsuspecting villains on the printed page. Referring to Hopkins in particular,

> He did not think that a 'chiel' was near, 'taking notes,' and will, doubtless, feel quite angry at having his character touched off in the ragged style of a slave's pen.[24]

Douglass clearly expected his readers to recognise this reference to Burns's poem, 'On the Late Captain Grose's Peregrinations Thro' Scotland', not least because Scott used it as the epigraph to each of the four volumes of *Tales of My Landlord*, a series in which *Old Mortality* was first published:

Hear, Land o' Cakes, and brither Scots,
Frae Maidenkirk to Johny Groats! –
If there's a hole in a' your coats,
      I rede you tent it:
A chield's amang you, taking notes,
      And, faith, he'll prent it.[25]

For Scott, the epigraph is presumably meant to allude to his own practice, whereby an obscure historical narrative, transmitted orally to the narrator by an unassuming source, is brought to the literary marketplace. In this way, some of the great episodes of Scottish history and the exploits of its most eminent families were rendered not according to an obsequious official chronicler but according to a popular oral tradition that was likely to expose flaws as well as the noble deeds of its protagonists.[26]

Douglass appropriated the line, as did some of his contemporaries, to draw attention to the truths that could only be revealed as a result of undercover reportage. A reviewer who quoted it in *Blackwood's Edinburgh Magazine* in 1842 suggested that the value of Charles Dickens's *American Notes* was compromised by the author's notoriety. Many of those he met would have been 'put on their guard, and by a thousand devices of courtesy, hospitality, and flattery, disabl[ed] their admired visitor from taking, or communicating to his countrymen, just and true observations on the men and manners of America'. If only he had gone 'under a strict *incognito*' – passed himself off as an inoffensive bystander jotting down his 'notes' on the sly – he would have caught them 'unconscious' and given his readers a more honest picture.[27]

This is precisely what Douglass describes himself doing in *My Bondage and My Freedom*. But it wasn't the first time. Recall the similar pleasure that flavours the speech where he invites his audience in Dundee to imagine him as a young boy spying on George Lewis and Thomas Auld through the keyhole as Lewis persuades his master to provide a contribution to the Free Church, neither of them suspecting that a slave's version of his fund-raising visit would ever find its way into print. And – to return to Douglass's invocation of 'the ancient "Black Douglass"' that he pasted into the second Dublin edition of his *Narrative* – here again is a picture of slave, once so lowly he 'hardly dared to look up' at a white man such as Mr Thompson of Wilmington, yet holding the memory close until one day, 'amid the free hills of Old Scotland', 'wearing the brave name' he shared with several of Scott's protagonists, he feels he could now summon the courage to look him 'full in the face' and publicly expose his moral and intellectual failings in the pages of his own international bestseller.

Writing from Edinburgh in July 1846, Douglass marvelled at the recently completed Scott Monument on Princes Street two weeks before its official opening. 'Just one conglomeration of architectural beauties,' he remarked.[28] But if Douglass brings something of the Waverley novels to his second autobiography, and volumes of Scott's works are found in his library at the great house, Cedar Hill, he later built in the leafy outskirts of Washington, DC, his declared interest in Scott does not appear to go much further than his choice of name.

He does not refer to Scott directly in the speeches he made in Scotland or in the letters he wrote there; nor does he quote him. Reporting in 1846 on her trip to Europe for the *New York Tribune*, Margaret Fuller implies that her 'pilgrimage to Abbotsford' was practically obligatory and claims that during the previous year, 'five hundred Americans inscribed their names in its porter's book'.[29] As we have seen, even the cynical Henry Clarke Wright deigned to visit Scott's residence and burial place on his speaking tour of the Borders; but Douglass, busy lecturing in Glasgow and Paisley, did not join him.[30]

Another Scottish author, however, does feature more prominently in his letters and speeches of 1846. It is to him we now turn.

Notes

1. Scott, *Waverley*, p. 36 (chapter 1). This historical distinction reappears in the novel as aspects of a single character, Bradwardine ('The pedantry of the lawyer superinduced upon the military pride of the soldier'), p. 87 (chapter 10).

2. Ferguson, *An Essay on the History of Civil Society*, esp. pp. 188–203 (Part IV, Sections 3 and 4).

3. See Brown, *Walter Scott and the Historical Imagination*; Kerr, *Fiction Against History*; Lincoln, *Walter Scott and Modernity*.

4. This point is made forcefully in Gordon, 'Scott, Racine, and the Future of Honor', pp. 260–4.

5. Wyatt-Brown, *Southern Honor*, p. 22.

6. Ibid. pp. 59, 88–114. Other studies of ethical culture in the antebellum South include Ayers, *Vengeance and Justice*; Bruce, *Violence and Culture*; Fox-Genovese, *Within the Plantation Household*; Greenberg, *Honor and Slavery*; Stowe, *Intimacy and Power*; Wyatt-Brown, *The Shaping of Southern Culture*.

7. For a useful selection of extracts from slave management manuals see Breeden, *Advice Among the Masters*.

8. B., 'Treatment of Slaves – Mr. Guerry', *Southern Cultivator* 18 (August 1860), p. 258, quoted in Breeden, *Advice Among the Masters*, p. 328.

9. John A. Calhoun et al., 'Management of Slaves', *Southern Cultivator* 4 (August 1846), p. 114, quoted in Breeden, *Advice Among the Masters*, p. 10.

10. Todd, 'The Transatlantic Context'. See also Landrum, 'Notes on the Reading of the Old South'.

11. Todd, 'Antebellum Libraries'.

12. Young, *Domesticating Slavery*, p. 138.

13. Ibid. p. 135.

14. For the way the interest in Scott extended to the man himself, his character and his domestic life, as demonstrated by the biographical sketches found in periodical literature in the United States, see Todd, 'The Transatlantic Context', pp. 126–31.

15. On medicine see e.g. Fett, *Working Cures*; Numbers and Savitt, *Science and Medicine in the Old South*; Savitt, *Medicine and Slavery*; Stowe, *Doctoring the South*; Wiener, *Sex, Sickness and Slavery*. On religion see e.g. Cornelius, *Slave Missions*; Loveland, *Southern Evangelicals and the Social Order*; Mathews, *Religion in the Old South*; Raboteau, *Slave Religion*; Touchstone, 'Planters and Slave Religion'.

16. BF, p. 182 (A, p. 242; FDP 2.2, p. 104).

17. BF, p. 81 (A, p. 172; FDP 2.2, p. 48).

18. BF, pp. 81–2 (A, pp. 172–3; FDP 2.2, p. 48). See also BF, pp. 174, 187 (A, pp. 236, 245–6; FDP 2.2, p. 99, 140). FD also talks of the slaveholders 'reading' the slaves: 'They watch, therefore, with skilled and practiced eyes, and have learned to read, with great accuracy, the state of mind and heart of the slave, through his sable face': BF, p. 277 (A, p. 307; FDP 2.2, p. 158).

19. BF, p. 257 (A, p. 293; FDP 2.2, p. 146).

20. BF, p. 258 (A, p. 293; FDP 2.2, p. 147).
21. BF, p. 262 (A, p. 296; FDP 2.2, p. 149).
22. BF, pp. 262–3 (A, pp. 296–7; FDP 2.2, pp. 149–50).
23. Scott, *Old Mortality*, pp. 70–2.
24. BF, p. 259 (A, p. 294; FDP 2.2, p. 147).
25. Currie, *Works* (1841), 1.134–5; Burns *Poems and Songs*, vol. 2, pp. 543–5. Not in Currie, *Complete Works* (1844). *Rede*: advise; *tent*: take care of; *chiel(d)*: child; *prent*: print.
26. See Takanashi, 'Circulation, Monuments'.
27. Q.Q.Q., 'Dickens's American Notes', p. 783.
28. FD to William A. White, Edinburgh, 30 July 1846 (FDP 3.1, p. 149).
29. Fuller, *At Home and Abroad*, p. 137.
30. The editors of FDP include appearances in Hawick, Galashiels, Coldstream and Kelso ('c. 1–14 April') in a list of FD's speaking engagements in 1846 (FDP 1.1, p. xcviii) which gives rise to the tantalising possibility that FD also visited Abbotsford. But while speeches by HCW in Galashiels, Selkirk and Melrose are documented in local newspapers of that month (*Border Watch and Galashiels Advertiser; Kelso Chronicle*), I have found no evidence that he was accompanied by Douglass. HCW's letters reporting his activities in the Borders (from Hawick, Kelso, Jedburgh, Coldstream, Galashiels and Berwick) printed in the *Liberator* (1 May 1846) make no reference to FD as a companion.

Chapter 13

A Visit to Ayr

Writing to Garrison in London, Douglass remarks of the freedom he enjoys in public places: 'There is no distinction on account of color. The white man gains nothing by being white, and the black man losing nothing by being black. "A man's a man for a' that."'[1]

Douglass was never afraid to flaunt his knowledge of Robert Burns. The first book he purchased after escaping from slavery was an edition of his works, which he later gave to his eldest son, Lewis.[2] In Dundee – to laughter and cheers – he says of the defenders of the Free Church 'that, to use the language of one of your own poets, "the De'il has business on his hands."'[3] But it is in the county of Burns's birth that Douglass dwells at length on the man and his work.

In March 1846 he visited Ayr, where he was shown the monument erected in Burns's memory two decades earlier, and called on Isabella Begg, the poet's youngest sister, then in her seventies, who lived in a cottage close by with her two daughters. 'I have felt more interest in visiting this place than any other in Scotland,' he wrote to an American friend, 'for, as you are aware [. . .] I am an enthusiastic admirer of Robt. Burns.' The second of two lectures he gave in the town's Relief Church on Cathcart Street was a long one, recounting the story of his life as a slave, his learning to read and write, his escape, his work in New Bedford, and then his new career as an abolitionist orator and author, and subsequent voyage to Britain. Wrapping up its coverage, the local newspaper reported: 'At some future time, he said, he might be again in Ayr; and he was proud of having been in the land of him who had spoken out so nobly against the oppressions and the wrongs of slavery – he alluded, of course, to Robert Burns.'[4]

Figure 13.1 Isabella Burns Begg.

Douglass's enthusiastic admiration may surprise some readers today. After all, it was widely known that in the summer of 1786, Burns had obtained a position on a sugar plantation near Port Antonio in Jamaica, owned by an Ayrshire doctor Patrick Douglas and managed by his brother Charles. He expected to sail in August or September, but in the end, the success of his first book of poems led him to change his plans and he headed instead for what he called the 'new world' of literary Edinburgh.[5]

Those closing words at the Cathcart Street church were neither the beginning nor the end of Douglass's engagement with Burns. But Douglass's responses were often fragmentary and evasive. Before we can examine them in more detail, we need to consider Burns's complicated attitudes to slavery, and the biographical and critical sources which would have shaped Douglass's assessment of the man and his work.

Some have doubted that Burns really intended to leave Scotland. After all, he postponed his departure several times.[6] But even so, his willingness to imagine himself, as he did his poem 'On a Scotch Bard, Gone to the West Indies', flourishing 'like a lily' as an agent of colonial slavery must be challenging for those who see him as a champion of liberty.[7] The position he was offered was that of 'assistant overseer; or, as I believe it is called, a book-keeper', recalled Burns's brother Gilbert.[8] According to a Baptist missionary who later published a survey of the colony, the job involved 'superintend[ing] the labours of the field, and the manufacture of its produce', wryly observing that 'the appellation is most inappropriate – a Jamaica book-keeper having no books to keep'.[9]

In a letter to Helen Maria Williams commenting on her 'A Poem on the Bill Lately Passed for Regulating the Slave-Trade' (1788), Burns took her to task for a somewhat glib reference to a 'generous' sailor. He reminded her that he 'is certainly not only an unconcerned witness but in some degree an efficient agent in the business', a phrase that he might have also intended to refer to himself, had he crossed the Atlantic.[10] It is possible that the experience might have transformed him into an abolitionist, as it did, eventually, for Zachary Macaulay, who had emigrated to Jamaica two years earlier.[11] But this may be wishful thinking, more suited to speculative fiction such as Andrew Lindsay's intriguing 2006 novel *Illustrious Exile*, which purports to reproduce a recently discovered diary kept by Burns in the Caribbean.[12]

Organised abolitionism would not emerge until the year following the publication of the Kilmarnock Edition of Burns's poems, with the formation in London of the Society for Effecting the Abolition of the Slave Trade in May 1787. It was perhaps not until its agent William Dickson spread the message on a tour of Scotland in 1792 that it had a popular impact north of the border.[13] Nevertheless, anti-slavery sentiment – in philosophy and poetry – was not uncommon in Scotland in the 1770s and 80s.[14] But, curiously, this left little trace in Burns's own work: one would be hard pushed to find a direct and unqualified abolitionist statement in any of his writings. While his exact contemporary John Marjoribanks, from Kelso, wrote *Slavery: An Essay in Verse*, a passionate twenty-page denunciation of the plantation system, while serving as an infantry officer in Jamaica in 1786, Burns could only manage the twelve sentimental lines of 'The Slave's Lament', beginning:

It was in sweet Senegal that my foes did me enthral
For the lands of Virginia–ginia O;
Torn from that lovely shore and must never see it more;
And alas I am weary weary O!

And even this song may not have been his: it was not included in collections of Burns's work until the 1850s, and doubts of his authorship remain.[15]

It is possible that the rousing democratic assertions of a poem like 'Honest Poverty' – with its famous refrain, 'A man's a man for a' that' – is open to an abolitionist interpretation, but for the most part the 'man' whose rights are passionately asserted is not only gendered but of a certain colour too.[16] When the word 'slave' appears in Burns's writings, it is deployed, more often than not, in accordance with a conventional metaphorical usage to suggest an individual failing, the weakness of one who – like the 'coward slave' who appears in the first verse of this well-known anthem – has too easily succumbed to the will of another, lacking the independent mind or physical courage to join the ranks of those prepared to fight for their freedom.[17]

White abolitionist rhetoric must take some of the blame for this infantilisation of the slave. Although it recognised that the slave was an unwilling victim of coercion, for which the slave was certainly not responsible, it did not imagine the slave as someone who could and did take an active role in securing his or her freedom. That role was reserved to the philanthropists who acted and spoke on their behalf. The abject, chained figure on Wedgwood's famous abolitionist medallion – distributed by Dickson in 1792 – pleads: 'Am I not a man and a brother?'[18] Instead of the bold ploughman who defiantly asserts his humanity, the slave meekly requests recognition.[19]

In his concluding flourish at the Cathcart Street church in March 1846, Douglass praised Burns for speaking out 'against the oppressions and the wrongs of slavery'. Coming from the mouth of one who not only documented those oppressions and wrongs, but who escaped, educated himself and travelled across the Atlantic to do so, this shrewdly realigns Burns as a critic of 'slavery' in a sense not actually congruent with the way he uses it in most of his writings. Still, Douglass makes no other explicit statement about Burns's relationship to Atlantic slavery – neither in Ayr nor elsewhere. Nor, for that matter, does he refer to the historic connections between Scotland and the colonial trade, which were deep and extensive, nor to the continuing dependence of the country's economy on the importation of cotton grown by slaves in the United States.[20]

This was not the result of ignorance. The treasured book purchased by Douglass in 1838 was an edition of James Currie's *The Works of Robert Burns*, and he was presented with another edition when he was in Scotland, possibly by George Gilfillan when he welcomed him to Dundee in January 1846 and later proclaimed Douglass to be 'the most powerful of natural orators, the self-taught, the Burns of the African race'.[21] First published in 1800, the *Works* includes Currie's long biographical essay on Burns, which, even half a century later, continued to serve as the one of the most influential interpretations of the poet and his work, especially in North America.[22]

No one reading Currie could have been left in any doubt of Burns's plans to work in the Caribbean. It is announced in the very first sentence of his biography:

> Robert Burns was, as is well known, the son of a farmer in Ayrshire, and afterwards himself a farmer there; but, having been unsuccessful, he was about to emigrate to Jamaica.[23]

And then, after a short preamble, Currie transcribes Burns's long autobiographical letter to Dr John Moore of August 1787, in which he imagines himself in the West Indies as 'a poor Negro-driver' ignorant of the critical and commercial success of his first book of poems.[24] How commonplace such a career choice was for Burns' contemporaries is evident from the passing references Currie makes to ways in which late eighteenth-century Scots were involved in the empire. His most telling example, perhaps, is an observation he quotes from Gilbert Burns regarding the colonial destinies of their childhood friends, most of whose careers took them to the East or West Indies.[25]

As an abolitionist, Currie might have been expected to pass comment on such matters. A leading surgeon in Liverpool, Britain's largest port in the triangular trade, he had become well acquainted with some of the consequences of that trade, including the horrific conditions of slave ships, which he sought to alleviate. He also furnished William Wilberforce with facts and figures to support his parliamentary campaign to outlaw the trade. Currie and his close friend William Roscoe, whose poem on the death of Burns he incorporated in his *Works*, risked the opprobrium of the Liverpool merchants. But they also earned the gratitude of Thomas Clarkson, who honoured both of them as pioneers in his famous genealogy of British abolitionism, in which its leading figures are represented as tributaries on a map of a fictional river system.[26]

But Currie neither condemned nor excused Burns's flirtation with colonial slavery. He records it without comment, undeserving of the kind of moral judgements he applies to other decisions Burns made in his life. Perhaps it was too close to home. As a young man Currie was employed as an apprentice by William Cunninghame & Company on their tobacco plantations in Virginia, before he returned home to study medicine at Edinburgh University. After graduating he tried hard to secure a position as a surgeon in Jamaica, and only when the job was given to another did he accept an alternative post in Liverpool.[27] And in that city, he would find it hard to keep a distance from every aspect of its maritime commerce. In 1789, for example, he accepted a position at Liverpool Infirmary as examiner of candidates seeking to be appointed surgeons on slave ships, which would have given him a reason for muting his abolitionist sympathies.[28]

Uncomfortably aware, perhaps, of the ways in which the path of his life echoed Burns's own, Currie resorted to euphemism in a letter to his friend Admiral Graham Moore, whose naval career had also taken him to the Caribbean. 'If I were to attempt to tell you the history of my own transactions in this business,' he wrote, 'I should consume more time than I can spare.' The similar phrasing in Burns's description, in his letter to Helen Maria Williams, of the sailor engaged in the slave trade as 'an efficient agent in the business', suggests they shared an unwillingness to articulate their complex feelings about slavery, critical of, but also to some degree complicit in, its operations.[29]

So there would be no question of Currie presenting Burns as a critic of slavery either. When leafing through the hundreds of songs Burns supplied to James Johnson for *The Scots Musical Museum*, issued in six volumes starting in 1787, Currie may have paused when he came upon 'The Slave's Lament', not least because he himself had composed, with Roscoe, a song he originally entitled 'The Negroe's Complaint' and published pseudonymously as 'The African' in 1788.[30] But he chose not to include it among the several dozen songs by Burns in his *Works*. It is possible he had doubts regarding its authorship. More decisively, it may have lacked what Currie believed were the distinctive features of Burns's songs, which, for him, typically depicted scenes of rural courtship in recognisably Scottish settings.

But in any case, Currie wanted to memorialise a Burns whose poetic genius was best observed when he stayed clear of politics and religion.[31] He plays down his radical ideas because they conflict with Currie's desire to avoid upsetting the family by invoking social explanations for his untimely death in reduced circumstances, preferring to blame Burns's own moral failings, which he exaggerated. His *Works* thus becomes a medium, as one critic put it, 'for translating a debate about politics into a debate about lifestyle'.[32]

That Douglass, in his speech in Ayr, chose not to interrogate Burns's attitudes towards colonial slavery may be an indication of how compellingly Currie framed his interpretation of his life and work. But Douglass had his own reasons for being circumspect. His main objective in his speeches was to appeal to his listeners' latent abolitionism and to rouse them to embrace it more vigorously. It would not have served him well to cast aspersions on a much-loved poet in a country where 'Burnomania' was already well established at the time of his visit. After all, he was speaking in his hometown, which two summers earlier had drawn crowds of 50,000 or more to a Burns Festival, organised by the same Lord Eglinton who had hosted that rain-drenched Scott-inspired jousting tournament in 1839.

Devised to mark the return home of two of the poet's sons, Colonel and Major Burns, after many years' service in the army of the East India Company, the festival featured a long colourful procession, musical and dramatic performances, and culminated in a banquet at which establishment figures took turns to eulogise Burns's life and work. It was a measure, perhaps, of how untouchable he had become that when the vice-president, Professor John Wilson, misjudging the occasion, spoke at too great a length on the poet's frailties, a restive audience forced him to cut short his speech before he had an opportunity to expound on his greater strengths.

The festival attracted bitter criticism from Chartists and other radicals, who recognised it as a cynical attempt to recruit Burns to a Tory agenda at a time when class divisions were threatening to engulf the nation. The police and army had been placed on high alert in Scotland during the summer of 1842, which saw large demonstrations of unemployed workers, a wave of strikes, and threats of civil disobedience.[33] Only three months before the festival the Chartist Henry Vincent – who would later work alongside Douglass in the formation of the Anti-Slavery League – contested a parliamentary by-election in neighbouring Kilmarnock for the Complete Suffrage Union, almost forcing the Liberal candidate to withdraw.[34] The poet who stood up for the rights of the oppressed was being transformed into a cosy celebrant of rural contentment, whose subversive barbs at the hypocrisy of the clergy and contempt of the rich for the poor were dismissed as little more than outbursts of provocative humour.[35]

Douglass would no doubt have shared these misgivings – he would later in the year share a platform in Paisley with Patrick Brewster, the outspoken Chartist and Church of Scotland minister who had lent his voice to the denunciations of the 1844 extravaganza.[36] In concluding his speech in Ayr on 24 March by invoking an antislavery Burns, Douglass casts aside Currie's reservations. While abolitionism in Britain was no longer the seditious movement it was in the 1790s, it was evidently compromised by its associations with the 'epoch of agitation' for conservatives like Wilson, who barely acknowledges any radical tendencies in Burns, not even in the full version of his speech, which was published in *Blackwood's*.[37] However, keenly aware perhaps of the range of political opinion represented in his audience at the Cathcart Street church, Douglass does not labour the point and declines to pursue the matter further.

Notes

1. FD to WLG, London, 23 May 1846 (FDP 3.1, p. 132). In a letter written shortly after his return to the United States, he adapts a couplet from 'Tam o'Shanter', replacing 'Tam' with 'I': 'Kings may be blest, but I was glorious, / O'er all the ills of life victorious': FD to Anna Richardson, Lynn, 29 April 1847 (FDP 3.1, p. 209).
2. Currie, *Works* (1841). The University of Rochester River Campus Libraries' Department of Rare Books, Special Collections, and Preservation has Douglass's copy of this edition, which is inscribed: 'This book was the first bought by me after my escape from slavery. I have owned it nearly thirty one years and now give it to my oldest son as a keep sake. F.D.' Dated October 1867, 'nearly thirty one years' cannot be correct, and FD may have been led astray in his calculation by the frontispiece of the volume which, unlike the title page, gives 1835 as the year of publication. See <http://rbscp.lib.rochester.edu/4646> and <https://catalog.lib.rochester.edu/vwebv/holdingsInfo?bibId=6384501> (last accessed 31 May 2018).
3. FD, Dundee, 10 March 1846 (FDP 1.1, p. 174).
4. FD, Ayr, 24 March 1846 (*Ayr Observer*, 31 March 1846).
5. Crawford, *The Bard*, pp. 222–37.
6. Carruthers, 'Burns and Slavery', p. 22; Daiches, *Robert Burns*, p. 93.
7. Burns, 'On a Scotch Bard, Gone to the West Indies', in Currie, *Works* (1841), vol. 1, pp. 47–8; Currie, *Complete Works (1844)*, p. 128; and Burns, *Poems and Songs*, vol. 1, pp. 238–9.

8. Currie, *Works* (1841), vol. 2, p. 22; Currie, *Complete Works* (1844), p. xxxviii.

9. Phillippo, *Jamaica*, p. 140. This view is echoed by a modern historian: 'Most estates had two book-keepers, whose occupation was anything but keeping books': Patterson, *The Sociology of Slavery*, p. 57.

10. Robert Burns to Helen Maria Williams, Ellisland, late July or early August 1789, in Burns, *Letters*, vol. 1, pp. 430–1. Williams's poem, 'A Poem on the Bill Lately Passed for Regulating the Slave-Trade' (1788), is reprinted in Richardson, *Slavery, Abolition and Emancipation*, pp. 83–98.

11. See Whyte, *Zachary Macaulay*.

12. Lindsay, *Illustrious Exile*.

13. Whyte, *Scotland and the Abolition of Black Slavery*, esp. pp. 70–106.

14. See Andrews, '"Ev'ry Heart Can Feel"'.

15. Marjoribanks, *Slavery*. See Williamson, 'The Antislavery Poems of John Marjoribanks'. Burns, 'The Slave's Lament', in Burns, *Poems and Songs*, vol. 2, pp. 647–8. James Kinsley notes that Burns's 'part in this song is uncertain' (Burns, *Poems and Songs*, vol. 3, p. 1405); and according to Donald Low, 'possibly not his work': Burns, *Songs*, p. 547.

16. Burns, 'For A' That and A' That', in Currie, *Works* (1841), vol. 1, pp. 100–1; Currie, *Complete Works (1844)*, pp. 230–1; Burns, *Poems and Songs*, vol. 2, pp. 762–3.

17. See Pittock, 'Slavery as a Political Metaphor'.

18. Marcus Wood describes the medallion as 'the central icon of slave passivity and disempowerment': 'Popular Graphic Images of Slavery', p. 144.

19. For a balanced assessment of Burns's attitude to slavery see Morris, *Scotland and the Caribbean*, pp. 98–140; see also Carruthers, 'Burns and Slavery'. Nigel Leask's close readings of the poems and letters are exemplary in this regard: see his 'Burns and the Poetics of Abolition' and '"Their Groves o' Sweet Myrtles"'.

20. See Graham, *Burns and the Sugar Plantocracy*; Mullen, *It Wisnae Us*; and Devine, *Recovering Scotland's Slavery Past*. Most of the recent work on Scotland and slavery has focused on the relationship with the North American colonies and the Caribbean before 1833. The importance to the British economy of slave-grown produce, especially cotton from the United States in the 1840s and 50s (and of the abolitionist campaign to persuade consumers and manufacturers to switch to 'free' cotton) has attracted less interest from Scottish historians.

21. In Douglass's library at Cedar Hill, Washington, DC, is an 1844 edition whose inscription indicates that it was presented to him in 'Jany 1846' by 'G. C.' See Petrie and Stover, *Bibliography of the Frederick Douglass*

Library, 20–1. I am grateful to the library for sending me a copy of the inscribed page. The second initial of the signature is unclear but the most likely donor was George Gilfillan, who himself went on to produce a critical edition of Burns a decade later. Gilfillan's effusive praise appeared in the *Dundee, Perth and Cupar Advertiser*, 24 January 1851.

22. 'Currie's *Works of Burns* provided a template through which Burns' poetry could be appreciated not just by Scots but by all people touched by the forces of modernity, including the metropolisation of the periphery and the increasing migrations of peoples around the globe': Davis, 'Burns and Transnational Culture', p. 162. On the popularity of Currie in North America until at least 1840s see also Davis, 'Negotiating Cultural Memory', esp. pp. 4–9; and McGuirk, 'Haunted by Authority', p. 144.

23. Currie, *Works* (1841), vol. 2, p. 10; Currie, *Complete Works* (1844), p. xxvii.

24. Robert Burns to John Moore, Mauchline, 2 August 1787 in Currie, *Works* (1841), vol. 2, p. 15; Currie, *Complete Works* (1844), p. xxxii; Burns, *Letters*, vol. 1, p. 144.

25. Currie, *Works* (1841), vol. 2, p. 23; Currie, *Complete Works* (1844), p. xxxix. During the second half of the eighteenth century between 10,000 and 20,000 Scots emigrated to the West Indies: Hamilton, *Scotland, the Caribbean and the Atlantic World*, p. 23.

26. Thornton, *James Currie*, pp. 189–99. Clarkson's map appears in Clarkson, *The History of the Abolition of the African Slave-Trade*, vol. 1, between pp. 258 and 259.

27. Thornton, *James Currie*, pp. 32–66, 92–4.

28. See Schwarz, 'Scottish Surgeons', which discusses Currie alongside other Scottish surgeons connected with the Liverpool trade.

29. James Currie to Graham Moore, Liverpool, 23 March 1788, in Currie, *Memoir*, vol. 1, p. 135. Burns's letter to Williams was written the following year. Admiral Graham Moore, to whom Currie dedicated his edition of Burns's *Works*, was the son of Dr John Moore, to whom Burns wrote his famous autobiographical letter in 1787. Admiral Moore's naval career included engagements in the Caribbean.

30. Thornton, *James Currie*, p. 191. For the words of the song and further details see Currie, *Memoir*, vol. 1, pp. 127–35. It is also reprinted, as 'The African', in Richardson, *Slavery, Abolition and Emancipation*, pp. 99–100.

31. For Currie's assessment of Burns's songs see esp. *Works* (1835), vol. 2, pp. 84–5; *Complete Works* (1844), pp. xci–xcii. For his dismissal of religious and political themes in Burns's poetry: 'Burns ought to keep clear of politics, and we may add religion, which, from its very nature, cannot be made the vehicle of good poetry' (James Currie to Graham Moore, 11 June 1787, quoted in Currie, *Memoir*, vol. 1, p. 241); and:

'I imagine it will be thought prudent to avoid all political allusions in the life' (James Currie to John Syme, September 1796, quoted in Currie, *Memoir*, vol. 1, p. 262).

32. Davis, 'James Currie's *Works of Robert Burns*'. See also Leask, '"The Shadow Line"'; and Carruthers and McKay, 'Re-reading James Currie'.

33. Wilson, *The Chartist Movement in Scotland*, pp. 189–91; Fraser, *Chartism in Scotland*, pp. 120–32.

34. Wilson, *Chartist Movement in Scotland*, pp. 203–4, 208. Vincent contested no less than eight parliamentary elections, but Kilmarnock was the one he had the best chance of winning. For a less charitable view of Vincent see Chase, *Chartism*, p. 237. On FD's relationship with Chartist leaders see Bradbury, 'Frederick Douglass and the Chartists'.

35. See Tyrrell, 'Paternalism'; and Whatley, 'The Political and Cultural Legacy of Robert Burns'.

36. FD and Brewster both addressed a 'Great Anti-Slavery Meeting' denouncing the Evangelical Alliance and the Free Church of Scotland in Paisley on 23 September 1846 (FDP 1.1, p. 426). On Brewster see Chase, *Chartism*, pp. 49–56. Brewster was also an honorary member of the Glasgow Emancipation Society.

37. 'The Burns Festival', *Blackwood's Edinburgh Magazine* (September 1844), pp. 378–87. 'Now and then' in his poetry, 'here and there peals forth the clangour of the war-trumpet. But Burns is not, in the vulgar sense, a military poet; nor are the Scottish, in a vulgar sense, a military people. He and they best love tranquil scenes and the secure peace of home' (p. 386).

Chapter 14

The Coward Slave and the Poor Negro Driver

In addressing meetings in Britain and Ireland, Douglass was well aware that his audience also included those who would read reports of his speeches in the United States. It was of great importance to him that these transatlantic readers would picture this black man, still legally a slave, cheered and applauded by supporters from all classes of society, welcomed as an equal in public places. He 'would wish them to know that one, who had broken from the bonds of slavery, was ranging through Great Britain exposing the enormities of the system'.[1] The word *ranging* here perfectly conveys the kind of limitless and unrestrained freedom he wants to wave before the pro-slavery lobby back home, shaming, even taunting, them with an image of him enjoying rights denied to him in the land of his birth. And if Douglass sarcastically dismissed the insulting language with which that lobby characterised his lecture tour – the *New-York Express* described him as a 'glib-tongued scoundrel [. . .] running a muck in greedy-eared Britain against America, its people, its institutions, and even against its peace' – he must have taken some pleasure from the fact that even his enemies acknowledged his popularity.[2]

It certainly appears that Douglass was always preaching to the converted, even when denouncing the leaders and supporters of the Free Church, who almost never seem to be in the halls in which he speaks. And this image of crowds unanimously fired up by his speeches – 'all this region is in a ferment', 'old Scotland boils like a pot' – is precisely the one that he wants to convey to American readers.[3]

But there are occasions where he expresses a more generalised frustration that doesn't let his audiences off so easily. 'When he left America for this country,' a Manchester paper reported him saying, 'he expected to find but one opinion about slaveholding and slave-holders in this country among all denominations; but he was disappointed.'[4] '[T]he anti-slavery spirit has scarcely a tangible existence in one town of twenty in all of England,' he declared in Leeds.[5] And in Glasgow: 'Not six years ago there were many in this city who did not hesitate to come forward and avow themselves the uncompromising advocates of emancipation, who were called Rev. Doctors of Divinity, and where are they now? They are among the missing.'[6] It was not enough to whisper the truth, he said, they had to 'speak with a trumpet tongue'.[7]

Such accusations may have made his audiences a little uneasy, especially when Douglass widened the scope of his criticism to target not just church leaders but a more diffuse set of attitudes that inhibit the development of a more vocal and committed abolitionism in the towns and cities he visits. At issue here is what he sees as the dilution of the term 'slavery' itself. At a large meeting in London he exaggerates the problem to good effect:

I have found persons in this country who have identified the term slavery with that which I think it is not, and in some instances, I have feared, in so doing have rather (unwittingly, I know) detracted much from the horror with which the term slavery is contemplated. It is common in this country to distinguish every bad thing by the name slavery. Intemperance is slavery (cheers); to be deprived of the right to vote is slavery, says one; to have to work hard is slavery, says another (laughter, and loud cheers); and I do not know but that if we should let them go on, they would say to eat when we are hungry, to walk when we desire to have exercise, or to minister to our necessities, or have necessities at all, is slavery. (Laughter.) I do not wish for a moment to detract from the horror with which the evil of intemperance is contemplated; not at all; nor do I wish to throw the slightest obstruction in the way of any political freedom that any class of persons in this country may desire to obtain. But I am here to say that I think the term slavery is sometimes abused by identifying it with that which it is not.[8]

It is crucial for Douglass that *slavery* is reserved for chattel slavery, a property relationship, maintained by violence, in which human beings are owned by others. And this is why the struggle against this, its most extreme form, must be carefully distinguished from the struggle for, say, higher wages, better working conditions or the extension of the franchise. Douglass was well aware that defenders of slavery in the United States eagerly pointed to the misery endured by the industrial wage-labourers in an attempt to undermine the priorities of the abolitionists. The treatment of the Dundee mill-workers in 1845 was recounted in a book containing many such examples, entitled *The Laboring Classes of England*, published in Boston, which pointedly remarked: 'Had they only been *black* instead of *white*, their case would have been taken into consideration long ago.'[9] The expression 'wage slave' or 'white slave' was common currency, even within the ranks of the Chartists and other radicals in Britain, even if they intended to emphasise their own grievances rather than endorse chattel slavery, which most of them abhorred. Patrick Brewster on one occasion offered the opinion that 'the fate of the English working man is worse than that of the Russian serf, the Hindoo pariah, or the negro slave'.[10]

However, the particular association of slavery with craven submission, not always present in the campaigns for social and political reform, but deeply embedded in Burns's poetry, is specifically addressed in Douglass's speech in Ayr on 24 March, when he tells the audience about the friend of his master's, Thompson, who published the letter that insisted that the boy he knew as Bailey could not be the author of *The Narrative of the Life of Frederick Douglass, An American Slave* because the latter 'had not the crouching character of the negro' and thus 'was very different from the generality of slaves'.[11] In this speech he elaborates on his previously published response to address a similar – and presumably fairly widely shared – scepticism on the part of his overseas audiences, who must have been a little surprised that the besuited and well-groomed man whose portrait adorned the title page of his autobiography did not at all resemble the standard images of the captive or runaway slave.

Douglass first reminds his listeners that the character of a slave is not fixed. His own story shows the transformation he underwent through education and experience. But then, he goes on, this 'crouching character' may not be all it seems. People like Thompson

> were greatly deceived if they judged of the minds of their slaves by their carriage before them. The poor wretches well knew, that if they showed the least symptoms of intelligence, heavy punishment awaited them, and thus they felt it to be [in] their interests to look as much as possible like insensible brutes.[12]

Indeed the recurring theme of the story he tells in Ayr is one of stealth – he impresses on his audience the need for slaves to conceal their actions, feelings and motivations from view. Their survival – and his own escape – depended on it. The figure of the 'crouching' or indeed 'coward slave' – may have suited those who preferred to imagine slaves as voluntarily acquiescing in their own condition, dependent on non-slaves to deliver their freedom, and Burns – along with many abolitionists – would appear to have been one of them. But Douglass forcefully reminds his listeners that what looks like an acquiescent victim may well be a plotting rebel.

Another expression used by Burns formed the subject of a letter Douglas wrote from Glasgow to Horace Greeley, the editor of the *New York Tribune*, a few weeks after his visit to Ayr. In it he recalls the 'low and vulgar epithets' flung at him by less sympathetic journalists in the United States. He airily dismisses them. After all, he says, he is used to them and their force is lost on him. But then he feels compelled to add some remarks that imply that he may have been troubled by them more than he cares to admit:

> They form a large and very important portion of the vocabulary of characters known in the South as plantation 'Negro drivers'. A slave-holding gentleman would scorn to use them. He leaves them to find their way into the world of sound, through the polluted lips of his hired 'Negro driver' – a being for whom the haughty slaveholder feels incomparably more contempt than he feels toward his slave. And for the best of all reasons – he knows the slave to be degraded, because he cannot help himself; but a white 'Negro driver' is degraded, because of original, ingrained meanness. If I agree with the slaveholders in nothing else, I can say I agree with them in all their burning contempt for a 'Negro driver,' whether born North or South.[13]

Or, for that matter, in Scotland. As we have noted, in his letter to Dr John Moore, Burns, now fêted by literary Edinburgh, referred to the possibility that he might have missed all the adulation, it being drowned by the Atlantic, as he laboured as a 'poor Negro driver'. The conceit relies on exaggerating the subordinate role he would have filled on the plantation. It is a passing flourish, but its flippancy may disturb the modern reader. Given that the occupation was one for which he reserved some of his most vitriolic prose, it may have disturbed Douglass too when he read it in Currie's volume. That

Douglass knew that his hero had seriously considered such an occupation, and casually joked about it later, suggests that some of his contempt may have attached to Burns. And while he tried hard to conceal it, traces of his strong feelings have left their mark. As a reader of Burns, Douglass is unlikely to have been any less forgiving of the joke about the 'poor negro-driver' than he would of scornful references to the 'coward slave'. But did this lead him to qualify his admiration of the poet?

Notes

1. FD, Bridgewater, Somerset, 31 August 1846 (FDP 1.1, p. 366). For similar formulations which stress the impact on Southern readers of the image of FD 'ranging' see FD, London, 22 May 1846 (FDP 1.1, p. 274); FD, Newcastle, 3 August 1846 (FDP 1.1, p. 322).
2. See FD to Horace Greeley, Glasgow, 15 April 1846 (FDP 3.1, p. 104).
3. FD to RW, Dundee, 16 February 1846 (BAA, p. 251); FD to Francis Jackson, Dundee, 29 January 1846 (FDP 3.1, p. 90; BAA, p. 248).
4. FD, Manchester, 12 October 1846 (FDP 1.1, p. 461).
5. FD, Leeds, 23 December 1846 (FDP 1.1, p. 475).
6. FD, Glasgow, 30 September 1846 (FDP 1.1, p. 442).
7. FD, Exeter, 28 August 1846 (FDP 1.1, p. 354).
8. FD, London, 22 May 1846 (FDP 1.1, p. 273).
9. Dodd, *The Laboring Classes*, p. 25.
10. Quoted in Chase, *Chartism*, p. 307. At one point, FD explains that he uses *slavery* 'not in the ordinary sense of the term, not in a political sense, but in its real and intrinsic meaning' (FD, Cork, 14 October 1846; FDP 1.1, p. 39). For a useful summary of mid-century contests over the term see Cunliffe, *Chattel Slavery and Wage Slavery*.
11. FD, Ayr, 24 March 1846 (FDP 1.1, p. 201).
12. Ibid.
13. FD to Horace Greeley, Glasgow, 15 April 1846 (FDP 3.1, p. 104).

Chapter 15

Crooked Paths

While he was in Ayr Douglass wrote a letter in which he described at length his visit to Burns's monument and to the cottage of Burns's surviving sister and her two daughters. Isabella Burns Begg, who had been a guest of honour at the 1844 festival, gave Douglass and Buffum a warm welcome. '[T]hough approaching 80, she does not look to be more than sixty,' Douglass remarks. 'She enjoys good health, is a spirited looking woman, and bids fair to live yet many days.'

'I am now in Ayr,' he begins. 'It is famous for being the birth-place of Robert Burns, the poet, by whose brilliant genius every stream, hill, glen and valley in the neighborhood have been made classic.' On their arrival, they were greeted by Rev. Renwick and immediately escorted to the monument, three miles distant, following a well-worn tourist route.[1] They would have passed the elegant house and grounds of Rozelle, the residence of Archibald and Lady Hamilton, named by her grandfather after his estate in Jamaica.[2] After pausing at the cottage where Burns was born, now an inn, the trio would have soon reached the roofless Alloway Kirk, and, a few hundred yards beyond, inspected the Auld Brig over the Doon. Between them was the imposing monument, well situated, thought Douglass, as it overlooked all these places immortalised by the poet, as well as affording a view of the Firth of Clyde and the mountainous outline of Arran shrouded in mist – a setting he finds 'admirably and beautifully adapted to the monument of Scotland's noble bard'.[3]

He goes on to dwell on inanimate memorials of the poet's life: a marble bust, two statues, letters in his own hand and an original portrait, but what moves him most is

a bible, given by Burns to his 'sweet Highland Mary' – there is also in the same case a lock of hair he so dearly loved, and who by death was snatched from his bosom, and up to his bust glowing with expression, I received a vivid impression, and shared with him the deep melancholy portrayed in the following lines . . .[4]

and Douglass quotes in full the poet's song *The Banks o' Doon*, in which the river serves as an unwelcome reminder of 'joys, / departed, never to return'.[5]

In the reference to 'deep melancholy' we might detect the imprint of Currie, a sufferer from depression himself who published medical papers on hypochondriasis and paid special attention to Burns's own susceptibility 'to those depressions of mind, which are perhaps not wholly separable from the sensibility of genius'.[6] There is some evidence that Douglass was likewise afflicted. From Edinburgh he wrote to Ruth Cox, the family friend he called 'Harriet', telling her how he 'got real low spirits a few days – ago – quite down at the mouth [. . .] There was no living for me.' It was clearly not an isolated episode, and if it was intensified by the pain of separation from Anna and the children, it seems more than this. Douglass talks of 'my fits of insanity I mean my fits of melancholy' (and in January he writes to her again in the same vein) – but his account of what helped him on this occasion is worth quoting:

> I went down the street and saw in the window of a large store – and old fiddle. The thought struck me – it has been so long since I played any that it might do me some good – you know when I get hungry at home I always play. Well I bought the fiddle[.] [G]ave a trifle for it – brought it to the Hotel, and struck up the 'Camels a coming.'[.] I had not played ten minutes before I began to feel better and – gradually I came to myself again and was lively as a crikit and as loving as a lamb. But Hatta. It is a terrible feeling and I advise every body to keep clear of it who can – and those who can[']t to buy a fiddle.[7]

If the words of one Burns's song evoke a state of mind that occasionally debilitated him, the tune of another, the Jacobite air 'The Campbells are Comin'', is here the means of his rejuvenation. A similar duality emerges in the letter from Ayr.

When he comes to assess Burns's life and work, Currie's influence is unmistakeable. Douglass's correspondent is Abigail Mott, a Quaker abolitionist who at the time was educating his daughter Rosetta in Albany, New York. He acknowledges that she is 'no admirer of

Burns's. Indeed she is addressed as one who is perhaps 'painfully' aware of Douglass's own enthusiasm, contrasting sharply with the local audience he would expect to address that night and the following. Currie provides a suitable template for his purposes in this respect because, as Currie writes at the very beginning of his 'Prefatory Remarks', Burns's readers are not exclusively Scottish, but are found in many 'other countries where the English language is spoken or understood'.[8] Many of his readers lack a familiarity with both his 'dialect' and the society in which he lived, and therefore might struggle to fully appreciate his work. Douglass would have been aware that this described Mott and others who would read his letter, an extract of which was published in the *Albany Evening Journal* and subsequently reprinted elsewhere.

To overcome this potential obstacle, Currie precedes his biographical essay with 'Some Observations on the Character and Condition of the Scottish Peasantry'. Douglass effectively confirms the wisdom of Currie's strategy – and indeed duplicates it – first by telling us that, according to one of the nieces, their uncle 'was more highly esteemed in America than in Scotland', and then by stating that

> I have ever esteemed Robert Burns a true soul but never could I have had the high opinion of the man or his genius, which I now entertain, without my present knowledge of the country, to which he belonged – the times in which he lived, and the broad Scotch tongue in which he wrote.

But as he goes on to elaborate, the Scottishness of this context fades into the background. The intention, though, is not to make Burns' story a universal one, but rather to allow another setting to take its place:

> Burns lived in the midst of a bigoted and besotted clergy – a pious, but corrupt generation – a proud, ambitious, and contemptuous aristocracy, who, esteemed a little more than a man, and looked upon the plowman, such as was the noble Burns, as being little better than a brute. He became disgusted with the pious frauds, indignant at the bigotry, filled with contempt for the hollow pretensions set up by the shallow-brained aristocracy. He broke loose from the moorings which society had thrown around him. Spurning all restraint, he sought a path for his feet, and, like all bold pioneers, he made crooked paths.

The clergy and aristocracy who are the villains in this piece have no obvious counterpart in Currie's biography, which sets his Burns in a much more congenial world that offered peasants more opportunities than elsewhere, even if Burns himself enjoyed a shorter period of formal education than many of his peers. The terms pretension, corruption and fraud are assuredly not Currie's; they are actually closer to the language of the Chartist *Northern Star* in its attack on the 1844 Festival and its attempt to 'whitewash' the 'flinty-hearted, selfish, arrogant aristocracy'.[9] But they are also drawn from the vocabulary Douglass elsewhere uses to condemn the class of slaveholders in the United States, who, as we have seen, often compared themselves to feudal nobility.

The antithetical pairing of 'man' and 'brute' recalls some of the most memorable rhetorical set pieces in Douglass's speeches and writings.[10] And here he comes close to quoting from his own apostrophe to the sailing ships in Chesapeake Bay in the *Narrative*, where he wrote: 'You are loosed from your moorings, and are free; I am fast in my chains, and am a slave!'[11] Anyone recognising the phrase (from what Garrison's Preface highlights as the most 'thrilling' episode in the book) might be forgiven for thinking that by the end of this passage, Douglass has imaginatively fused his own escape from slavery with Burns's exceptional rise from rural obscurity. Somehow Ayrshire has turned into Maryland's Eastern Shore. The transformation reinforces the claim made by the editor of the *Albany Evening Journal*, who felt it necessary to tell his readers that Douglass is 'qualified' to write about Burns precisely because he is '"a Runaway Slave," who, during his eight years of stolen freedom, in defiance of all the disadvantages under which his class labor'.[12]

Mindful of his sceptical reader, as well as showing how much he had learnt from Currie, Douglass feels obliged to acknowledge Burns's much-discussed moral shortcomings, which he renders euphemistically as 'crooked paths', and continues:

We may lament it, we may weep over it, but in the language of another, we shall lament and weep with him. The elements of character which urged him on are in us all, and influencing our conduct every day of our lives. We may pity him, but we can't despise him. We may condemn his faults, but only as we condemn our own. His very weakness was an index of his strength. Full of faults of a grievous nature, yet far more faultless than many who have come down to us in the pages of history as saints. He was a brilliant genius, and like all of his class, did much good and much evil. Let us take the good and leave the evil – let us adopt his virtues but avoid his vices – let us pursue his wisdom but shun his folly; and as death has separated his noble spirit from the corrupt and contemptible lust with which it was encumbered, so let us separate his good from his evil deeds – thus may we make him a blessing than a curse to the world.[13]

In the opening sentence, Douglass may be alluding to Christ's warning to his disciples that they will soon 'lament and weep' over his death. In John's Gospel, he goes on to reassure them that sorrow will turn to joy, just as the trials of childbirth give way to celebrations.[14] Perhaps Douglass feels it appropriate to make this parallel with the man already by the 1840s commonly dubbed the 'immortal Bard', and reassurance is precisely the tone he appears to be striving for here.[15] But the allusion is a clumsy one, for Douglass is making a different point. It is Burns's 'faults' which preoccupy him in what immediately follows.

Currie has plenty to say about – and is a little more explicit in giving a name to – the 'intemperance', 'dissipation', even 'orgies' in which the poet was tempted to indulge, a weakness which he attributes to the particular temperament of men of genius. For Douglass, however, they are failings to which we are all prey, and by saying that he lends them an everyday normality which deprives them of their force. And then he suggests we can, in any case, offset them against Burns's merits. Now he is dead – and here the transformation on which his biblical allusion rests comes into play – 'let us take the good and leave the evil – let us adopt his virtues but avoid his vices'. And yet as the pattern goes on repeating (wisdom and folly, noble and corrupt, blessing and curse), the reader is reminded of the one as much as the other. In a rather unexpected use of what students of rhetoric call paralepsis, the qualities we are supposed to forget are mentioned as often as those we are supposed to remember, and so, despite closing his letter by urging his correspondent to 'read his poems' – if only 'to gratify your friend Frederick' – Douglass leaves us with an impression of a man we're not sure is worthy of imitation or not.

Notes

1. See, for example, 'Route to and from Burns' Monument', in *Guide to the Glasgow & Ayrshire Railway*, pp. 95–106.

2. Graham, *Burns and the Sugar Plantocracy*, pp. 23–59, 103.
3. FD to Abigail Mott, Ayr, 23 March 1846 (FDP 3.1, p. 112). The letter is dated 23 April, but on 23 April FD was in Glasgow; his speaking engagements in Ayr were on 23 and 24 March. The more likely date of composition is 23 March.
4. FD to Abigail Mott, Ayr, 23 March 1846 (FDP 3.1, pp. 111–12).
5. Robert Burns, 'The Banks of Doon' in Currie, *Works* (1841), vol. 1, pp. 113–14; Currie, *Complete Works* (1844), p. 169; Burns, *Poems and Songs*, p. Vol. 2, pp. 575–6.
6. Currie, *Works* (1841), vol. 2, p. 27; Currie, *Complete Works* (1844), p. xliii. On Currie's scientific researches (and his own susceptibility to depression) see Thornton, *James Currie*, pp. 81–2, 140–1, 153, 158–9, 174–5. Thornton makes suggestive remarks on the way the genre of the medical case history left its trace on the ethics and practice of Currie's biographical writing: *James Currie*, pp. 184–8.
7. FD to Ruth Cox, Edinburgh, 6 May 1846 (FDP 3.1, p. 125); see also FD to Ruth Cox, Leamington, 31 January 1847 (FDP 3.1, pp. 200–1). The editors of FDP 3.1 do not indicate from where the 6 May letter was sent, but all of FD's known speaking engagements between 27 April and 7 May inclusive were in Edinburgh (see Appendix I).
8. Currie, *Works* (1841), vol. 2, p. 1; Currie, *Complete Works* (1844), p. xvii.
9. 'Burns, the Poor Man's Poet', *Northern Star and Leeds General Advertiser*, 24 August 1844.
10. Most famously: 'You have seen how a man was made a slave; you shall see how a slave was made a man': N, p. 107 (A, p, 60; FDP 1.1, p. 50).
11. N, p. 106 (A, p. 59; FDP 1.1, p. 49).
12. *Albany Evening Journal*, 13 June 1846.
13. FD to Abigail Mott, Ayr, 23 April 1846 (FDP 3.1, pp. 113–14).
14. John 16:20–1.
15. Currie himself talks of Burns's 'immortal verse' and 'works of genius which seem destined to immortality': *Works* (1835), vol. 2, pp. 87, 89; *Complete Works* (1844), pp. xciii, xcv.

Chapter 16

The Sons and Daughters of Old Scotia

We have so far discussed two occasions on which Douglass directly commented on Burns and passed judgement on him, attuned to different audiences in each case: the enthusiastic devotees in the meeting he addressed at the Cathcart Street church in Ayr, and the more sceptical family friend who received his letter in Albany.

Two and a half years later, back in the United States, Douglass spoke of Burns in front of a different audience yet again. In Rochester, New York he was invited to the second annual gathering of the 'sons and daughters of Old Scotia in this city and land of their adoption', wrote Edinburgh-born John Dick, printer of *The North Star*.[1] Dick was closely involved in the running of the paper, which Douglass edited with Martin Delany, and contributed numerous articles.[2] From his account, it is clear Dick attended the gathering as a proud Scot and not just as a dispassionate reporter of his employer's speaking engagements. Two thirds of the three hundred present to celebrate the ninetieth anniversary of the poet's birth, he estimated, had been born in Scotland. 'I could almost have believed,' he continued, 'when I heard the Scotch voices, and saw the Scotch faces, and listened to the wild notes of the pibroch, which was played at intervals during the evening, that I was in the "auld toon of Ayr" itself.'

But which Burns was being celebrated here? It seems clear from the speech of a Mr Sidey, which takes up nearly half of Dick's report, that it is a boldly egalitarian Burns. Sidey describes him as 'freedom's poet [. . .] whose greatest joy was in the triumph of right', who despised British tyranny and sung the glory of the American and French revolutions; a defender of the oppressed and 'friend to universal brotherhood'. The evening featured recitations and songs including some from the Scottish singer William Dempster, who happened to be in town and whose

> 'Highland Mary' brought the sympathizing tear to the eyes of more than one of his delighted listeners; and that song of Burns which is, and will always be, the admiration of all men – 'A man's a man for a' that,' brought raptures of applause from the audience.[3]

And then, reported Dick, calls of 'Douglass, Douglass!' arose, that ancient war cry once again transformed, this time to cajole a speech from their special guest, who rose and began: 'I regard it as a pleasure, not less than a privilege, to mingle my humble voice with the festivities of this occasion.' Certainly, Sidey's speech might have made Douglass feel freer to endorse a more radical Burns than he did before his audience in Ayr; and it would have relieved him of the obligation to excuse the poet's 'crooked paths' that he was under in his letter to the sceptical Abigail Mott. And some of his pleasure might have derived from the contrast with another event in Rochester the previous year. Douglass had been initially refused admittance to a celebration of Benjamin Franklin's birthday on the grounds that it was 'a violation of the rules of society for colored people to associate with whites'.[4]

Yet there is something about Sidey's speech that may have bothered Douglass. It employs a rhetoric he had heard all too many times in the United States, not least on that anniversary when patriots commemorate the Declaration of Independence. As Douglass famously pointed out in his 'What to a Slave is the Fourth of July?' speech, delivered in Rochester in 1852, the rights it asserted were not extended to members of 'the negro race', and therefore these celebrations take place as if black people simply do not exist. In that speech he confronts the audience head on: 'The rich inheritance of justice, liberty, prosperity and independence, bequeathed by your fathers, is shared by you, not by me [. . .] This Fourth July is *yours*, not *mine*. *You* may rejoice, *I* must mourn.' On this occasion, Douglass's tactics are rather more subtle. Rather than confronting his adversary, he outflanks him.

Like Sidey, he begins by declaring his admiration not for Burns, but for Scotland. Just as Sidey praised the country 'whose every hill and glen bears record of where a martyr fell and patriot died in defence of freedom and fatherland', so Douglass, adapting a turn of phrase he has used before, speaks of how, during his travels 'through that land', he 'learned that every stream, hill, glen and valley, had been rendered classic by heroic deeds in behalf of Freedom'.[5] Coming from Sidey's lips, this invocation of Scotland does nothing to disrupt the convention that such rhetoric is racially exclusive. But the almost identical words spoken by Douglass have a different meaning; they insist otherwise.

> Although I am not a Scotchman, nor the son of a Scotchman, (perhaps you will say 'it needs no ghost to tell us that,') (a laugh,) but if a warm love of Scotch character – a high appreciation of Scotch genius – constitute any of the qualities of a true Scotch heart, then indeed does a Scotch heart throb beneath these ribs.

Only then does he go on to mention his 'pilgrimage' to Ayr and have the audience picture him 'seeing and conversing' with Burns's sister. In doing so Douglass implies he enjoys a closer connection to Burns than many of those present would ever have enjoyed, making a claim not only to be Scottish but more Scottish than this gathering of emigrants. And then, in a *coup de grâce*, he fashions the perfect response to those who might suspect this Scottish Douglass is rather far-fetched.

> But, ladies and gentlemen, this is not a time for long speeches. I do not wish to detain you from the social pleasures that await you. I repeat again, that though I am not a Scotchman, and have a colored skin, I am proud to be among you this evening. And if any think me out of my place on this occasion (pointing at the picture of Burns), I beg that the blame may be laid at the door of him who taught me that 'a man's a man for a' that.' (Mr. D. sat down amid loud cries of 'go on!' from the audience).

In the end it is the democratic Burns that Douglass invokes, one that justifies his presence at an event from which he might have been doubly excluded – for being neither white nor Scottish. It may provide a reassuring conclusion to our discussion of the often restrained and indirect ways in which Douglass publicly engages with Burns in the 1840s. But we must not lose sight of the fact that his admiration was not unbounded. He may have had good reasons for not openly condemning Burns's lukewarm and superficial abolitionism. But it is unlikely, given the strength of his distaste for two particular expressions ('coward slave', 'poor negro driver') used so casually by the poet, that he was not troubled by his attenuated concept of human rights.

Douglass demonstrated an impressive knowledge of Scottish literature and history, and an extraordinary facility for adapting it to shed light on his own situation and to power his transformation from an 'American slave' to a cosmopolitan intellectual. His persistent, and barely critical, allusions to Scott and Burns may puzzle those modern readers alert to the associations of Scott with the Southern plantocracy on the one hand and Burns's ambiguous relationship to Caribbean slavery on the other. But these allusions are not primarily intended to illuminate their writings or dissect their ideologies, even though they sometimes lead Douglass to important insights. Rather, they are designed to help Douglass connect with his Scottish audiences.

However, he is not only seeking appreciative nods of recognition from the crowd. Douglass chooses these authors because he knows he can rely on his listeners and readers to recognise them as bearers of values he holds dear. In Ayr and Rochester he signals his love for Burns as a poet of human rights. In Dundee and the revised editions of his *Narrative* he invokes the 'heroic deeds' of his mediaeval namesake, made classic by Scott, in passionate defence of the struggle for freedom.

When Douglass was in Ireland, his attempts to connect with audiences along the same lines were less successful, and it is worth considering why.

Already, before he had left Boston, Douglass had in his *Narrative* written of the impact on him as a young teenager of Caleb Bingham's *The Columbian Orator*, the school textbook that included selections from famous speeches, dramatic dialogues and poems, chosen as models for students to imitate. Of two texts in particular which Douglass said he 'read over and over with unabated interest' was 'one of Sheridan's mighty speeches on and in behalf of Catholic emancipation'.[6] Actually Douglass confused Richard Brinsley Sheridan (represented elsewhere in the volume) with another Irishman, Arthur O'Connor, whom Bingham correctly credits as the author of the 1795 speech.[7] There is no evidence that Douglass made anything of this in his lectures in Ireland in 1845, but he did take care on at least two occasions, when giving an account of the disturbance on his outward voyage, to let audiences know that the soldier Captain Gough, who intervened on his behalf, was a 'noble-hearted Irishman'.[8]

Much more important, however, were Douglass's expressions of admiration for 'The Liberator', Daniel O'Connell. Within a month of his arrival in Dublin he had seen the elderly O'Connell speak at the Repeal movement's new headquarters, Conciliation Hall. The account Douglass gives Garrison of the occasion focuses on the impact of his oratory:

> It was a great speech, skilfully delivered, powerful in its logic, majestic in its rhetoric, biting in its sarcasm, melting in its pathos, and burning in its rebukes. [. . .] I have heard many speakers within the last four years – speakers of the first order; but I confess, I have never heard one, by whom I was more completely captivated than by Mr. O'Connell. [. . .] It seems to me that the voice of O'Connell is enough to calm the most violent passion, even though it were already manifesting itself in a mob. There is a sweet persuasiveness in it, beyond any voice I ever heard. His power over an audience is perfect.[9]

If one Irishman, O'Connor, gave him his first lessons in public speaking on the printed page, another, O'Connell, followed it with a practical demonstration from the lecture platform. But it is O'Connell's bold stance against slavery that animates most of Douglass's invocations in his subsequent speeches, including the unscheduled short address he gives at the invitation of O'Connell himself later in the proceedings. In Cork, for example, he says: 'I feel grateful to him, for his voice has made American slavery shake to its centre. – I am determined wherever I go, and whatever position I may fill, to speak with grateful emotions of Mr O'Connell's labours.'[10] And indeed he honoured his pledge, continuing to praise the man and invite others to follow his example throughout the rest of his tour – in Newcastle, as we noted in Chapter 5, applauding his commitment to refuse the 'blood-stained offerings' from pro-slavery supporters in the United States, in order to shame the Free Church; in Exeter repeating his conviction that 'O'Connell was the friend of the negro'; and borrowing his image of 'the track of a wounded man through a crowd' in his farewell address in London in March 1847.[11]

Still, despite his immense popularity, O'Connell was a controversial figure. If Douglass was happy to praise his abolitionism, he tends to avoid making public remarks about his stance on Repeal or on Catholic Emancipation. After all, his audiences, especially in Belfast, were largely Protestant and Unionist. Even at Conciliation Hall, he finds it advisable not 'to speak of Repeal as a political question'.[12] His host, Richard Webb, may have advised him to steer clear of the matter in any case: Webb was not a supporter of Repeal, in contrast to his colleague in the Hibernian Anti-Slavery Society, James Haughton. Furthermore, within the Repeal movement, O'Connell was increasingly under fire from a more radical, younger generation ('Young Ireland') who were to break away the following year. Douglass may also have been aware of Chartists' hostility to O'Connell, especially in Scotland, after his denunciation of the Glasgow cotton spinners' strike in 1837. Even as an abolitionist, O'Connell's reputation was not unsullied. Garrison thought that his steadfast support of anti-slavery wavered in the face of the levels of support for repeal among pro-slavery Irish in the United States. As we saw in Chapter 5, it was only under pressure from William Haughton that O'Connell took the stand against the 'blood-stained' donations, and there is little evidence that he afterwards actually returned those he received.[13]

If Douglass held firm to an antislavery O'Connell, well after his departure from Ireland, he must have found his public affiliation with 'The Liberator' awkward, requiring some tact, given that not all those who were warm to his abolitionist message shared Douglass's enthusiasm.

In Cork he paused in a lecture to remark: 'I cannot proceed without alluding to the man who did much to abolish slavery. I mean Daniel O'Connell.'[14] In Ayr, needing a Scottish hero to draw to his side, he, as it were, rewinds and begins again; this time choosing someone less divisive. Using what seems like an almost identical formulation (allowing for the shift from direct to indirect speech of the reporter), he declares that 'he was proud of having been in the land of him who had spoken out so nobly against the oppressions and the wrongs of slavery – he alluded, of course, to Robert Burns'.[15] In both cases the attribution of abolitionist sympathies is extravagant, given that the priorities of both O'Connell and Burns lay elsewhere. But Burns, as well as being conveniently dead, was venerated more universally by his compatriots than O'Connell. Political divisions in Ireland were expressed as for and against O'Connell; in Scotland, by contrast, everyone claimed Burns, they just adapted him to suit their various, often opposed, purposes, as the responses to the 1844 Festival suggest.

We began this Part by referring to Douglass's various surnames: Bailey, Stanley, Johnson, Douglass. But emerging public figures are often compared, not always favourably, with more celebrated individuals, identified by adaptations of *their* names, rather than their own. The actor Mary Webb, for example, was known as the 'coloured Siddons', after the better-known white performer Sarah Siddons.[16] The 'black Swan' was Marjorie Greenfield in a revision of the 'Swedish nightingale', the nickname of soprano Jenny Lind.[17] Douglass was no exception, and we will conclude with some remarks on how he manipulated this convention to his own purposes.

At a public meeting in Glasgow in 1835, O'Connell famously expressed (to great cheers) the hope that one day 'some black O'Connell might rise among his fellow slaves, who would cry, agitate, agitate, agitate'.[18] When invited by O'Connell to address the audience at Conciliation Hall, after Buffum had engineered an introduction, Douglass suggests that his words travelled far and wide:

> He had often heard of the Liberator when he was a slave in a way that was dear to his heart; he had heard of him in the curses of his masters, and thus he was taught to love him (loud cheers). O'Connell was denounced by those in this country who hated Repeal. – The poor trampled slave of Carolina had heard the name of the Liberator with joy and hope, and he himself had heard the wish that some black O'Connell would yet rise up amongst his countrymen, and cry 'Agitate, agitate, agitate.'[19]

Recalling the occasion many years later, Douglass claimed that O'Connell 'playfully' introduced him as 'the "Black O'Connell of the United States"'.[20] Whether this was true or not, Douglass did nothing at the time to dispel the impression that he was the leader O'Connell had wished for.

Douglass, O'Connell and their audience would have known the oft-told story of how, during the revolution in colonial Saint-Domingue, the French general Laveaux claimed that the rebel commander Toussaint Louverture was the 'black Spartacus' predicted by the Enlightenment *philosophe* Abbé Raynal.[21] George Didbin Pitt's play *Toussaint L'Ouverture, or the Black Spartacus* was staged in London June 1846, suggesting the parallel was still compelling, although there is no evidence that Douglass went to see it.[22] In her 'historical romance' *The Hour and the Man* (1839), Harriet Martineau imagines that Toussaint 'heard these words; and in his heart also were they glowing', but no one suggested that he adopted the nickname himself.[23] Another example, equally familiar to contemporaries, was the tragedian Ira Aldridge. The London *Times* had dubbed him, unkindly, 'the African Roscius' (after the Roman actor Quintus Roscius Gallus). But he, in contrast to Toussaint, turned the nickname to his advantage and used it to advertise his shows, and even spun an increasingly elaborate and fictitious biography to suit.[24]

Although Douglass was happy to remind his audience at Conciliation Hall of O'Connell's famous invocation of a hypothetical black counterpart, he did not adopt the designation. To call himself 'the black O'Connell' – however 'playfully' – would have trapped him within the terms of a contemporary whose agenda he must have realised was not always congruent with his own.

Spartacus and Roscius, on the other hand, were classical models, polished by the centuries in a way the contentious Irish leader was not. Douglass had already been compared to Spartacus in a newspaper report of one of his earliest speeches in Massachusetts, the writer reminded of Edwin Forrest's performance in Robert Montgomery Bird's drama *The Gladiator* (1831), premiered in New York in the wake of Nat Turner's slave insurrection in Virginia.[25] The example of Aldridge (who was touring the west of Scotland when Douglass arrived in January 1846) may have alerted him to the possibilities of appropriating for oneself a name bestowed by another.[26]

But Douglass already bore the name of an 'ancient' forebear. He did not have to wait for a theatre critic or a political leader to apply it to him, with kind intentions or not. Nathan Johnson in New Bedford had already encouraged him to embrace the resonant patronymic several years before he took to the public stage. In Scotland, the briefest reference and a metaphorical wink was all Douglass needed to exploit his name before audiences long spell-bound by the 'heroic deeds' it conjured up, absorbing the literary prestige it had accumulated in the work of Burns and Scott and others. No wonder, then, that it is as a 'black Douglas' and not a 'black O'Connell' that he declares his freedom and independence.

Notes

1. J[ohn] D[ick], 'Burns' Anniversary Festival', *North Star*, 2 February 1849. FD's speech is reproduced in FDP 1.2, p. 148 but not the rest of the report, which is briefly summarised in an editorial note.

2. On Dick's work for the *North Star* extending well beyond printing duties see Fagan, 'The *North Star* and the Atlantic 1848', pp. 53–4. According to his obituary in the *Otago Times* (8 April 1895), Dick later worked on the Toronto *Globe* and in 1861 he emigrated to New Zealand. The obituary does not mention Douglass or the *North Star*, misleadingly claiming that Dick 'start[ed] an Anti-Slavery paper at Rochester'. Also closely involved in the running of the *North Star* were the sisters Julia and Eliza Griffiths, who came from England to assist Douglass in 1848. Dick married Eliza in 1850 (*North Star*, 27 June 1850).

3. William Richardson Dempster was also well known as a composer of songs, particularly his setting of Tennyson's 'May Queen', which was in the repertoire of (and indeed made famous by) the Hutchinson Singers when they toured Britain and Ireland in 1845–6. See Ross, *The Scot in America*, p. 346; Hutchinson, *Story of the Hutchinsons*, vol. 1, pp. 174, 186, 208. FD warmly reviewed a public concert by 'this sweet songster' at Rochester's new concert hall the following week in the same issue of the *North Star*, 2 February 1849.

4. William C. Nell to WLG, Rochester, 23 January 1848 (*Liberator*, 11 February 1848).

5. For earlier uses of variations on 'rendered classic' see FD to Francis Jackson, Dundee, 29 January 1846 (FDP 3.1, p. 89); FD to Abigail Mott, Ayr, 23 March 1846 (FDP 3.1, p. 111).

6. N, pp. 83–4 (A, p. 42; FDP 2.1, p. 35).

7. For a detailed discussion of O'Connor's speech and Douglass's response to it see Coughlan, 'Frederick Douglass and Ireland, 1845', pp. 17–71.

8. FD, Dublin, 9 September 1845 (*Freeman's Journal*, 13 September 1845). See also FD, Belfast, 5 December 1845 (FDP 1.1, p. 91). Gough's intervention is described above, in Chapter 1.

9. FD to WLG, Dublin, 29 September 1845 (FDP 3.1, p. 57).

10. FD, Cork, 17 October 1845 (FDP 1.1, p. 44).

11. FD, Newcastle, 7 August 1846 (FDP 1.1, pp. 337–8); FD, Exeter, 25 August 1846 (FDP 1.1, p. 352); FD, London, 30 March 1847 (FDP 1.2, p. 27).

12. FD, Dublin, 29 September 1845 (*Freeman's Journal*, 30 September 1845). In Newcastle, he similarly tempers his praise for O'Connell, warning that 'I am not here to indorse Mr. O'Connell or his agitation': FD, Newcastle, 7 August 1846 (FDP 1.1, p. 337).

13. On Douglass and O'Connell see Riach, 'Daniel O'Connell'; Jenkins, '"The Black O'Connell"'; Quinn, '"Safe in Old Ireland"'; Kinealy, *Daniel O'Connell*, pp. 113–40; Chaffin, *Giant's Causeway*, pp. 54–66; Fenton, *Frederick Douglass in Ireland*, pp. 84–99. On the hostility of Scottish Chartists towards O'Connell see Wilson, *Chartist Movement in Scotland*, p. 141; Fraser, *Chartism in Scotland*, pp. 30, 95, 194.
14. FD, Cork, 17 October 1845 (FDP 1.1, p. 44).
15. FD, Ayr, 24 March 1846 (Ayr *Observer*, 31 March 1846).
16. Merrill, '"Most Fitting Companions"', p. 156.
17. Stoever, *The Sonic Color Line*, p. 112.
18. Daniel O'Connell, Glasgow, 23 September 1835 (*Glasgow Chronicle*, 25 September 1835, repr. *Liberator*,14 November 1835).
19. FD, Dublin 29 September 1845 (*Freeman's Journal*, 30 September 1845, repr. *Liberator*, 31 October 1845).
20. LT2, p. 296 (A, p. 682; FDP 2.3, p. 185). If this was the case, surely the report in the *Freeman's Journal* (which merely states: 'The LIBERATOR introduced to the meeting Mr. Douglas [sic], who had been an American slave') would have mentioned such a striking characterisation?
21. The story was popularised by Rainsford, *An Historical Account of the Black Empire of Hayti*, p. 247; and widely circulated in abolitionist literature, especially in Martineau, *The Hour and the Man*. For a discussion of the 'black Spartacus' motif in the nineteenth century see Daut, *Tropics of Haiti*, pp. 49–62.
22. See Gibbs, *Performing the Temple of Liberty*, pp. 214–66.
23. Martineau, *The Hour and the Man*, vol. 1, p. 191.
24. Lindfors, *Aldridge: The Early Years*, pp. 83–5. The term was already a common one for anyone who showed unusual theatrical talent; on playbills of the era one finds 'an American Roscius, a Scottish Roscius, a Hibernian Roscius, an Equestrian Roscius, a Kentucky Roscius, a Manchester Roscius, and a pair of infant Rosciae', but on this occasion the usage was intended to be ironic (pp. 84–5).
25. 'As this Douglas stood there in manly attitude, with erect form, and glistening eye, and deep-toned voice, telling us that he had been secretly devising means to effect his release from bondage, we could not help thinking of Spartacus, the Gladiator; his whole bearing reminded us of Forrest's noble personation of that daring insurgent' (*Liberator*, 3 December 1841, from the *Hingham Patriot*). On the play and its abolitionist resonances see Gibbs, *Performing the Temple of Liberty*, pp. 185–92. In one English newspaper, he was referred to as a 'Negro Hercules' (*Manchester Examiner*, 11 July 1846). See Murray, 'A "Negro Hercules"'.

26. Aldridge performed in Greenock, Dumbarton, Airdrie and Glasgow during the first two months of 1846 according to the weekly roundups of the provincial theatres in the *Era* (11 January 1846; 1 February 1846; 15 February 1846). The two men never met, on this occasion or any other, as far as I know, and I have found no example of FD making reference to Aldridge before the 1850s.

Part IV

Measuring Heads, Reading Faces

I was not a bad reader of the human face.
Frederick Douglass, My Bondage and My Freedom.

Chapter 17

Breakfast with Combe

It was love at first sight. Frederick Douglass's surviving letters don't often depart from antislavery matters, but barely a day into his first visit to Edinburgh in April 1846, he wrote to his friend Amy Post: 'It is a beautiful city, the most beautiful I ever saw – not so much on account of the buildings as on account of its picturesque position. I have no time even had I the ability to discribe it.'[1] The impression must have been a strong one, for a few weeks later, in London, he reported meeting an artist who confidently asserted that Boston was 'the handsomest city in the world'. Douglass agreed 'that Boston is a very handsome city, but I thought not the most handsomest in the world – and proceeded to speak of Edinburgh', whence he was bound the following day.[2] He was back again in the Scottish capital in July, extolling its virtues in a letter to William White. 'The Calton Hill – Salsbury Craggs and Arthur Seat give the city advantages over any City I have ever visited in this or in your country.'[3] By then, he was beginning to make plans to return to the United States – later postponed, as it turned out, until the following Spring – but not before he had considered bringing Anna and the children over and settling in Britain indefinitely.[4] If he had, it is hard to imagine him choosing to live anywhere but Edinburgh.

Douglass had rushed back to Edinburgh from London to attend the General Assembly of the Free Church on 30 May, after which he made several speeches condemning Cunningham and Candlish for refusing to cut ties with the pro-slavery churches. On Saturday 6 June, Douglass attended a special meeting at the town's Council Chambers to confer the freedom of the city upon George Thompson. The next day, Thompson and Buffum joined him as they took up an invitation to breakfast.

Picture them that Sunday morning stepping out of the York Hotel on Nicolson Street. The month had begun warm and sunny and the settled weather looked set to continue. After several weeks of intense campaigning, the three men must have welcomed the opportunity to relax and enjoy the pleasures of a leisurely stroll. They would have crossed North Bridge, looking down on the new railway station beneath, still under construction, from which passengers would soon be able to travel to Newcastle and London, as well as Glasgow to the west. From the bridge they would have enjoyed a fine view of the hills Douglass so admired, the Castle glued to the summit of its enormous rock, and the pleasure-grounds in the valley below, and, on the other side, the recently completed Scott Monument, towering two hundred feet high above Princes Street.

Princes Street would have led them towards their destination, but a turn right to St Andrew Square would have allowed them to continue their promenade along the road parallel to it: George Street, the broad principal thoroughfare of the late eighteenth-century New Town, offering at each junction glimpses north towards the Firth of Forth and the hills of Fife. The fine stone buildings included St Andrew's Church, out of which Chalmers led the exodus of his Evangelical supporters on that momentous day in 1843, and the Music Hall, with its Doric portico, where Douglass and his friends had addressed enthusiastic meetings the previous week. Beyond Charlotte Square, at its western end, was laid out a newer neighbourhood, largely comprising the private homes of Edinburgh's commercial bourgeoisie.[5]

At 45 Melville Street was the residence of a man whom Douglass later described as an 'eminent mental philosopher', whose best-known work had 'relieved my path of many shadows'. The meeting, he wrote, gratified a 'very intense desire', and turned out to be 'one of the most delightful I met in dear old Scotland'. And he reflected: 'I look back with much satisfaction to the morning spent with this singularly clear-headed man.'[6] A few years after his visit, his friend William Wells Brown – another fugitive slave who sought refuge in Britain – accepted a similar invitation. In a letter he published ('out of its proper place') at the very end of his *Three Years in Europe* (1852), Brown warmly recalled this 'great champion' and remarked that 'few foreigners are more admired in America' than his lively host, approaching seventy, but 'as active and as energetic as many men of half that age'.[7] The subject deemed fit to be given such prominent,

Figure 17.1 George Combe.

if brief, mention in the memoirs of two of the best-known black abolitionists to visit Britain in the three decades before the Civil War is George Combe, the leading British exponent of phrenology, an influential science of mind that claimed to identify mental dispositions and talents on the basis of the examination of heads.

Originally devised as 'craniology' by Franz Joseph Gall in Vienna in the 1790s and popularised by his disciple Johan Gaspar Spurzheim on lecture tours across Europe and North America, it secured its first institutional base in Edinburgh, where Combe established the first Phrenological Society in 1820.[8] The following year he bought Clyde Street Hall to give the society a permanent home and house his personal collection of casts and skulls.[9] Thomas Chalmers was an early enthusiastic visitor, although he would later repudiate the increasingly secular path taken by the phrenologist.[10] Another eminent Scot to make his way to the collection, if not of his own accord, was Robert Burns, a cast of whose skull was made when his vault was opened to allow the burial of his widow beside him in 1834, and passed on to Combe for analysis.[11]

By the mid-1830s there were twenty-four societies in Britain and Ireland, sixteen of them in Scotland.[12] Further afield, phrenology found enthusiastic adherents from St Petersburg to Buenos Aires, but above all in the United States, where, under the leadership of the brothers Lorenzo Niles Fowler and Orson Squire Fowler, it swelled, giving birth to a hugely successful publishing empire and mail-order business.[13] In 1842 Charles Dickens encountered a Scottish phrenologist in Belleville, Illinois, remarking in *American Notes* that a 'Doctor Crocus' advertised lectures, charging 'so much a head'.[14] Such puns became *de rigueur* in any discussion of the science, and detectable perhaps in Douglass's reference to Combe as 'that clear-headed man'.[15]

Through lecture tours, articles in his *Phrenological Journal*, and dozens of books and pamphlets, Combe elaborated the theory that the brain consisted of thirty to forty localisable intellectual and moral organs or faculties (the list was frequently revised) bearing the names of common abstract nouns such as 'destructiveness' and 'self-esteem' or more outlandish monikers such as 'philoprogenitiveness' or 'amativeness'. Their relative sizes were specific to each individual and their unique configuration could be analysed through an informed examination of the shape of the head. Though little read today, his *Constitution of Man* (1828) was one of the most influential works of popular science published in the nineteenth century, more popular than either Robert Chambers's *Vestiges of the Natural History of Creation* (1844) or Charles Darwin's *Origin of Species* (1859), with more than 300,000 copies being sold in over twenty editions by 1860.[16]

That Douglass and Brown sang Combe's praises will puzzle many modern readers, certainly more than Douglass's admiration for Scott and Burns; for phrenology has long been associated with practices of racial classification and ideologies of Anglo-Saxon supremacy. The standard view today is that phrenology was a 'pseudoscience [. . .] determined to prove, from the size and shape of their heads, that black people were innately inferior'.[17] Even in its own time, the scientific pretensions of phrenology came under fire from antislavery campaigners – including the man later to become Douglass's close associate, the medical practitioner James McCune Smith. In an 1837 lecture, delivered on his return to the United States after five years studying medicine at the University of Glasgow, Smith 'demonstrated the false philosophy of the system, and its inconsistency with

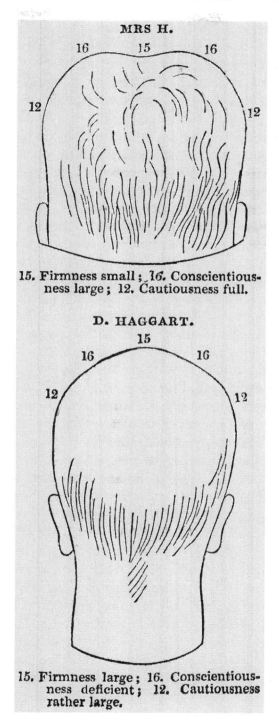

Figure 17.2 Phrenological illustration from *The Constitution of Man*.

the organic and functional laws of the animal economy'.[18] A few years before, the British abolitionist poet James Montgomery challenged phrenological generalisations about 'Hindoos and Negroes' by presenting historical and contemporary examples of Indian and African achievement that conflicted with the apparent craniological evidence.[19]

Combe's work was comfortably embedded in a busy transatlantic network that linked cutting-edge medical research in Edinburgh, London and Paris with what later became known as the 'American School of Ethnology'. In their writings of the 1840s and 1850s, US writers such as Samuel G. Morton, Josiah Nott, George R. Gliddon and Louis Agassiz broke free of religious orthodoxy to lend scientific credibility to the claim that the 'human family' was divided into several distinct, even incompatible, species or types that had remained relatively fixed over the course of recorded history. And while they acknowledged that 'amalgamation' clearly took place, they argued that the resulting hybrid offspring (at least in the case of less 'proximate' races) became increasingly infertile and died out within several generations.[20]

Some of these arguments had been anticipated in *Intermarriage* (1838) by the Edinburgh-trained physiologist Alexander Walker.[21] One of Walker's admirers was Robert Knox, a popular lecturer in anatomy at the private school at 10 Surgeons' Square. Knox, best known today for dissecting bodies supplied by the murderers Burke and Hare, had a long-standing interest in racial classification, based on his observations of 'Hottentots' and 'Bushmen' while on military service in Cape Colony, and later perusing Combe's collection of skulls at Clyde Street Hall.[22] While Douglass was concluding his British tour in 1847, Knox embarked on his own tour of England, starting in Newcastle, delivering lectures that were subsequently published as *Races of Men* (1850), which has been described as 'the first substantively racialist scientific work in Britain'.[23] In 1821–2 Knox had studied in Paris, where he became close friends with the white Jamaican William Frédéric Edwards, whose arguments on the infertility of hybrids in *Des caractères physiologiques des races humaines* (1829) was a formative influence on his subsequent theories of permanent racial types. Edwards's importance was acknowledged by Nott, who also studied in Paris, as did Morton, after taking his medical degree at Edinburgh.[24]

Combe himself made a point of visiting Morton in Philadelphia during the winter of 1838–9, supplying him with skulls he had shipped from Scotland, and contributed a phrenological appendix to his first book, *Crania Americana* (1840), an expensive folio volume, with actual-size lithographs of over seventy carefully measured skulls, which Morton hoped would contribute to the improved classification of 'the varieties of the human species'.[25] Yet when Douglass gave an important speech in 1854 that witheringly exposed the prejudiced assumptions on which the work of 'American Ethnologists' such as Morton were based, he nevertheless singled out Combe as a noteworthy exception.[26]

It is true that Douglass's and Brown's enthusiasms were not unqualified. Douglass refers, somewhat pointedly, to the way Combe 'did the most of the talking' and indeed 'spoke as not expecting opposition to his views'. On the printed page, decades later, Douglass hints that he did not entirely share these views, referring to Combe's 'peculiar mental science' and the way it 'explained everything to him'.[27] And if Douglass waited until 1881 to do so (choosing not to include the episode in his second autobiography of 1855), Brown repositions the Combe meeting in the revised (US) edition of his travel narrative five chapters from the end, reducing its symbolic importance.[28] But still, the fact that they seem to overlook the well-rehearsed arguments against phrenology and do not more emphatically distance themselves from its chief exponent requires some explanation.

Notes

1. FD to Amy Post, Edinburgh, 28 April 1846 (FDP 3.1, p. 122). FD had arrived in Edinburgh and checked into the York Hotel on Nicolson Street the previous evening (*Manstealers*, p. 45).
2. FD to WLG, London, 23 May 1846 (FDP 3.1, p. 132)
3. FD to William White, Edinburgh, 30 July 1846 (FDP 3.1, p. 149).
4. See FD to WLG, Glasgow, 16 April 1846 (FDP 3.1, p. 108); FD to WLG, London, 23 May 1846 (FDP 3.1, p. 131); FD to Ruth Cox, Belfast, 17 July 1846 (FDP 3.1, p. 144).
5. For this recreation of FD's walk across Edinburgh, I have drawn on *Black's Economical Guide through Edinburgh*; *The Land We Live In*, vol. 2, pp. 75–107; Willox, *Guide to the Edinburgh and Glasgow Railway*, pp. 18–24; 'The Weather and Crops', *Witness*, 24 June 1846.

6. LT2, pp. 299–300 (A, pp. 685–6, FDP 2.3, pp. 187–8). Recalling events some thirty-five years later (the account is the same in LT1, published in 1881), FD's memory is unreliable: he claims he visited Combe in the company of GT, JB and WLG, but WLG did not arrive in Britain until 31 July. For Combe's address see *Post-Office Edinburgh and Leith Directory*, p. 246. The Combes had taken possession of the house in 1844: see Kaufman, *Edinburgh Phrenological Society*, p. 106. For Combe's own brief account of the meeting with FD (and the date) see George Combe to WLG, Edinburgh, 7 June 1846 (*Liberator*, 31 July 1846).

7. Brown, *Three Years in Europe*, p. 311.

8. For useful background on Combe and phrenology see Cooter, *The Cultural Meaning of Popular Science*; Van Wyhe, *Phrenology*; Stack, *Queen Victoria's Skull*; Tomlinson, *Head Masters*, esp. pp. 97–182.

9. On Clyde Street Hall see Stack, *Queen Victoria's Skull*, pp. 50–2. The museum closed in 1831 and the collection did not find a new home until 1849, when it was moved 'into a large back room at the back of what had formerly been John Lizars' Anatomy classroom in Number 1 Surgeons' Square'. In 1878 it moved again, to 25 Chambers Street. See Kaufman, *Medical Teaching in Edinburgh*, pp. 166–9.

10. On Chalmers's visit to the museum see Gibbon, *The Life of George Combe*, vol. 1, p. 135. Combe later noted, with some bitterness, that Chalmers made no reference to phrenology in his *Bridgewater Treatise* (1833) despite its claim to address (as its title had it) 'The Adaptation of External Nature to the Moral and Intellectual Condition of Man', even if he took some comfort in the fact that Chalmers did not directly criticise his science. See Combe, *The Constitution of Man*, 8th edn, p. 17. See also Cooter, *Cultural Meaning*, pp. 128–9; Stack, *Victoria's Skull*, p. 58.

11. George Combe, 'Observations on the Skull of Robert Burns'; see also Cox, 'Observations on Combativeness'.

12. Watson, *Statistics of Phrenology*, p. 118.

13. On phrenology in the United States see Stern, *Heads and Headlines*; and Falkoff, 'Heads and Tales'.

14. Dickens, *American Notes*, p. 223.

15. Puns slip easily into the titles of modern books on phrenology: Stern's *Heads and Headlines*; Falkoff's 'Heads and Tales'; Tomlinson's *Head Masters*.

16. Cooter, *The Cultural Meaning of Popular Science*, p. 120.

17. Henry Louis Gates, Jr, 'Foreword' to Smith, *Works*, p. xi.

18. From a report in the *Commercial Advertiser* of a lecture delivered by Smith in New York, repr. *Colored American*, 30 September 1837. Combe himself refers to Smith (whom he believes studied medicine at

Edinburgh University) and (a different?) 'attack on phrenology' in the *Colored American* of 30 March 1839: see Combe, *Notes on the United States*, vol. 1, p. 329.

19. Montgomery, *An Essay on the Phrenology of the Hindoos and Negroes*, pp. 9–31.

20. For a useful overview see Young, *Colonial Desire*, p. 18. On the 'American school' in particular see Dain, *A Hideous Monster of the Mind*; Horsman, *Josiah Nott of Mobile*; Fabian, *The Skull Collectors*; Fredrickson, *The Black Image in the White Mind*; Stanton, *The Leopard's Spots*.

21. Walker, *Intermarriage*.

22. The best biography of Knox is Bates, *The Anatomy of Robert Knox*. On his admiration for Walker see p. 148. On his military service in the Cape see pp. 32–41. On his 'careful examination of the very excellent collection of crania at present in the rooms of the [Edinburgh] Phrenological Society' see Knox, 'Lectures on Physiological Anatomy', p. 55.

23. Young, *Colonial Desire*, p. 119. On Knox's racial thought see Bates, *Anatomy*, which tends to follow scholars such as M. D. Biddis and Evelleen Richards by pointing out that he was not as racist as James Hunt and the Anthropological Society (who appropriated his arguments in the 1860s) and in fact was opposed to slavery and imperialism and did not believe one race was superior to another. Still, they acknowledge that he did claim that 'race was everything', that races were different species which were intrinsically antagonistic to each other and could never successfully interbreed. See Biddiss, 'The Politics of Anatomy'; Richards 'The "Moral Anatomy" of Robert Knox'; and Callanan, *Deciphering Race*, pp. 44–75. For the broader mid-Victorian context of Knox's views see Lorimer, *Colour, Class and the Victorians*, pp. 131–61; Stocking, *Victorian Anthropology*, pp. 46–77.

24. Young, *Colonial Desire*, pp. 13–18, 122–3. Histories that chart the emergence of racial science during this period tend to underplay the extent of transatlantic connections; Young's work is a refreshing exception, but see also Rusert, *Fugitive Science*, pp. 11–15. On Knox's debt to Edwards see Knox, *The Races of Men*, pp. 148, 181, 277, 504. For more background on Edwards see Blanckaert, 'On the Origins of French ethnology'. On Nott's training in Paris see Horsman, *Josiah Nott of Mobile*, pp. 43–5. Edwards's influence is acknowledged in Nott and Gliddon, *Types of Mankind*, p. 89. And on Morton's medical training in Europe see Fabian, *Skull Collectors*, pp. 21–3.

25. Morton, *Crania Americana*. Combe's appendix is at pp. 269–91; references to Combe donating skulls and casts are at pp. 201, 247, 262. Combe refers to collecting from the Custom House in Boston 'five large packages of skulls, casts, and drawings, which I had shipped

from the Clyde' (*Notes on the United States*, vol. 1, p. 47) and records his meetings with Morton (see *Notes on the United States*, vol. 1, pp. 86–7, 307–8, vol. 2, pp. 4–15). See also Fabian, *Skull Collectors*, esp. pp. 94–103.

26. FD, Hudson, Ohio, 12 July 1843 ('The Claims of the Negro Ethnologically Considered') (FDP 1.2, p. 510).
27. LT2, pp. 299–300 (A, pp. 685–6, FDP 2.3, pp. 187–8).
28. Brown, *The American Fugitive in Europe*, pp. 266–7.

Chapter 18

The Physiological Century

To understand Douglass's and Brown's attitude to phrenology, we need to recognise that phrenology contained a number of contradictions. Its tendency to attribute fixed characters to nations and races co-existed with an approach which stressed that human capacities and propensities were shaped by the environment. Furthermore, its detailed individual 'readings' rarely supported the generalisations it was often tempted to make, and Combe himself saw no conflict between his scientific claims and his commitment to a wide range of social reform causes, including abolitionism.[1]

But it was not just the flexibility of its theory or clinical practice that stopped Douglass and Brown rejecting this 'peculiar mental science' outright. Phrenology was far more embedded in their world than we often realise. Indeed, it has been called the psychoanalysis of the nineteenth century, as influential as Freud's theories were in the twentieth.[2] The parallels are quite extensive. Like psychoanalysis, phrenology was initially developed in Vienna by a single individual, but within fifty years had become widely practised in Western Europe and North America. In both cases, they acquired status as a theory or body of knowledge, promulgated by means of lectures and specialist journals and as an effective specialist technique, deployed in private consultations with trained practitioners. But their cultural significance lies in the way they provided a widely adopted idiom used to assess the personality, intelligence and moral worth of strangers and acquaintances. Just as today we easily speak of people 'projecting' or 'overcompensating' or of having a 'complex' of one sort or another, without necessarily subscribing to the metapsychological theories from which such terms derive, so our nineteenth-century counterparts talked of their 'organ of reference' or 'large self-esteem' without always accepting the craniological hypotheses that they apparently presuppose. Furthermore, phrases of phrenological origin, such as 'need your head examined' and 'low-brow'/'high-brow' survive in contemporary speech.[3]

If the medium of psychoanalytical interpretation is listening, then that of phrenology was looking; instead of the talking cure, its method was the examination of heads. As such it was closely associated with physiognomy – the scrutiny of faces. Physiognomy has a much longer history than phrenology, although it remained of merely specialist interest until it was popularised by Johann Kaspar Lavater in his *Physiognomische Fragmente* (1775–8), which was translated into many languages. It shared with phrenology the assumption that outward appearances could – if skilfully interpreted by someone with sufficient knowledge of anatomy – disclose aspects of a person's character that were not otherwise immediately evident. Indeed, the distinction between phrenology and physiognomy was not clear-cut and the two were – and still are – routinely confused, the names of Lavater and Gall frequently conjoined.[4]

We might situate phrenology and physiognomy in a broader culture that might be called – to borrow a more supple term that was current at the time – 'physiological': a culture which lent credibility to the practice of determining character by means of an informed analysis of outward manifestations that included the shape of the head, facial expression, clothing, gait and demeanour. Periodicals and cheap paperbacks offering 'physiologies' of occupational types, from pickpockets to bankers, were enormously popular in Europe during the 1840s and 50s. Their scope extended to include personified sketches of particular city neighbourhoods or social institutions, such as Balzac's *Physiologie du mariage* (1829) or Albert Smith's *The Physiology of Evening Parties* (1846), their essential nature revealed – like those of individuals – through their appearance and associated behaviour.[5] By the same token, it expanded the range of techniques novelists, artists and actors used to *convey* character, techniques which could of course be used by individuals in their daily interactions, to conceal their weaknesses or emphasise their strengths, or indeed to mislead others with malicious intent.[6]

The appeal of phrenology may indeed be rooted, as one author puts it, in the 'perennial human need' to find 'some simplified means of organizing our perceptions of our fellows'.[7] But there are more historically and culturally specific explanations why it took off where and when it did. The same author suggests – as do several other scholars, if only in passing – that phrenology and physiognomy became so important in the nineteenth century because of new challenges thrown up by accelerating industrialisation and urbanisation.[8] When increasing numbers of people leave behind small rural communities where everyone is known to each other for city streets where most encounters are between strangers, the need for a reliable – or at least reassuring – way of determining whether one can trust another is obvious.

While the membership of phrenological societies tended be dominated by professional middle-class men, mainly interested in the philosophical implications of the new science, its practical application appealed to a much broader constituency.[9] Phrenology – especially in the United States – became big business, selling expert advice on hiring prospective employees, choosing a marriage partner, raising children, deciding on a career, and identifying deviants such as criminals or the insane.[10] In Glasgow David George Goyder supplemented his income as a Swedenborgian minister by lecturing on phrenology. By his own account he was 'inundated with visitors' to the Society's museum at 104 Brunswick Street, 'eager to test phrenology by an examination of their own cranium' and 'in the space of two years I could not have measured less than a thousand heads'.[11] Of the surviving record he kept of several hundred Glaswegians who came to him for consultations, most of them were young manual workers, or servants sent by prospective employers to obtain a character reference.[12] Combe himself read his fiancée's head on the day he proposed; and later, when married, he took over Cecilia's responsibility for appointing domestic servants, with results – it must be said – that suggested his judgement was not always as sharp as he liked to think.[13]

Of all those facing the anxieties of the modern city, none felt them more acutely than the fugitive slave – for whom a betrayal of trust could entail not just a loss of dignity or belongings, but of freedom itself. Douglass evokes this situation brilliantly as he describes the situation in which he found himself on arriving in New York, a few days after his escape from slavery in Maryland:

A sense of my loneliness and helplessness crept over me, and covered me with something bordering on despair. In the midst of thousands of my fellow-men, and yet a perfect stranger! In the midst of human brothers, and yet more fearful of them than of hungry wolves! I was without home, without friends, without work, without money, and without any definite knowledge of which way to go, or where to look for succor.[14]

He is befriended by a fellow fugitive, Jake, whom he knew from Baltimore, who warns him of the very real danger of being recaptured and returned to slavery. Not even 'the black people in New York were [. . .] to be trusted' for 'there were hired men on the lookout for fugitives from slavery, and who, for a few dollars would betray me into the hands of the slave-catchers.' Jake advises him to 'trust no man with [his] secret,' and, fearing Douglass himself may be a threat or at least a liability, quickly disappears.[15]

But Douglass needs the assistance of others; eventually he is 'forced to go in search of an honest man'. How does he identify such a man? 'I was not a bad reader of the human face,' he says, and fortunately finds a sailor, Stewart, who makes the connections that allow him to make his onward journey to New Bedford.[16]

Douglass's conviction that he was able to assess character on the basis of physical appearance was no doubt pressed on him by the extreme circumstances in which he was placed. But his belief was shared by many of his contemporaries, as the frequent deployment of phrenological and physiognomical terminology and assumptions in nineteenth-century literature would suggest.

Certainly, several eminent authors (including George Eliot, Charlotte Brontë, Lydia Maria Child and Walt Whitman) went for phrenological readings themselves.[17] And it has been argued that even where the terminology is absent, these emerging sciences or techniques left their mark on the developing complexity of characterisation in the novel. Changes in physical appearance and the ways in which characters observe each other and share their observations became increasingly significant, even in the work of authors who otherwise had little time for phrenology or physiognomy.[18]

Their influence on those avowedly sceptical or hostile is evident in the arguments of antislavery campaigners too. A critical abolitionist reviewer of Combe's lectures in New York, for instance, baldly states that they offered 'nothing [. . .] which led us to change any of our views regarding the fallacies of Phrenology' but goes on to describe his physical appearance, referring to 'a head of singular symmetry' that might easily be taken as an explanation of the 'far-famed logical acumen' the author admits admiring.[19] Lydia Maria Child owed her inability to identify some eminent individuals to the fact that her 'organ of reverence, though pretty largely developed, never occupies itself with great names', while William Lloyd Garrison confessed that '[p]hrenologically speaking, my caution is large, and my combativeness not very active.'[20] Even slave narratives adopted the same language on occasion, with Solomon Northup noting that the 'African race is a music-loving one, proverbially; and many there were among my fellow-bondsmen whose organs of tune were strikingly developed,' and Sojourner Truth referring to another slave as having 'not then sufficiently cultivated her organ of time to calculate years, or even weeks or hours'.[21]

Douglass's associate Martin Delany wrote appreciatively of Simon Foreman Laundrey, a fourteen-year-old boy he encountered in Troy, Ohio, whom he described as 'a natural Phrenologist, who examines heads, reads out the organs, and delivers lectures on the science', and was hoping to publish a work to be entitled *Geography of the Brain*. Delany allowed himself to be examined, and the boy 'passed his little hands over the organs, reading them with as much facility as Fowler or Melrose', Melrose being the real name of the 'Doctor Crocus' Dickens had poked fun at in *American Notes*.[22]

Even James McCune Smith, who was highly critical of the scientific pretensions of phrenology, nevertheless absorbed the broader 'physiological' assumptions of the day. Between 1852 and 1854 he published a series of sketches in *Frederick Douglass' Paper* under the title 'Heads of the Colored People', a (presumably deliberate) echo of *Heads of the People; or, Portraits of the English* (1840), which went through several editions over the next four decades. Smith's series was not accompanied by illustrations, but the textual portraits adopted the same format. They were intended, in part, as parodies of phrenological descriptions, but if they challenged racially prejudiced conclusions, his portraits of a black news-vendor, a boot-black, a washerwoman, a sexton, a steward, an editor, an inventor, a white-washer and a schoolmaster nevertheless presuppose that character can be read from appearance.[23]

Notes

1. See Hamilton, '"Am I Not a Man and a Brother"'.
2. Falkoff, 'Heads and Tales', pp. 1–2. For other comparisons between phrenology and psychoanalysis see Dallenbach, 'Phrenology versus Psychoanalysis'; and Stern, *Heads and Headlines*, pp. x, xii.
3. On the former see Partridge, *A Dictionary of Catch Phrases*, p. 563. On the latter see Levine, *Highbrow/Lowbrow*, pp. 221–2.

4. The ease with which the two co-existed is evident from the following titles: Chaussier, *Nouveau manuel du physionomiste et du phrénologiste*; and Ysabeau, *Lavater et Gall: Physiognomie et phrénologie rendues intelligibles pour tout le monde*. Godwin's 'On Phrenology' was reprinted as 'On the Systems of Lavater and Gall'. That phrenology and physiognomy were inextricably linked is stressed in Heier, *Literary Portraiture*, 8–9.

5. See Wechsler, *A Human Comedy*, pp. 31–4; Benjamin, 'The Paris of the Second Empire in Baudelaire', pp. 67–70; Heier, *Literary Portraiture*, pp. 113–25; Cowling, *The Artist as Anthropologist*, p. 208 n.). In 1855 the waxwork exhibit at Madame Tussaud's was renamed the Chamber of Comparative Physiology: see Pearl, *About Faces*, p. 38.

6. See House, 'Toward a "Modern" Lavater?'; Tytler, *Physiognomy in the European Novel*; Colbert, *A Measure of Perfection*; Cowling, *Artist as Anthropologist*; Heier, *Literary Portraiture*; Wechsler, *Human Comedy*. Combe himself wrote a book on *Phrenology Applied to Painting and Sculpture* in which he lavished his highest praise on the work of Raphael and the famous actor Sarah Siddons (who happened to be his mother-in-law).

7. Cowling, *Artist as Anthropologist*, p. 31.

8. See Cowling, *Artist as Anthropologist*, p. 120; Cooter, *Cultural Meaning*, p. 176; Pearl, *About Faces*, pp. 26–32; Burbick, *Healing the Republic*, pp. 141–3. For the wider nineteenth-century context see Sennett, *The Fall of Public Man*, pp. 123–255, which makes no reference to phrenology or physiognomy, although Sennett does in his foreword to Wechsler, *Human Comedy*, pp. 7–8.

9. See Parssinen, 'Popular Science and Society', pp. 1, 8.

10. See Stern, *Heads and Headlines*, pp. 37–48.

11. Goyder, *My Battle for Life*, pp. 293. For the address of the museum see *The Post-Office Glasgow Annual Directory*, p. 103.

12. Cooter, *Popular Science*, p. 176.

13. Stack, *Queen Victoria's Skull*, pp. 112, 120.

14. BF, pp. 338–9 (A, p. 351; FDP 2.2, p. 195).

15. BF, p. 338 (A, p. 351; FDP 2.2, p. 194).

16. BF, pp. 340–1 (A, p. 352; FDP 2.2, p. 196).

17. For George Eliot (consultation with James DeVille, 1844) see Ashton, *George Eliot*, p. 3 and Postlethwaite, 'George Eliot and Science', pp. 104–5. For Charlotte Brontë (consultation with J. P. Browne, 1851) see Kronshage, *Vision and Character*, Chapter 2. For Lydia Maria Child (consultation with Lorenzo Fowler, 1841) see Karcher, *The First Woman in the Republic*, p. 295; and for Walt Whitman (consultation with Lorenzo Fowler, 1849) see Stern, *Heads & Headlines*, pp. 101–5.

18. See Tytler, *Physiognomy*, esp. pp. 166–315.

19. 'Mr George Combe's Lectures', *Colored American*, 18 May 1839.

20. Lydia Maria Child, 'Lewis Clark[e]: Leaves from a Slave's Journal of Life', *Anti-Slavery Standard*, 20 October 1842; WLG to HCW, Bristol, 26 August 1846 (BAA, p. 280).

21. Solomon Northup, *Twelve Years a Slave* [1853] in Taylor, *I Was Born a Slave*, vol. 2, p. 258; Truth, *The Narrative of Sojourner Truth*, pp. 19–20.

22. Martin R. Delany to FD, Milton, OH, 18 June 1848 (*North Star*, 7 July 1848; repr. in Delany, *A Documentary Reader*, pp. 101–2. Laundrey is discussed in relation to other black phrenologists in Rusert, *Fugitive Science*, pp. 121–6. For the identification of Melrose see Dickens, *American Notes*, p. 353 n. 3.

23. James McCune Smith, 'Heads of the Colored People' [1852–4], in Smith, *Works*, pp. 187–241. For the editor's claim that the series 'parodies the language of phrenology', see p. 188. *Heads of the People* featured illustrations by Kenny Meadows accompanied by texts describing 'The Dress-Maker', 'The Omnibus Conductor', 'The Chimney-Sweep', 'The Post-Man' and so on (the chapter headings are similar to Smith's) by Douglas Jerrold, William Thackeray and others. Smith is in more decidedly satirical mode in an earlier article in which he uses explicitly phrenological and physiognomical language to support his claim that the fêted Hungarian nationalist Louis Kossuth was in fact a 'Mongol' rather than a 'Caucasian'. See Smith, 'Outside Barbarians' [1851], in Smith, pp. 81–2. He also draws on phrenological terminology in 'Chess' [1859], in Smith, *Works*, p. 287.

Chapter 19

Travelling Phrenologically

In order to give us a better understanding of phrenological readings and the contexts in which they took place, let us consider some of the verbal portraits which abound – predictably enough – in George Combe's account of his tour of the north-eastern United States between 1838 and 1840. We will then compare them to the ways in which Douglass and William Wells Brown, travelling in the opposite direction, described the people they met in Britain and Ireland. Attending to the methods of characterisation used by these three writers reveals not only how Douglass and Brown both challenged phrenological conventions, but that they did so very differently.

A mixture of business and pleasure, Combe's 'phrenological visit' (as he titled it) involved giving numerous lectures, inspecting a large number of disciplinary institutions such as asylums, prisons and schools, and enjoying more recreational excursions, at which points Combe's narrative often defers to that of his wife Cecilia, whose journal he quotes frequently.

Here, for example, is Dr Samuel B. Woodward, the superintendent of the state lunatic asylum at Worcester, Massachusetts:

> He is in the prime of life, and has large limbs, a large abdomen, large lungs, and a large head. His temperament is sanguine-bilious, with a little of the lymphatic. The organs of the propensities are well-developed, but those of the moral sentiments and intellect decidedly predominate.[1]

Silas Jones, who runs the Asylum for the Blind in New York, 'has a large head, ample anterior lobe, large Benevolence, and Love of Approbation'.[2] Of the reformer Dr W. E. Channing, he writes: 'The anterior lobe of his brain is well developed, the lower region predominating; Ideality is prominently conspicuous, and the organs of all the moral sentiments are large.'[3]

What is noteworthy about his narrative is the way it reveals how diverse is Combe's notion of physical appearance. Although his readings give priority to the shape and size of (different parts of) the head, they also frequently take account of tone of voice, facial expressions, posture, gait, gesture, voice and clothing.[4] Of his assessment of Aaron Burr, whom he first describes on the basis of his death mask, he finds confirmation of the former Vice-President's secretive character in a remark in the *New York Mirror*: 'He glided rather than walked; his foot had that quiet, stealthy movement which involuntarily makes one think of treachery.'[5] Attending a Unitarian meeting with Edward Everett, the Governor of Massachusetts, Combe finds it significant that his companion 'had no insignia of office' and indeed, 'the audience, although composed of persons in every variety of pecuniary circumstances, appeared, to the eye of a stranger, nearly all equal; they were well dressed, and none ostentatiously attired'.[6] These observations are not incidental to his phrenological concerns but in line with his theory that each faculty had a 'natural language' of bodily expression associated with it as well as a measurable location on the cranium.[7]

Combe distinguishes his own approach from that of the 'practical phrenologists', who charge a fee for their ill-informed and superficial readings of customers' heads. His method is not just more scientific, involving the careful measurement and close examination of skulls, but also more sensitive to the feelings of the individuals he subjected to analysis.[8] For instance, Combe, on principle, 'declined giving opinions about the heads of living men, unless they had permitted authentic casts or busts of themselves to be published'.[9] In the course of describing the appearance of senior public figures he meets in Washington (including president Martin Van Buren, and senators John C. Calhoun, Henry Clay and Daniel Webster), he reminds us that their 'busts and portraits [. . .] abound in the United States', thus excusing him 'of any indelicacy'.[10] He once admitted to scrutinising the head of Queen Victoria in person, but it was not likely she was aware of it, as he was observing her through a pair of opera glasses in a London theatre at the time.[11]

Combe's sense of propriety, however, was highly variable, according to a person's social standing. The descriptions of less eminent men such as Dr Woodward and Mr Jones were probably based on face-to-face encounters alone, and the observations of those who were confined in the kind of institutions they ran certainly so. Combe does not express any reservations when offering phrenological characterisations of unnamed individuals and groups, either in this account of his visit to the Eastern Penitentiary in Philadelphia:

> The convicts whom I saw in this prison presented the usual deficiencies in the organs of the moral sentiments in relation to those of the animal propensities which distinguish criminals in general. One man, in whom the superior organs were very deficient, and Acquisitiveness, Secretiveness, and Destructiveness very large, with a good intellectual development, said, in answer to a question from me, that it would depend on circumstances whether he would steal again after he was liberated.[12]

Or in this report on a Shaker settlement between Troy and Schenectady:

> About half a dozen of the men whom we saw were past the middle period of life: they had large, round, portly figures, with regularly-formed and well-developed brains, and the external aspect of good sense. They were obviously the leaders. The rest presented heads such as one generally sees in Lunatic Asylums [. . .] The heads of the women were covered by their caps; but the general size and outline could be seen through the thin muslin. The great majority of them had well-developed foreheads; but in some the head was small.[13]

His portraits of black people clearly show him guilty of the 'indelicacy' he professes to avoid. Firstly, the 'colored man' who manages the apartments he stays in in Philadelphia:

> Our apartments [. . .] are under the charge of a colored man, who, although a complete negro, has a brain that would do no discredit to a European. It is of a full size; the moral and intellectual regions are well developed; and his manner of thinking, speaking, and acting, indicates respectfulness, faithfulness, and reflection.[14]

And secondly, Cinqué, the leader of the recent slave mutiny on the *Amistad*, whom Combe visits in prison in Hartford, Connecticut:

> They are genuine Africans, and little more than three months have elapsed since they left their native shores. Their heads present great varieties of form as well as of size. Several have small heads, even

for Africans; some short and broad heads, with high foreheads, but with very little longitudinal extent in the anterior lobe. Their leader Cinquez or Jinquez, who killed the captain of the schooner, is a well-made man of 24 or 25 years of age. His head is long from the front to the back, and rises high above the ear, particularly in the regions of Self-Esteem, and Firmness. The breadth is moderate and Destructiveness is large, but not excessive. Benevolence and Veneration are well marked, and rise above the lateral organs; but the coronal region is altogether narrow. The anterior lobe is also narrow; but it is long from front to back. The middle perpendicular portion, including Comparison and Eventuality, is decidedly large. Individuality is full. The temperament seems to be nervous-bilious. This size and form of brain indicate considerable mental power, decision, self-reliance, prompt perception, and readiness of action.[15]

Combe's readings of individuals sometimes slip into generalisations about the groups to which he assigns them. His narrative is not short of phrenological remarks on national character or the differences between the sexes.[16] But the temptation is perhaps strongest when he encounters people of other 'races'. The descriptions here rely on assumptions of what a 'complete Negro' or a 'genuine African' could be expected to be like, even while going on to sketch a unique individual configuration that in some ways might challenge these expectations. Elsewhere, crude typologies of 'African and native American Indian races' are presented without qualification.[17]

It is true that Combe's underlying position appears to be an environmentalist one. What appear to be innate characteristics are actually the product of circumstance rather than a fixed essence. That the brains of slaves appear to be smaller on average than those of freemen and women he explains with reference to the latter's greater opportunities – and competitive pressures – to exercise their mental faculties.[18] Furthermore, the descriptions take place in a narrative that frequently signals Combe's firm abolitionist convictions and his objections to segregation in the North.[19]

However, any attempt to rescue Combe from the racial theories that he undoubtedly helped to promulgate may detract from a more fundamental weakness: his failure to fully recognise the implications of the different social contexts in which his phrenological readings took place. Whom he chose to phrenologise, and how, involved choices he did not scrutinise as closely as he did foreheads. While everyone seemed to come indiscriminately under his analytical gaze, there are big differences between examining a portrait or a bust and the discreet observation of a fellow professional, between the gentle perusal of a client who requests a personal reading and the blunt, uninvited inspection of a stranger judged to be socially inferior.

If for Combe travelling phrenologically involves crossing the Atlantic to examine 'Negro' heads in the United States, then perhaps instructive comparisons can be made with the accounts of black abolitionists familiar with its idioms when they describe their encounters in Europe. Given Douglass's and Brown's acquaintance with Combe and phrenology, they are obvious authors to examine in this context. If we read the accounts of their own travels in Britain in the 1840s and 50s in conjunction with Combe's *Notes*, we are immediately alerted to significant differences not only between their narratives and Combe's, but between each other's. They illustrate two contrasting ways of challenging the physiological culture that tended to objectify them.

Brown's travel narratives – *Three Years in Europe* (1852) and *The American Fugitive in Europe* (1855) – frequently betray phrenological preoccupations, if somewhat narrow in range. Take these opening remarks on Dr Pusey, the Anglican theologian, whom he meets in Oxford:

> His profile is more striking than his front face, the nose being very large and prominent. As a matter of course, I expected to see a large nose, for all great men have them. He has a thoughtful, and somewhat sullen brow, a firm and somewhat pensive mouth, a cheek pale, thin, and deeply furrowed.[20]

His more didactic 'chapter on American slavery' includes thumbnail sketches of leading reformers which fix on those features that were of special significance to Combe and others.[21] Thus, of Garrison he writes: 'He has a high and prominent forehead, well developed, with no hair on the top of the head, having lost it in early life; with a piercing eye,' and of Elihu Burritt: 'His stature is of the middle size, head well developed, with eyes deeply set.' Douglass himself is not excluded, his 'vast and well-developed forehead announc[ing] the power of his intellect'.[22]

These descriptions, like Combe's, are intended to do more than help the reader imagine what the person looks like; they are meant to convey something of their moral and intellectual character. But unlike Combe, Brown shows no compunction in expressing opinions based on the observation of living individuals, perhaps especially eminent ones. Indeed, he often represents himself as their equal, or even on occasion, somewhat playfully, as their superior.

Consider his description of Queen Victoria, coming ashore in Ireland, which appealingly demystifies her as 'a lady rather small in stature, with auburn or reddish hair, attired in a plain dress, and wearing a sky-blue bonnet, standing on the larboard paddle-box, by the side of a tall good-looking man with mustaches'.[23] The next day, joining the throngs lining the streets in Dublin, he remarks: 'My own colour differing from those about me, I attracted not a little attention from many; and often, when gazing down the street to see if the Royal procession was in sight, would find myself eyed by all around,' as if he and the Queen were equally compelling objects of interest.[24]

Brown reverses the usual phrenological scenario – where he would normally have been the anonymous object of the scientific gaze – by turning that gaze back at the kind of people who might have phrenologised him. While Combe – in his travel narrative at least – seems most comfortable when composing detailed portraits of the powerless, Brown tends to specialise in major public figures. In fact, when he does dwell on 'ordinary' people – even when they become significant minor characters with a rich back story, such as the enterprising African-born crossing-sweeper, preacher, band-leader and Shakespearean actor 'Joseph Jenkins' ('the greatest genius I had met in Europe') – he does not disclose their facial appearance at all.[25]

Douglass did not compose a travel narrative as Brown did. But he included a chapter on his 'Twenty-One Months in Great Britain' in *My Bondage and My Freedom*, a chapter he suggested he could easily have expanded into a book, and admits a similar temptation when including a revised version in *Life and Times*.[26] However, what strikes the reader, coming to them after *Three Years in Europe* or *American Fugitive*, is that Douglass does not provide physical descriptions of people at all. Furthermore, they rarely appear in the reports of speeches he made during his tour, or in the letters he sent home, many of which were published in the abolitionist press.

This is especially surprising, perhaps, since the accounts of his experiences in Britain are full of incident, recording dramatic encounters with other individuals, such as the confrontations with the pro-slavery mob on the *Cambria*, the debates with leaders of the Free Church of Scotland, and what Douglass called the 'point blank collision' with Rev. Dr Samuel Hanson Cox at the World's Temperance Convention.[27] The interpretability of physical appearances is not entirely absent from his work, as the evocation of New York City quoted earlier shows. Nevertheless, when Douglass portrays real people – whether friend or foe – it is their words and deeds which make up the portrait, not what they look like.[28]

When Brown describes the Members of Parliament from the public gallery at Westminster, his emphasis is on appearance:

> There, in the centre of the room, shines the fine, open, glossy brow and speaking face of Alexander Hastie, a Glasgow merchant, a mild and amiable man, of modest deportment, liberal principles, and religious profession. [. . .] On the right of the hall, from where we sit, you see that small man, with fair complexion, brown hair, gray eyes, and a most intellectual countenance. It is Layard.[29]

And he continues for several pages in the same vein, hardly pausing before going on to describe those near him in the gallery. When Douglass reports on his visit to the same place, he simply lists the names of some of the 'distinguished members' present and describes the mode of proceeding: 'I was much pleased with the respectful manner with which members spoke of each other,' pointedly contrasting it to the Congress in Washington which would, of course, have never allowed him in the building at all.[30]

Both Brown and Douglass had good reasons to distrust approaches such as physiognomy and phrenology, judging by the frequency with which they recorded the routine discrimination they faced in the United States on the basis of their appearance. Their ability to enjoy public facilities such as hotels or railroad cars is always determined by individuals who are authorised to refuse admittance or assign them a place after the (sometimes close) scrutiny of their head and face. No doubt their experiences in Europe – where, as neither of them tired of pointing out, racial discrimination was largely absent – granted them a welcome reprieve from such scrutiny. Nevertheless, they would still have been particular objects of curious attention. Douglass may have winced when he read in the *Liberator* Combe's description of him in his account of their Edinburgh meeting: 'He has an excellent brain. His benevolence and veneration are both large, and his conscientiousness is full, while his intellect is vigorous and practical, and his propensities all of subordinate dimensions.'[31] But

Combe would not have been the only Scot to feel free to look at him this way.

Accustomed to being the object of a demeaning gaze, Brown and Douglass respond to it in contrasting ways. Brown – at least in the relative safety of the written page – looks back, and phrenologises his spectators with the same lack of sensitivity they have shown him. Perhaps he hoped it would demonstrate to them its intrusive and reductive character. Douglass, on the other hand, avoids phrenological descriptions almost entirely. No one, he seems to suggest, should assess a person's character unless it is on the basis of a scrupulous attention to their words and deeds.

Notes

1. Combe, *Notes on the United States*, vol. 1, p. 45.
2. Ibid. vol. 1, p. 142.
3. Ibid. vol. 1, p. 114.
4. Perhaps the most relevant passage is the one where he talks of the overlap between phrenology and physiognomy: ibid. vol. 1, pp. 148–9.
5. Ibid. vol. 1, p. 144; vol. 2, p. 51.
6. Ibid. vol. 1, pp. 51–2.
7. Ibid. vol. 2, pp. 148–9. In his *Lectures on Phrenology* Combe specifies the 'natural language' associated with each organ or faculty in some detail.
8. Combe encounters 'practical phrenologists' on several occasions and his references are invariably dismissive: see Combe, *Notes on the United States*, vol. 1, p. 148; vol. 2, pp. 54–5, 67–8, 191.
9. Ibid. vol. 1, p. 118.
10. Ibid. vol. 1, p. 271 n. See also his *System of Phrenology*, where he insists that his observations are based on 'the printed works, and published busts or casts, of the individuals alluded to; and both of these being public property, there appeared no impropriety in adverting to them. In instances in which reference is made to the cerebral development of persons, whose busts or casts are not published, I have ascertained that the observations will not give offence', p. v.
11. Stack, *Queen Victoria's Skull*, p. xi. Concern over impropriety did not extend to her children, however. In 1846 (a month before the meeting with FD) the Combes were invited to Buckingham Palace, 'where George was allowed to determine the Phrenological Development of the Princess Royal and the Prince of Wales, then aged 6 and 4, respectively. This exercise was repeated in subsequent years at the request of

the Queen, when Combe was consulted about his views on the best course of education for the Royal children.' See Kaufman, *Edinburgh Phrenological Society*, p. 107.

12. Combe, *Notes on the United States*, vol. 1, p. 227.
13. Ibid. vol. 1, p. 59.
14. Ibid. vol. 1, p. 243.
15. Ibid. vol. 2, pp. 138–9.
16. On national character see ibid. vol. 1, pp. 41, 284; on gender see ibid. vol. 1, pp. 86–7; on class see ibid. vol. 1, pp. 128–9.
17. Ibid. vol. 1, pp. 59–60, vol. 2, pp. 192–3.
18. Ibid. vol. 1, pp. 280–1; see also the comparison between Africans and African Americans, ibid. vol. 2, p. 192.
19. Thus: his forthright criticisms of slavery (ibid. vol. 1, pp. 158–61, 265–6); his opposition to piecemeal abolition (ibid. vol. 2, pp. 295–6) and to colonisation (ibid. vol. 2, pp. 34–5); his rejection of the anti-abolitionist argument that abolition would lead to a 'war of extermination' (ibid. vol. 1, pp. 259–60); his objection to segregation in the North, for example, in schools (ibid. vol.1, p. 103) and public meetings, including his own lectures (ibid. vol. 1, p. 243).
20. Brown, *Three Years in Europe*, p. 232.
21. Ibid. pp. 250–73.
22. Ibid. pp. 253–4, 272, 259.
23. Ibid. p. 16.
24. Ibid. p. 17. See also his remarks on encountering Thomas Carlyle, mistaking him for an Ohio farmer: Brown, *American Fugitive*, pp. 199–200.
25. Brown, *American Fugitive*, pp. 268–75. 'Joseph Jenkins' was probably a fictionalised character based on several individuals: see Pettinger, '"The Greatest Genius that I Had Met in Europe"'.
26. BF, p. 373 (A, p. 376; FDP 2.2, p. 215); LT2, pp. 305, 314 (A, pp. 690, 698; FDP 2.3, pp. 192, 199).
27. BF, p. 387 (A, p. 385; FDP 2.2, p. 222).
28. One rare exception is his description of Burns's nieces in his letter from Ayr: 'Coal black hair, high foreheads, and yet black eyes, sparkling with the poetic fire which illumined the breast of their brilliant uncle. Their deportment was warm and free, yet dignified and lady-like': FD to Abigail Mott, Ayr, 23 March 1846 (FDP 3.1, p. 113).
29. Brown, *American Fugitive*, p. 282.
30. FD to WLG, London, 23 May 1846: FDP 3.1, p. 133.
31. George Combe to unidentified correspondent, Edinburgh, 7 June 1846 (*Liberator*, 31 July 1846).

Chapter 20

A Glut of Ethiopians

Douglass's deep suspicion of physical appearance as a key to character is evident in the reservations he expressed regarding Smith's 'Heads of the Colored People' articles that he published in his newspaper. Commenting on the portrait of the washerwoman, he implies that Smith's 'faithful pictures of contented degradation' might not meet the approval of the woman in question. Douglass hints that Smith would be entirely to blame if 'he should occasionally get a rap or two over his head with a broom-stick, or a few drops of moderately hot "suds" upon his neatly-attired person'. 'Look out,' he concludes with a flourish, 'look out for "suds" and "broom-sticks!"'[1]

He returned to the subject in a more serious vein the following year. 'Very little', he writes, 'can be learned of the colored people as a whole from merely seeing them in the streets of this or any other city.' On the basis of such a fleeting acquaintance, one would simply confirm the common view formed after seeing them

> either in rags and idleness, or dressed up in the gaudy trappings of waiters and flunkys, dancing attendants behind their chairs at table, in hotels or steamboats, or forming a part of their grand equipages (the ebony to set off ivory), rolling down the life-thronged Broadway.

If we really want to know about them, he insists, we must 'see them at their homes, in their places of business, at their churches, and in their literary benevolent societies'.[2]

If Douglass is – perhaps unusually – acutely sensitive to the misleading impression that can be conveyed by one's appearance and conduct in public, he knows that, of all people, blacks cannot escape the tyranny of the gaze. What he suggests is that it should be directed elsewhere. Instead of looking at heads, faces, clothes – the things immediately visible when encountering 'colored people' in public – his readers ought to look indoors to the places they live, work, and worship, where one may find 'order, neatness, and intelligence' and 'the marks of material prosperity' that the 'rags' and 'gaudy trappings' of the city street obscure. We might say that Douglass is recommending we shift from a physiology of heads to a physiology of institutions. In his closing line, addressed directly to Smith, he suggests these other locations are where he would find the 'real "heads of colored people"', although, on the basis of what he has already said, it would seem that 'heads', wherever they may be found, are not so singularly informative as Smith believes.

As a prominent public figure himself, Douglass could not rely on people judging him solely on the basis of his domestic arrangements or the content of his articles or speeches. He was keenly aware that his own physical appearance – especially on the lecture platform – would inevitably be interpreted by audiences in order to draw conclusions about him and 'colored people' more generally. And, notwithstanding his frequent claims that racial discrimination was absent, this would have been true in Britain and Ireland as well as the United States. A lecture by Frederick Douglass was clearly a draw, in towns large and small. But abolitionist lectures competed for attention with other kinds of entertainment, instruction and moral and political uplift. We need to take these into account if we are to get a sense of what expectations Douglass's audiences brought with them to his lectures.

The notice of a lecture by 'Frederick Douglass, a self-liberated American slave', on Thursday 15 January at Glasgow's City Hall appeared in the *Glasgow Argus* next to one announcing a 'Great Anti-Corn Law Meeting' scheduled the evening before in the same building.[3] An almost identical advertisement for Douglass was printed on the day of the lecture. Below it was a notice of an event the same evening, the first of a series of lectures on 'General History' by Professor Reid of Glasgow University at the Montrose Street Secession Church.[4] The previous week Rev. David Russell delivered his second monthly lecture to the young on the history of Moses at Nicholson Street Congregational Chapel, and George Combe addressed a 'crowded auditory' at Anderson's University on the subject of phrenology.[5]

Readers of the Glasgow papers were also tempted by lighter, more relaxing forms of recreation. On 5 and 7 January, a 'respectable crowded audience' at the Assembly Rooms on Ingram Street was entertained by the 'celebrated pianist and vocalist' Henry Russell, much admired by the Hutchinson Family, and who would perform at Douglass's farewell soirée at the London Tavern the following year.[6] On 9 January the *Herald* announced a 'grand new moving diorama and panorama' at the Monteith Rooms, Buchanan Street, depicting the Israelites receiving the Ten Commandments, scenes from the Battle of Amoy and the 'Great Porcelain Pagoda' of Nankin.[7]

And, although it was not his first visit to Glasgow, 'General Tom Thumb' drew large audiences to City Hall through January and beyond. This was Charles Stratton, born in Connecticut in 1838, who, as the advertisements proclaimed, 'has not increased one inch in height nor an ounce in weight since he was seven months old!'[8] His manager, P. T. Barnum, doubled his age to make him seem more remarkable, but also perhaps to make more plausible his precocious talents as a singer, dancer and comic actor, best loved perhaps for his quick-witted, sometimes saucy responses to questions about himself. They had been on tour in Europe for two years and would stay a year more, delighting audiences, and several royal households, with the 'little personage's' impersonations of various characters including an Oxford professor, a Spanish dandy, a kilted Scottish Highlander and, most famously, Napoleon. Between the thrice-daily 'exhibitions' or 'levees', the General promenaded the streets in a specially made miniature carriage drawn by four small ponies.[9]

Of particular interest to anyone investigating the cultural milieu into which Douglass plunged is another form of popular entertainment on offer that month which was advertised in the *Argus* of 22 January. As well as carrying a detailed report of the previous week's antislavery meeting, it advised its readers of a series of 'Grand Ethiopian Concerts' alongside the panorama on display at the Monteith Rooms. The concerts featured R. W. Pelham and the 'Five Celebrated and Unrivalled Sable Brothers, Mr Brennie, Banjo; Mr Green, Violin; Mr Williamson, Tambourine; Mr Secole, Triangle; and Mr Dwight, Castinets'.[10] In the *Herald*, audiences were promised they would 'give their unrivalled Delineations and Characteristics of the Slave Population of the United States (unmixed with the slightest vulgarity), and will not offend the most fastidious taste'.[11]

Richard – or, more commonly, Dick – Pelham was a former member of the Virginia Minstrels, one of the first blackface minstrel troupes in the United States, and which had toured Britain and Ireland in 1843–4, entertaining audiences who had already

been introduced to the new phenomenon by three earlier visits of
Thomas Dartmouth Rice performing his 'Jump Jim Crow' and other
popular routines, including eight nights in Edinburgh.[12] Members
of the Virginia Minstrels performed in various configurations, end-
ing with a show at Glasgow's City Hall, after which they returned
home – except Pelham, who stayed, got married and teamed up
with local talent, performing under different names well into the
1850s.[13]

The same month Douglass arrived in Glasgow, Pelham's younger
brother Gilbert – often known simply as 'Pell' – disembarked in Liverpool with another troupe, the Ethiopian Serenaders. They played
in London, then toured the provinces, with a number of dates in
Edinburgh, Glasgow and Aberdeen between August and November
1846. They were successful enough to spawn a number of imitators;
Dick Pelham, for instance, changed the name (and line-up) of his
troupe from 'Sable Brothers' to 'Ethiopian Delineators' in the hope
of capitalising on the confusion.[14]

Blackface entertainers and Douglass followed each other around
Britain. Sometimes a minstrel show would directly compete with
Douglass for an audience, sometimes only a few streets away, with
advertisements for the two attractions printed side by side in the
local paper.

At first glance, an abolitionist lecture and a blackface minstrel
show would seem to be worlds apart. The one an earnest moral
and political gathering aimed at protesting the injustice of slavery
and affirming the humanity of 'the Negro'; the other a form of light
entertainment that is notorious for its sentimental view of the plantation and dehumanising portrayal of black people, both enslaved and
free. And yet these events often took place in the same venues, their
audiences overlapped and, as we shall see, they were enjoyed (as
were the panoramas) as forms of virtual travel, providing instructive
representations of unfamiliar lands and peoples.[15]

Studies of blackface performance as it emerged as a popular form
of entertainment in the United States in the 1830s and 40s suggest
that the phenomenon was more complex than is generally assumed.
To be sure, its songs and routines revolved around a small number of
stock characters: the humble plantation elder ('Old Uncle Ned', 'Aunt
Dinah Roe'), the flirtatious mulatta ('Lucy Long'), the trickster ('Ole
Dan Tucker'), the abandoned slave girl ('Lucy Neal', 'Mary Blaine'),
and the aspirational urban freeman ('Dandy Jim', 'Zip Coon'). But

KINGSTOWN ASSEMBLY ROOMS
LAST APPEARANCE OF THE INITIMABLE BATEMAN.

THE Proprietor of the above Rooms, being anxious to meet the wishes of all Classes, has reduced the price for Children and Servants as described underneath.

MONSTER CONCERT
On THIS EVENING (Friday), 12th Sept., 1845,
both Vocal and Instrumental,

In addition to which the Inimitable Bateman, from the American, English, Scotch Theatres, and Theatre Royal, Hawkins's-street, Dublin, will perform, and delineate the various characteristics of Negro life, manners, and customs.

By the kind permission of Colonel Bunbury, K.H., the fine band of the 67th Regiment will be in attendance.
Doors open at half-past Seven o'Clock.
Concert commences at Eight.
Tickets, 1s.; Reserved Seats, 2s.; Children and Servants half price.

AMERICAN SLAVERY.

FREDERICK DOUGLASS, recently a Slave in the United States, intends to deliver a Second Lecture on American Slavery, in the Friends' Meeting House, EUSTACE-STREET, on THIS EVENING (Friday) the 12th instant, at Eight o'Clock.
Doors to be open at half-past Seven o'Clock.
Admission Free. No collection.

Freeman's Journal, Dublin, 12 September 1845

MONTEITH ROOMS, 67, BUCHANAN STREET,

LAST WEEK of Mr. PELHAM'S Celebrated AMERICAN SABLE BROTHERS, who will give their unrivalled delineations of Negro Life and Character: in addition to MARSHALL'S interesting new PANORAMA of MOUNT SINAI with its Wilderness: the Siege of Amoy; Nankin, &c. Accompanied by a full Military Band.

Admission, 1s.; Gallery, 6d.; Children, Half-price.
Fashionable Morning Performance at 1 and ½ past 2.
—— Evening do. at 7 and 9 o'clock.

SLAVERY.
LADIES' MEETING.

MR. FREDERICK DOUGLASS (a Self-liberated Slave,) will DELIVER an ADDRESS to the LADIES, on WEDNESDAY first, at one o'clock afternoon, IN THE ASSEMBLY ROOMS,
on the Subject of SLAVERY in AMERICA.
Glasgow, 14th Feb., 1846

Glasgow Herald, 16 February 1846

they were designed to elicit a range of different responses, from derision to nostalgia, from pity to admiration.

To the extent that the minstrel show resolved, or at least managed, some of the anxieties and confusions unleashed by growing demands for racial equality, it appealed to whites who were faced with the prospect of forging new relationships with the fugitives and free blacks with whom they had to live and work. While the show often mocked the antislavery orator, it was flexible enough to also harness abolitionist sentiment: its songs were adapted by abolitionist campaigners including Douglass's companions on the *Cambria*, the Hutchinsons (their popular anthem 'Get Off the Track' was sung to the tune of 'Dan Tucker'), and *Uncle Tom's Cabin* was deeply indebted to its conventions, especially its many theatrical adaptations.[16] Furthermore, although black people were the vehicle of its satire, they were not its only target. The burnt cork (like the older whiteface personae such as the cowboy and the stage Irishman, which they partially displaced, but perhaps more effectively) gave performers the courage to articulate forms of social comment that they might not otherwise have got away with. Their anarchic, rowdy routines sent up bourgeois pretensions or gleefully cast aside the industrial work ethic in ways that appealed to their working-class spectators.[17]

Travelling to Europe, blackface performers encountered audiences with different preoccupations and expectations. They found themselves playing in civic theatres and gardens as well as less reputable saloons and 'free and easies'. Venues in Scotland included the Theatre Royal in Edinburgh, Glasgow's City Hall and the Botanic Gardens.[18] Much was made of the fact that the Ethiopian Serenaders performed for the Queen at Arundel Castle, and, as we have seen, advertisements took pains to stress the tasteful character of their shows, 'unmixed with the slightest vulgarity' as the Glasgow notice had it.[19] Visiting artists – and the many local performers who imitated them – adapted the lyrics and dialogue to address local and topical concerns. For example, Rice added new verses to his signature routine, such as this one, which condenses the experiences of many fugitive slaves, including Douglass –

Den I jump aboard de big ship,
And cum across de sea,
And landed in ole England,
Where de nigger be free.[20]

– while *Punch* rewrote popular minstrel songs to lampoon politicians including the Prime Minister Robert Peel and the Irish MP William Smith O'Brien.[21]

Outside the United States, minstrelsy's ability to assuage white concerns over racial equality was largely moot because, while abolitionism was an issue of prominent public debate, it related to the status of black people in another country. But if its political valence in this respect was much weaker, its cultural allure was correspondingly more pronounced. After all, because they generally *were* elsewhere, and therefore to a large extent unfamiliar to British and Irish audiences, the performers' 'delineations and characteristics of the slave population' (as the *Glasgow Herald*'s notice had it) – and, perhaps especially, of the distinctive harmonic and rhythmic peculiarities of the African American traditions of music and dance they drew on, however superficially – had to satisfy a keener ethnic curiosity in Glasgow and Manchester than in New York or Philadelphia.[22]

London advertisements for the Virginia Minstrels in 1843 announced that they were 'the only representatives of the Negro that have appeared in this country'.[23] 'Representatives' is a curious choice of word that blurred, perhaps intentionally, the distinction between example and impersonation. But in neither sense was it accurate, for black and blackface Americans had been appearing on stage in Britain for many years. In any case, they couldn't plausibly claim to be unique for long. By 1847, the *Glasgow Theatrical Review* was asking, 'Where do all the American serenaders come from?':

[W]hence proceeds this astounding importation of musical exotics – a question as intense in interest, and as unlikely to meet with a satisfactory reply, as the celebrated query of where do all the pins go to? We may surmise, with the editor of the Theatrical Beauties, that the King of Ethiopia must have perceived a terrible diminution in the number of his subjects of late. Can it be so? Are the Venuses of Africa left widows, and the picaninnies about the sources of the Nile abandoned to dusky orphanhood, that we may listen to the epic of Daniel Tucker, or weep over the hapless fate of Mary Blane? [. . .] The nigger school of song is, indeed, decidedly in the ascendant. Where people once raved of 'Lucia of Lammermoor,' they now weep over 'Lucia of Alabama,' and instead of Norma in a Druid circle, we have 'Lubbly Dinah,' in a rice plantation.[24]

This 'glut of Ethiopians' or 'serenading mania' (as *Punch* scurrilously called it) clearly owed something to a broader fascination with the exotic – the same kind of curiosity that drew audiences to anatomical museums and freakshows that featured African and other 'primitive' peoples.[25] For example, an estimated 96,000 spectators came to peer at a group of four 'Bosjesmans' or 'Bush People' when they were exhibited for two weeks at Glasgow Fair in July 1847 – as part of an extensive British tour. On sale at performances was a sixpenny pamphlet outlining the history, habits and dispositions of this 'extraordinary race of human beings', featuring 'copious extracts from the best authors', including the text of a lecture by Robert Knox.[26]

The 'Bosjesmans' really were from Southern Africa, although such shows often featured more easily available 'primitives' closer to home, with those from the Celtic fringes considered to require the least adjustment to their appearance to play the part. The Glasgow promoter of the spectacle recalled that '[s]ome would say they were Paisley weavers dressed up; others that they were Irishmen, sweeps, &c., &c. . . . [O]thers there were who asserted that the savages were Highlandmen, and I really believe that many of their words are very similar to the Gaelic.' He especially enjoyed the story that one disappointed customer was convinced that the man 'crouching at a fire, clothed in skins, and smoking a short dhudee' was actually a fellow 'Patlander' who had robbed him of his wallet in Manchester some months before.[27]

It is tempting to insist on a clear difference between human zoos and blackface minstrel shows – the one promising *examples* of individuals of exotic appearance, which audiences expected to be authentic (expressing displeasure when they thought they were being cheated); the other offering *impersonations* of purported racial types that claimed to accurately depict their characteristic attitudes, demeanour and modes of cultural expression. However, as the ambiguous term 'representative' suggests, exhibits like the 'Bosjemans' were trained to perform in a certain way, while blackface minstrels, despite advertising their artifice by publishing images of themselves out of character, were often believed to be actually black.

Notes

1. FD, [editorial], *Frederick Douglass' Paper*, 17 June 1852. The item appears with no heading and is not signed.

2. FD, 'Letter from the Editor', *Frederick Douglass' Paper*, 27 May 1853 (repr. Smith, *Works*, pp. 233–5. For a different interpretation of Douglass's objections to Smith's portraits, which emphasises his discomfort with Smith's frankness about sexuality and his refusal to prefer bourgeois over working-class blacks, see Rusert, *Fugitive Science*, pp. 55–6.

3. *Glasgow Argus*, 12 January 1846.

4. *Glasgow Argus*, 15 January 1846.

5. *Glasgow Herald*, 9 January 1846. Combe was delivering a lecture penned by his brother Andrew, who was unable to attend due to illness. Part of it was published in the *Lancet*, 17 January 1846. The occasion marked the inauguration of a new lecture series on phrenology at the University.

6. *Glasgow Herald*, 9 January 1846. On the admiration of the Hutchinsons see Cockrell, *Excelsior*, pp. xxxiii, 66, 137, 287. On Henry Russell's contribution to Douglass's final London appearance ('Mr Henry Russell, who, among other songs, sang "The Slave Ship" with more than his accustomed pathos') see *Report of the Proceedings*, p. 3. For further background on Russell see Scott, *The Singing Bourgeois*, pp. 38–41.

7. *Glasgow Herald*, 9 January 1846.

8. *Glasgow Herald*, 2 January 1846.

9. See Saxon, *P. T. Barnum*, pp. 123–55; Eric D. Lehman, *Becoming Tom Thumb*, esp. 18–71.

10. *Glasgow Argus*, 22 January 1846.

11. *Glasgow Herald*, 16 January 1846.

12. Graham, 'The "Black Minstrelsy" in Scotland', p. 21. Rice was in Britain in 1835–6, 1838–40 and 1842–3.

13. Nathan, *Dan Emmett*, pp. 135–42; Graham, 'Black Minstrelsy', pp. 22–3.

14. See the playbill for their show in Liverpool in June 1846, available at <https://minstrels.library.utoronto.ca/content/ethiopian-delineators-pelhams-1846-26-jun-1846-27-jun-1846-lancashire> (last accessed 16 February 2018). Dick Pelham's group was referred to as 'Ethiopian Serenaders' in the *Glasgow Herald*, 20 March 1846, although this may have been the newspaper's own confusion.

15. See Nowatzki, *Representing African Americans*, esp. pp. 10–79.

16. Meer, *Uncle Tom Mania*, pp. 25–6.

17. The most influential studies of minstrelsy focus on the United States: Toll, *Blacking Up*; Lott, *Love and Theft*; Cockrell, *Demons of Disorder*; Lhamon, *Raising Cain*.

18. See Graham, 'The "Black Minstrelsy"', pp. 21–30. Performances in Glasgow Botanic Gardens (22, 24 and 26 September 1846) were advertised in the *Glasgow Argus*, 21 September 1846.

19. For the royal performance see White, 'Negro Minstrelsy', p. 196.

20. Quoted in Bratton, 'English Ethiopians', p. 135.

21. *Punch*, 16 May 1846.
22. The distinctiveness of the character and reception of blackface min-strelsy in the British Isles is addressed by: Bratton, 'English Ethiopians'; Pickering, *Blackface Minstrelsy in Britain*, esp. pp. 85–108; Pickering, 'White Skin, Black Masks'; Graham, 'The "Black Minstrelsy"'; Rehin, 'Harlequin Jim Crow'; Rehin, 'Blackface Street Minstrels'; Scott, *Sounds of the Metropolis*, pp. 144–70; Waters, *Racism on the Victorian Stage*, esp. 94–113.
23. *London Morning Post*, 24 June 1843.
24. 'Where Do All the American Serenaders Come From?', *Glasgow Theatrical Review* 30 (16 June 1847), pp. 233–4. For articles in a similar vein (which may have inspired this article) see 'Glut of Ethiopians', *Punch*, 20 March 1847; and 'Serenading Mania', *Punch*, 27 February 1847.
25. On ethnic freakshows in Victorian times see Durbach, *Spectacle of Deformity*, pp. 147–70; Altick, *The Shows of London*, esp. pp. 268–87; Lindfors, 'Hottentot, Bushman, Kaffir'.
26. *History of the Bosjesmans*.
27. Miller, *The Life of a Showman*, pp. 132–4. Miller subsequently toured England, performing in a troupe that included his son, 'who played the character of a Bosjesman', for which 'curious deceit' he attracted the censure of a Leeds newspaper (pp. 149–50). For more background on the 'Bosjesmans' see Durbach, *Spectacle*, pp. 163–4; Lindfors, 'Hottentot', pp. 10–16.

Chapter 21

Douglass on Stage

Familiarity (and fascination) with such stylised impersonations and one-dimensional 'exhibits' must have shaped audience expectations when black men and women from the United States appeared before the British and Irish public on what they hoped would be their own terms. Many of them came under pressure to conform to these expectations, and Douglass was no exception. In the theatricality of his performances he negotiated the demand that he correspond to the popular image of the blackface minstrel, acceding to it and resisting it at the same time. Sometimes he directly comments on his predicament, showing distaste for the way that terms such as 'runaway' and 'fugitive' – most often used to introduce him in the press – demean him as much as the comic impersonators did. To the extent that he successfully disrupts audience preconceptions, however, he faces a new challenge: the accusation that he is an 'imposter'.

The month Douglass first spoke at Glasgow's City Hall, the actor Ira Aldridge was also appearing in theatres in the West of Scotland, although their paths never quite crossed. When Aldridge starred in *Zaraffa*, *Mungo* and *Three-Fingered Jack* at the Adelphi, the *Glasgow Dramatic Review* noted his habit of following his moving performances with renditions of 'Jumping Jim Crow' and 'Opposum up a Gum Tree'.[1] The celebrated New York dancer William Lane ('Juba'), allegedly the same man described by Dickens in *American Notes* (1842), performed solo but enjoyed more success alongside the Ethiopian Serenaders (appearing with members of the group in Edinburgh in 1848), and also artificially darkened his complexion (at least earlier in his career), suggesting that his appeal was greatest when he seemed to conform to the conventions of blackface.[2] The composer and bandleader Frank Johnson, whose five-piece American Minstrels played in London in 1837–8 with exquisite arrangements of operatic classics and military marches, found that audiences seemed more delighted with his arrangement of 'Jim Crow', and he later wrote versions of 'Miss Lucy Long', 'Dandy Jim' and 'Ole Dan Tucker'.[3] To what extent such concessions to popular taste were coupled with a wry attempt to satirise the form that dehumanised them – and, if so, whether this was evident to the crowds that went to see them – is hard to determine.[4]

Douglass must have found himself in a similar position, although he rarely refers to his predicament directly. He left almost no record of his opinion of Dick Pelham, the Ethiopian Serenaders or other similar artists who were touring Britain at the same time as him, although there may be a sly reference to Pelham's American Sable Brothers when, sarcastically employing a euphemistic adjective more commonly used by apologists for slavery, he referred to slaves on one occasion as 'my sable brethren'.[5] However, in November 1845, at a speech in Limerick, he did regret that a blackface entertainer (or 'one of these apes of the negro', as he described him) had recently performed in that town, even if 'the reptile was only supported by those of his own kind'.[6] The performer Douglass chooses not to name was the 'Inimitable Bateman', whose tour schedule had closely entwined with his own during the first three months in Ireland.[7] And at his farewell soirée in London, even the self-declared abolitionist Henry Russell, whose repertoire, like that of the Hutchinsons, included minstrel songs (but not in blackface) did not escape censure, with Douglass chiding him for remarks which, 'unjustly, by the by', represented 'the negro, simple in his understanding'.[8]

Back in the United States eighteen months later Douglass famously denounced blackface performers as 'the filthy scum of white society, who have stolen from us a complexion denied to them by nature'.[9] Perhaps the invective was powered by an uncomfortable awareness that the minstrel show was fast becoming the standard against which audiences judged any representations of slavery, including his own. Perhaps he was coming to realise that his success as a lecturer depended not only on the cogency of his political message but on whether he looked the part.[10] Introducing one of his speeches, the *Dundee Courier* observed that '[t]he novelty of a slave addressing a Scottish audience, altogether apart from the interest felt in the subject, could not fail to draw together a numerous assembly.'[11] Audiences clearly came for the spectacle of his appearance as well as the content of his address. And to this extent, abolitionist lecturers like Douglass were so many bodies to be gawped at by paying customers as much as blackface entertainers.[12]

Douglass was accustomed to being regarded in this way, and to some extent reconciled to it: 'I am willing to be regarded as a curiosity, if I may thereby aid on the high and holy cause of the slave's emancipation,' he wrote, even before his transatlantic tour, in 1844.[13] And sometimes he could create humour from the situation. It was after one of those speeches in Dundee that he made a wry reference to this aspect of his popularity in a letter to the Boston abolitionist Francis Jackson:

> It is quite an advantage to be a 'nigger' here. I find I am hardly black enough for British taste, but by keeping my hair as woolly as possible, I make out to pass for at least half a negro at any rate. My old Fr[iend] Buffum finds the tables turned upon him here completely, the people lavish nearly all their attention on the negro.[14]

He had little control over what drew people to his lectures, but, once on stage, how did Douglass respond to these expectations? He did not share a platform with minstrel troupes the way Lane did, or absorb minstrel songs or routines into his repertoire on a regular basis like Aldridge or Johnson. But, as we have seen, he did delight audiences with semi-theatrical performances, notably during the speech in Dundee where he imagines George Lewis visiting Thomas Auld in Maryland, his younger self eavesdropping on their conversation, and then later finding himself for sale at a slave auction, throughout expertly impersonating all the characters involved.[15] And his portrayal of a pro-slavery minister was a regular feature of his speeches: 'He then buttoned up his coat, twisted his countenance into a grave and canting aspect, and with a most inimitable tone of voice, and a genuine Yankee twang, gave the following sermon amidst shouts of laughter.'[16] And there were occasions when acting out an anecdote, Douglass would slip on, as it were, a minstrel mask and briefly become a more conventional figure of fun. Sometimes, he would avail himself of the words of a stage Irishman in order to make a point, but on at least one occasion, he assumed the persona of the faithful plantation 'uncle', telling his audience that some slaves are ignorant enough to unthinkingly accept the message of the pro-slavery preacher, saying '"Me hear a good sermon to day, de Minister make ebery thing so clear, white man above a Nigger any day."'[17]

On occasion Douglass sang at meetings. In Limerick the local paper reported that at the close of an antislavery soirée, 'Mr Douglass then sang a beautiful sentimental air.'[18] At a temperance meeting in Cork, when a John Donovan welcomed Douglass with his own composition, 'Céad Míle Fáilte', sung to the tune 'Old Dan Tucker', the distinguished guest 'was so moved that he sang unsolicited with great effect, and power, a noble *Abolition* song' to the same tune.[19] This was almost certainly 'Get Off the Track', one of the Hutchinsons' best-known songs, itself a parody of the campaign song of 1844 presidential candidate Henry Clay, 'Get Out of the Way!'[20] In doing so, Douglass offered a polite acknowledgement of the welcome offered him, while diplomatically transforming the mood of the occasion from one of self-congratulation to passionate abolitionist commitment. Such subtlety was not always appreciated. That Douglass's song was met with 'infinite amusement', according to one report, suggests the novelty of the performance was what struck the audience most.[21] Another report, referring to a similar occasion the week before, noted merely that he 'sang a Nigger Song', as if he were no more than a blackface minstrel like Bateman.[22] Perhaps this is why he seems to have stopped singing in public after this; certainly, there is no record of him having done so in Scotland.[23]

If the 'delineations' promised by blackface performance tended to rely on a certain way of speaking or singing (which Douglass occasionally adopted), they also offered a powerful image of what an American slave was supposed to *look* like. And every time Douglass is referred to as a 'fugitive' or 'runaway', he remains caught in that image. Unlike his teasing appropriations of minstrel theatre, his response to this stereotype was much more direct and confrontational.

Consider the Virginia Minstrels as they are pictured on the cover of the sheet music of *The Celebrated Negro Melodies*: dressed in rags, in contorted postures, occupying a humble setting, indicated by the damaged plasterwork and broken floorboards.

Such images were not strikingly discontinuous with those circulated in the mainstream white abolitionist movement. We have already mentioned Wedgwood's medallion representing the suppliant, enchained half-naked slave, which circulated widely after 1787. A contrasting, though hardly less demeaning, image was of the runaway slave, frequently depicted in flight, with one foot raised, his belongings gathered in a bundle tied to a stick. And while he is running, the impression that he is taking control of his own destiny is undermined by the vulnerability: out in the open, on foot, during daytime, pushed by the wind rather than his own effort. Standard typesetter symbols were used to depict runaways in slave advertisements in the

Figure 21.1 The Virginia Minstrels.

United States, which were quoted and reproduced – with a rather different purpose – in abolitionist campaign material on both sides of the Atlantic.[24]

Douglass's description of the printer's emblem as of 'a human being *as if* in the act of running' suggests he found it an unsuitable symbol of emancipation, and he declined to reproduce it alongside the runaway notices he reprinted in the *North Star*: 'We have no such figures nor prints in our office, to enable us to follow copy; but the reader must supply them for himself.'[25] When he did include an image of a runaway slave on the newspaper's masthead, which he did for nine months in 1850, he chose a more dynamic one than the stock typographic figure.[26] So he must have been less than pleased with the demeaning picture of himself that the publisher chose to put on the cover of the sheet music for 'The Fugitive's Song' by his friends The Hutchinson Family.

One can perhaps imagine then the expectations generated by the promise of a novel appearance of a 'runaway slave' – which was how Douglass was frequently introduced to Scottish audiences and readers of local newspapers.[27] There is some evidence to suggest that he was not happy with this, and other designations from the language of slaveholders which treated him as lost property or an object for sale. In Cork he had already criticised a newspaper for referring to him as a 'fine specimen' – a charge the editor strongly denied, although the term he admitted using ('fine young negro') was almost as bad, both of them straight from the lexicon of the slave market.[28]

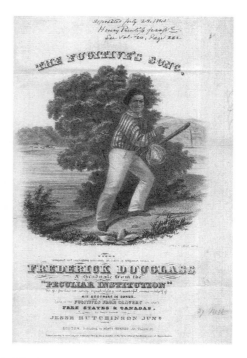

Figure 21.2 The Fugitive's Song.

Another phrase was the target of Douglass's invective at a speech in Edinburgh in May the following year that took a swipe at the Free Church minister, Rev. John McNaughtan. After telling one his favourite stories – travelling in a coach at night in the United States, his fellow passenger accords him all the respect due to a human being until dawn breaks, and then, seeing the colour of his skin, abruptly turns abusive – he reminds his listeners:

> The feeling of prejudice, however, against the slave was not altogether confined to the United States [. . .] there were men in this country, too, ministers of the Gospel of Christ, who could point the finger of scorn at the 'fugitive slave.' There was the Rev. Mr M'Naughton of Paisley [. . .] who did not hesitate to brand him (Mr. Douglas[s]) when he visited Paisley as a poor ignorant, miserable fugitive slave [. . .] Now he (Mr. Douglas[s]) did not expect such things as these when he came to this country – he did not expect to hear them from a minister of the gospel, but least of all did he expect to hear them from the Rev. Mr. M'Naughton – (hear, hear) – a minister of the Free Church – a man who had loaded his altar with the gold which, produced by

the labour of the 'fugitive slave,' should have been employed in his education, and yet turns round and calls him ignorant – (loud cheers) – who built his churches with the earnings of the slave – wrung from him amidst tears of blood and sounds of woe – and yet slanders him now as a miserable fugitive (immense cheering). He (Mr. D.) would not say that to a dog.[29]

The repetition of 'fugitive', as well as the reporter's decision to place it in inverted commas, suggest that Douglass gave it sarcastic emphasis in his speech. He did not always voice his displeasure at being called a 'fugitive' or 'runaway slave', but he makes it clear on this occasion, talking of being 'branded' and 'slandered' by the use of such terms. Like 'fine specimen', they reduce him to a commercial asset. Furthermore, as we saw in Part III, the terms 'fugitive' and 'runaway' carried for him a charge of cowardice that was anathema to the codes of Southern masculinity Douglass absorbed as a youth: he and other male authors of slave narratives took great care to recount their escapes from slavery, not as a shameful running away,

Figure 21.3 John McNaughtan.

but as the culmination of a manly struggle they won fair and square. For his listeners in Edinburgh, Douglass's point was that fugitives and runaways were nearly always qualified as 'poor ignorant, miserable': epithets that would disqualify him from being considered a gentleman, even while the touchstones of Victorian masculinity such as politeness and refinement (nurtured by high birth and the elite education that went with it) were being displaced by sincerity and moral and physical courage (qualities more widely distributed). As Douglass says, not even a dog deserved to be so described.[30]

After being announced this way, the subsequent impact of his stepping up to the platform in a frock coat, necktie and waistcoat must have challenged his audiences even before he said a word.[31] But in disrupting their preconceptions, he faced a new problem. Some onlookers may have been confused. As the *Glasgow Argus* put it, but presumably adapting Douglass's own words: 'The abolitionists had knocked so much of the rust off him, and polished him to such an extent, that the friends of slavery would not believe he had ever been a slave.'[32] Whispered accusations that he was an imposter hung around Douglass like a cloud of midges.

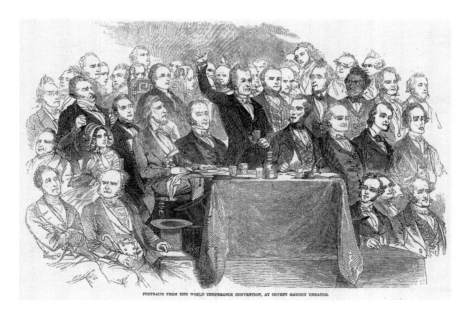

PORTRAITS FROM THE WORLD TEMPERANCE CONVENTION, AT COVENT GARDEN THEATRE.

Figure 21.4 Frederick Douglass at the World Temperance Convention, Covent Garden Theatre, 1846.

Figure 21.5 'Frederick Douglass, the escaped slave, on an English platform, denouncing slaveholders and their religious abettors'.

According to the *Dundee Courier*, the Free Church newspapers the *Scottish Guardian* and the *Witness* regularly maligned Douglass as 'an imposter, a lying scoundrel, or a vagabond'.[33] In Ayr, the Rev. Robert Renwick introduced Douglass to his audience by reassuring them that he was 'not an imposter'.[34] In a letter to Maria Weston Chapman, Mary Ireland, writing from Belfast, reports, 'It was first whispered, but *dare not now be repeated*, that Frederick Douglass was an imposter.'[35] It was clear to him that this response was a measure of how much the minstrel craze had shaped British people's expectations of what a slave was supposed to act and sound like. As he 'did not answer the Jim Crow description which was given of negroes at New York, and in theatres in this country', Douglass found it hardly surprising that some found his story hard to believe.[36]

Perhaps the most public accusation of this sort was that of A. C. C. Thompson of Delaware who, in his review of the *Narrative*, claimed that its author was (in the paraphrase of Douglass's cool reply) 'an imposter – a free negro who had never been south of

Mason & Dixon's line'.[37] But, as Douglass wrote in his 1855 autobiography, Thompson was certainly not the only one who

> said I did not talk like a slave, look like a slave, nor act like a slave
> . . . 'He don't tell us where he came from – what his master's name
> was – how he got away – nor the story of his experience. Besides, he
> is educated, and is, in this, a contradiction of all the facts we have
> concerning the ignorance of slaves.' Thus, I was in a pretty fair way
> to be denounced as an imposter.[38]

Douglass attests that some friends suggested, '"Better have a little of the plantation manner of speech than not; 'tis not best that you seem too learned."'[39] Apart from the occasional light-hearted anecdote, he did not follow their advice. They might have made similar recommendations on how he should dress – donning cut-off trousers, perhaps, or rolling up his shirt-sleeves. But if they did, he must have ignored them too.

If we follow the lead of some fashion historians, that Douglass wore a suit would hardly be worthy of remark. By the 1840s, mass production had allowed clothing to become increasingly standardised. For men, the frock-coat, vest, shirt and necktie became the norm among the upper and middle classes, and most working-class men would have had at least one suit for Sunday best. Masculine attire was becoming plainer, darker, more anonymous, at a time when 'gentleman' was increasingly signified not by the outward signs of high birth or inherited wealth but by moral worth. People were being judged on the basis of behaviour rather than appearance. But this story is misleading. It is true that any attempt to advertise one's superior social rank or distinctive personality ran the risk of appearing feminine, extravagant or foppish – and conduct books cautioned against this repeatedly ('overdressing [. . .] is a very serious evil [. . .] Do not affect singularity in dress [. . .] and so become contemptibly conspicuous,' wrote the author of *Hints on Etiquette*).[40] Subtle clues could be left for those who cared to notice: the quality of fabric, the type of button, the cleanliness of gloves, the manner in which one carried a cane. However, what counted as improperly ostentatious would vary considerably. A factory worker who paid a little too much attention to (and spent more money on) his Sunday best would meet ridicule faster than his employer – though more so in Britain than the United States.[41]

In Douglass's case, the difficulties in avoiding 'contemptibly conspicuous' dress were compounded. Commonly represented in popular iconography in the loose, cheap clothes of an agricultural labourer, a black man in a suit – however plain, inexpensive and unaccessorised – could be nothing but a fop or a dandy in the eyes of many. And Douglass, we know, took considerable care over his appearance. In a letter from Belfast he told Webb that 'I bought a watch yesterday, a right down good one, 7L–10 shillings.' And then added, using a verb that often signified a certain pomposity and self-importance, 'I swell, but I think I shall not burst.'[42] Far from merging with the crowd, a well-dressed former slave would be considered by many to be wearing laughably inappropriate dress. Contemporary verbal and pictorial depictions of urban free black men in the United States were often caricatures whose humour depended on an assumed incongruity between race and dress, a humour shared with blackface minstrel routines.[43] For, alongside the plantation stereotypes promulgated by one set of minstrel characters ('Jim Crow', 'Uncle Ned ') were the mocking images of free blacks embodied in another ('Zip Coon', 'Dandy Jim').

If Douglass's appearance on stage offered a striking contrast to the slave 'delineated' by the tatterdemalion Virginia Minstrels, those cries of 'imposter' suggest that he probably found it hard to avoid being identified with the would-be gentleman lampooned by the besuited Ethiopian Serenaders. Historians and biographers who describe Douglass as a 'black dandy' hint as much, if they don't always appreciate

Figure 21.6 The Ethiopian Serenaders

the double bind he faced.[44] To adopt the language Douglass used later in his criticism of Smith's 'Heads of the Colored People', he disdained 'rags' only to find himself adorned with 'gaudy trappings'.

Notes

1. *Glasgow Dramatic Review*, 11 February 1846, p. 333. For a more detailed account of Aldridge's adaptation of minstrel songs in his repertoire see Lindfors, *Ira Aldridge: The Vagabond Years*, pp. 67–80; Evans, 'Ira Aldridge'.
2. Lott, *Love and Theft*, pp. 113–18; Gilmore, *The Genuine Article*, pp. 49–50. Lott's source for Barnum's blacking-up of Lane is Nichols, *Forty Years of American Life*, vol. 2, pp. 231–2. On Lane see also Winter, 'Juba and American Minstrelsy'; and Johnson, 'Death and the Minstrel', pp. 75–82.
3. Jones, *Francis Johnson*, pp. 161–2, 209, 236, 242.
4. Lindfors suggests that Aldridge subverted the codes of minstrelsy and robbed them of their power; and since for many in Britain and Ireland (except perhaps London), Aldridge was their first exposure to minstrelsy, he served, as it were, to inoculate them against its insidious effects. See Lindfors, *Aldridge: The Vagabond Years*, pp. 77–80. For an argument that minstrel idioms could be harnessed to abolitionist ends (taking examples from the writings and performances of William Wells Brown) see Gilmore, *The Genuine Article*, pp. 37–66.
5. FD to Horace Greeley, Glasgow 15 April 1846 (FDP 3.1, p. 103).
6. FD, Limerick, 10 November 1845 (FDP 1.1, p. 82).
7. See *Freeman's Journal*, 1, 12 and 13 September 1845; *Limerick Reporter*, 11 November 1845; Cork *Examiner*, 10 December 1845. The Limerick *Reporter* defended Bateman. 'We do not think he deserved the language applied to him. Mr. BATEMAN is a clever actor, and his representation of a particular negro character, debased by his white despot, is no more to be considered as a description of negros generally than the representation of *Macheath* in the "Beggar's Opera," can be regarded as a delination of the character of Englishmen, or any of the Irish buffoons represented by LEONARD or Miss HERON be viewed as types of Irish character.'
8. FD, London, 30 March 1847 (FDP 1.2, p. 39). On Russell's antislavery stance see Scott, *Singing Bourgeois*, p. 39.
9. FD, 'The Hutchinson Family. – Hunkerism', *North Star*, 27 October 1848. For other pronouncements on minstrelsy by Douglass – which were not consistently negative – see 'Gavitt's Original Ethiopian Serenaders', *North Star*, 29 June 1849; FD, Newcastle, 23 February 1860 (FDP 1.3,

p. 336); and FD to 'Friends Hayden and Watson', Paris, 19 November 1886 (LWFD4, pp. 444–5). For an analysis of FD's attitudes to blackface performance see Nyong'o, *The Amalgamation Waltz*, pp. 123–34.

10. On minstrelsy becoming the standard by which representations of African Americans were judged see Meer, *Uncle Tom Mania*, p. 22.

11. 'American Slavery', *Dundee Courier*, 3 Feb 1846. See also: 'the novelty of his appearance on the platform' – 'a tall young man, intelligently featured, with a dark complexion': *Ayr Advertiser*, 26 March 1846.

12. See Nowatzki, *Representing African Americans*, pp. 25–6.

13. FD to James Miller McKim, Chester County, Pennsylvania, 5 September 1844 (FDP 3.1, p. 28).

14. FD to Francis Jackson, Dundee, 29 January 1846 (FDP 3.1, p. 90).

15. FD, Dundee, 10 March 1846 (FDP 1.1, pp. 179–80). See also FD, Paisley, 20 March 1846 (FDP 1.1, pp. 193–4).

16. FD, Exeter, 28 August 1846 (FDP 1.1, p. 360). The same virtuosity thrilled those who went to see General Tom Thumb, who was also known to include well-known minstrel songs in his performance: Saxon, *Barnum*, pp. 83–4.

17. FD, Cork, 14 October 1845 (FDP 1.1, p. 43). For a fuller discussion of Douglass's adoption of the minstrel mask see Sweeney, *Frederick Douglass and the Atlantic World*, pp. 94–137.

18. *Limerick Reporter*, 25 November 1845.

19. *Cork Examiner*, 29 October 1845; *Southern Reporter and Cork Commercial Courier*, 30 October 1845.

20. See Gac, *Singing for Freedom*, pp. 179–81.

21. *Southern Reporter and Cork Commercial Courier*, 30 October 1845.

22. *Cork Examiner*, 24 October 1845.

23. But there is evidence that he continued to sing in private, for example at the London home of the Chartist sympathiser, John Humffreys Parry, where FD, 'who had a fine voice, sang a number of negro melodies': Lovett, *Life and Struggles*, p. 268.

24. On the iconography of the runaway slave see Wood, *Blind Memory*, pp. 78–142.

25. FD, [Editorial], *North Star*, 22 February 1850. Italics added.

26. For a fuller discussion see Blackwood, 'Fugitive Obscura', pp. 102–6.

27. GT 'concluded by introducing to the meeting Mr. Frederick Douglass, the runaway slave' (*Caledonian Mercury*, 7 May 1846); 'In the course of last week, four public meetings have been held, at which addresses on the subject of American slavery have been delivered by a Mr Frederick Douglass, a runaway slave' (*Dundee Courier*, 3 February 1846); 'During the last few days much interest has been excited by the visit to our town of Mr Frederick Douglass, a run-away slave' (*Ayr Advertiser*, 26 March 1846).

28. See FD, Cork, 17 October 1845 (FDP 1.1, p. 50); FD, Cork, 23 October 1845 (FDP 1.1, p. 66).
29. FD, Edinburgh, 1 May 1846 (FDP 1.1, p. 247). See also FD, Paisley, 23 September 1846 (FDP 1.1, pp. 432–3); FD to Horace Greeley, Glasgow, 15 April 1846 (FDP 3.1, pp. 103–4).
30. See esp. John Tosh, 'Gentlemanly Politeness', pp. 455–72. When WLG introduces FD to Clarkson in a letter, he takes care to choose adjectives that offset that expectation, referring to him as 'the gifted and eloquent fugitive slave': WLG to Thomas Clarkson, London, 19 August 1846 (GL3, p. 381).
31. See Powell, *Cutting a Figure*, p. 64.
32. FD, Glasgow, 15 January 1846 (FDP 1.1, p. 133).
33. *Dundee Courier*, 18 August 1846.
34. *Ayr Advertiser*, 26 March 1846 (FDP 1.1, p. 195).
35. Mary Ireland to MWC, Belfast, 24 January 1846 (BAA, p. 248).
36. FD, Limerick, 10 November 1845 (FDP 1.1, p. 82).
37. FD to WLG, Perth, 27 January 1846 (FDP 3.1, p. 83). See also appendix to second Dublin and subsequent editions of the *Narrative* where the letter is reprinted with revisions: D2, pp. cxxv–zxviii (FDP 2.1, pp. 156–60).
38. BF, p. 362 (A, p. 367; FDP 2.2, p. 208).
39. Ibid.
40. Day, *Hints on Etiquette*, pp. 63–4.
41. On masculine dress in the nineteenth century see Kuchta, *The Three-Piece Suit*; Ribeiro, *Dress and Morality*; Ewing, *Everyday Dress*; Ginsberg, *Victorian Dress in Photographs*; Hall, *Common Threads*; Harvey, *Men in Black*. For a criticism of the 'democratisation' argument (and also differences between Britain and the United States) see Crane, *Fashion and its Social Agendas*. See Adams, *Dandies and Desert Saints* for the anxieties concerning everyday 'performance' especially as indicated in conduct books (esp. pp. 13–14), drawing on Curtin, *Propriety and Position*, pp. 129–30.
42. FD to RW, Belfast, 7 December 1845 (LWFD5, p. 15).
43. See White and White, *Stylin'*, pp. 92–116.
44. See, for example, Powell, *Cutting a Figure*, pp. 64–71.

Chapter 22

The Suit and the Engraving

A public figure like Douglass faced dilemmas at every turn. No matter how he looked, he could never escape censure, and this would seem to apply both to his appearances on the lecture platform and to representations of him on canvas or the printed page. In an essay of 1849 he stated his belief that 'Negroes can never have impartial portraits, at the hands of white artists. It seems to us next to impossible for white men to take likenesses of black men, without most grossly exaggerating their distinctive features.' He went on:

And the reason is obvious. Artists, like all other white persons, have adopted a theory respecting the distinctive features of Negro physiognomy. We have heard many white persons say, that 'Negroes look all alike,' and that they could not distinguish between the old and the young. They associate with the Negro face, high cheek bones, distended nostril, depressed nose, thick lips, and retreating foreheads. This theory impressed strongly upon the mind of an artist exercises a powerful influence over his pencil, and very naturally leads him to distort and exaggerate those peculiarities, even when they scarcely exist in the original. The temptation to make the likeness of the Negro, rather than of the man, is very strong; and often leads the artist, as well as the player 'to overstep the modesty of nature.'[1]

He later expressed the hope that photography would displace these stereotypes with more honest depictions. He was particularly excited about the democratising potential of this new technology, allowing ordinary people to fill their homes with portraits of themselves and their ancestors, a privilege previously reserved to the rich. Alluding to a line by Burns that was also used in advertisements for daguerreotypists, Douglass wrote:

Men of all conditions may see themselves as others see them. What was once the exclusive luxury of the rich and great is now within reach of all. The humbled servant girl whose income is but a few shillings per week may now possess a more perfect likeness of herself than noble ladies and court royalty, with all its precious treasures could purchase fifty years ago.[2]

When Douglass toured Britain and Ireland in 1845–7, this new technology was in its infancy, although even then, newspaper advertisements testify to the rapid spread of photographic studios. In February 1846 a notice in the *Glasgow Herald* advertised the reopening of the Daguerreotype Rooms at Andersonian University, offering portraits from 7s 6d to £4 2s.[3]

In Edinburgh, David Octavius Hill and Robert Adamson had already produced hundreds of calotypes: negatives which could generate multiple prints, unlike the one-off daguerreotype. Their subjects included architecture, landscape, family groups, characters from Scott's novels, soldiers, labourers and fish-sellers; and they executed portraits of several prominent individuals mentioned in this book: Thomas Chalmers, William Cunningham, Robert Candlish, George Lewis, John McNaughtan, George Gilfillan, George Combe, Isabella Burns Begg, Henry Vincent, Hugh Miller and Robert Knox. These early photographs often called for physical supports to help sitters remain motionless during the long exposure times required, and had to be taken outdoors in places where there would be few distractions; cemeteries were favoured locations. That the subjects could remain at ease in such contrived environments has been attributed to Hill's warm, empathetic personality. When we imagine the circumstances in which these affecting images were captured and the careful work later, brushing out imperfections in the negative, sharpening outlines, lengthening garments or concealing mechanical aids, mixing chemicals, washing prints over and over – we might wonder if the artifice involved in producing such a 'perfect likeness' was actually greater than that involved in drawing or painting.[4]

The German cultural critic Walter Benjamin admired these early photographs. He remarks how they compel the viewer to connect with the empirical reality that exists independently of the camera in a way that paintings never do. 'No matter how artful the photographer,' he wrote, 'no matter how carefully posed his subject, the beholder feels an irresistible urge to search such picture for the tiny spark of contingency, of the Here and Now, with which reality has so to speak seared the subject, to find the inconspicuous spot where in the immediacy of that long-forgotten moment the future subsists so eloquently that we, looking back, may rediscover it.'[5] The more photographs aspired to art, the weaker this 'spark of contingency' would become.

But if many photographers wanted to be acknowledged as fine artists, fine artists were becoming more dependent on photography. Before he met Adamson, Hill was a noted landscape painter, but his best-known work, *The First General Assembly of the Free Church of Scotland*, which he didn't complete until 1866, was based on hundreds of calotype portraits he and his partner took of those involved in 1843–5.[6] And there is something in that eleven-foot-wide masterpiece that draws the viewer into the lives of the people so precisely fixed at a particular moment in a way that Benjamin seems to think is unique to mechanically captured images: 'a painting in which everyone is special', as one critic puts it.[7] Certainly they are more captivating than earlier group portraits that did not make use of photographs such as Robert Haydon's painting of the World Anti-Slavery Convention in London in 1840, in which those faces not in the foreground are rendered somewhat generically.[8]

Engravings also came to be increasingly based on photographs and sought to imitate the characteristics of the new medium, such as its range of continuous tones.[9] As early as 1839 one finds engravings 'printed in rust to imitate the look of the original photograph.'[10] It has also been suggested that the conventional practice of leaving the upper body less well defined than the face was exaggerated in a way that led portraits to resemble a photographic image in the process of being formed.[11] And it was the engraving that preoccupied Douglass when he was in Scotland, specifically the engraved portraits of himself that were printed in the first editions of his *Narrative*. For if he was dismayed at the vast majority of images of black people, and alert to how narrow that gap was between 'rags' and 'gaudy trappings', he did not conclude that one image was as bad as another. On the contrary, he took great care over these images, not only in his choice of clothes and pose as a sitter, but also in demanding a say in how they were reproduced on the printed page.[12]

By the time Douglass arrived in Scotland in January 1846, Webb's first Dublin edition of the *Narrative* had almost sold out. This edition was substantially the same as the one that had appeared in

Boston earlier that year, but subsequent Irish and English editions show Douglass struggling to free himself from the sometimes suffocating patronage of his Garrisonian mentors and define himself as a thinker in his own right. Although the title of his book forcefully indicates that it was 'written by himself', the reader of the original edition had first to read the twelve pages of the preface by Garrison and an introductory letter from Wendell Phillips before reaching Douglass's own words. For the reprinting (also dated '1845' although it did not appear until March), Douglass wrote a new preface of his own, which was inserted first. Against Webb's advice, he introduced more changes in the second Dublin edition – published in May – extending his preface and including notices from leading Irish clergy as well as an appendix with Douglass's 'refutation' of the charges of his adversary A. C. C. Thompson. An English edition published in Leeds later in the year incorporated further material, namely a report of the meeting addressed by Douglass in London on 22 May 1846.[13]

The first Irish edition probably did not originally include a frontispiece author portrait. As it was printed within a month of Douglass's arrival in Dublin, Webb would not have had time to order a new engraving based on the portrait that had appeared in the original Boston edition (even if Douglass and Buffum had brought with them the steel plate that was used for it).[14] But in the copies he printed, bound and distributed in early 1846 he inserted a completely new portrait.

In a letter to Chapman, Webb, referring to James Haughton, chair of the Hibernian Anti-Slavery Society, of which Webb was secretary, explains that one of Haughton's relatives was an amateur artist. Although he doesn't name her, he must have been referring to Bessie Bell, a sister-in-law of James's brother William (with whom he was in partnership as a flour merchant). Evidently, Bell offered to draw or paint Douglass's portrait, probably when he returned from his tour of Munster in November 1845, before heading to Belfast. This required several visits to William Haughton's country house and the brothers' offices on City Quay. 'The result', wrote Webb, 'was a good likeness and as I am told a very good specimen of art.' It was then suggested that he arrange to have it engraved so it could serve as the frontispiece of his *Narrative*. As it bears the name of 'H[enry] Adlard', as well as 'B. Bell', it is likely the portrait (or a copy) was sent to the London workshop of this renowned engraver, where, for £9, a steel plate was produced and proofs returned to Dublin. Webb reports that 'the result pleased those who saw it a good deal – and is really very well executed', and he duly ordered a thousand copies.[15] Plate printing was a specialist job for which his own business was not equipped, and indeed most Irish engravings at the time were produced in London, Birmingham, Edinburgh or Glasgow.[16]

Webb probably placed the order without consulting Douglass, who, when he received a copy in Belfast in December, was not at all pleased. According to Webb he expressed his feelings in a letter 'full of abuse of the portrait to which he applied every epithet of deprecation he could think of'. Webb assured him that it had pleased his friends in Dublin and he urged him not to throw away £9 on a whim. Douglass retorted that if their friendship 'consisted in endeavouring to force a thing on him he did not like [then] it was of too pictorial a nature to be worth much'. This was almost the last straw for Webb, whose relationship with Douglass, as we have seen, had been prickly since he had arrived in Ireland four months earlier. 'I was greatly hurt by this,' he wrote, 'for I made nothing by this portrait. I had nothing but trouble by it.'[17]

In Glasgow, on the eve of his first big meeting there in January, Douglass shows no sign of changing his mind, while implying that his friend had overreacted and unnecessarily personalised the issue:

> You ask my opinion of the portrait. I gave it, and still adhere to it, – though I hope not without due deference to yourself, and those who think with you. That the picture don't suit is no fault of yours – or loss of yours. – I am displeased with it not because I wish to be, but because I cant help it. I am cirtain the engraving is not as good, as the original portrait. I dont like it, and I have said so without heat or thunder.[18]

On the other hand, Douglass doesn't want to hold up the publication unduly. The 300 copies of the first edition he asked for in Glasgow (possibly all that was left of the intial print run of 2,000) had not arrived by the time he left.[19] The consignment, not for the first time, was delayed because Webb bound the volumes in batches as required. In Perth on 20 January Douglass complains he has no copies of his *Narrative* to sell, and is clearly anxious that the remaining copies, when he receives them, will not last long in any case. Hoping to speed up the production of the reprint, he decides not to press Webb further on the changes they have discussed (which involve shorter pages and better quality paper as well as adjustments to the portrait he dislikes): 'If you cannot get the edition off in time and make the alteration, I know no better way than to get it out in the old form.' And he adds: 'When the next edition is published, I wish you to have it all bound up at once, so that I may not have to wait, as I have had to do for the last edition.'[20]

From Dundee on 10 February he resigns himself in a postscript: 'I have seen the new portrait. It has its faults – but I'll try no more – it must answer.'[21] He acknowledged receipt of the first batch of the 2,000 copies of the reprinted first edition (with his own preface, and the Adlard engraving) at the end of March.[22] As he expected they sold very quickly, hastening a second edition in May. He had made his point, though, for in this edition Webb replaced the portrait with a close copy of the one used in the original Boston edition, commissioned from the Glasgow engraver Joseph Swan.

Frontispiece portraits had evolved considerably by the time Douglass and Webb clashed over the Dublin editions. For most of the eighteenth century, frontispieces typically set the (male) author in an architectural frame, stressing his classical antecedents and situating him in public space. The development of stipple engraving (using dots and short flicks rather than lines) paved the way for delicate gradations of tone and shading associated with a feminine sensibility and characterised the portraits that appeared in authoritative editions of women poets that began to appear in the 1790s, often placed in an oval frame, giving them a more intimate character and situating them in domestic space. The feminine connotations attached to the portraits of romantic male authors too, such as Byron and Shelley, which increasingly dispensed with a frame altogether, depicting the subject emerging imperceptibly from an undefined background which in turn shades into the blank margins of the page – a change facilitated by the development of steel engraving, which was especially suited to stipple techniques. By the 1830s this practice had become the norm for frontispiece portraits in general. 'These engravings', writes one critic, 'are clearly not images of hanging portraits or busts but rather depictions of a fluid, emotive self that melds into a mysterious, romantic background.'[23]

If such portraits had long served to reinforce the idea that when reading a book, the author is talking to you ('if someone talks to you, you turn to the speaker to see who it is, and so when reading his words you turn equally naturally to the portrait frontispiece to see who is addressing you'[24]), the decontextualised unframed portraits of the nineteenth century would seem particularly suited to this conceit. But for this reason, it may have loaded them with expectations that could bring publishers and authors into conflict, as what served well as a marketing device may not have accorded with the effect the writer wanted from the text. Douglass was in good company when he expressed his displeasure with the Adlard engraving: Samuel Richardson (again, blaming the engraver rather than the artist) decided not to use the sketches he had commissioned from Hogarth to illustrate scenes in his novel *Pamela* probably for similar reasons.[25]

What was it that so vexed Douglass? One noticeable difference from the original portrait is the facial expression, Adlard's Douglass sporting a distinct smile compared to the more serious and determined look of its predecessor. It was later reprinted by the Leeds abolitionist Wilson Armistead in *A Tribute for the Negro* (1848), an impassioned 'vindication of the moral, intellectual and religious capabilities of the coloured portion of mankind', supported by biographical documents and 'superior engravings' of eminent individuals.[26] Reviewing the book, Douglass expressed disappointment in the portraits, which are mostly of 'the commonest sort' and fall far short of providing a true likeness of the subject. Of his own image, he 'shall leave to others to criticise, begging only to remark that it has a much more kindly and amiable expression, than is generally thought to characterize the face of a fugitive slave'.[27] There may be some sarcasm in 'generally thought' here, given that images of happy, contented slaves circulated widely in blackface performance, and it is precisely this popular association that compromises Adlard's engraving, especially when portraits of Douglass's contemporaries usually featured a more neutral expression.[28]

But it was probably not only the facial expression that displeased him. It is true that in other respects both the Dublin frontispieces depict the sitter in the pose and dress typical of men of substance of the day. And yet there are differences between them, which may further explain Douglass's strongly felt objections.[29]

In the Adlard portrait (Fig. 22.1) he wears what looks like a heavier jacket, perhaps of more expensive material. It is closely buttoned and his arms hang stiffly at his side. The necktie is smaller, and more carefully symmetrical. His hair is oiled and relaxed, and there

Figure 22.1 Frederick Douglass, variant first Dublin edition of his *Narrative*.

Figure 22.2 Frederick Douglass, second Dublin edition of his *Narrative*.

is a hint of makeup. Adlard's engraving presents a more static, sedentary Douglass, a more fashionable, more affluent Douglass. Perhaps even a little ingratiating.

In the original Boston portrait, copied by Swan (Fig. 22.2), Douglass has a more casual appearance. His jacket is open and of lighter material, offering more freedom of movement. His hair is worn naturally ('more woolly', as his earlier joking remark had it). His folded arms – clearly visible, in defiance of convention – appear comfortable, perhaps even slightly defiant. And while Douglass's social status was not assured enough for him to risk the open-necked look of a poet like Shelley or Whitman, movement and informality is suggested by the flopping necktie, faintly reminiscent of Byron.[30]

In an essay entitled 'The Suit and the Photograph', John Berger considered several photographs by August Sander to illustrate the ways in which working men look awkward or uncomfortable in suits. Their bodies, used to effort and free movement, appear misshapen when wearing clothes that symbolise 'sedentary power', as he put it, 'cut to follow the idealised shape of a more or less stationary body and then hang from it'. In the case of middle-class men, on the other hand, he argues that 'the suits actually confirm and

Figure 22.3 Lord Byron   **Figure 22.4** Walt Whitman

enhance the physical presence of those wearing them. The clothes convey the same message as the faces and as the history of the bodies they hide.'[31]

These images of Douglass, however, do not neatly fall into either category. By all accounts, Douglass, as a manual labourer in his youth, certainly had the physique to match, and in many of his speeches in Britain and Ireland he did not want his audiences to forget this (he made numerous references to the scars on his back), but he also sought to be recognised for his intellectual abilities (bristling at references to himself as a 'poor fugitive'). He may have appreciated the way the first portrait managed a careful balance between the two: seated and suited and yet not awkwardly confined by his clothes, someone whose physical strength is not entirely suppressed, and who appears ready to move at any moment. By contrast, in the second portrait the contours of his chest, arms and hands are barely visible. He wears the suit with bourgeois nonchalance, the traces of his slavery past erased as if he had been to the manor born. But, despite his tamed hair and lighter complexion, he would not escape those taunts of imposter that never troubled his white counterparts.

One can imagine – and perhaps Douglass did too – why Webb preferred Adlard's portrait. The smile, the buttoned-up, almost uniform-like suit, and the intimacy suggested by its sitter positioned closer to the viewer, represents the Douglass he preferred to imagine: docile and disciplined, rather than the aloof and defensive man that emerges from the characterisation of him in Webb's letters. But Douglass may also have been reminded of the caricatures of free black men that appeared in Northern US periodicals and in the performances of the Ethiopian Serenaders, in which the more elegant the dress, the more the intended incongruity with the dark complexion would create the required comic effect.

In March 1848 Charles Dickens wrote to his friend the actor William Charles Macready, enclosing a copy of Douglass's *Narrative*, apparently in response to his desire to learn more about the United States, where he was about to go on tour (though it was not his first visit). But before doing so, Dickens took an unusual precaution. 'There was such a hideous and abominable portrait of him in the book, that I have torn it out, fearing it might set you, by anticipation, against the narrative.'[32]

It is impossible to know which edition – and therefore which portrait – he was referring to (although many more copies of the

Narrative with Swan's engraving had been sold in Britain by 1848 than the variant first Dublin edition with Adlard's). Dickens's language is strong, and he clearly thinks the portrait strikingly at odds with his own conception of a fugitive if not the specific author of the text (whom he probably never met in person). Neither portrait would seem to answer Dickens's idea of a 'wretched slave'; neither conforms to the fictionalised versions of the younger Douglass that later figure in *Great Expectations*.[33] But it does seem more likely that a reader sympathetic to the abolitionist cause – and one not duly concerned about Douglass's growing independence within it – would find Adlard's portrait more jarring than the other. If that 'hideous and abominable' engraving is a measure of Douglass's failure to control his public image, then the Boston engraving – and its Scottish copy – reminds us that he also helped to fashion portraits that he felt did him justice, capturing the passage from 'slave' to 'man' without erasing either.

Notes

1. FD, 'A Tribute for the Negro', *North Star*, 7 April 1849 (LWFD1, p. 380).
2. FD, Boston, 3 December 1861 ('Pictures and Progress') (FDP 1.3, p. 455). The Burns poem is, of course, 'To a Louse': Burns, *Poems and Songs*, vol. 1, pp. 193–4. On the use of this line in daguerreotype advertisements see Dinius, *The Camera and the Press*, p. 208.
3. Glasgow *Herald*, 6 February 1846.
4. See Bruce, *Sun Pictures*; Fowler, *Mr Hill's Big Picture*; Crawford, *The Beginning and the End of the World*.
5. Benjamin, 'A Small History of Photography', p. 243.
6. David Octavius Hill, *The First General Assembly of the Free Church of Scotland* (1866; Presbytery Hall, Free Church of Scotland, Edinburgh).
7. Crawford, *The Beginning and the End of the World*, p. 155.
8. Robert Haydon, *The Anti-Slavery Society Convention, 1840* (1841; National Portrait Gallery, London).
9. See Koivunen, *Visualizing Africa*, p. 173; Moser, *Wood Engraving*, p. xi.
10. Batchen, 'Origins Without End', p. 76.
11. See Folsom, 'Portrait of the Artist as a Young Slave', pp. 58–9; and Meehan, *Mediating American Autobiography*, p. 169. Folsom and Meehan make this observation in regard to FD's early portraits. I have not seen this claim made about mid-century engravings more generally.

12. In what follows, I have drawn on the important work on the portraits of Douglass in Bernier, 'A "Typical Negro"'; Bernier, *Characters of Blood*, esp. pp. 251–98; Bernier, 'A Visual Call to Arms'; Casmier-Paz, 'Slave Narratives'; Fried, 'True Pictures'; Hill, '"Rightly Viewed"'; Stauffer, 'Creating an Image in Black'; John Stauffer et al., *Picturing Frederick Douglass*; Westerbeck, 'Frederick Douglass Chooses His Moment'; Folsom, 'Portrait of the Artist'; Meehan, *Mediating American Autobiography*; and Dinius, *The Camera and the Press*.

13. Most discussions of the British and Irish editions of the *Narrative* (including the editors of FDP 2.1) assume there were simply two Irish editions, but it is clear that the reprinted first edition includes important variations: Sweeney, *Frederick Douglass and the Atlantic World*, pp. 13, 15, 38, 52.

14. The (unsigned) engraving for this portrait may have been based on one or both of the oil paintings (the first, at Howard University, attributed to Elisha Livermore Hammond, the second, at the Smithsonian Institute, previously attributed to him) reproduced in Stauffer et al., *Picturing Frederick Douglass*, pp. 78–9 (Plates 2.1 and 2.3), where it is also suggested that it may have been based on a daguerreotype by Lorenzo Chase; see also Westerbeck, 'Frederick Douglass Chooses His Moment', p. 148; Folsom, 'Portrait of the Artist', p. 58; Powell, *Cutting a Figure*, pp. 65–6.

15. RW to MWC, Dublin, 26 February 1846 (BPL Ms. A.9.2 v. 22, p. 26 (A & B): available at <https://archive.org/details/lettertomydearfr00webb28> (last accessed 17 February 2018), quoted courtesy of the Trustees of the Boston Public Library/Rare Books. The portrait is signed 'B. Bell, del^r. H. Adlard, sc', identifying the artist and the engraver respectively. Henry Adlard was a well-known engraver, with works in the National Portrait Gallery in London. From various genealogical websites, it appears that Elizabeth (Bessie) Bell was born in Belfast in 1817; her sister Anna married William Haughton in 1840 and it seems likely that Bessie followed her to Dublin after the death of their mother in 1842, herself subsequently marrying, in 1855, another Haughton, William's and James's nephew Frederick. She died in 1894 and is buried at Killeshin Parish Church, County Laois.

16. On Irish engravings needing to be produced in Scotland or England see Hunnisett, *Steel-Engraved Book Illustration*, p. 203. This work has served as my main guide to the subject.

17. RW to MWC, Dublin, 26 February 1846 (BPL Ms. A.9.2 v. 22, p. 26 (A & B): available at <https://archive.org/details/lettertomydearfr00webb28> (last accessed 17 February 2018), quoted courtesy of the Trustees of the Boston Public Library/Rare Books. We only have Webb's (retrospective) account of these exchanges (presumably in December), the originals not having survived.

18. FD to RW, Glasgow, 14 January 1846 (FDP 3.1, p. 79). The editors of FDP date this as 'mid-January', although in the letter FD says that his 'first meeting here will be held tomorrow Ev. in the City Hall' which, as an editorial note explains, was on 15 January.

19. Although in a letter of 24 December 1845, FD refers to 'the remaining 1000' – which suggests more than 300 remained by the time he left Glasgow, unless he sold 700 in the intervening five meetings, which is unlikely. See FD to RW, Belfast, 24 December 1845 (BPL Ms. A.1.2 v. 15, p. 91) available at <https://archive.org/details/lettertomydearfr-00doug_3> (last accessed 1 June 2018), quoted courtesy of the Trustees of the Boston Public Library/Rare Books.

20. FD to RW, Perth, 20 January 1846 (FDP 3.1, p. 81); see also FD to RW, Glasgow, 14 January 1846 (FDP 3.1, pp. 79–80) for earlier references to these changes, including the quality of paper.

21. FD to RW, Dundee, 10 February 1846 (FDP 3.1, p. 93).

22. FD to RW, Kilmarnock, 29 March 1846 (FDP 3.1, p. 102).

23. Egan, 'Radical Moral Authority and Desire', p. 196.

24. David Piper, quoted in Egan, 'Radical Moral Authority and Desire', p. 192.

25. Barchas, 'Prefiguring Genre', pp. 272–3.

26. Armistead, *A Tribute for the Negro*.

27. FD, 'A Tribute for the Negro', *North Star*, 7 April 1849 (LWFD1, pp. 379–80).

28. The image of the happy, contented slave was also promulgated by some travel narratives. In his speech in Glasgow on 15 January 1846, FD criticised Charles Lyell for this (FDP 1.1, p. 136).

29. Very few scholars have paid attention to the difference between the two portraits, typically referring to the '1845 frontispiece' as if there was only one, and more commonly compare this with the portrait used in BF ten years later. On the original Boston portrait (copied by Swan) see Dorsey, 'Becoming the Other'; Folsom, 'Portrait of the Artist'; and Meehan, *Mediating American Autobiography*. In 'Creating an Image in Black', John Stauffer compares the Boston portrait and the one appearing in *Tribute for the Negro*, apparently unaware that the latter was previously used for the reprint of the first Dublin edition. As far as I know only Sweeney (*Frederick Douglass and the Atlantic World*) and Lee (*American Slave Narrative*) have noted that the first editions of the *Narrative* included different portraits, although Lee (p. 4) somewhat misleadingly refers to them as the 'American' and the 'British' portraits.

30. For an interesting comparison between Douglass and Whitman's portraits see Folsom, 'Appearing in Print'.

31. Berger, 'The Suit and the Photograph'.

32. Charles Dickens to W. C. Macready, 17 March 1848, in Dickens, *Letters*, vol. 5, pp. 262–3. This letter is discussed by Lee, *American Slave Narrative*, pp. 3–9. Lee assumes Dickens must have been presenting the 'British' edition (i.e., the one with the Adlard portrait), while the editors of Dickens's letters assume he is talking of the 'one of the American edns, containing a very grim and aggressive-looking head and shoulders portrait as frontispiece, as against the comparatively relaxed portrait in the English edns': Dickens, *Letters*, vol. 5, p. 263 n.

33. For 'wretched slave' see Charles Dickens to Mrs Edward Cropper, 20 December 1852, in *Letters*, vol. 6, p. 826, quoted in Lee, *American Slave Narrative*, p. 114. For the influence of the slave narrative (and of Douglass in particular) on *Great Expectations* see Lee, *American Slave Narrative*, pp. 113–30.

Part V

The Voyage Home

I go, turning my back upon the ease, comfort, and respectability which I might maintain even here, ignorant as I am. Still, I will go back, for the sake of my brethren.

Frederick Douglass, 'Farewell speech' at the London Tavern, 30 March 1847

Chapter 23

A Disconnected Farewell

On Tuesday 30 March 1847, five days before his departure for the United States, Frederick Douglass addressed several hundred distinguished guests at a soirée organised in his honour at the London Tavern, Bishopsgate Street. The *London Morning Advertiser* reported that 'Very many elegantly dressed ladies graced the scene with their presence, and, in addition to an excellent band stationed in the gallery, Mr. Henry Russell was engaged, and sang the "Slave Ships," and several others of his exquisite American songs.'[1]

On the platform beside Douglass were a number of leading Garrisonians including the chairman George Thompson, John Estlin, William Howitt and W. H. Ashurst, as well as rival abolitionists aligned with the British and Foreign Anti-Slavery Society, such as Thomas Binney and its founder Joseph Sturge. Also present was Rungo Bapojee, the agent of Pratap Singh, the deposed Maharaja of Satara, for whose reinstatement Thompson had (as his official ambassador in London on a salary of £1,200 per annum) campaigned – unsuccessfully – for a number of years. A number of invited notables – Charles Dickens among them – sent their apologies.[2]

Thompson called the meeting to order and after several introductory remarks from some of his friends and supporters, Douglass had the floor. He told his audience that he was not returning to a country he admired – it was a place where slavery was vigorously upheld by the constitution, aided and abetted by the Northerners who sent fugitives back to their masters, and unapologetically defended by the churches. He paid tribute to the courageous abolitionists, especially William Lloyd Garrison, 'the foremost, strongest, and mightiest among those who have completely identified with the negroes in the United States'. He went on:

He has thrown himself, as it were, over the ditch as a bridge; his own body, his personal reputation, his individual property, his wide and giant-hearted intellect, all were sacrificed to form a bridge that others might pass over and enjoy a rich reward from the labours that he had bestowed, and the seed which he had sown.[3]

He reminded his listeners that for his 'uncompromising hostility to slavery', Garrison had faced opprobrium not only in the United States, but also in 'this country'.[4] Douglass pulled no punches. If the occasion conventionally demanded that he conclude by warmly thanking his hosts, he did not do so before reminding them of their shortcomings. There was no room for complacency. He could have mentioned the dogged refusal of the Free Church of Scotland to return the money donated by slaveholders in the United States. Instead – he was in London, after all – he singled out the weakness of British Christians in not facing up to their American pro-slavery counterparts at the Evangelical Alliance which had met in the capital the previous year. He called on them to support the struggle for black emancipation and take advantage of the increasing commercial traffic across the Atlantic to use every means possible to loudly denounce their slaveholding colleagues, for slavery 'is not so disreputable out of the United States as it should be'.[5]

Only then did he acknowledge the generous welcome he received everywhere in the British Isles, in stark contrast to the contempt and discrimination he faced back home. But though kind friends had offered every inducement for him to stay, he had chosen to 'go home; to return to America'.

I go, turning my back upon the ease, comfort, and respectability which I might maintain even here, ignorant as I am. Still, I will go back, for the sake of my brethren. I go to suffer with them; to toil with them; to endure insult with them; to undergo outrage with them; to lift up my voice in their behalf; to speak and write in their vindication; and struggle in their ranks for that emancipation which shall yet be achieved by the power of truth and of principle for that oppressed people. (Cheers.) But, though I go back thus to encounter scorn and contumely, I return gladly, I go joyfully and speedily.[6]

Douglass bookended his speech with ritual apologies for its lack of finesse. 'I do not [. . .] promise to make you a very connected speech,' he began.[7] 'Pardon me, my friends, for the disconnected manner in which I have addressed you,' he concluded, pleading that any indelicacies be attributed to 'the free upgushings of a heart over-borne with grateful emotions'.[8] The apology was rhetorical; it was of course a finely constructed oration and the indelicacies may have been carefully planned. But it may have alluded to other kinds of connection and disconnection that were on his mind.

His tribute to Garrison was a powerful one, yet Douglass com-bined it with remarks that might have suggested a growing distance from his great friend. In the midst of his tribute he turns attention to himself:

> I have now been in this country for nineteen months; I have gone through its length and breadth; I have had sympathy here and sym-pathy there; co-operation here, and co-operation there; in fact, I have scarcely met a man who has withheld fellowship from me as an abolitionist, standing unconnected with William Lloyd Garrison. (Hear.) Had I stood disconnected from that great and good man, then numerous and influential parties would have held out to me the right hand of fellowship, sanctioned my proceedings in England, backed me up with money and praise, and have given me a great reputation, so far as they were capable; and they were men of influence.[9]

That Douglass draws attention to the personal disadvantages he suffered through his 'connection' with Garrison may simply be a sign of his loyalty, of the sacrifices he gladly made for a man more able and experienced than himself. But that he imagines the advantages he might have enjoyed had he been 'disconnected' from him could also hint at the frustration of an ambitious and increasingly inde-pendent-minded protégé who felt that his mentor was holding him back. Naming two of Garrison's abolitionist rivals, Gerrit Smith and Arthur Tappan, as 'intrepid champions of the slave' in this speech further marks his distance.[10]

Earlier in his speech, Douglass seems to be expressing some impa-tience with the white abolitionist's pacifist approach. When he calls for the renewed campaign against slavery in the United States, he aban-dons the language of peaceful non-resistance for that of the stage Irish-man 'Pat', who, he says (to 'loud cheers and laughter'), wades into a heated dispute, calling out 'Wherever you see a head, hit it!' This is a good example of how a minstrel mask might be used; in this case allowing Douglass to voice support for violence without, as it were, saying it himself, humorously breaking the ice before continuing, in his own (more tempered) voice (to 'renewed cheering'), to spell out his meaning: 'So, the abolitionists have resolved, that wherever slavery manifests itself in the United States, they will hit it.'[11]

Garrisonian rhetoric may have deployed violent metaphors to express the urgency of its demand for the immediate abolition of slavery, but Douglass here pushes that language to the limit. If caution demands that he talk of abolitionists metaphorically hitting an institution, his listeners won't forget the more corporeal form of persuasion practised by Pat. The effect is reinforced when later in the speech Douglass – not for the first time in Britain – invokes Madison Washington, who in 1841 led a slave mutiny on board the *Creole* while it was on its way from Richmond, Virginia to New Orleans. Garrison, despite his pacifism, never condemned slave revolts, but nor did he glorify them, as Douglass does here, referring to 'the noble Madison Washington, who broke his fetters on the deck' and 'achieved liberty for himself and one hundred and thirty-five others'.[12] In fact, the only times during his overseas trip that Douglass spells out the non-violent Garrisonian position are during the late summer and early autumn when Garrison is touring the country with him, if not always in his presence.[13]

Douglass increases his distance from Garrison towards the end of the speech, when it becomes clear that he envisages his own role in the coming struggle as one that builds on and goes beyond that of the older man. While Garrison comes across as a largely subservient figure (a bridge over whom others walk, a sower of seeds the fruits of which others will enjoy), Douglass puts himself in the front line, fighting alongside other blacks rather than merely supporting them.

As Douglass turns his thoughts westward across the Atlantic, he begins to redefine his relationship with the man who has done much to bring him on as a lecturer and author in Massachusetts, and created the network that allowed him to flourish in Britain and Ireland. But his journey has also given Douglass a breathing space, and the opportunity to build new relationships independently of Garrison and his circle, even while they continued to advise him, sometimes with a heavy-handedness that may have sharpened his resolve. The three main subjects of this book – Douglass's reshaping of the 'Send Back the Money' campaign; his imaginative engagements with Scottish literature, history and landscape; and the ways in which he takes control of his own image – were defiantly Douglass's initiatives, not Garrison's.

By the time Garrison joined him in August 1846, the chance that their old relationship would resume as it had been in Lynn the year before had probably gone. With his legal freedom secured in December, after Garrison's departure – a freedom secured largely through the assistance of supporters outside the Garrisonian orbit – the dynamic between the two men would have changed again. Douglass would return home not as 'Frederick Douglass, the fugitive slave' but 'Mr Frederick Douglass's, 'emancipated' and a 'gentleman'. It was a change of status Garrison was happy to publicly endorse, but one which lay the ground for their later estrangement. Already, on his return, at a meeting at the Tabernacle, New York City, welcoming Douglass home, the audience quickly grew impatient during Garrison's introduction, called out 'Douglass, Douglass's, echoing that ancient Scottish war cry, forcing him to cut short his remarks and give way to the guest of honour himself.[14]

Douglass says he returns home 'for the sake of my brethren' – to suffer, toil and endure insult with them. But he is also returning home to be with his wife and children, whom he hasn't seen for nearly two years. Slavery broke up families in many ways, not just on the auction block as sentimental abolitionist narratives seemed to imply. Not long after his first arrival in Ireland, his host in Cork, Isobel Jennings, noticed the 'suffering on his countenance' and explained: 'He is anxiously expecting letters from home. He did not think he could be so uncomfortable.'[15] The separation troubled Douglass more than he thought possible, and, judging by the glimpses of homesickness he allows us in his few surviving private letters, the feeling never left him.

Notes

1. *London Morning Advertiser*, 31 March 1847 (repr. *Liberator*, 30 April 1847).
2. The names of those sharing the platform with Douglass and those offering apologies for not being able to attend are listed in *Report of Proceedings*, pp. 3–5. On GT, Rungo Bapojee and Pratap Singh see Fisher, *Counterflows to Colonialism*, pp. 275–92.
3. FD, London, 30 March 1847 (FDP 1.2, p. 33).
4. Ibid. p. 33.
5. Ibid. p. 45.
6. Ibid. p. 51.

7. Ibid. p. 21.
8. Ibid. pp. 51–2.
9. Ibid. p 33.
10. Ibid. p. 40. See also Levine, *Lives of Frederick Douglass*, p. 112.
11. FD, London, 30 March 1847 (FDP 1.2, p. 31). Sweeney discusses this passage in *Frederick Douglass and the Atlantic World*, pp. 114–15.
12. FD, London 30 March 1847 (FDP 1.2, pp. 46–7). I return to Washington and the *Creole* in Chapter 26.
13. FD, Bridgewater, 31 August 1846 (FDP 1.1, p. 369); FD, Taunton, 1 September 1846 (FDP 1.1, p. 373); FD, Liverpool, 19 October 1846 (FDP 1.1, p. 468). In Taunton, FD's language ('we cast aside carnal weapons') echoes that of WLG's 'Declaration of Sentiments' (*Liberator*, 14 December 1833), which speaks of the need to reject 'the use of all carnal weapons'.
14. FD, New York City, 11 May 1847 (FDP 1.2, p. 58). For a detailed consideration of this speech as marking a decisive stage in FD's development see Wright, *Lecturing the Atlantic*, pp. 63–72.
15. Isobel Jennings to MWC, Cork, 15 October 1845 (BPL Ms. A.9.2 v. 21, p. 70B), available at <https://archive.org/details/lettertomydearmr00jenn4> (last accessed 17 February 2018), quoted courtesy of the Trustees of the Boston Public Library/Rare Books. Jennings's first thought was that this suffering made FD 'more interesting' before allowing her own fascination to give way to a more sensitive appreciation of FD's situation.

Chapter 24

Cabin 72

Douglass's appearance at the London Tavern was not his last speech in Britain. Promising to keep his closing remarks brief, he reminds his audience that 'I have to speak again to-morrow night almost 200 miles from this place.'[1] This meeting was in Huddersfield, and the day after, Thursday, he headed for Bristol, and another 'farewell address'. On Friday he must have taken the train to Manchester, for, according to the *Manchester Express*, it was from there the next morning he left, 'accompanied by several friends, and proceeded to Liverpool, where he was joined by other friends from Glasgow, Perth, Cork, Dublin, Sheffield, Wrexham, Rochdale, &c who assembled to witness his departure'.[2]

It was a month since he had visited the Cunard office in London and paid £40 19s for his first-cabin passage on the *Cambria*. Douglass had made a point of booking his return voyage on the same vessel that brought him over. He may have felt reassured that Captain Judkins, who had defended him so heroically two years before, would not permit a repeat of the insulting treatment he had faced then. But he also took care to ask Mr Ford, the London agent, whether 'my colour would prove any barrier to my enjoying all the rights and privileges enjoyed by other passengers'. He was assured it would not.[3]

Douglass must then have been genuinely surprised to find that when he carried his luggage on board that Saturday afternoon, and inquired after his berth, he was told that it had been given to another passenger and the London agent had no right to have sold him his ticket. The captain offered to accompany Douglass to the office of the Liverpool agent on Water Street, but Judkins's presence made no difference. Charles MacIver was in bullish mood. The company was not a reformatory society, he explained. It had to take account of the feelings – even the prejudices – of other passengers, and it was for

Figure 24.1 The *Cambria*.

this reason they were excluding him. Judkins was in no position to overrule his superior, but it appears that he brokered a compromise, offering his own state rooms to Douglass, a proposal MacIver agreed to on condition that he remained there during the voyage and did not come into contact with other passengers.[4]

Douglass may have appreciated Judkins's impossible position, but the compromise brought him no relief. He returned to his friends at Brown's Temperance Hotel in Clayton Square and told them what had transpired. While sympathising with his feelings, some of them at least were probably secretly pleased that the incident offered a marvellous opportunity to highlight the company's discriminatory policy. At any rate, there must have been lengthy discussions over the most effective way to make the matter public. William Bevan, secretary of the Liverpool Anti-Slavery Society, suggested he help Douglass compose a letter. 'Sir,' it began. 'I take up my pen to lay before you a few facts.' It was addressed to the editor of *The Times*.

The next morning, Easter Sunday, they breakfasted together. Douglass and fifteen of his friends boarded the *Cambria*, where they noted the satanic sneers of some of the other passengers. As they said their final goodbyes in the captain's state rooms – recently occupied, it seems, by the Governor-General of Canada – they sought to console Douglass, who declared that he would rather be in the poorest hold of the ship and able to move freely than confined in luxurious quarters. But as the ship moved slowly down the Mersey, he knew he had left in their hands a smouldering missive that would soon start a forest fire. If his arrival in Liverpool in August 1845 had attracted little notice even in the local press (and subsequent coverage of the confrontation on board was largely confined to reports of Douglass's speeches in the towns where he lectured), his departure made headlines across the country.

One of the small group of supporters was the Scottish social reformer William Logan, author of *An Exposure of Female Prostitution* (1843) and a delegate, like Douglass, at the World Temperance Convention in London in August 1846. Back at the hotel, Logan made a copy of Douglass's letter to *The Times* and entrusted it to the penny post. The original he took home to Rochdale and on Monday morning arranged for 250 copies to be printed, and after endorsing them, mailed at least fifty copies to other newspapers and journals, and the rest to friends across the country. Then all he had to do was wait.

On Tuesday the first notices appeared in the *Manchester Express* and *Liverpool Mercury*, which, Logan noted, 'excited considerable interest'. Later the same day he would have seen Douglass's letter at the head of a column in *The Times*, whereupon 'the subject became the topic of conversation'. Two days later, a 'thundering leader' in the same paper shared Douglass's outrage, condemning the company for allowing its agents to succumb 'to a miserable and unmeaning assumption of skin-deep superiority by the American portion of their passengers'.[5] Upon which, Logan, alluding to the welcome Paul the Apostle received on his arrival in Rome, remarked: 'every British abolitionist "thanked God and took courage"'.[6]

The following week, three more letters appeared in *The Times*, each claiming to tell the company's side of the story, the first two on the Tuesday. One was from Charles MacIver, complaining that Douglass had suppressed an earlier conversation in which it had been explained to him that the reason for the precaution was the incident on the outward voyage in which Douglass 'was the cause, whether intentionally or unintentionally on his part, of producing, by the observations he made use of, serious disturbance on board, which required the authority of the captain to quell, in order to restore peace and safety'.[7] Another was from Charles M. Burrop, 'of Asgill, Virginia, United States, Head Manager of the Cunard Company of Liners', defending the action of the company, claiming it could not afford to ignore the 'absolute and invincible disgust on the part of the great majority of white men, and particularly of white women, not less in England than in America, to come into close contact with blackamores' if it meant profits would be affected by travellers cancelling tickets when they discovered that blacks had booked a passage on the same vessel.[8]

The next day the *The Times* allowed Samuel Cunard himself to respond. He made no reference to MacIver's letter, but he did expose 'Burrop', pointing out that 'no such person, or any other individual in the United States, holds any share or interest in the steam ships alluded to, and that the statements set forth in that letter are entirely untrue'. And he continued: 'No one can regret more than I do the unpleasant circumstances respecting Mr Douglass's passage; but I can assure you that nothing of the kind will again take place in the steam-ships with which I am connected.'[9]

Logan observed with satisfaction the shockwaves breaking across the nation. Douglass's letter, he claimed, was reprinted in 'every influential paper in Britain'. When passing through Manchester, Edinburgh and Glasgow the following week he visited the public reading rooms in those cities and observed articles on the affair in over a hundred English and Scottish newspapers. He assembled a large collection of cuttings, with a sample of the editorial indignation suggested by headlines studded with phrases such as 'disgraceful prejudice', 'villainous conduct', 'outrage' and 'dishonour', and forwarded them to the *Liberator* newspaper in Boston, which dedicated nearly three of its large, densely printed pages to them on 14 May.[10] One of them was a letter claiming that a brother of MacIver had been a planter in Alabama, whose family inherited a considerable fortune on his death, and went on to suggest that MacIver himself having spent some years there explained his inclination to sympathise with pro-slavery sentiment.[11]

Douglass's departure inspired at least two poems, and even prompted an irreverent sidelong glance in *Punch* which reworked the episode into its standing joke about another topic of public interest that year:

BLACK AND WHITE DISTINCTIONS. Four of four thousand Ethiopian Serenaders at present in England applied for berths on board the *Cambria*, to return to their native Ethiopia, but were refused on account of their colour. It was only when they had taken the soot off their faces, and had washed their hands of the foul disgrace of being genuine blacks, that they were allowed to associate with the American passengers. We wonder the Yankees, in their hatred of everything black, do not, when they represent *Othello*, make him a white General.[12]

The *Glasgow Argus*, which three years earlier had published the remonstrance condemning the treatment of a Haitian passenger on the Cunard ship *Acadia*, took a particular interest in the affair.[13] In January 1846, the paper had taken notice of Douglass's arrival in Glasgow with a small announcement that 'Frederick Douglass, a self-liberated American slave, will deliver a lecture on American slavery at a public meeting.'[14] We can measure something of the impact of his British and Irish tour when we compare this to the more expansive description of the man less than eighteen months later. Under the headline 'Shameful Violation of the Rights of Man', the *Argus* begins:

> Frederick DOUGLASS, a *gentleman*, (and if Christian conduct, manly honesty, and cultivated intellect, combine to form a gentleman, he is eminently worthy to be so designated,) has been refused by Englishmen a passage on board a steam-ship bound to his native land, because his skin is not white – because he was once a slave.

The parenthesis indicates a degree of special pleading that suggests the extent that 'gentleman' was a contested term, caught between an older sense that associated it with high birth and inherited wealth, and a newer, more democratic conception, defined in terms of a certain mode of behaviour. Cunard's own list of passengers departing on the *Cambria* on 4 April prefers the former, reserving the title of 'gentleman' for those of independent means who did not have to work for a living; as a 'lecturer' Douglass, like those described as 'merchant', 'physician', 'clerk, 'ship-builder', 'shoe-maker', 'geologist' (or with no designation at all in the case of women), is assigned to the lower rank of those who are effectively reliant on commercial transactions or matrimonial relationships with others.[15]

The *Argus* reprinted Douglass's letter from *The Times*, together with the account of his departure in the *Manchester Express*, which supplied some details missing from the letter, perhaps most notably the fact that the captain had stepped in and offered Douglass his own rooms. It meant that Douglass was not deprived of comfort, but of course it did little to soften the insult, especially as he was apparently still forbidden to mix with the other passengers.

The following week it reprinted the letters from Burrop and MacIver. The *Argus* quickly dismissed that of Burrop as 'a gross and abominable fabrication' (an allegation, as we have seen, confirmed by Cunard), but engaged more closely with MacIver, examining his and Douglass's letters with the forensic precision of a barrister.

> The letter of Mr. M'Iver is written with some snappishness, but that perhaps is not to be wondered at under all the circumstances. Mr. M'Iver impugns the accuracy of the statement of Mr. Douglass; accuses him of 'withholding the entire conversation,' of 'suppressing the most material facts,' and of 'giving a spurious version which has misled the public.' We shall endeavour, by comparing very carefully the letter of Mr. Douglass with that of Mr. M'Iver, to discover wherein the spurious-ness or inaccuracy of the statement of Mr. Douglass consists.[16]

The paper goes on to challenge MacIver's claim that Douglass was 'satisfied' with the arrangements that were made, insisting that if he was satisfied at all, it was with Judkins's offer to give up his state rooms, not the company's initial refusal to accommodate him. And it was not at all convinced by MacIver's argument that his restriction was motivated entirely by a desire not avoid a repeat of the distur-bance on the outward voyage; whatever his private motivations, the exclusion of Douglass 'from the sight or the society of his super-refined and white fellow passengers' effectively discriminated against a man 'whose sole crime was the colour of his skin'.

Douglass was in no position to comment, of course, but, as we have seen, they did not have to wait long for a resolution. But, as if serialising a novel, the *Argus* did not reprint Samuel Cunard's letter (which had actually appeared in *The Times* the day before) until the next issue, prolonging the suspense, keeping the issue in the limelight a little longer, and possibly making it seem as if Cunard was taking more time to respond to a public outcry than he actually did. What-ever the reason, the scandal had reached a climax and it then fizzled out as suddenly as it had started. The *Argus* concluded:

> The British public will be glad to learn that Mr Cunard, the chief proprietor and original projector of the line of mail steamers ply-ing between this country and America, has made the *amende* to the national feelings for the outrage recently committed upon them by the agents of the Company at Liverpool. Mr Cunard's letter appeared in the morning papers of Thursday last, and contains a distinct avowal of the injustice perpetrated upon Mr Douglass, and as dis-tinct a promise that so outrageous a proceeding should not occur again. Let, then, by-gones be by-gones.[17]

Notes

1. FD, London, 30 March 1847 (FDP 1.2, p. 47).
2. *Manchester Express*, repr. Glasgow *Argus*, 8 April 1847.
3. FD to editor, Liverpool, 3 April 1847 (*The Times*, 6 April 1847; FDP 3.1, pp. 201–2). 'It is doubtful, whether Frederick will return till the next steamer afterward, as he is desirous of crossing in the Cambria with Capt. Judkins – the same vessel which brought him over': WLG to Helen E. Garrison, Sheffield, 10 September 1846 (GL3, p. 405).
4. My account of what happened on 3–4 April in Liverpool is based mainly on FD to editor, Liverpool, 3 April 1847 (*The Times*, 6 April 1847; FDP 3.1, pp. 201–2); William Bevan to editors of *Liverpool Mercury*, 7 April 1847 (*Liverpool Mercury*, 13 April 1847); William Logan to WLG, Rochdale, 17 April 1847 (*Liberator*, 14 May 1847).
5. Editorial, *The Times*, 8 April 1847.
6. Acts 28:15.
7. Charles MacIver to editor, Liverpool, 12 April 1847 (*The Times*, 13 April 1847).
8. Charles M. Burrop to editor, Maidenhead, 8 April 1847 (*The Times*, 13 April 1847).
9. Samuel Cunard to editor, London, 13 April 1847 (*The Times*, 14 April 1847).
10. A selection of over thirty of them were reprinted in the *Liberator*, 14 May 1847.
11. 'F.R.' of Bristol, apparently from *Jerrold's Magazine*. I have not been able to trace such a letter in the pages of that newspaper, nor confirm the allegation.
12. M.C., 'Farewell to Frederick Douglass', *Howitt's Journal*, 17 April 1847, pp. 222–3; *Poem on the Embarkation at Liverpool of Mr. Frederick Douglass upon his return to America, by F. N. D.*, Manchester, 8 July 1847 (cited in LWFD1, p. 433 n. 28); 'Black and White Distinctions', *Punch*, 17 April 1847.
13. *Glasgow Argus*, 5 August 1844.
14. *Glasgow Argus*, 12 January 1846.
15. The passenger list is available at: <http://www.immigrantships.net/v3/1800v3/cambria18470421.html> (last accessed 17 February 2018).
16. *Glasgow Argus*, 15 April 1847.
17. *Glasgow Argus*, 19 April 1847. Most modern assessments of the episode tend to side with Douglass, but for a provocative defence of MacIver see Butler, *The Age of Cunard*, pp. 66–8.

Chapter 25

Never Again

Meanwhile Douglass was pacing his commodious accommodations, in a stormy crossing of sixteen days. It would be at least a week after his arrival in Boston on 20 April that the extent of the furore would have been known in the United States, and not till the 14 May, when the *Liberator* reprinted the news items forwarded to it by Logan, would it become general knowledge.

When Douglass wrote of the incident in his second autobiography several years later, he described how public outrage at the 'contemptible conduct' of the shipping company led Mr Cunard to apologise, 'promising that the like should never occur again on board his steamers'.[1] It is hard to tell from the small number of documents from this period in the Cunard Archives whether Cunard took steps to ensure his promise was kept. In a private letter to MacIver written less than three weeks after the exchanges in *The Times*, Cunard makes no mention of the affair, preferring to share his concerns about the threat of competition from 'American ships'. However, a passing mention of the 'national prejudices', which might refer to the inclination of at least some would-be passengers from the United States to prefer their commercial rivals, hints at other prejudices the company considered indulging in order to retain their custom.[2]

In any case, Douglass was convinced: 'and the like, we believe,' he continued, 'has never since occurred on board the steamships of the Cunard Line'.[3] It was a claim he repeated in both editions of his third autobiography, published in 1881 and 1892.[4]

It is true that some African American travellers reported trouble-free passages. Henry Highland Garnet, for instance, recorded this voyage from 1861:

> My ticket was given me without a remark; an elegant state-room with *six berths* was placed at my disposal, and my seat at the table

was between two young American gentlemen [. . .] . And I am happy to say that I did not receive a look, or hear a word during the whole voyage, that grated upon my very sensitive feelings.[5]

But Douglass's faith in Cunard was misplaced, for cases of racial discrimination on his ships were recorded at least until the Civil War. Garnet himself noted that his experience contrasted markedly with an earlier voyage in 1850 during which he had been 'caged up in the steward's room of one of Cunard's vessels, and although a first class passenger, I was not allowed to go into the saloon, or to eat at the table with white humanity'.[6] The same year, William and Ellen Craft faced problems obtaining tickets in Halifax, where

> they baffled us shamefully at the Cunard office. They at first said that they did not book till the steamer came; which was not the fact. When I called again, they said they knew the steamer would come full from Boston, and therefore we had 'better try to get to Liverpool by other means.' Other mean Yankee excuses were made, to whom Mr Francis Jackson, of Boston, kindly gave us a letter, went and rebuked them, that we were able to secure our tickets.[7]

In 1851, Clarissa and Josephine Brown were denied passage by the Cunard agent in Boston unless they were classified as servants of their white companion, Rev. Charles Spear.[8] Two years later, Samuel Ringgold Ward was prevented from taking his meals with the rest of the passengers on the *Europa*. The decision was defended by Edward Cunard, son of Samuel, who managed the business in Halifax, Boston and New York, by drawing Ward's attention to the

> prevalent feelings in this country in respect to coloured people, and if you eat at the cabin table Americans will complain. We cannot allow our ship to be the arena of constant quarrels on this subject; we avoid the difficulty by making the rule that coloured passengers shall eat in their state rooms, or we can't take them.[9]

The following year James Watkins arranged to be joined by his wife and children who, having initially planned to travel on 'one of the Cunard line of steamers', found that the company 'refused to bring them across, on account of their colour'.[10]

In November 1859, Caroline Putnam and her party purchased first-class tickets for a passage on the *Europa* to Liverpool, only to receive, a few days before sailing, a letter from the Cunard agent informing her that they would be required to eat separately from the other passengers. On board Putnam protested but to no avail. On arrival in England, her sister Sarah Parker Remond (who had preceded her the year before) persuaded friends to make the details public. In an open letter to Samuel Cunard, the authors reminded him of the promise he made in 1847, 'that no more offences such as that committed against Mr. F. Douglass should take place on board your steamers'.[11] Cunard was not moved. 'I do not see that any advantage would result from discussing the subject matter of those letters, therefore I must decline entering into any correspondence on the subject.'[12] With the renewal of his government contract currently being debated in Parliament, perhaps he wanted to avoid drawing further attention to it. Lord Henry Brougham raised the matter of Putnam's treatment in the House of Lords but was told that it was 'not in the power of the Government to interfere', and no sanctions were imposed on the company.[13]

There is some evidence that the company continued to discriminate against black passengers long after the Civil War. When in Paris in 1937 the African American poet Langston Hughes met Nancy Cunard – a great-granddaughter of the shipping magnate – he told her

I had come to France on a Cunard Line vessel, thinking it would please her, since I knew she was of that family. To my surprise, she had never set foot on a Cunard liner and never intended to do so, she said, because the line segregated Negroes. Instead she travelled on French boats.[14]

Why did Douglass persist in his belief that Cunard changed its policies after 1847? Many of those who encountered discrimination on its ships in the 1850s and 60s were his friends. The case of Caroline Putnam was even reported in his own newspaper, *Douglass' Monthly*.[15]

When Douglass wrote his first account of his return voyage in a letter to Garrison – this was before he could have known of the impact of his letter to *The Times* – he admits that, apart from the restriction that prevented him from leaving the captain's state-rooms,

I was as well provided for as any other passenger. Indeed, my apartments were much to be preferred to any which I saw on board. I was

treated with the utmost politeness by every officer on board, and
received every attention from the servants during the whole voyage.[16]

In *My Bondage and My Freedom* in 1855, he describes himself,
somewhat less equivocally, as being 'cooped up in the stern', refashioning the episode so as to make it the climax of a narrative of his
'Twenty One Months in Great Britain' that charts his emergence as
a defiantly independent abolitionist leader, someone who must demonstrate that he can make a difference.

The chapter begins by reminding his readers of the dangers that
led him to 'seek a refuge from republican slavery in monarchical
England' in the summer of 1845, and continues:

> A rude, uncultivated fugitive slave was driven, by stern necessity, to
> that country to which young American gentlemen go to increase their
> stock of knowledge, to seek pleasure, to have their rough democratic
> manners softened by contact with English aristocratic refinement.[17]

If Douglass's motivations are rather different from those of the
'gentlemen' he compares himself to, the contrast is intensified as
soon as he begins to describe his departure.

> On applying for a passage to England, on board the *Cambria*, of the
> Cunard line, my friend, James N. Buffum, of Lynn, Massachusetts,
> was informed that I could not be received on board as a cabin passen-
> ger. American prejudice against color triumphed over British liberality
> and civilization, and erected a color test and condition for crossing the
> sea in the cabin of a British vessel.[18]

That it was a ship flying the colours of the country that had
abolished slavery in the colonies more than a decade before (and at
home much further back than that) certainly aroused his indignation, but he had endured much more severe cases of racial prejudice
in Massachusetts, and he makes light of the proscription, no doubt
anticipating the more established freedoms he would enjoy once he
disembarked in Liverpool.

> The insult was keenly felt by my white friends, but to me, it was
> common, expected, and therefore, a thing of no great consequence,
> whether I went in the cabin or in the steerage. Moreover, I felt that if

I could not go into the first cabin, first cabin passengers could come into the second cabin, and the result justified my anticipations to the fullest extent. Indeed, I soon found myself an object of more general interest than I wished to be; and so far from being degraded by being placed in the second cabin, that part of the ship became the scene of as much pleasure and refinement, during the voyage, as the cabin itself. The Hutchinson Family, celebrated vocalists – fellow-passengers – often came to my rude forecastle deck, and sung their sweetest songs, enlivening the place with eloquent music, as well as spirited conversation, during the voyage. In two days after leaving Boston, one part of the ship was about as free to me as another. My fellow-passengers not only visited me, but invited me to visit them, on the saloon deck. My visits there, however, were but seldom. I preferred to live within my privileges, and keep upon my own premises. I found this quite as much in accordance with good policy, as with my own feelings.[19]

As the chapter proceeds, Douglass makes a point of paying tribute to those who helped him during his sojourn – the 'gallant' Captain Judkins, who saved him from the mob on the *Cambria*, the 'remarkable' Anna Richardson, who raised funds to buy his freedom, the 'much abused republican friend of freedom' George Thompson, 'honest' John Murray of the Glasgow Emancipation Society, and many others.[20] Detailing his abolitionist campaigns, he singles out three confrontations for special mention. In the first two cases he plays down his own role – focusing on George Thompson's intervention at the Free Church assembly in 1846, and reporting the meeting of the Evangelical Alliance in the third person. But with the World Temperance Convention, and his own 'point blank collision' with Rev. Dr Cox, Douglass, with a little help from Shakespeare, turns attention on himself:

Thus did circumstances favor me, and favor the cause of which I strove to be the advocate [. . .] I became one of that class of men, who, for the moment at least, 'have greatness forced upon them'.[21]

He follows this by acknowledging the help of his British friends in raising funds 'to enable me to start a paper, devoted to the interests of my enslaved and oppressed people' – at a time, he reminded them, when 'there was not, in the United States, a single newspaper regularly published by the colored people'.[22] And by the end of the year, his plans came to fruition, causing some discomfort to Garrison and his associates in the American Anti-Slavery Society in Boston. Pointedly, Douglass moved his family from Massachusetts to the shores of Lake Ontario, basing the *North Star* more than three hundred miles from his mentor, in Rochester, New York. Although it would be several years before the two men fell out in public, their paths had begun to diverge.[23]

As the chapter draws to its conclusion, Douglass's transformation is almost complete – from an agent of the Massachusetts Anti-Slavery Society serving the white abolitionist cause to a man looking forward to editing his own newspaper. It is true that his British lectures failed to reverse the policies of the Free Church, the Evangelical Alliance and the World Temperance Convention, but their achievement, he insists, was the more diffuse one of rousing public opinion. What better way, then, to end his account than with a story that forcefully demonstrated the power of the press? The events in Liverpool in Easter 1847, specifically his letter to *The Times*, offered the perfect opportunity to conclude the narrative of his tour with the first decisive act of his new career. The 'gallant' Judkins is conspicuously absent from this account of the return voyage because in this later autobiographical reinvention, Douglass wants to be seen as the sole protagonist.

'Cooped up in the stern', Douglass interprets his return passage not as an 'insult [. . .] of no great consequence', but one that encapsulates the entire history of his subordination to date. 'The lash of proscription', he writes, 'has a sting for the soul hardly less severe than that which bites the flesh and draws the blood from the back of a plantation slave,' coming as it did, he points out, after nearly two years' freedom from discrimination on grounds of colour. 'The reader,' he concludes, 'will easily imagine what must have been my feelings.'

But, as befits his emerging role as the leader of 'my enslaved and oppressed people', it is not ultimately about his personal feelings. Because his privations led to what he presents as Cunard's historic pronouncement – which, he insists, freed others in his wake – he can represent them as an effective martyrdom: 'It is not very pleasant to be made the subject of such insults; but if all such necessarily resulted as this one did, I should be very happy to bear, patiently, many more than I have borne, of the same sort.'[24]

Notes

1. BF, pp. 390–1 (A, pp. 387–8; FDP 2.2, p. 225).
2. Samuel Cunard to Charles MacIver, London, 1 May 1847 (MacIver Papers, D138/4/1).
3. BF, p. 391 (A, p. 388; FDP 2.2, p. 25).
4. LT1, p. 263; LT2, p. 319 (A, p. 702; FDP 2.3, p. 202). The claim is sometimes repeated uncritically by biographers. For example: 'On his return voyage [. . .] Douglass caused the *Cunard* steamship line to end its discriminatory policy toward "colored" people forever, and he had first-class cabin accommodation,' Ross, 'European Lecture-Circuit (1845–47)', p. 61.
5. Henry Highland Garnet to Julia Garnet, 13 September 1861 (BAP1, p. 497). This was on a New York to Liverpool run on a British vessel, but Garnet does not specify the shipping company involved.
6. Ibid. p. 497.
7. Craft, *Running a Thousand Miles for Freedom*, p. 108.
8. See Farrison, *William Wells Brown*, pp. 192–3; Greenspan, *William Wells Brown*, p. 258.
9. Ward, *Autobiography of a Fugitive Negro*, p. 228.
10. Watkins, *Struggles for Freedom*, p. 41.
11. M. D. Hill and Edwin Chapman to Samuel Cunard, Bristol, 11 June 1860, quoted in 'Coloured Persons and Cunard Steamers', *Lloyd's Weekly Newspaper*, 8 July 1860. The letter was composed at the evident request of Remond. The article also reprints the letter they received from Putnam, and the letter she received from the Cunard agent. Remond also wrote to the press directly: see Sarah Parker Remond to editor, *Scottish Press*, 4 December 1859 (BAP 1, pp. 470–1).
12. Samuel Cunard to Edwin Chapman, Edmonton, 29 June 1860, quoted in 'The Cunard Company's Subserviency to the American Doctrine of Caste', *Economist*, 7 July 1860.
13. House of Lords Debates, 25 June 1860, vol. 159, c. 933, available at <http://hansard.millbanksystems.com/lords/1860/jun/25/motion-for-papers> (last accessed 21 February 2018); for Lord Granville's response on 17 July see *Illustrated Times*, 21 July 1860. 'We are glad to record that on her return, in a mail-packet belonging to the Company by which she had been thus treated, Mrs Putnam was permitted to take her place at table without objection, although American slaveowners were among the passengers. An auspicious omen!': Hill, *Our Exemplars Poor and Rich*, p. 286. For a summary of the episode see Salenius, *An Abolitionist Abroad*, pp. 76–9.
14. Hughes, *I Wonder as I Wander*, p. 318.

15. 'The Cunard Steamship Company and Colored Passengers', *Douglass' Monthly* (September 1860).
16. FD to WLG, Lynn, 21 April 1847 (*Liberator*, 30 April 1847).
17. BF, pp. 365–6 (A, p. 370; FDP 2.2, p. 210).
18. BF, p. 366 (A, p. 370; FDP 2.2, p. 210).
19. BF, pp. 366–7 (A, pp. 370–1; FDP 2.2, p. 210).
20. BF, pp. 368, 374, 378, 381 (A, pp. 372, 376, 379, 381; FDP 2.2, pp. 211, 215, 218, 220).
21. BF, p. 388 (A, p. 386; FDP 2.2, p. 233). The quotation is from *Twelfth Night*, II, v and III, iv.
22. BF, pp. 388–9 (A, pp. 386–7; FDP 2.2, p. 223). The careful wording doesn't quite excuse his neglecting to acknowledge the *Ram's Horn*, which was launched by Willis A. Hodges and Thomas Van Rensselaer in January 1847, and to which Douglass himself subsequently contributed. The newspaper closed in June 1848. Other African American newspapers published, intermittently, at this time included David Ruggles's *Genius of Freedom* and Martin R. Delany's *The Mystery*. See Penn, *The Afro-American Press and its Editors*, pp. 55–65; Simmons, *The African American Press*, pp. 11–12.
23. For a study of the relationship between FD and WLG see Anadolu-Okur, *Dismantling Slavery*.
24. BF, p. 391 (A, p. 388; FDP 2.2, p. 225).

Part VI

The Affinity Scot

But, ladies and gentlemen, this is not a time for long speeches. I do not wish to detain you from the social pleasures that await you. I repeat again, that though I am not a Scotchman, and have a colored skin, I am proud to be among you this evening. And if any think me out of my place on this occasion (pointing at the picture of Burns), I beg that the blame may be laid at the door of him who taught me that 'a man's a man for a' that.'

Frederick Douglass, Rochester, New York, 25 January 1849

The change wrought in me is truly amazing. If you should meet me now, you would scarcely know me. You know when I used to meet you near Covey's wood-gate, I hardly dared to look up at you. If I should meet you where I now am, amid the free hills of Old Scotland, where the ancient 'Black Douglass' once met his foes, I presume I might summon sufficient fortitude to look you full in the face. It may be that, wearing the brave name which I have assumed, might lead me to deeds which would render our meeting not the most agreeable. Especially might this be the case, if you should attempt to enslave me. You would see a wonderful difference in me. I have really got out of my place; that is, I have got out of slavery, which you know is 'the place' for negroes in Christian America.

Frederick Douglass, Perth, 27 January 1846

Chapter 26

Recitals of Blood

In its report on Douglass's speech at the Cathcart Street Church on 24 March 1846, the *Ayr Advertiser* remarked on his skills as an orator:

> He brought every possible view of the subject before the audience, sometimes harrowing up their feelings with recitals of blood, and again persuasively and mildly reasoning the point; at one time cutting with the most vigorous sarcasm, and again assuming all the solemnity of a man deeply in earnest.[1]

It is the 'recitals of blood' I want to dwell on here, for 'blood', both literally and metaphorically, signifies many things of importance to Douglass. The word *blood* and its cognates occur over fifty times in his *Narrative*, mostly in the course of his accounts of acts of brutality towards slaves. The pattern continues in his speeches, but while he occasionally recites the kinds of verbal description he has already committed to print, he amplifies them in ways that are only possible on the lecture platform.

The *Dundee Courier* reported how, alongside his 'pathetic, earnest, and impressive' descriptions of 'the horrid scenes he had witnessed, the sufferings of the slaves', Douglass held up in his hands 'instruments of torture', including 'a collar to prevent repose, handcuffs and anklets, with the lash, all commonly in use.'[2] Such displays were a common feature of his – and Buffum's – lectures.[3] On some occasions, he strove for more dramatic effect by explaining that the instruments they brought with them were not mere theatrical props, but items that bore traces of their former use. In Limerick, for instance, Douglass produced 'an iron collar taken from the neck of a young woman who had escaped from Mobile. It had so worn into her neck that her blood and flesh were found on it.'[4] Some of them had been used on people he knew well, even in his presence.[5] When Buffum displayed some implements at a church in Edinburgh, it elicited 'a most painful sensation in the immense congregation'.[6] Even more sensational were the moments when Douglass declared that his own body still bore the marks of the slave-driver's whip.[7]

Douglass is not just looking for a raw emotional response here. These bloody scenes provide a graphic illustration of the difference between chattel slavery and other forms of subordination. Keenly aware that British and Irish opponents often countered abolitionist arguments by suggesting that they ignore privations suffered by wage labourers or peasants – 'We have slavery here too' – he repeatedly insists on the distinctive character of the system he is describing. It is not about how hard the work is or about the lack of political rights, it is about one person holding property in another.[8] But as this property relation is one that can only be maintained by violence, or the immediate threat of it, examples of this violence are among the most powerful images of the distinctiveness of chattel slavery. Thus, as Douglass says in Paisley in March 1846, 'the best evidence of a man being a slave is the scar on his back'.[9]

No wonder, then, that the language of the campaign against the Free Church drips with blood, with its calls to return the 'blood-stained money' and the 'bloody gold', donations 'wrung from the sinews, and muscles, and blood of the slaves', its slogans scrawled on walls in 'blood red capitals'.[10]

But these stories are not just about cruelties passively borne. They also record resistance. In his *Narrative* Douglass makes much of his fight with the brutal Covey, who hired him as a field hand in 1833, calling it 'the turning-point in my career as a slave', after which the man does not dare lay a finger on him again. 'He had drawn no blood from me, but I had from him,' he remarks, emphasising the reversal grammatically.[11] His speeches in Britain and Ireland, by contrast, choose to highlight two other moments of resistance. They both take place at sea, and on at least one occasion Douglass couples them together, as if one is incomplete without the other.

The first is the riot that followed his attempt to deliver a lecture on the *Cambria* on the last evening of his voyage from Boston. As we saw in Part I, the hostility of slaveholders which forced him to abandon his speech turned nasty indeed, with some of them threatening to throw him overboard. In contrast to the fight with Covey, though, it is not Douglass who fights back, but Captain Judkins on his behalf.

If Douglass enjoys picturing Judkins threatening the abusive slave-holders with irons – and often takes this opportunity in his lecture to exhibit instruments used for torturing slaves – the episode does not match his own act of rebellion as an adolescent.

Perhaps this is why he supplements it with the story of Madison Washington and the mutiny on board the *Creole*, which he does several times, not only in his farewell speech in London. In recounting the events, Douglass does not conceal the violence involved: 'He got on deck, and seizing a handspike, struck down the captain and mate, secured the crew, and cheered on his associates in the cause of liberty.'[12] But what is especially important is that the rebellion was successful. The mutineers guided the ship to a British port – Nassau in the Bahamas – where the slaveholders had no jurisdiction and thus 'found shelter under the British lion', having 'fled from a republican government and have chosen a monarchical, and are basking under the free sun amid the free hills and valleys of a free monarchical country'.[13] In Cork Douglass tells the story immediately after recounting his own voyage across the Atlantic. In doing so, he invites his audience to draw a parallel between Washington and himself who also found shelter under the British lion, but places Douglass at the centre of the narrative rather than Judkins.[14]

These stories sit uneasily with the claim he makes elsewhere that the 'abolitionists of America did not contemplate physical force' but rather 'relied on God and truth and humanity for the overthrow of slavery in the United States'.[15] Sometimes, when Douglass seems to come close to endorsing violence, he hastily retracts:

> If a foreign enemy were to land in America and plant the standard of freedom, the slaves would rise to man [. . .] a strong fire would be kindled within their breasts, which would remind them that their fathers and mothers had been tortured by the oppressors, that the white face had been guilty of grinding the poor blacks – they would not spare the guilty traders in human blood. But you are not to infer from this that I am an advocate for war, no I hate war, I have no weapon but that which is consistent with morality, I am engaged in a holy war; I ask not the aid of the sword, I appeal to the understanding and the hearts of men – we use these weapons, and hope that God will give us the victory.[16]

To even imagine an armed insurrection of slaves places strain on Garrison's doctrine of non-resistance, to which Douglass publicly adhered. By the end of his time in Britain and Ireland, as we saw in Part V, it is possible to detect signs of him beginning to assert his independence, on this issue among others. In private, he was already admitting as such. In a letter to Elizabeth Pease from Belfast in July 1846 he wrote:

> You ask me if I go with friend Garrison on the nonresistant principle. In answer, I think there is a slight difference between us. I am against taking life – against all war offensive or defensive – against retaliation of every kind, and yet I can concieve of circumstances when it would not only be right – but our bounden duty to use Physical force to restrain persons bent upon the commission of crime. But about this we may speak face to face should a kind Providence permit us to meet. I may say that although I do not go the whole length of repudiating the use of physical force I am regarded in the U.S. as being in the fullest manner identified with the nonresistant school of reformers.[17]

Given that we know that Douglass ultimately parted ways with Garrison, breaking with him definitively in 1851, it is tempting to over-read early signs of this during his British and Irish tour. But surely the fact that he was an ocean away from him for nearly a year before Garrison joined him in August 1846 gave Douglass an opportunity to reflect on his relation to the American Anti-Slavery Society whose concerns and suspicions over a Douglass on the loose (we learnt in Chapter 6 how Chapman and Webb in particular expressed fears that he would be led astray by money and women) must have weighed heavily on him. For that reason, his letter to Pease is revealing, especially when he goes on to suggest that his experience overseas has made him more aware of the prejudice of white Americans he considered his friends. He tells her of a recent encounter with the peace campaigner Elihu Burritt, then touring Britain to launch a new organisation, the League of Universal Brotherhood:

> I have seldom met with an American in whose presence I felt more at home. They are all more or less tainted with prejudice against color so that I generally feel like keeping my distance from them – for fear of being repulsed. Persons who seemed in America – pretty free from that feeling – when compared with people here – disclose the taints. They have it – but don't know it. They speak to and of colored people differently, from what they do of & to persons of their own complexion.[18]

Burritt had stood as Liberty Party candidate in the US presidential election of 1844, and so was associated with a rival branch of abolitionism which the Garrisonians abhorred. That Douglass singles out Burritt as an exception and not Garrison or any other of his allies in the American Anti-Slavery Society indicates an important reassessment had been taking place.

If a speech by Douglass is rarely complete without someone being manacled, whipped, beaten or shot, he delivers 'recitals of blood' in a different sense too. For another persistent theme he articulates during this period is that of kinship or consanguinity. There are two reasons why it preoccupies him.

First and foremost, his own ruptured family background. As he explains repeatedly, he did not know who his father was; he was separated from his mother at an early age and, according to his own account, recalled seeing her only 'four or five times in my life; and each of those times was very short in duration, and at night'.[19] 'The ties that ordinarily bind children to their homes', he wrote in his *Narrative*, 'were all suspended in my case.'[20] Such experiences were common. 'Genealogical trees do not flourish among slaves,' as he put it, making it hard for them to establish their own ancestry with any certainty.[21] Given that they grew up in a distinctively Southern culture that placed particular emphasis on lineage, this difficulty caused them especial pain, as slave narratives often pointed out.

> In the northern and middle states, so far as I have known them, very little respect is paid to family pretensions; and this disregard of ancestry seems to me to be the necessary offspring of the condition of things. In the plantation states, the case is widely different.[22]

Thus Charles Ball in his *Slavery in the United States* (1835). Slaves might indeed be expected to offer a critical perspective on this ideology; for, despite the 'patriarchal' rhetoric of plantation management in the antebellum period (which increasingly represented slaves as part of the extended household), they could never be fully part of the families they belonged to, as were their white contemporaries with whom they played as children, even as they were half brothers and sisters.

'My father, ___, was one of the most wealthy planters in Virginia,' writes William Grimes at the start of his narrative, a sentence that might announce a very different autobiography, if the omission of his father's name did not already warn us that despite this connection, 'I was in law, a bastard and slave, and owned by Doct. Steward.'[23] Invoking the generic male slave, James Pennington dwells at length on the way the plantation system

> throws his family history into utter confusion, and leaves him without a single record to which he may appeal in vindication of his character, or honour. And has a man no sense of honour because he was born a slave? Has he no need of character? Suppose insult, reproach, or slander, should render it necessary for him to appeal to the history of his family in vindication of his character, where will he find that history? He goes to his native state, to his native country, to his native town; but no where does he find any record of himself as a *man*. On looking at the family record of his old, kind, Christian masters, there he finds his name on a catalogue with the horses, cows, hogs and dogs.[24]

Now Pennington, like many other authors of slave narratives, escaped from the South at a relatively early age. When he came to write his story, he had been living in the North for some twenty years, joined the community of abolitionists, and learned to address Northern audiences in an idiom that would appeal to them.

What is interesting about this passage is that Pennington believes that his 'character' can only be vindicated by reference to his 'family history' rather than, say, his own actions. This suggests that he places an importance on kinship which may have seemed strange to his Northern readers. His reference to 'honour' indicates that he is not simply asserting the value of the ties of affection between relatives (which slavery often ruthlessly cut, as abolitionists never tired of pointing out) but subordinating individual achievement to family reputation. His condemnation of slavery here draws less on a Northern, sentimental conception of family, which emphasised the private emotional bonds between individuals, than a Southern one, for which it was the seat, as one historian puts it, of 'corporatist values that legitimated white men's personal power over dependents'.[25] This suggests that he absorbed this ideology as a child and did not entirely abandon it as a free adult in the North.

Pennington was not an exception. As Douglass explained to an audience in later life, 'the Negro [. . .] is preeminently a Southern man. He is so both in constitution and habits, in body as well as

mind. He will not only take with him to the North southern modes
of labor, but southern modes of life.'[26]

A second reason Douglass engaged with the language of kinship
is the emergence in the 1840s of the so-called 'American School' of
Ethnology which, as we saw in Chapter 17, mounted a scientific
challenge to the long-established Christian doctrine of the unity of
the human species, proposing instead the existence of several distinct, and to some extent incompatible, races. Douglass criticised the
school's assumptions at length in a speech entitled 'The Claims of
the Negro Ethnologically Considered' before an audience in Ohio in
1854, suggesting that virtually all its supporters belong to 'those who
hold it to be the privilege of the *Anglo-Saxon* to enslave and oppress
the African', for whom the temptation 'to read the negro out of the
human family' is very strong.[27]

But, already, in his pronouncements in Britain and Ireland, we can
hear Douglass insistently proclaim 'God has made of one blood all
nations of the earth' – perhaps the line most cited from the New Testament by abolitionists since at least the late 1830s, but echoing the
earlier slogan 'Am I not a man and brother?' from the 1790s.[28] From
Dublin he writes that he finds himself 'not treated as a color, but as a
man – not as a thing but as a child of the common Father of us all'.[29]

Universal siblinghood rarely turns out to be as universal as it
makes out: some people nearly always turn out to be endowed with
less humanity than others, the circle of kinship often restricted to
those of the same faith, nation or ethnicity.[30] When Douglass uses
that language to describe his relationship to others devoted to the
abolitionist cause, he often crosses the colour line, perhaps with a
small measure of defiance. Of Garrison, even after the two men had
fallen out, he declared, 'I stand in relation to him something like that
of a child to a parent.'[31] And in letters he writes from abroad in 1846
Douglass repeatedly asserts a sibling-like connection to several other
white correspondents: 'You have been to me – a brother' (Wendell
Phillips); 'You loved me and treated me as a brother before the world
knew me as it now does' (Amy Post); 'I shall never forget how like
two very brothers we were ready to dare-do, and even die for each
other' (William A. White).[32]

But if Douglass counters the American Ethnologists by turning
his white associates into blood relatives, he also, on one occasion,
executes the opposite gesture. When he comes to write of his mother
in his second autobiography he describes her as 'tall, and finely

proportioned; of deep black, glossy complexion'. In the absence of a portrait to remember by, Douglass says that he relied instead on a figure in James Cowles Prichard's *Natural History of Man* (1843), in which he saw a resemblance.[33] But, as James McCune Smith points out in his introduction to Douglass's autobiography, the figure in question was the Pharoah, Ramesses the Great, and the same illustration had been used by the American Ethnologists Nott and Gliddon in *Types of Mankind* (1854) as an example of a profile that '"like Napoleon's, is superbly European".'[34] If Douglass – albeit momentarily – conjures with the idea that his mother is white, we might note that, in changing her sex, Douglass was all too conventional in thinking that the ancestors worth searching for were men, not women.

The two kinds of blood – bloodlines and bloodshed – often run in separate grooves. But one place they converge for Douglass is mediaeval Scotland.

Already in New Bedford, Douglass had – in perhaps the most audacious and public of his 'kin' fictions – taken a new name, imaginatively grafting himself onto one of Scotland's most famous family trees. And not just any famous family, but one famous for its violence. As we saw in Chapter 10, the story of the Douglases is littered with acts of unwarranted savagery arising from struggles with rival Scottish nobles as well as invading English armies. As he worked on his *Tales of a Grandfather*, Scott wrote:

> The morning was damp, dripping and unpleasant; so I even made a work of necessity, and set to the *Tales* like a dragon. I murdered McLellan of Bomby at Thrieve Castle; stabbed the Black Douglas in the town of Stirling; astonished King James before Roxburgh; and stifled the Earl of Mar in his bath in the Canongate. A wild world, my masters, this Scotland of ours must have been.[35]

With these events long past, Scott can relish the bloodshed as if he were writing fiction. Not so a peace campaigner like Henry Clarke Wright who, in his letters from the Scottish Borders in 1846, cannot withhold his solemn judgement of a different age: 'It has been a golgotha and a field of blood,' he wrote from Jedburgh, while in Berwick he is reminded of 'Wallace, Bruce, Edward, Northumberland, and Douglass, and many other of the butchers and tigers of mankind'.[36]

As a non-resistant, Douglass might have wanted to avoid being identified with such butchers and tigers. In January 1846 we can see him wrestling with the moral and political ramifications of choosing such a violent man as a fictional ancestor. Recall that his first reference to the Black Douglas was in the letter he wrote to Garrison from Perth, enclosing a draft of his reply to Thompson, the man who had cast doubt on his identity:

> If I should meet you now, amid the free hills of old Scotland, where the ancient 'black Douglass' once met his foes, I presume I might summon sufficient fortitude to look you full in the face; and were you attempt to make a slave of me, it is possible you might find me almost as disagreeable a subject, as was the Douglass to whom I have just referred.[37]

In order to make the reversal of their relationship as dramatic as possible, Douglass contrasts their former encounters in Maryland, in which the young slave 'hardly dared to lift my head, and look up at you', with a hypothetical one now in Scotland, in which Thompson is the one quaking before a powerful man capable of awesome retribution should he be wronged. Some readers of the letter might have been reminded of the episode known bleakly as Douglas's Larder, in which the Good Sir James recaptured his fortress from the English, 'and, putting the garrison to the sword, mingled the mangled bodies with a large stock of provisions which the English had amassed, and set fire to the castle'.[38] But Douglass, who hints at a possible justification for ancient violence by implying it was in the cause of freedom, can only refer to this threat euphemistically as 'disagreeable'. He may have chosen the word carefully to spare the blushes of the Garrisonians, but, like many euphemisms, it may also signal a conspiratorial wink that knows all too well what terrors lie behind it.

Two days later, in Dundee, the free hills of Scotland once more make their way into a letter, this time to Francis Jackson, an abolitionist colleague of Garrison's. Not intended for publication, as the letter from Perth was, it may have offered Douglass the opportunity to express himself more honestly, although he would still have been tailoring his views to match those of his addressee.

> I am now as you will perceive by the date of this letter in old Scotland – almost every hill, river, mountain and lake of which has been made classic by the heroic deeds of her noble sons. Scarcely

a stream but what has been poured into song, or a hill that is not associated with some firce and bloody conflict between liberty and slavery. I had a view the other day of what are called the Grampion mountains that devide east Scotland from the west. I was told that here the ancient crowned heads use to meet, contend and struggle in deadly conflict for supremacy, causing those grand old hills to run blood, each warming cold steal in the others heart.[39]

In this passage, Douglass's namesake disappears into the more generic 'noble sons', but their cause, at least initially, is defined as 'heroic' and implicitly in defence of 'liberty' against 'slavery' (Douglass allowing himself to use the word to mean political oppression, a usage he normally strongly criticised). The violence, though, is more openly acknowledged: blood runs freely in Douglass's prose here. At the same time, the noble cause becomes more ambiguous, less a struggle for freedom from foreign rule than 'a deadly conflict for supremacy'. Douglass seems to be admitting here that the foes of his illustrious forebears were not just the English invaders but rivals competing for personal power and wealth. Having gone much further than his earlier letter in recognising what this ancient violence entailed, he now feels compelled to reflect on what what it means for him to celebrate it.

My soul sickens at the thought yet I see in myself all those elements of character which were I to yeild to their promptings might lead me to deeds as bloody as those at which my soul now sickens, and from which I now turn with disgust and shame. Thank God liberty is no longer to be contended for and gained by instruments of death. A higher, a nobler a mightier than carnal weapon is placed into our hands – one which hurls defiance at all the improvements of carnal warfare. It is the rightious appeal to the understanding and the heart – with this we can withstand the most firey of all the darts of perdition itself. I see that America is boasting of her naval, and military power – let her boast. She may build her walls and her forts, making them proof against ball, and bomb. But while there is a single voice in her midst to charge home upon her the duty of emancipation neither her army, nor her navy can protect her from the knawing of a guilty conscience.[40]

Douglass here – with his reference to 'carnal weapons' – echoes the defiantly pacifist language of Garrison's 'Declaration of Sentiments'. And yet in the speech he made the following day these misgivings seem to be cast aside. Douglass is pleased to stand before his audience at the Bell Street Chapel and recycle the phrases which had caused him such disgust and shame the night before, in order to massage his listeners' patriotism. In that standard ritual of the touring performer, Douglass declares himself happy to be in

> a land whose every hill has been made classic by heroic deeds performed by her noble sons – a land whose every brook and river carry the songs of freedom as they pass to the ocean – a land whose hills have nearly all been watered with blood in behalf of freedom.[41]

Although Douglass is quick to qualify the bloodshed as 'heroic' and 'in behalf of freedom', he risks blunting the force of his argument against the Free Church, which he condemns immediately afterwards for striking 'hands in good Christian fellowship with men whose hands are full of blood'.[42] The blood of slavery and the blood of freedom are uncomfortably close together.

Two months later in Ayr, he invokes the Scottish landscape once more, but this time steers away from danger, suggesting that it has been 'made classic' not by 'heroic deeds' but by the 'brilliant genius' of a poet, seeking safety in the pen rather than the sword.[43]

Notes

1. FD, Ayr, 24 March 1846 (FDP 1.1, p. 204).
2. FD, Dundee, 30 January 1846 (*Dundee Courier*, 3 February 1846).
3. See also FD, Dublin, 9 September 1845 (*Freeman's Journal*, 13 September 1845); FD, Dublin, 1 October 1845 (FDP 1.1, p. 35); FD, Cork, 23 October 1845 (FDP 1.1, p. 66); FD, Limerick, 10 November 1845 (FDP 1.1, pp. 85–6); FD, Ayr, 24 March 1846 (Ayr *Advertiser*, 26 March 1846); JB, Edinburgh, 29 April 1846 (*Manstealers*, p. 52).
4. FD, Limerick, 10 November 1845 (FDP 1.1, p. 85).
5. For example, handcuffs that had been broken by a fugitive slave he knew well; and a whip that he had seen his master apply to a young woman, probably his cousin Henny: FD, Limerick, 10 November 1846 (FDP 1.1, pp. 85–6).
6. JB, Edinburgh, 29 April 1846 (*Manstealers*, p. 52).
7. FD, Dublin, 1 October 1845 (FDP 1.1, p. 36); FD, Cork, 14 October 1845 (FDP 1.1, pp. 37, 41–2); FD, Limerick, 10 November 1845 (FDP 1.1, p. 77); FD, Exeter, 28 August 1846 (FDP 1.1, p. 357); FD, Sheffield, 11 September 1846 (FDP 1.1, p. 400); FD, Sunderland, 18 September 1846 (FDP 1.1, p. 418).

8. See FD, Belfast, 5 December 1845 (FDP 1.1, p. 93); FD, Glasgow, 15 January 1846 (FDP 1.1, pp. 134–5); FD, Paisley, 17 March 1846 (FDP 1.1, pp. 183–4); FD, London, 22 May 1846 (FDP 1.1, p. 273); FD, Newcastle, 3 August 1846 (FDP 1.1, pp. 317–20); FD, Bristol, 25 August 1846 (FDP 1.1, pp. 343–4); FD, Bridgewater, 31 August 1846 (FDP 1.1, p. 365); FD, Sheffield, 25 March 1847 (FDP 1.2, pp. 9–10).

9. FD, Paisley, 20 March 1846 (FDP 1.1, p. 190).

10. For 'blood-stained money' see e.g. FD, Paisley, 25 April 1846 (FDP 1.1, p. 243); for 'bloody gold' see e.g. FD, Paisley, 19 March 1846 (FDP 1.1, p. 189); for 'blood red capitals' see FD, Paisley, 25 April 1846 (FDP 1.1, pp. 242–3); for 'wrung from the sinews' see FD, Dundee, 28 January 1846 (*Dundee, Perth and Cupar Advertiser*, 30 January 1846).

11. N, p. 113 (A, p. 65; FDP 2.1, p. 54).

12. FD, Edinburgh, 1 May 1846 (FDP 1.1, p. 245).

13. FD, Paisley, 6 April 1846 (FDP 1.1, pp. 211–12). The story may have gained extra significance for FD when in Liverpool on 19 October 1846 he had a chance encounter with a former slave he had known in Baltimore, who (FD discovers), around the time of FD's own escape to the North, had been hired out by his master as a ship's cook, and when a storm forced the vessel to shelter in Nassau, like Washington (also the ship's cook) he took the opportunity to claim freedom on British soil. FD, Edinburgh, 21 October 1846 (*Scotsman*, 24 October 1846; *Edinburgh Evening Post*, 24 October 1846).

14. FD Cork, 23 October 1845 (FDP 1.1, pp. 67–9). For other references to the *Creole* mutiny in FD's speeches see FD, Dundee, 9 February 1846 (*Dundee, Perth and Cupar Advertiser*, 10 February 1846; *Dundee Courier*, 10 February 1846), FD, London, 30 March 1847 (FDP 1.2, pp. 46–7). And for a useful discussion of these speeches see Levine, *The Lives of Frederick Douglass*, pp. 135–8. For a historical account of the *Creole* mutiny see Hendrick and Hendrick, *The Creole Mutiny*. FD later fictionalised the life of Madison Washington in his novella *The Heroic Slave* (1853).

15. FD, Bridgewater, 31 August 1846 (FDP 1.1, p. 369).

16. FD, Paisley, 19 March 1846 (FDP 1.1, p. 187).

17. FD to Elizabeth Pease, Belfast, 6 July 1846 (FDP 3.1, pp. 141–2).

18. Ibid. p. 142.

19. N, p. 48 (A, p. 16; FDP 2.1, pp. 13–14).

20. N, p. 73 (A, p. 34; FDP 2.1, p. 28).

21. BF, p. 34 (A, p. 140; FDP 2.2, p. 22).

22. Charles Ball, *Slavery in the United States* [1835] in Taylor, *I Was Born a Slave*, vol. 1, pp. 383–4.

23. William Grimes, *Life of William Grimes, the Runaway Slave* [1825], in Taylor, *I Was Born a Slave*, vol. 1, p. 187. Compare him with the

father of William Wells Brown, who was 'connected with some of the first families in Kentucky': William Wells Brown, *Narrative of William Wells Brown, a Fugitive Slave* [1847], in Taylor, *I Was Born a Slave*, vol. 1, p. 684.

24. J. W. C. Pennington, *The Fugitive Blacksmith* [1849], in Taylor, *I Was Born a Slave*, vol. 2, p. 111.

25. Fox-Genovese, *Within the Plantation Household*, p. 63.

26. FD, Saratoga, NY, 12 September 1879 (FDP 1.4, p. 530); also quoted in LT2, p. 531 (A, p. 872; FDP 2.3, p. 343).

27. FD, Hudson, OH, 12 July 1854 (FDP 1.2, pp. 506–7).

28. FD, Paisley, 17 April 1846 (FDP 1.1, p. 230). FD is quoting Acts 18:26. For a history of US abolitionism that pays particular attention to the use of this phrase see Goodman, *Of One Blood*.

29. FD to WLG, Dublin, 16 September 1845 (FDP 3.1, p. 54).

30. For a stimulating discussion see Shell, *Children of the Earth*.

31. FD to Charles Sumner, Rochester, NY, 2 September 1852 (LWFD2, p. 210). The phrase may betray a certain impatience at WLG's patronising attitude as well as recognising him as a role model; the precise context here refers to the pressure FD feels to maintain silence regarding their disagreements.

32. FD to Wendell Phillips, Glasgow, 28 April 1846 (FDP 3.1, p. 117); FD to Amy Post, Edinburgh, 28 April 1846 (FDP 3.1, p. 122); FD to William A. White, Edinburgh, 30 July 1846 (FDP 3.1, p. 148).

33. BF, p. 52 (A, p. 152; FDP 2.2, p. 31).

34. James McCune Smith, 'Introduction' to BF, p. xxx (A, p. 136; FDP 2.2, p. 18).

35. Scott, *Journal of Sir Walter Scott*, vol. 2, p. 39 (entry for 29 September 1827).

36. HCW to WLG, Jedburgh, 19 March 1846 and Berwick, 22 March 1846 (*Liberator*, 1 May 1846).

37. FD to WLG, Perth, 27 January 1846 (FDP 3.1, p. 85).

38. Scott, *History of Scotland*, vol. 1, p. 96. That the episode was well known is indicated by the reference to it in an article in the *Witness* ridiculing the 'mingled devotion and diversion' of a typical Relief Church service: 'We do think there are things very good in themselves, which are yet all the better for being kept apart. Corn is a very good thing, and so is malt, and casks of wine are very good things too, so are fat beeves and brave soldiers; but they made at best but a sorry mess when mixed up together in the Palm-Sunday larder of the Black Douglas' ('A New Order of Christian Union: Soirees in the Relief Church', repr. *Northern Warder*, 21 January 1845).

39. FD to Francis Jackson, Dundee, 29 January 1846 (FDP 3.1, p. 89).

40. Ibid. pp. 89–90.

41. FD, Dundee, 30 January 1846 (FDP 1.1, p. 148).
42. FD, Dundee, 30 January 1846 (FDP 1.1, p. 149).
43. FD to Abigail Mott, Ayr, 23 March 1846 (FDP 3.1, p. 111). JB echoes FD in a letter of his own, referring to Scotland's 'hills and valleys made classic by the genius of Scott, Burns, and others of her gifted sons': JB to WLG, Bowling Bay, 14 April 1846 (*Liberator*, 15 May 1846).

Chapter 27

Choosing Ancestors

Douglass's occasional claim to be of Scottish descent was playful and not meant to be taken literally, exploiting a pun offered by the historical existence of a 'Black Douglas'. But some other American slaves did not have to invent a Scottish ancestry. One such was Lewis Clarke, who begins his autobiography thus:

> I was born in March, as near as I can ascertain, in the year 1815, in Madison county, Kentucky, about seven miles from Richmond, upon the plantation of my grandfather, Samuel Campbell. He was considered a very respectable man, among his fellow-robbers, the slaveholders. It did not render him less honorable in their eyes, that he took to his bed Mary, his slave, perhaps half white, by whom he had one daughter, Letitia Campbell. This was before his marriage.
> My father was from 'beyond the flood' – from Scotland, and by trade a weaver. He had been married in his own country, and lost his wife, who left to him, as I have been told, two sons. He came to this country in time to be in the earliest scenes of the American revolution. He was at the battle of Bunker Hill, and continued in the army to the close of the war. About the year 1800, or before, he came to Kentucky, and married Miss Letitia Campbell, then held as a slave by her *dear* and *affectionate* father. My father died, as near as I can recollect, when I was about ten or twelve years of age. He had received a wound in the war, which made him lame as long as he lived. I have often heard him tell of Scotland, sing the merry songs of his native land, and long to see its hills once more.[1]

Given that Campbell is an unmistakably Scottish name, this passage indicates that three of Clarke's grandparents were of Scots descent. Lewis Clarke was widely, if over-enthusiastically, believed to be the model for George Harris in *Uncle Tom's Cabin* (and Clarke certainly made the most of the association).[2] But he is not mentioned anywhere in Duncan A. Bruce's bestselling *The Mark of the Scots*, a book which lists famous people of Scots ancestry in an attempt to demonstrate – as its subtitle has it – 'their astonishing contributions to history, science, democracy, literature and the arts', as if the nation were somehow vindicated by a careful selection of its talented progeny.[3] Nor does he (or any other African American) appear in most of the recent academic literature on the Scottish diaspora. It is as if only white Scots ever emigrate, and when they do, mate exclusively with their own kind.[4]

To his credit, Bruce does – if only with a single example, that of Colin Powell – admit the possibility that people racialised as black in the United States can still have Scottish ancestors.[5] And it is in less scholarly work that we glimpse other exceptions to the rule. For instance, in *Scottish Exodus* (2005), James Hunter pauses briefly to acknowledge that 'African-American McLeods [. . .] include people of Highlands and Islands descent', and speculates that the civil rights campaigner Mary McLeod Bethune was among them.[6] More boldly, Billy Kay, writing in *The Scottish World* (2006) of his journeys in the 'Scotch South', reminds us that 'there are hundreds of thousands of people in the South who share an African and a Scottish heritage'. He quotes a communication he received from one of them – named, as it happens, Marian Douglas – who refers to her 'combined African, American Indian and European cultural and physical heritage' and remarks:

> As a Black American, I truly like the hybrid I am. But I don't accept the rejection and feigned ignorance I often encounter, whether from institutions and individuals in the US or in Britain. Even today I know that in more than a few places in Scotland and in the US there are plenty of people who would still look askance at and overtly or covertly resist the participation of Black Scots descendants in Scottish-related events and affairs.[7]

Among the participants of Scottish heritage events in a 'Northern US state' interviewed by Euan Hague in 1997, a proud member of a Clan MacDonald society reflected:

> I supposed there are not many African Americans though – one defining feature must be that most of those at the Games are white, but that doesn't mean that African-Americans have no connection. Alex

Haley explored and told of his *Roots*. Now, he was half Irish but these were not the roots he explored. There were, of course, good reasons for his choice to explore the African side.[8]

Perhaps Haley, like Malcolm X (whose autobiography he edited, and whose own maternal grandfather was rumoured to be Scottish) 'learned to hate every drop of that white rapist's blood that is in me'.[9] The 'one-drop rule' in the United States – which for a long time dictated that a single black great-grandparent would determine one's categorisation as black – already disqualified that ancestor from counting for legal purposes.[10]

The advent of genetic ancestry testing since the early 2000s has done little to break this habit. Rick Kittles, the co-founder of African Ancestry, Inc., advises customers that 'more than 20 percent of Y chromosomes of men of African descent will trace to Europe', and he alludes to his own German ancestry on his paternal side.[11] But it is clear that his customers are primarily interested in knowing more about their African ancestry, and some experience 'genealogical disorientation' when test results point elsewhere.[12]

The success of books like *The Mark of the Scots* illustrate how much we remain in thrall to genealogy: not just by being curious about tracing our ancestors, but by continuing to believe that it can ground moral judgements. It is still common to swell someone's status by pointing to their exalted pedigree or (if you live in Scotland) to punctuate their pretension by disclosing their lowly origins ('I kent his faither'). But it should also remind us that, even since the commercialisation of DNA sequencing, genealogy has little to with genetics. Social and legal conventions govern who counts as a relative and often some relatives count more than others. Wherever ancestry is at issue, lines of descent are unevenly valued and documented, perhaps most obviously in naming practices (the naming of children after fathers, wives after husbands).

Note Lewis Clarke's distribution of sympathy in his mini-genealogical narrative. He is careful to distinguish the slaveholding maternal grandfather, whose respectability, honour and capacity for sentiment is heavily ironised, from the revolutionary father, courageous not only in the field of battle but in marriage too. Others may reject their ancestry or disown their ancestors altogether because of associations with a life they want to leave behind, and change their name, thus frustrating efforts of their descendants to trace their family tree.

So, genealogies are selective, not simply because of incomplete information but because some ancestors count more than others – more virtuous, more distinguished, more interesting. It is also true for many of those people who claim what might be called 'symbolic ethnic identity'. In the United States, for example, we find many people classifying themselves as 'Italian-' or 'Irish-' or 'Polish-American' and so on. Given the multiple origins of those whose ancestors settled in the country several generations ago, these affiliations are not straightforwardly dictated by descent, but chosen from a range of options, if not always consciously. Many Americans enjoy a freedom to, as it were, freely shop in the ethnicity market, adopting an identity in accordance with, say, family tradition or religious affiliation, but they are also influenced by the fact that some ethnicities are felt to be more attractive than others.[13]

For white Americans such choices are recreational. They can, so to speak, practice – and indeed change – their ethnicities at will in their spare time. People of colour are more constrained in their choices because they experience ethnicity differently. European ancestry will struggle to have more than private significance when your legal status and economic opportunities are shaped by a racism that discriminates on the basis of certain arbitrary physical features.[14] Alex Haley did eventually follow *Roots* with another multi-generational family saga, *Queen*, that explored his Irish antecedents on his father's side of his family, but, going against the grain, it was never going to strike a chord the way its predecessor did.[15]

Studies suggest that Scottish ancestry was held in rather low esteem for much of the twentieth century, but its status has risen rapidly since the 1970s.[16] The clan member interviewed by Hague in the late 1990s recalled 'one woman who came to our tent who was clearly Sicilian, but she had a great grandparent who she felt was important'.[17] In *Scottish Exodus*, James Hunter tells of meeting a lawyer, Katherine McLeod, in North Carolina. He discovers that she grew up as Edna Bryan, and took her husband's name when she got married. Now divorced, she changed her name again.

> I've always been impressed by the way my McLeod ancestors handled themselves in the face of hardship and adversity [. . .] That's why, though I don't have to confront what she confronted, I've taken my McLeod great-grandmother's name. By doing this, I'm making a statement about who I am, who I'd like to be, how I aim to live my life.[18]

With his admiration of his namesake's 'heroic deeds', Douglass is similarly motivated, although the ancestral bonds he invokes are wholly, rather than partly, fictionalised. But kinship has always extended beyond the biogenetic, to relationships engendered by, for example, adoption and remarriage (whether legally recognised or not); more recently, kinship has been adapted to embrace distant 'cousinage' disclosed by DNA ancestry tests.[19]

Many living outside Scotland who feel a strong emotional connection to the emblems, rituals and narratives of 'Highlandism' have no ancestral connection to the country. This was acknowledged by the organisers of Homecoming Scotland 2009, a major government initiative to attract visitors from the diaspora, who made a point of reaching out to what it called 'affinity Scots'.[20] Douglass was probably not the kind of aficionado it had in mind (and if he was alive today, one wonders if the Home Office processing his visa application would have given any weight to the 'affinity' he proclaimed). But the prominent inclusion of his image on the banner of the Douglas Archives website ('A collection of historical and genealogical records') hints at what an elastic and inclusive conception of kinship could look like.[21]

Disraeli's *Sybil* (1845), published a few months before Douglass's arrival in Liverpool, was one of many eighteenth- and nineteenth-century novels to use the plot device where a lowly protagonist is revealed to have noble ancestry. A contemporary reviewer, W. R. Greg, complained, of one of its principal male characters, that its author cannot 'portray a high-minded, able, virtuous, educated Chartist-artizan' without making him 'descend with an unbroken pedigree from a Norman baron, – by representing him as proud of his descent, – and as the rightful heir, – and ultimately the successful claimant to an English earldom!'[22] Greg might have complained that Douglass is only able to justify himself by imaginatively buying into a romanticised history that allows him to claim the heritage of a Scottish mediaeval knight. But Douglass is not exploiting the connection in pursuit of wealth or title. It is true that his teasing identification with the 'Black Douglas' cannot be explained solely in terms of the 'strategic Anglophilia' or 'Celtophilia' deployed by Douglass and others, who crafted an idealised Britain and Ireland, free of prejudice, in order to more forcefully condemn racism in the United States.[23] But nor is it quite the same as the obsessive fascination with aristocratic manners and royal intrigue evident in the writings of white American visitors during the same period.[24] The Highlandism of black abolitionists like Douglass is different not because it offers an allegorical contrast to chattel slavery but because in the very act of invoking it, they occupy and lay claim to an ideological terrain as important as the streets, churches and railroad cars that are equally denied to them at home. It carries the same charge as the 'impudent' act of walking down Broadway 'with two white women resting on his arms', which so scandalised the *New York Globe* in 1850 when Douglass was sighted there in the company of Eliza and Julia Griffiths.[25]

As the Clan MacDonald member observed, one does not see many African Americans at Highland Games in the United States. This was not always the case. The Scottish-American associations which flourished in the nineteenth century (such as St Andrew's Societies, and Caledonian Clubs), often serving to support first-generation immigrants, were never exclusive organisations, as the welcome given to Douglass in Rochester by the Sons and Daughters of Old Scotia might suggest. One historian remarks that the Caledonian Games in Philadelphia were open

> to all comers without distinction of creed, nationality, or previous condition of servitude. The result was that those who in the Quaker City, went to see *Scotch* games saw a general scramble for the prizes by negroes, Irishmen, and Germans, as well as Scots.[26]

From the 1880s the games become more 'Scottish' as others were drawn to emerging 'national' sports such as baseball and football, and 'Scottish-American' activities themselves declined, especially once immigration slowed after 1920s. When they revived in the 1970s – the growth of the Highland Games has been spectacular – they catered not for immigrants but Americans who had discovered Scottish roots, often only recently due to the broader explosion of interest in tracing ancestry. At the same time, their centre of gravity had shifted from the north and east to the south and west. In the process they became increasingly middle-class in character and attracted more women than their nineteenth-century counterparts.[27]

At least one commentator has argued that part of the appeal of such events (especially in the South) is that they offer a de facto whites-only space for those still troubled by the desegregation that, starting in 1954, has been enforced by the courts.[28] This appeal can only be reinforced by the way the Highland Heritage movement likes to construe parallels between the 'lost causes' of Bonnie Prince Charlie, the Jacobite rebel crushed at Culloden in 1746, and Jefferson Davis, President of the Confederacy, defeated at Appomattox in 1865.[29] More broadly, this is congruent with the tendency of some ethnically conscious white Americans to imagine their history as shaped by ancestral traumas that match those of the Holocaust or the Middle Passage, with Scots promulgating highly mythical narratives of the Highland Clearances and of 'white slavery' in an attempt to emphasise the similarity.[30]

Indeed, since at least the Civil War, the idea of 'Scotland' has played a modest, if persistent, role in the white supremacist imagination in the United States, indicated, as numerous commentators have pointed out, by the incorporation of the saltire in the Confederate Battle Flag, the apparently 'Celtic' rituals of the Ku Klux Klan, and the special place awarded the film *Braveheart* by certain hate groups.[31] Less noticed are the ways in which these gestures draw on a more diffuse tendency for Scotland to be invoked as a particularly appealing haven of racial purity. When Washington Irving visited Abbotsford in 1817, Walter Scott told him that 'a real old Scottish song [. . .] shows what the national visage was in former days, before the breed was crossed', while the English have no 'national airs [. . .] because they are not natives of the soil, or, at least, are mongrels'.[32] Henry James, when confronted by the melting pot that was turn-of-the-century New York City, expressed a yearning for 'the luxury of some such close and sweet *whole* national consciousness as that of the Switzer and the Scot'.[33]

James takes it for granted that his readers will understand his choice of example; and nearly a century later, the expectation of a similar recognition lies behind the provocations of the right-wing historian (and Holocaust denier) David Irving when he told the *Sunday Herald* that he was thinking of moving to Edinburgh 'to get away from "Arabs and blacks"' and the British National Party's Nick Griffin's tweeting of an image of black men in kilts in an attempt to persuade voters that Scotland's Scottishness was under threat from 'asylum-seekers and refugees'.[34]

However, while anecdotal evidence suggests that white supremacist groups have targeted some Highland Games as potential recruiting grounds, studies of the Scottish-American cultural revival tend to agree that those taking part take care to distance themselves from such politics, and stress other, more benign, motivations for their involvement.[35]

The official recognition in 1998 of 6 April as National Tartan Day in the United States (following the example of several Canadian provinces) is interesting because it may signal the beginnings of a realignment. In the terms of Senate Resolution 155, the importance of 'Scotland' is not tethered to the Confederacy, but to the founding of the Republic, its Declaration of Independence, allegedly modelled on the Declaration of Arbroath (6 April 1320), and signed by Americans of mostly Scottish descent. And moreover, while Tartan Day provides a pretext for many local heritage-style celebrations across the country, the highest profile events take place in Washington, DC and, especially, New York City where, after some initial suspicion, the Scottish government (enlarging it to become 'Scotland Week') takes the opportunity to promote contemporary theatre, music, literature, fashion in the context of promoting Scotland as a place to visit, to study, to work, and to do business with, while declining to acknowledge Tartan Day events hosted by other organisations. The occasion has steadily increased in popularity, attracting a number of Scottish celebrities and public figures, but remains dwarfed by the St Patrick's Day celebrations that take place three weeks earlier. [36]

One of the images that featured on the Scottish government's website for Scotland Week 2017 was a photograph of the annual Tartan Day parade along Sixth Avenue, showing a pipe band led by a man of colour. A quiet rebuke, perhaps, to anyone who might strive too hard to define Scottish-America as a whites-only affair.[37]

As a further illustration of this stumbling realignment, let me refer to another official Scottish-American occasion, one with a slightly more pronounced black presence. I am thinking of the speech given in 2009 by Scotland's First Minister Alex Salmond at the Library of Congress, marking the 250th anniversary of the birth of Robert Burns. As befitting the occasion, Salmond emphasises how much Burns has been loved and honoured in the United States. As well as referring to more predictable admirers, such as Abraham Lincoln and Walt Whitman, he twice invokes Maya Angelou, whose pilgrimage to the land of Burns was the subject of a television documentary broadcast in Scotland a decade earlier.[38] In the film, Angelou makes no mention of her nineteenth-century forebear, but the First Minster makes amends:

For Frederick Douglass, Burns was esteemed as a 'true soul'. The first book Douglass bought after he escaped slavery was a copy of Burns' poetry – which he later passed on to his oldest son.

And speaking at a Burns Supper in New York in 1849, Mr. Douglass said, 'Though I am not a Scotchman, and I have a coloured skin, I am proud to be among you this evening.' He then pointed to a portrait of Burns and continued, 'And if any think me out of my place at this occasion I beg that the blame be laid at the door of him who taught me that "a man's a man for a' that".'[39]

Here, perhaps for the first time, Douglass is called forth at an official event, in a move that couples Scotland, not with those neo-Confederate warriors that like to imagine it untainted by those with 'a colored skin', but with those countervailing forces aligned with affirmative action and civil rights.

Notes

1. Lewis Clarke, *Narrative of Lewis Clarke* [1846] in Taylor, *I Was a Slave*, vol. 1, p. 608.
2. Eric J. Sundquist, 'Introduction' to Sundquist, *New Essays on Uncle Tom's Cabin*, p. 17.
3. Bruce, *The Mark of the Scots*.
4. Hewitson, *Tam Blake & Co*; Fry, *'Bold, Independent, Unconquer'd and Free'*; Calder, *Scots in the USA*; Basu, *Highland Homecomings*; Sim, *American Scots*; Devine, *To the Ends of the Earth*; Bueltman et al., *The Scottish Diaspora*; Leith and Sim, *The Modern Scottish Diaspora*; McCarthy and Mackenzie, *Global Migrations*.
5. Bruce, *Mark of the Scots*, p. 163.
6. Hunter, *Scottish Exodus*, pp. 244–5.
7. Kay, *The Scottish World*, p. 146.
8. Hague, 'The Scottish Diaspora', pp. 147–8, 154 n. 3.
9. Malcolm X, *The Autobiography of Malcolm* X, p. 81. The rumours of Malcolm's mother being the product of the rape of her mother by a Scotsman: see Marable, *Malcolm X*, p. 16. The *Autobiography* itself does not identify the man as Scottish but does refer to him as the source of his reddish skin and hair colour: Malcolm X, *Autobiography of Malcolm X*, p. 80.
10. See Davis, *Who is Black?*; Gross, *What Blood Won't Tell*.
11. Nelson, *The Social Life of DNA*, pp. 90, 34.
12. Ibid. p. 90.

13. See Waters, *Ethnic Options*, esp. pp. 147–54.
14. Ibid. pp. 155–64.
15. Haley and Stevens, *Queen*. In an interview in *Penthouse* (December 1976) Haley said, 'One of my ancestors was an Irish colonel', available at <http://www.alex-haley.com/alex_haley_penthouse_interview.htm> (last accessed 17 February 2018). More recently, DNA analysis seems to confirm Haley's Scottish ancestry too: see Rita Rubin, 'DNA Testing: "Roots" Author Haley Rooted in Scotland, Too', *USA Today*, 6 April 2009, available at <http://usatoday30.usatoday.com/tech/science/genetics/2009-04-06-haley-dna_n.htm> (last accessed 17 February 2018); and 'Roots Author Had Scottish Blood', *BBC News*, available at <http://news.bbc.co.uk/1/hi/scotland/7917605.stm> (last accessed 17 February 2018).
16. In her study of 'white ethnics' in Philadelphia and San José, CA, based on research in 1986–7, Mary Waters found that Scottish ancestry had a relatively low popularity ranking (and claimed that it had declined through the twentieth century): Waters, *Ethnic Options*, pp. 11, 82–3. But Duncan Sim, writing twenty years later, suggests this trend has now reversed: Sim, *American Scots*, pp. 10–13, 116–18. See also Hague, 'Scottish Diaspora', pp. 139–46; Basu, *Highland Homecomings*, p. 44; Devine, *Ends of the Earth*, pp. 276–85. Signs of this reversal, boosted in the 1990s, include the international success of films such as *Braveheart* and *Rob Roy* (both released 1995) and the *Outlander* series of novels by Diana Gabaldon (1991–).
17. Hague, 'Scottish Diaspora', p. 148.
18. Hunter, *Scottish Exodus*, p. 102.
19. Nelson, *The Social Life of DNA*, pp. 152–5.
20. Hesse, *Warrior Dreams*, pp. 170–92.
21. 'The Douglas Archives', <http://douglashistory.ning.com> (last accessed 2 December 2017).
22. W. R. G., 'Review of *Sybil*', p. 73.
23. For 'strategic Anglophilia' or 'Celtophilia' see Rice, *Radical Narratives*, pp. 172–87, 213.
24. See Tamarkin, 'Black Anglophilia'.
25. 'Equality in New York', *New York Globe*, repr. *The Times*, 10 June 1850. See Nyong'o, *The Amalgamation Waltz*, p. 126.
26. Ross, *The Scot in America*, p. 427.
27. My account here draws on Berthoff, 'Under the Kilt'; Hague, 'Scottish Diaspora'; Ross, *The Scot in America*, esp. pp. 411–41; Redmond, *The Caledonian Games*; Ray, *Highland Heritage*.
28. 'Highland games now provide, besides their more obvious attractions, an acceptable refuge from the courts and commissions that since 1954 have been ordering racial integration in other public and quasi-private

places. There may be black Macleans and Macleods, but they are tacitly assumed to have no properly Scottish ancestors and no place at Scottish-American gatherings': Berthoff, 'Under the Kilt', p. 26.

29. Ray, *Highland Heritage*, pp. 17–18, 182–9.

30. On the tendency of ethnically conscious white Americans to imagine their history as one of oppression that is equivalent to that of African Americans or native Americans, see Waters, *Ethnic Options*, pp. 155–68. On the tendency of some diasporan Scots to equate the Clearances with genocide see Basu, *Highland Homecomings*, pp. 187–216; Ascherson, *Stone Voices*, pp. 172–87. The 'white slavery' myth is succinctly debunked in Stephen Mullen, 'The Myth of Scottish Slaves', *Sceptical Scot*, March 2016, available at <http://sceptical.scot/2016/03/the-myth-of-scottish-slaves> (last accessed 3 December 2017), following the example of Liam Hogan who has analysed the origin and development of the 'Irish slaves' myth in great detail. See his '"Irish Slaves": The Convenient Myth', *OpenDemocracy*, 14 January 2015, available at <https://www.opendemocracy.net/beyondslavery/liam-hogan/%E2%80%98irish-slaves%E2%80%99-convenient-myth> (last accessed 17 Feburary 2018); and 'Two Years of the "Irish Slaves" Myth', *OpenDemocracy*, 7 November 2016, available at <https://www.opendemocracy.net/beyondslavery/liam-hogan/two-years-of-irish-slaves-myth-racism-reductionism-and-tradition-of-diminis> (last accessed 17 February 2018).

31. See Diane Roberts, 'Your Clan or Ours?', *Oxford American* (September/October 1999); Hook, 'Troubling Times', pp. 224–30.

32. Irving, *Abbotsford and Newstead Abbey*, pp. 27–8. Scott's remarks are anticipated by Irving's earlier observations on his host's dogs: 'Scott was too true a sportsman, and had too high a veneration for pure blood, to tolerate a mongrel' (pp. 5–6).

33. James, *The American Scene*, p. 86.

34. On Irving see Rob Edwards, 'Anti-Green Activist in Links with Nazi Writer', *Sunday Herald*, 5 May 2002. In 2017, Irving, by then living in Nairn, was quoted expressing similar views at a private function: Paul Hutcheon, 'Holocaust Denier David Irving Rants about Jews at Secret Glasgow Talk', *Sunday Herald*, 12 February 2017. Griffin's tweet was posted in April 2015, available at <https://twitter.com/NickGriffinBU/status/583610176189681664/> (last accessed 17 February 2018), making unacknowledged use of a photograph by Daniele Tamagni of members of the 'Piccadilly' group of Congolese *sapeurs* in Brazzavile: see Tamagni, *Gentlemen of Bacongo*.

35. On white supremacist recruitment see Hague, 'Scottish Diaspora', p. 153. For an emphasis on the more benign attractions see Berthoff, 'Under the Kilt', pp. 26–8; Ray, *Highland Heritage*, pp. 14, 89–90,

117–18, 191–2, 207–8; and Sim, *American Scots*, pp. 30–1. Even Hague takes care to point out 'the "racial" character of Scottish and Celtic identities in the USA is not representative and does not reflect the political beliefs of the persons with whom I spoke or the Scottish-American community as a whole': 'Scottish Diaspora', p. 156 n.

36. On Tartan Day see Hague, 'National Tartan Day'; Cowan, 'Tartan Day in America'; Sim, *American Scots*, pp. 95–114; Fry, *Bold, Independent, Unconquer'd and Free*, 225–7; Ascherson, *Stone Voices*, pp. 262–74.

37. The image on the Scottish Week website is archived at <https://web.archive.org/web/20160912052921/http://www.scotland.org/assets/3883/img_9861__gallery.jpg> (last accessed 17 February 2018). In 2008, Jamaica-born Geoff Palmer of Heriot-Watt University in Edinburgh noted that the planned Homecoming 'is being marketed in Canada, New Zealand, Australia. Why are they not inviting people from Jamaica with Scottish names?' According to David Hesse, the organisers did not reply directly, but subsequently 'adjusted the campaign's main advertisement by digitally inserting a young man with a dark complexion into what had been until then an exclusively white crowd of homecomers': see Jackie Kemp, 'New Centre for Study of Scottish Diaspora is Mired in Controversy', *Guardian*, 25 November 2008; Hesse, *Warrior Dreams*, p. 174.

38. *Angelou on Burns*, film, directed by Elly M. Taylor. UK: Taylored Productions, 1996.

39. Frank Shaw, 'Alex Salmond speaks at Burns symposium in Washington, DC', available at <http://www.electricscotland.com/familytree/frank/burns_lives40.htm> (last accessed 17 February 2018). See also Crawford, 'America's Bard', which is partly based on a lecture given at the same event and, judging by the similarities, probably shared with Salmond's speechwriter.

Chapter 28

Remembering Douglass

In remarks made at an event to mark Black History Month in February 2017, Donald Trump name-checked Frederick Douglass with a vagueness that led many to believe he had no idea who he was.[1] Demonstrating rather more knowledge of Douglass than the forty-fifth president of the United States, Alex Salmond in 2009 quoted both his letter from Ayr and his address in Rochester, and alluded to the inscription in the first copy of Currie's *Works* he owned. None of these texts was widely known at the time. They had only recently been reprinted or reproduced, and barely discussed even within academia. More broadly, this political intervention would not have been possible without decades of research and public engagement in Scotland excavating the country's slavery past.

Scholars have illuminated the efforts of Scots who campaigned for the abolition of slavery, as well as those who made their fortunes from it and left their mark on town and country alike. In turn this has inspired artists, creative writers, film-makers and musicians, while literary critics have teased out the frequent, if subdued, references to slavery in Scottish literature. It has generated exhibitions, conferences, talks, walking tours, street performances, websites, mobile apps, radio and television programmes, and resource packs for teachers and youth leaders. Activities gathered momentum in 2007, the 200th anniversary of the British abolition of the slave trade, and a wide variety of initiatives formed part of the Empire Cafe, a programme of events at Glasgow's Briggait during the Commonwealth Games 2014. Black History Month has, predictably, served as the focus for many of these undertakings, which eventually achieved a level of official recognition in 2017 when Glasgow's Lord Provost hosted an evening at the City Chambers and announced plans for a working group to look into how best civic authorities can better acknowledge the city's colonial and imperial history.[2]

Some of this work has recognised the importance of Douglass. George Shepperson wrote three pioneering articles on Douglass and the 'Send Back the Money' campaign in the 1950s, and further research since has built on his work.[3] Douglass's Scottish visit has been the subject of two BBC radio documentaries, and marked by several events during Black History Month, including the re-enactment of a speech by Jim Muotune.[4] Songs printed during the 'Send Back the Money' campaign were recorded by traditional singers for one of the radio programmes, and were subsequently revived by a women's history group, which has taken a keen interest in the relationship between Douglass and Scottish women abolitionists (and re-enacted the episode in which he dug the turf on Arthur's Seat with Jane and Eliza Wigham and imprinted 'Send Back the Money' on its grassy slopes).[5] The *Merchant City Voices* project drew on the words of Douglass's writings and speeches, spoken by the Glasgow-based writer, teacher and performer Tawona Sithole and others, and left behind a sign bearing his name on the wall of the City Hall. Another venue at which he spoke, the former Bell Street Chapel in Dundee (now the Bell Street Music Centre) also bears a token of his presence in the form of a plaque, its unveiling forming one of several such set pieces in the BBC television series *Black and British*, broadcast in November 2016, also featuring Sithole.[6] The lecture Douglass delivered there was excerpted in a collection of *Great Scottish Speeches*, published in 2011, and it forms the subject of a poem by Aonghas MacNeacail, 'saor bho shaorsa'/'free from freedom', commissioned by the Empire Cafe in 2014.[7]

While impressive, this is rather meagre compared to the extent to which Douglass's sojourn in Ireland is commemorated there, the subject of three books, numerous scholarly articles, and a full-length documentary.[8] It is therefore not surprising that Douglass has featured somewhat more prominently in the work of Irish artists and writers, honoured by two republican murals in west Belfast, commemorative plaques in Cork and Waterford, and a touring resin 'monument' sculpted by Andrew Edwards.[9] Douglass also appears as a central character in Donal O'Kelly's play *The Cambria* (2005) and Colum McCann's novel *Transatlantic* (2013).[10]

It is hard to assess the long-term impact of these attempts to bring this history to the broader public, in Scotland and elsewhere.

Many of them are ephemeral: web pages go out of date or disappear, unarchived; radio and television programmes are taken offline after a short interval; exhibitions and performances are often poorly documented and remembered only by the small numbers of people who attend them. This is perhaps one of the reasons why, despite all this activity, there are growing calls for a permanent memorial or dedicated museum in Glasgow that would recognise the city's debt to slavery, both directly, through the ownership of enslaved persons, and indirectly, through the importation and consumption of the products of their labour, generating fortunes which were invested in Scotland's domestic infrastructure, such as heavy industry and the railways.

Certainly, Scotland does not boast a slavery museum like Liverpool or Bristol or a research centre like the Wilberforce Institute in Hull, nor has it honoured Douglass the way Ireland has. Historical scholarship has only recently begun to explore in detail what are sometimes vaguely called the 'connections' between Scotland and slavery. But can we speak, as some do, of 'collective' or 'popular amnesia'? The word *amnesia* occurs more than a dozen times in an important collection of essays devoted to *Recovering Scotland's Slavery Past* (2015), implying a sudden, involuntary loss of a particular set of memories.[11] And yet some of the book's contributors suggest that a reluctance to address this past took effect gradually over several decades following West Indian Emancipation, and for reasons that include wilful denial. In one essay Tom Devine talks of 'shame' and 'discretion', in another Michael Morris refers to 'euphemism, elision and misrepresentation', terms which indicate a degree of discomfort and self-consciousness that 'amnesia' seems to rule out.[12] They allow us to think of these 'connections' not as silenced or forgotten, but managed, excused and, sometimes, openly debated. To refer disparagingly to 'Scotland's image of itself as an abolitionist nation',[13] as if the Scottish campaigns against slavery required the exculpation of all Scots from any complicity in its manifold operations in a deluded fantasy of collective goodwill, is misleading and risks marginalising dissenting voices.

In the 1840s and 50s, while almost no one of substance in Scotland voiced unequivocal support for slavery in the United States, there was considerable public disagreement over what should be done about it. Abolitionism came in many varieties, some more radical than others. When Douglass arrived in 1846, he came not to congratulate its people on their having broken with a slavery past, but to accuse them of their continued alliance with a slavery present. As we have seen, most of his efforts were directed at the Free Church's refusal to cut ties with Southern Presbyterians, but Douglass also expressed disappointment that the antislavery spirit in the country at large was not as strong as it had once been. Later, other black abolitionists, including James Pennington and Samuel Ringgold Ward, toured Scotland in support of the Free Produce movement, again targeting Scots, imploring them to stop importing and consuming slave-grown cotton. Their audiences were left in no doubt as to the many ways in which they were helping to delay emancipation in the United States. Many of them were troubled. Some of them heeded the call and collected donations, shopped ethically, submitted resolutions, gave speeches, published pamphlets and wrote letters to the press. Others preferred to direct their energies elsewhere.

It is true that one might cast entities such as the Free Church as aberrations, deviants who do not really represent 'Scotland', in order to imagine a national moral consensus. This is the move that Dr Mudie makes at the Anti-Slavery Soirée addressed by Douglass in Dundee in March 1846, referring to the church's 'alliance with slaveholding seminaries and slaveholding churches' as something of which 'Scotland knew nothing – whom she never recognised – whom she never delegated – to whom she gave no authority.' Mudie goes on:

> We are bold to pronounce that Scotland indignantly disowns all such representations. Her independence, her piety, her honour, never will be soiled by an alliance with manstealers. No; the voice that comes forth from her mountains, her glens, her villages, her cities, proclaims in accents loud as the roaring of seven thunders, that the blood-stained slaveholder shall never fill a place in her fellowship, nor find an avenue to her intercourse; that such are the unalterable sentiments of Scotland this great and enthusiastic assembly will testify.[14]

In Belfast three months later Douglass himself proclaims, to great cheers: 'The Free Church of Scotland is not the People of Scotland. The people of Scotland are with us.'[15] While Douglass sometimes flatters his audiences by talking about his warm welcome in Scotland, and the country's noble history of struggles on behalf of freedom, we need to recognise this as strategic, a gesture that is often followed by more critical, rebuking remarks that charge his listeners with being too quiet and weak over the issue of slavery.

Notes

1. See, for example, Jacey Fortin, 'Trump's Black History Talk: From Douglass to Media Bias and Crime', *New York Times*, 1 February 2017, available at <https://www.nytimes.com/2017/02/01/us/politics/trump-black-history-douglass.html> (last accessed 11 February 2018); David A. Graham, 'Donald Trump's Narrative of the Life of Frederick Douglass', *The Atlantic*, 1 February 2017, available at <https://www.theatlantic.com/politics/archive/2017/02/frederick-douglass-trump/515292/> (last accessed 11 February 2018).

2. For an overview of this activity since 2000 see 'Scotland, Slavery and Abolitionism: A Timeline of Public Engagement' available at <http://www.bulldozia.com/douglass/timeline> (last accessed 20 February 2018).

3. Shepperson, 'Frederick Douglass and Scotland'; Rice, *Scots Abolitionists*; Blackett, *Building an Anti-Slavery Wall*; Pettinger, 'Send Back the Money'; Whyte, *'Send Back the Money!'*.

4. *Send Back the Money*, produced by Vicky Davidson (BBC Radio Scotland, 11 December 1996); *A Man's a Man for A' That: Frederick Douglass in Scotland*, presented by Andrea Baker (BBC Radio 4, 25 October 2015); 'Reliving the Past', *Glasgow Herald*, 9 October 2002.

5. 'Anti-Slavery Songs', sung by Bob Blair and Gordeanna McCulloch for *Send Back the Money* (BBC Scotland, 11 December 1996), available at <https://soundcloud.com/90millionfrancs/anti-slavery-songs/> (last accessed 27 February 2018); DRB Scottish Women's History Group, *Women on the Platform* (2014), available at <https://drbgroup1.files.wordpress.com/2014/02/drb_booklet.pdf> (last accessed 11 February 2018).

6. *Merchant City Voices* (2012), available at <https://vimeo.com/collectivearchitecture> (last accessed 1 June 2018); *Black and British: A Forgotten History*, a series of four programmes produced and directed by Naomi Austin, presented and written by David Olusoga (BBC 2, 9–30 November 2016). Douglass figured in Part III, 'Moral Mission' (23 November 2016).

7. FD, 'If there was to be found a house open for him, he would yet raise the cry "send back the blood-stained dollars"' in Torrance, *Great Scottish Speeches*, pp. 48–50; Aonghas MacNeacail, 'saor bho shaorsa'/'free from freedom' in Welsh, *Yonder Awa*, pp. 34–7.

8. Sweeney, *Frederick Douglass and the Atlantic World*; Chaffin, *Giant's Causeway*; Fenton, *Frederick Douglass in Ireland*; Coughlan, 'Frederick Douglass and Ireland'; Quinn, '"Safe in Old Ireland"'; Jenkins, '"The Black O'Connell"'; Lee Jenkins, 'Beyond the Pale', pp. 80–95; Ferreira, 'Frederick Douglass and the 1846 Dublin Edition'; Liam Hogan, 'Frederick Douglass and his Journey from Slavery to Limerick', *Old Limerick Journal* (Winter 2015), pp. 21–6; *Frederick Douglass and the White Negro*, film, written and directed by John J. Doherty (Ireland: Camel Productions, 2008).

9. For photographs of the Belfast murals see Stauffer et al., *Picturing Frederick Douglass*, p. 109; for the memorial plaques in Cork and Waterford see Dan Buckley, 'Plaque Recalls Anti-Slavery Activist's Visit', Irish Examiner, 1 September 2012, available at <https://www.irishexaminer.com/ireland/plaque-recalls-anti-slavery-activists-visit-206074.html> (last accessed 11 February 2018) and Barry Roche, 'Anti-Slavery Campaigner Frederick Douglass Remembered in Waterford', *Irish Times*, 8 October 2013, available at <https://www.irishtimes.com/news/ireland/irish-news/anti-slavery-campaigner-frederick-douglass-remembered-in-waterford-1.1553226> (last accessed 11 February 2018). For Edwards's statue see Chris Butler, 'There are Superheroes', available at <https://crucibletheblog.com/2015/11/25/there-are-superheroes/> (last accessed 11 February 2018). In England, Douglass is honoured by two plaques, on the houses once owned by George Thompson in London and the Richardsons in Newcastle: see 'Frederick Douglass Gets London Blue Plaque', African Diaspora Tourism, 10 February 2013, available at <http://www.africandiasporatourism.com/index.php?option=com_content&view=article&id=910:frederick-douglass-gets-london-blue-plaque-gets-london-blue-plaque&catid=124:news-bites&Itemid=73> (last accessed 27 February 2018) and Brian Ward, 'Frederick Douglass: The Ex-Slave and Transatlantic Celebrity who Found Freedom in Newcastle', The Conversation, 21 February 2018, available at <https://theconversation.com/frederick-douglass-the-ex-slave-and-transatlantic-celebrity-who-found-freedom-in-newcastle-90886> (last accessed 27 February 2018).

10. Donal O'Kelly, *The Cambria* (2005), available from Playography Ireland <http://www.irishplayography.com/> (last accessed 11 February 2018); Colum McCann, *Transatlantic* (London: Bloomsbury, 2013).

11. Devine, *Recovering Scotland's Slavery Past*.
12. Devine, 'Lost to History', pp. 22, 28; Morris, 'Yonder Awa', p. 44.
13. Devine, 'Lost to History', p. 22.
14. Anti-Slavery Soirée, pp. 20–1 (FDP 1.1, p. 494).
15. FD, Belfast, 16 June 1846 (*Belfast News-Letter*, 19 June 1846).

Chapter 29

Out of My Place

Beginning in July 1846, a series of intriguing letters appeared in the New York *Mirror*. Signed by Ferdinand Mendez Pinto, they recorded his impressions of Britain, France and Italy as he travelled in Europe, encountering (or referring to) many of the individuals we have mentioned in this book: Robert Peel, Lord Eglinton, Elihu Burritt, P. T. Barnum and General Tom Thumb, Charles Dickens, the Hutchinson Singers and the Ethiopian Serenaders. The missives are full of incident, if somewhat implausible, giving a version of the 'hungry forties' that might disturb a historian. And no wonder. Pinto was the fictional creation of Charles Briggs, a journalist, magazine editor and author of three novels, who wrote the letters at his home on Staten Island. He based Pinto partly on Nathaniel Parker Willis, a previous editor of the *Mirror*, a dandy and a snob who worshipped the English nobility and whose own letters from abroad were obliquely satirised in the travel accounts of William Wells Brown (discussed in Chapter 19). But the letters also mock Margaret Fuller, whose despatches from Europe were appearing concurrently in the New York *Tribune*.[1]

Like Fuller, Pinto undertakes a tour of the Highlands, and, as the guest of the Duke of Argyll at his castle near Inveraray, spends two weeks shooting game on his estate. One day he is told that among some newly arrived visitors is 'one of the Douglasses, from America, a very famous gentleman'. Pinto cannot recall 'any celebrity of that name', although he has 'a glimmering recollection of [a] rich family of Douglasses on Long Island'. At dinner, the honoured guest is seated too far away for Pinto to identify him, and he asks the Free Church minister beside him who he is. '[D]ark enough to be a relation of the family, and a lineal descendant from the black Douglas himself,' he replies, but even when he goes on to denounce him for 'trying to make us send back the money', Pinto is none the wiser. So when he is later introduced to the man in the intimacy of the drawing room he is shocked and insulted to discover that he is 'a dark mulatto [. . .] no other than the notorious runaway slave, Frederick Douglas'.

Abruptly withdrawing his offered hand, Pinto turns pompously to his host, expressing disappointment that 'the days of exclusiveness and gentility are gone, and in their place those of reformers and abolitionists and amalgamations have come', and promptly storms out of the castle, only to lose his way in thick fog and find himself up to his waist in a bog. Despite Douglass's notoriety, Pinto had been unable to imagine him in such company and surroundings.[2]

That it was so unthinkable for him is underscored when he later encounters Douglass again in London, tellingly introduced, as if he has already forgotten their previous meeting, as a 'black man named Douglas, who pretends to be a philanthropist and an orator'. Pinto tells him he has heard of his 'slanders about the glorious institutions of my country' and advises him to 'keep dark' in future. Douglass, wryly exploiting the ambiguity of the word, assures him he will, and Pinto is cheered by his response. '"Very well," said I, "if you do, I will speak a good word for you to some of my friends, and I may get you a good place as a *valet*."'

When Douglass points out his misunderstanding with an epigrammatic declaration of black pride, Pinto is infuriated and makes to assault him with his cane, but his adversary is the stronger. Scandalised that no one else at the London Tavern will come to his assistance, Pinto again walks out of the room, and after entering 'a protest at the Home Office against the insult put upon my country', he leaves immediately for Paris.[3]

Briggs's satire presents Pinto's racism as a spectacular cognitive failure. It is simply impossible for him to recognise Douglass in Scotland, despite all evidence to the contrary, because he is in the wrong place; the right place being that of a 'valet', and even that is a position he believes Douglass could not secure without the recommendation of Pinto's friends. And Briggs intends his readers to relish the carnivalesque reversal that follows both encounters as Pinto discovers that it is actually himself who is out of place, an unwanted intruder in the castle and the tavern, forced into an ignominious retreat.

During his time in Britain and Ireland, Douglass must have been used to insinuations that he was 'out of place', perhaps especially in Scotland, since it is in this connection that he twice uses the phrase with special emphasis. At the Burns Supper in Rochester, he takes care to refute any suggestion that the fact that he is 'not a Scotch-man, and [has] a colored skin' makes him 'out of my place' there, insisting he has every right to celebrate Scottish history, literature and landscape, and even choose to identify as a Scot, invoking the poet's famous declaration of human rights in his defence.[4]

The same four words appear in the letter he included in the appendix to the second Dublin edition of his *Narrative*, addressed in Perth on 27 January 1846 to Mr A. C. C. Thompson of Delaware, in which he refutes the latter's allegations contesting Douglass's claims to authorship. To quote from it one last time:

> The change wrought in me is truly amazing. If you should meet me now, you would scarcely know me. You know when I used to meet you near Covey's wood-gate, I hardly dared to look up at you. If I should meet you where I now am, amid the free hills of Old Scotland, where the ancient 'Black Douglass' once met his foes, I presume I might summon sufficient fortitude to look you full in the face. It may be that, wearing the brave name which I have assumed, might lead me to deeds which would render our meeting not the most agreeable. Especially might this be the case, if you should attempt to enslave me. You would see a wonderful difference in me. I have really got out of my place; that is, I have got out of slavery, which you know is 'the place' for negroes in Christian America.[5]

For most of his life, Douglass had been told that his 'place' was slavery – or the 'Jim Crow' car or the 'negro pew'. Here, 'amid the free hills of Old Scotland, where the ancient "Black Douglass" once met his foes,' he is finally out that place, the place to which many insist he belongs and from which he had no right to stray. And it is not just slavery he has escaped from, but the continuous, if uneven, prejudice of the Northern states, where his freedom to go out in public, and who with, was always open to challenge – by a look, a remark, a command or a blow. Finally, he could begin to relax, knowing that he could enter a hall to attend a meeting without any-one blocking his path or walk along a main street in the company of white women without facing a mob. The patronising concern of so-called friends and the insults in the Free Church press, though they must have stung, did not disturb his tranquility for long. But we must not forget that Douglass was 'out of his place' in a third sense too: away from his family and closest friends in Massachusetts. We know from some of his letters and speeches that he missed home and, in the end, looked forward to his return, especially once his legal freedom was secured.

Douglass lays before us different kinds of belonging. The place he is consigned to by slaveholders and racists. The place of refuge and safety abroad to which he flees. And the place to which he wishes to return, not yet a place of genuine freedom but one where he must resume the struggle as a stronger, more confident, accomplished and independent-minded campaigner.

What of Douglass's 'place' for us, today, in the twenty-first century? Here we can find similar sets of tensions and ambiguities. Is there a place for him in the gap between Scottish historiography (which ignores Douglass) and Douglass studies in the United States (which has little to say about Scotland)? Is this a gap in the scholarship that we just need to fill in and leave with a smooth finish?

But Douglass was not interested in the past for its own sake. 'We have to do with the past only as we can make it useful to the present and to the future,' he famously declared in his 'What to the Slave is the Fourth of July?' speech, delivered in 1852.[6] What matters is how to make it work for us. In the same spirit we might treat Douglass himself as our contemporary too, someone who can be, and is, invoked, reimagined, recruited by the politics of the present.

It is tempting to suggest that two paths are open to us. On the one hand we have the official memorialisation of Douglass, the recognition of his ambition and achievements through initiatives funded by public bodies. In the United States he has been honoured by stamps, coins, banknotes, plaques or statues that display his likeness, and by schools, parks, roads, bridges, prizes and research institutes that bear his name.[7] Such acts of recognition can seem tokenistic or gestural, signalling that the sponsoring body – and perhaps society at large – is congratulating itself on finally recognising 'diversity', celebrating a new civic multicultural orthodoxy. On the other, we might delve into Douglass's life and writings to find strength and inspiration to challenge the complacency sometimes nurtured by that orthodoxy, and support campaigns that, as in Douglass's time, are geared to asserting rights and claiming freedom. This approach might give rise to what has been called 'guerrilla memorialisation', one which is more likely to take the form of local, largely self-funded short-lived interventions, including performances, ceremonies, occupations, marches, low-budget films and murals.[8]

But things are not so simple. Official recognition is often a begrudging response to long campaigns from the grassroots and even radical small-scale initiatives usually rely on some degree of government funding. In any case the two approaches are often intertwined. In the absence of substantial recognition of Douglass in Scotland, two examples from Ireland may be illuminating.

The Frederick Douglass Ireland Monument was created by the sculptor Andrew Edwards in 2011. It is a striking, nine-foot-high representation of Douglass as a young man, striding forward, and holding forth, book in hand, his coat flapping in the wind. The plan was to cast it in bronze and install it permanently at University College Cork, and the US president Barack Obama was invited to unveil it during his state visit to Ireland that Spring. In the event, Obama did not make it to Cork and the monument was cast in resin instead, allowing it to be transported to Farmleigh, near Dublin, the official guest house for foreign dignitaries. Douglass duly posed for photographs with Obama and the Taoiseach Enda Kenny. If this ran the risk of demeaning him as a servant of the tourist industry and international public relations, Obama hinted at a more historically dynamic Douglass in his speech before a large crowd on College Green, referring to 'that escaped slave and our great abolitionist, [who] forged an unlikely friendship [. . .] with your great liberator, Daniel O'Connell'. The same week, Douglass's great-great-granddaughter Nettie Washington Douglass and her son, Kenneth B. Morris, Jr, founders of an organisation that promotes awareness of human trafficking, met Irish President Mary McAleese in Dublin and attended the launch of a commemorative edition of the 1845 *Narrative*. The resin monument was subsequently displayed at various events in Ireland and the United States, and a bronze incarnation now stands at the University of Maryland, College Park.[9]

The monument was an initiative of the Frederick Douglass Ireland project, established by humanitarian campaigner Don Mullan and policy consultant Kristin Leary, who took full advantage of Obama's visit to raise the profile of Douglass in Ireland, lobbying the White House, co-ordinating the visit of the descendants and arranging the publication of the souvenir volume. In doing so they not only ensured that Frederick Douglass was remembered as a figure of historical importance in his own time, but presented him as someone of continuing significance. Mullan's introduction to the *Narrative* places Douglass alongside Desmond Tutu, Martin Luther

King, Jr and Rosa Parks, but Douglass's primary purpose in all this seems to be to act as a catalyst for contemporary educational and development programmes. Royalties from the book, we are told, will go to support Concern Worldwide's work in Haiti, another part of the world in which Douglass took a deep interest, notably through his service as US minister to that country from 1889 to 1891.[10]

If the monument offers one way in which Douglass can be honoured as someone of contemporary relevance, Donal O'Kelly's play *The Cambria* (2005) suggests another. Commissioned by Dublin's St Patrick's Festival, where it was first performed, before going on tour, it also received funding from Abhann, the company that owns and produces Riverdance, and (echoing the monument's concerns) from Afri, an organisation that 'seeks to inform debate and influence policy and practice in Ireland and internationally on human rights, peace, global justice, and sustainability issues'.[11] Drawing on the events of Douglass's outward voyage in 1845, the drama addresses a number of themes explored in this book: the extent to which Douglass is motivated by – or can be persuaded to abandon his principles by – the promise of making money; his need to change names and the circumstances which dictated when it was safe to reveal himself and when not; and the element of performance that is common to both Douglass's lectures and blackface minstrel shows. This fluidity of identity and motivation is expertly conveyed by a cast of ten characters, representing captain, crew and passengers, played by just two actors, shifting rapidly between them, across sexes, nationalities and races.

But what is most innovative about *The Cambria* is the way it is framed by events in the audience's present. For it opens in an 'airport environment' with Colette, explaining to Vincent, engaged in decorating the immigration section, that her friend Patrick has just been deported to Lagos, last-minute appeals notwithstanding. She's a history teacher and Patrick was one of her prize pupils – and well integrated into Irish society, as his name suggests (his party piece was Robert Emmet's famous 1803 *Speech from the Dock*). When she quotes Douglass, Vincent asks who he was, and the action slips back a century and a half as Colette invites him and the audience to imagine 'if Frederick Douglass . . . came to Ireland NOW . . .' And if Douglass at the end of the play steps off the boat to be greeted by Daniel O'Connell, this moment gives way and we return to

Vincent and Colette, who completes her introduction by announcing his arrival thus: 'Frederick Douglass, one-time asylum-seeker and refugee.'[12]

In Scotland, as we have seen, Douglass has barely made his mark in the two decades of activity that have sought to understand and recognise the country's historical involvement in Atlantic slavery and the struggles for emancipation. This book has explored some of the ways in which Douglass's experiences in Scotland helped to sculpt the public figure who was to become so significant in the second half of the nineteenth century in the United States and across the world. It has tried to suggest that Scotland – with its radical abolitionist culture, its globally recognised literature and its fast-evolving science and technology – provided Douglass with a stimulating environment in which he seized every opportunity to refashion himself as a public speaker, independent thinker and political campaigner who knew how to engage with different audiences. In doing so the book tells many shorter stories – recounting journeys, encounters, transactions, bondings, disagreements, performances – which shed light on the immediate impact of his visit on those around him. Each of them could serve as the starting point of further research, perhaps leading to cultural interventions that will spark wider debates.

In the main body of *Frederick Douglass and Scotland, 1846*, I have tried to situate its protagonist firmly in the mid-nineteenth century and, as far as possible, to interpret his words and understand his actions in the context of his own time. I have allowed myself to roam a few years before and after, but even Douglass's second visit to Scotland in 1860 I chose to consider beyond the scope of this volume, given the very different circumstances in which it took place.[13] I have tried in particular not to lose sight of the way his own sense of self was unsettled by contending and changing notions of manhood, including the Southern codes of masculinity that shaped his upbringing and the norms of behaviour associated with the Victorian gentleman – attracting, but also disconcerting, those men and women around him. When he wrote to Maria Weston Chapman, insisting that 'I am trying to preach and practice a genuine antislavery life', Douglass reminds us how powerful the ethical impulse was for him. Abolitionism was not just about campaign slogans and declarations of principle, but involved the trickier grey areas of compromise that inevitably inform its adherents' strategic decisions and personal conduct.

In these closing chapters, I have turned to explore what Douglass might mean to those reading about him today. Again, it might be less the soundbites – 'Send Back the Money!' or 'No Fellowship with Slaveholders' – that stir people two centuries on, than the way Douglass sought to define and assert his place in his relationships with those he encountered, in private and public. O'Kelly's play *The Cambria* provides a compelling illustration of how Douglass's experiences might be represented in order to amplify the resonance his example might have for those who find themselves in similar situations today in the context of the so-called 'refugee crisis' that has politicised Europe, especially since 2015.

Leaving the country of his birth where he faced persecution, he undertook a perilous journey to seek refuge and safety abroad. On arrival, he expressed a sense of relief at the freedom he could now enjoy, even while feeling the wrench of leaving his family behind. He would need to create for himself new affiliations to his new home – to its people, its history, its landscapes – forging fresh and imaginative ties of kinship. Douglass declined to accept the obligation to be grateful and discreet. He was unafraid to speak out against the way he was sometimes treated, challenging those who questioned the credibility of his testimony, rebuking those who repeatedly defined him as no more than a 'fugitive' or 'runaway'. He delivered rousing speeches in cities and towns that criticised his hosts for their complacency and demanded that they recognise him as a fully human being. When Douglass invites us to imagine him 'amid the free hills of old Scotland', he is celebrating not what Scotland is, but what he hopes it might become.

Notes

1. Weidman, 'Pinto Letters'. On Brown and Willis see Stadler, *Troubling Minds*, pp. 88–94.
2. Weidman, 'Pinto Letters', pp. 114–16.
3. Ibid. pp. 127–8.
4. FD, Rochester, NY, 25 January 1849 (FDP 1.2, p. 148).
5. D2, p. cxxvii. The phrase 'out of my place' does not appear in what was probably an earlier draft of the letter he sent to WLG on 27 January 1846 (FDP 3.1, pp. 81–6), only in the revision of it he submitted to RW from Glasgow soon afterwards (FD's preface to the new edition is dated 'Glasgow, Feb. 6th, 1846').

6. FD, Rochester, NY, 5 July 1852 ('What to the Slave is the Fourth of July?') (FDP 1.2, p. 366).

7. For a brief sketch of FD's current standing in the 'national consciousness' in the United States see Barnes, *Frederick Douglass*, p. 6.

8. For 'guerrilla memorialisation' see Rice, *Creating Memorials*, esp. pp. 15–16.

9. Chris Butler, 'There are Superheroes', available at <https://cruciblethe-blog.com/2015/11/25/there-are-superheroes/> (last accessed 11 February 2018); Kevin Whelan, 'Bringing It All Back Home: O'Connell, Douglass and Barack Obama', *History Ireland* 4 (July/August 2011), available at <http://www.historyireland.com/20th-century-contemporary-history/bringing-it-all-back-home-oconnell-douglass-and-barack-obama/> (last accessed 11 February 2018); Lara Marlowe, 'All Parties Got What They Wanted Despite Brevity of Visit', *Irish Times*, 24 May 2011, available at <https://www.irishtimes.com/news/all-parties-got-what-they-wanted-despite-brevity-of-visit-1.580141> (last accessed 11 February 2018).

10. Don Mullan, 'Introduction'. The official website of 'The Frederick Douglass Ireland Project' is no longer online but is archived at <https://web.archive.org/web/20170131055129fw_/http://douglassoconnellmemorial.org:80> (last accessed 11 February 2018).

11. 'Welcome to Afri', available at <http://www.afri.ie> (last accessed 11 February 2018).

12. O'Kelly, *The Cambria* (2005). For a careful reading of the play see Sweeney, 'Other People's History'.

13. For a brief account of the second visit see Blackett, 'Cracks in the Anti-slavery Wall'.

Speaking Itinerary, 1846

Douglass made several tours of Scotland, the first and longest lasting four months. He spent a total of nearly six months in Scotland between January and October 1846, addressing at least seventy meetings, probably many more.

Douglass and his fellow campaigners spoke mostly at two kinds of venue. They held public meetings at civic halls and meeting rooms, such as the City Hall and the Assembly Rooms in Glasgow, the Exchange Rooms in Paisley, the Music Hall (now the Assembly Rooms) and Waterloo Rooms in Edinburgh, the City Hall in Perth and the Assembly Rooms (now the Music Hall) in Aberdeen – and many of them still exist today.

They also addressed audiences in numerous churches, usually belonging to the United Secession Church or the Relief Church (the two denominations merged in 1847 to form the United Presbyterian Church). Most of these church buildings have since been demolished or rebuilt beyond recognition.

In drawing up a list of his speaking engagements, my starting point was the list published in *The Frederick Douglass Papers. Series One: Speeches, Debates and Interviews. Volume 1: 1841–46*, under the general editorship of John W. Blassingame (New Haven: Yale University Press, 1979).

But some meetings are listed there which certainly did not take place: Douglass did not accompany fellow antislavery campaigner Henry Clarke Wright on his tour of the Borders in March and April, for instance. I have not included them here, nor a few others for which I have been unable to find independent confirmation. On the other hand, I have found evidence of meetings which are not listed in the *Frederick Douglass Papers*.

An asterisk indicates that the exact date is not certain. One may assume the meetings took place in the evening unless specified otherwise.

Accompanied by his white abolitionist friend James Buffum, Douglass arrived in Ardrossan from Belfast on Saturday 10 January and proceeded by train to Glasgow.

> Thursday 15 January: Glasgow, City Hall.
> Thursday 22 January: Glasgow, City Hall.
> Friday 23 January: Perth, City Hall.
> *Saturday 24 January: Perth.
> *Sunday 25 January: Perth.
> Monday 26 January: Perth, City Hall.
> Tuesday 27 January: Dundee, School Wynd Chapel.
> Wednesday 28 January: Dundee, School Wynd Chapel.
> Thursday 29 January: Dundee, School Wynd Chapel.
> Friday 30 January: Dundee, Bell Street Chapel.
> Monday 9 February: Dundee, McGavin's Chapel, Tay Square.
> Tuesday 10 February: Arbroath, Trades' Hall.
> Wednesday 11 February: Arbroath, Abbey Church.
> Thursday 12 February: Arbroath, Abbey Church.
> Wednesday 18 February: Glasgow, Assembly Rooms (afternoon). 'Ladies' Meeting'.
> Wednesday 18 February: Glasgow, City Hall.
> *Thursday 26 February: Montrose.
> *Friday 27 February: Montrose.
> *Saturday 28 February: Montrose.
> *early March: Aberdeen, Music Hall, George Street and Assembly Rooms, Union Street.
> Monday 9 March: Montrose, Mr Hyslop's Chapel.
> Tuesday 10 March: Dundee, School Wynd Chapel. 'Anti-Slavery Soiree'.
> Tuesday 12 March: Perth (afternoon). 'A meeting of ladies'.
> Tuesday 12 March: Perth, City Hall. 'Anti-Slavery Soiree'.
> Tuesday 17 March: Paisley, William Nisbet's Church, 16 Abbey Close.
> Thursday 19 March: Paisley, William Nisbet's Church, 16 Abbey Close.

Friday 20 March: Paisley, William Nisbet's Church, 16 Abbey Close.

Monday 23 March: Ayr, Relief Church.

Tuesday 24 March: Ayr, Relief Church.

Monday 30 March: Paisley, Secession Church, 21 George Street.

Tuesday 31 March: Bonhill. Probably the first of several meetings in the Vale of Leven.

*Sunday 5 April: Fenwick, Secession Meeting House.

Monday 6 April: Paisley, Secession Church, 21 George Street.

Friday 10 April: Greenock, West Blackhall Street Chapel.

Friday 17 April: Paisley, Exchange Rooms.

Tuesday 21 April: Glasgow, City Hall.

Thursday 23 April: Glasgow, Assembly Rooms (afternoon).

Thursday 23 April: Glasgow, City Hall.

Tuesday 28 April: Edinburgh, McGilchrist's Church, 19 Rose Street.

Wednesday 29 April: Edinburgh, McGilchrist's Church, 19 Rose Street (afternoon). 'Ladies' Meeting'.

Friday 1 May: Edinburgh, Waterloo Rooms. 'Public breakfast' followed by meeting of the Edinburgh Ladies' Emancipation Society (afternoon).

Friday 1 May: Edinburgh, Music Hall.

Thursday 7 May: Edinburgh, McGilchrist's Church, 19 Rose Street.

Douglass left for London on 17 or 18 May to attend the anniversary meeting of the British and Foreign Anti-Slavery Society, although he had scheduled meetings in Kirkcaldy (19 May) and Edinburgh (20 and 22 May) which went ahead without him. He returned on 23 or 24 May.

Monday 25 May: Edinburgh, Music Hall.

Wednesday 27 May: Edinburgh, Music Hall.

Tuesday 28 May: Leith.

Monday 1 June: Kirkcaldy, Bethelfield Chapel.

Tuesday 2 June: Edinburgh, Music Hall.

Wednesday 3 June: Edinburgh, Music Hall.

Thursday 4 June: Edinburgh, Music Hall.

Tuesday 9 June: Edinburgh, Music Hall.

His next known engagement was in Belfast on 16 June. He was back in Liverpool on 4 July seeing off his friend Buffum, heading back to Massachusetts, after which he returned to Belfast for the General Assembly of the Presbyterian Church in Ireland. Douglass then sailed to Ardrossan and thence to Edinburgh via Glasgow.

> Friday 31 July: Edinburgh, Brighton Street Chapel. Scottish Anti-Slavery Society meeting 'to commemorate the anniversary of the emancipation of the slaves in the West Indies'.

Douglass left Edinburgh for Newcastle on 1 August, and thence travelled to London where he met William Lloyd Garrison, newly arrived from Boston. The following month they both travelled to Scotland, but while Garrison went directly from London to Glasgow, arriving on the evening of 19 September, Douglass spoke in Sunderland on 18 September and did not rejoin him until 21 September. They had hoped to speak at City Hall, Glasgow on 21 September, but the meeting had to be postponed because the building 'was to be occupied during the week with an exhibition of statuary'.

> Tuesday 22 September: Greenock.
> Wednesday 23 September: Paisley, Secession Church, 21 George Street.
> Thursday 24 September: Edinburgh, Brighton Street Chapel.
> Friday 25 September: Edinburgh. Edinburgh Female Anti-Slavery Meeting.
> Monday 28 September: Dundee, Bell Street Hall.
> Tuesday 29 September: Edinburgh.
> Wednesday 30 September: Glasgow, City Hall.
> Thursday 1 October: Glasgow, City Hall (afternoon).
> Thursday 1 October: Glasgow, City Hall.
> Friday 2 October: Glasgow, Eagle Temperance Hotel (morning).
> Friday 2 October: Kilmarnock (afternoon).

Douglass and Garrison then took the overnight steamer from Ardrossan to Belfast, where they spoke on 3 October. After speaking in Liverpool on 19 October, Douglass, Garrison and George Thompson took the train to Fleetwood on 20 October, then the overnight boat to Ardrossan, and headed for Edinburgh via Glasgow arriving just in time for the evening meeting.

> Wednesday 21 October: Edinburgh, Brighton Street Chapel.
> Thursday 22 October: Kirkcaldy.
> Friday 23 October: Dundee, James' Chapel, Bell Street.
> Saturday 24 October: Perth, City Hall.
> Monday 26 October: Perth.
> Wednesday 28 October: Glasgow, City Hall.
> Thursday 29 October: Edinburgh.

Douglass and Garrison then headed south to Carlisle, probably by train (the line, via Dumfries, having opened in August), and Douglass was one of many supporters who saw Garrison off when he departed from Liverpool for Boston on 4 November.

Maps

Scotland

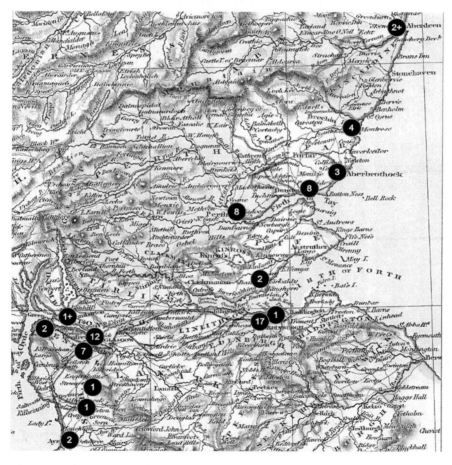

Showing locations of Frederick Douglass's speaking engagements and approximate number of times he spoke in each place, 1846.

Glasgow

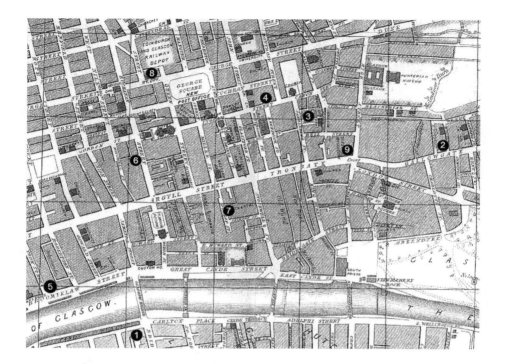

1. Terminus of the Glasgow–Ayr railway.
2. 161 Gallowgate, home of William Smeal, FD's probable base when in Glasgow.
3. City Hall: FD spoke here numerous times during January, February (with JB), April (with JB, GT, HCW), September and October (with WLG).
4. Assembly Rooms, Ingram Street: FD spoke here on 18 February and 23 April.
5. Eagle Temperance Hotel: FD spoke here on 2 October (with WLG).
6. Monteith Rooms, Buchanan Street: Dick Pelham and his 'Sable Brothers' performed here from January to March.
7. Adelphi Theatre Royal: Ira Aldridge performed here in March.
8. Terminus of the Glasgow–Edinburgh railway.
9. Tontine Hotel and Reading Room.

Edinburgh

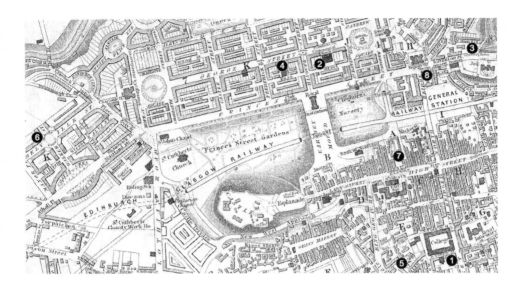

1. York Temperance Hotel: FD's base when in Edinburgh.
2. United Secession Church, Rose Street (Rev. John McGilchrist): FD spoke here on 28 and 29 April, and 7 May (with JB, GT and HCW).
3. Waterloo Rooms: FD spoke here on 1 May (with GT).
4. Music Hall: FD spoke here numerous times in May and June (with JB, GT and HCW).
5. Brighton Street Chapel: FD spoke here on 31 July (alone), 24 September and 21 October (with WLG).
6. 45 Melville Street: home of George Combe, visited by FD, JB and GT on 7 June.
7. Council Chambers: FD attends ceremony conferring freedom of the city on GT, 6 June.
8. Theatre Royal: Ethiopian Serenaders performed here in October.

Paisley

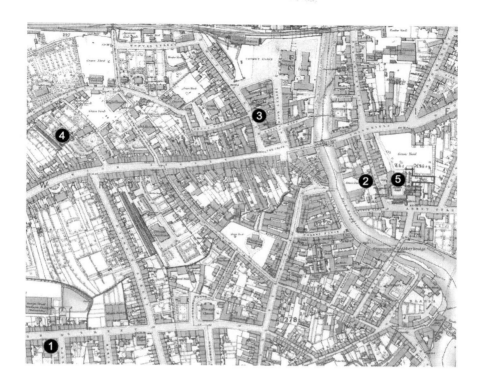

1. United Secession Church, 21 George Street (Rev. Robert Cairns):
   FD spoke here on 9 February (with JB) and 23 September
   (with WLG).

2. United Secession Church, 16 Abbey Close (Rev. William Nisbet):
   FD spoke here on 17, 18, 19, 20, 30 March and 6 April
   (with JB).

3. Exchange Rooms: FD spoke here on 17 April (with JB).

4. Free Church of Scotland, High Church, Orr Square
   (Rev. John McNaughtan).

5. Church of Scotland, Abbey (Rev. Patrick Brewster).

Dundee

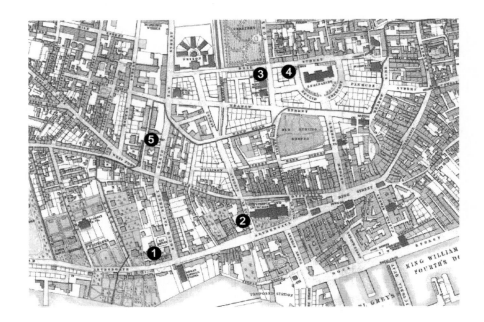

1. United Secession Church, Tay Square (Rev. James R. McGavin): FD spoke here with JB on 9 February 1846.

2. United Secession Church, 'George's Chapel', School Wynd (Rev. George Gilfillan): FD spoke here on 27, 28, 29 Jan (with JB) and 10 March 1846 (with JB).

3. United Secession Church, Bell Street (Rev. W. B. Borwick): FD spoke here on 30 January (with JB and HCW) and 28 September (with WLG).

4. Relief Church, 'James' Church', Bell Street (Rev. James Reston): FD spoke here on 23 October 1846 (with WLG and GT).

5. Free Church of Scotland, St David's Church, Ward Road (Rev. George Lewis)

Bibliography

Works by Douglass

A   *Autobiographies* (New York: Library of America, 1994).
BF   *My Bondage and My Freedom* [1855] (New York: Dover, 1969).
D1   *Narrative of the Life of Frederick Douglass, an American Slave, Written by Himself* (Dublin: Webb and Chapman, 1845).
D2   *Narrative of the Life of Frederick Douglass, an American Slave, Written by Himself* (Dublin: Webb and Chapman, 1846).
FDP 1.1   *The Frederick Douglass Papers. Series One: Speeches, Debates, and Interviews, Volume 1: 1841–46*, ed. John W. Blassingame (New Haven: Yale University Press, 1979).
FDP 1.2   *The Frederick Douglass Papers. Series One: Speeches, Debates, and Interviews, Volume 2: 1847–54*, ed. John W Blassingame (New Haven: Yale University Press, 1982).
FDP 1.3   *The Frederick Douglass Papers. Series One: Speeches, Debates, and Interviews, Volume 3: 1855–63*, ed. John W. Blassingame (New Haven: Yale University Press, 1985).
FDP 1.4   *The Frederick Douglass Papers. Series One: Speeches, Debates, and Interviews, Volume 3: 1864–80*, ed. John W. Blassingame (New Haven: Yale University Press, 1991).
FDP 1.5   *The Frederick Douglass Papers. Series One: Speeches, Debates, and Interviews, Volume 3: 1881–95*, ed. John W. Blassingame and John R. McKivigan (New Haven: Yale University Press, 1992).
FDP 2.1   *The Frederick Douglass Papers. Series Two: Autobiographical Writings, Volume 1: Narrative*, ed. John W Blassingame, John R. McKivigan and Peter P. Hinks (New Haven: Yale University Press, 1999).
FDP 2.2   *The Frederick Douglass Papers. Series Two: Autobiographical Writings, Volume 2: My Bondage and My Freedom*, ed. John W. Blassingame, John R. McKivigan and Peter P. Hinks (New Haven: Yale University Press, 2003).

FDP 2.3   *The Frederick Douglass Papers. Series Two: Autobiographical Writings, Volume 3: Life and Times*, ed. John R. McKivigan (New Haven: Yale University Press, 2012).

FDP 3.1   *The Frederick Douglass Papers. Series Three: Correspondence, Volume 1: 1842–52*, ed. John R. McKivigan (New Haven: Yale University Press, 2009).

LT1   *Life and Times of Frederick Douglass: His Early Life as a Slave, His Escape from Bondage, and His Complete History to the Present Time* (Harford, CT: Park Publishing Co, 1881).

LT2   *Life and Times of Frederick Douglass, Written By Himself* (Boston: De Wolfe & Fiske Co., 1892).

LWFD1   *The Life and Writings of Frederick Douglass. Volume I: Early Years, 1817–1849*, ed. Philip S. Foner (New York: International Publishers, 1950).

LWFD2   *The Life and Writings of Frederick Douglass. Volume II: Pre-Civil War Decade, 1850–1860*, ed. Philip S. Foner (New York: International Publishers, 1950).

LWFD4   *The Life and Writings of Frederick Douglass. Volume IV: Reconstruction and After*, ed. Philip S. Foner (New York: International Publishers, 1955).

LWFD5   *The Life and Writings of Frederick Douglass. Volume V: Supplementary Volume, 1844–1860*, ed. Philip S. Foner (New York: International Publishers, 1975).

N   Frederick Douglass, *Narrative of the Life of Frederick Douglass, an American Slave, Written by Himself* [1845], ed. Houston A. Baker, Jr (New York: Penguin, 1982).

Collections of Abolitionist Writings and Speeches

BAA   Taylor, Clare (ed.), *British and American Abolitionists: An Episode in Transatlantic Understanding* (Edinburgh: Edinburgh University Press, 1974).

BAP1   Ripley, C. Peter (ed.), *The Black Abolitionist Papers, Vol 1: The British Isles, 1830–1865* (Chapel Hill: University of North Carolina Press, 1985).

GL3   Merrill, Walter M. (ed.), *The Letters of William Lloyd Garrison. Volume III: No Union with Slave-Holders, 1841–1849* (Cambridge, MA: Belknap Press of Harvard University Press, 1973).

Manstealers   *Free Church Alliance with Manstealers. Send Back the Money. Great Anti-Slavery Meeting in the City Hall, Glasgow, Containing Speeches Delivered by Messrs. Wright, Douglass, and Buffum, from America, and by George Thompson, Esq. Of*

London, with a Summary Account of a Series of Meetings
Held in Edinburgh by the Above Named Gentlemen (Glasgow:
George Gallie, 1846).

Manuscript Collections

Smeal Collection   William Smeal Collection, Mitchell Library, Glasgow
Chalmers Papers   Chalmers Collection, New College Library, Edinburgh
BPL   Anti-Slavery Collection, Boston Public Library
MacIver Papers   University of Liverpool Library, MacIver Papers

Other Sources

Adams, James Eli, *Dandies and Desert Saints: Styles of Victorian Manhood* (Ithaca: Cornell University Press, 1995).

Alexander, James E., *L'Acadie; or, Seven Years' Explorations in British America*, 2 vols (London: Henry Colburn, 1849).

Altick, Richard, *The Shows of London* (Cambridge, MA: Belknap Press of Harvard University Press, 1978).

American and Foreign Anti-Slavery Society, *Letter from the Executive Committee of the American and Foreign Anti-Slavery Society to the Commissioners of the Free Church of Scotland* (Edinburgh: Myles Macphail, [1844]).

American Slavery: Report of a Public Meeting Held at Finsbury Chapel, Moorfields, to Receive Frederick Douglass, the American Slave, on Friday May 22, 1846 (London: C. B. Christian, 1846).

Anadolu-Okur, Nilgün, *Dismantling Slavery: Frederick Douglass, William Lloyd Garrison, and the Formation of Abolitionist Discourse, 1841–1851* (Knoxville: University of Tennessee Press, 2016).

Andrews, Corey, '"Ev'ry Heart Can Feel": Scottish Poetic Responses to Slavery in the West Indies, from Blair to Burns', *International Journal of Scottish Literature* 4 (2008): 1–22.

Andrews, William (ed.), *Critical Essays on Frederick Douglass* (Boston: G. K. Hall, 1991).

Anti-Slavery Soirée: Report of the Speeches Delivered at a Soirée in Honour of Messrs Douglass, Wright, & Buffum, Held in George's Chapel, Dundee, on Tuesday the 10th March, 1846 (Dundee: D. Hill at the Courier Office, 1846).

Anti-Slavery Songs (Edinburgh: J. Fairgrieve & Co., 1846), transcription available at <http://www.bulldozia.com/douglass/songs> (last accessed 24 February 2018).

Anstruther, Ian, *The Knight and the Umbrella: An Account of the Eglinton Tournament, 1839* (London: Bles, 1963).

Armistead, Wilson, *A Tribute for the Negro: Being a Vindication of the Moral, Intellectual, and Religious Capabilities of the Coloured Portion of Mankind* (Manchester: William Irwin, 1848).

Ascherson, Neil, *Stone Voices: The Search for Scotland*, revised edn (London: Granta, 2014).

Ashton, Rosemary, *George Eliot: A Life* (London: Hamish Hamilton, 1996).

Ayers, Edward L., *Vengeance and Justice: Crime and Punishment in the 19th-Century American South* (New York: Oxford University Press, 1984).

Babcock, F. Lawrence, *Spanning the Atlantic* (New York: Knopf, 1931).

Bacon, Margaret Hope, *But One Race: The Life of Robert Purvis* (Albany: State University of New York Press, 2007).

Bailey, Kenneth K., 'Protestantism and Afro-Americans in the Old South: Another Look', *Journal of Southern History* 41.4 (1975): 451–72.

Baines, Edward, *History of the Cotton Manufacture in Great Britain* (London: H. Fisher, R. Fisher and P. Jackson, 1835).

Barbour, John, *The Bruce* [1375], ed. A. M. M. Duncan (Edinburgh: Canongate, 1997).

Barchas, Janine, 'Prefiguring Genre: Frontispiece Portraits from *Gulliver's Travels* to *Millennium Hall*', *Studies in the Novel* 30.2 (1988): 260–86.

Barnes, L. Diane, *Frederick Douglass: Reformer and Statesman* (New York: Routledge, 2013).

Barnum, P. T., *Struggles and Triumphs or Forty Years' Recollections* (London: Sampson, Low, Son, and Marston, 1869).

Basu, Paul, *Highland Homecomings: Genealogy and Heritage Tourism in the Scottish Diaspora* (Abingdon: Routledge, 2007).

Batchen, Geoffrey, 'Origins Without End', in Tanya Sheehan and Andrés Mario Zervigón (eds), *Photography and its Origins* (Abingdon: Routledge, 2015), pp. 67–81.

Bates, A. W., *The Anatomy of Robert Knox: Murder, Mad Science and Medical Regulation in Nineteenth-Century Edinburgh* (Brighton: Sussex Academic Press, 2010).

Bates, Stephen, *Penny Loaves & Butter Cheap: Britain in 1846* (London: Head of Zeus, 2014).

Baxter, Terry, *Frederick Douglass's Curious Audiences: Ethos in the Age of the Consumable Subject* (New York: Routledge, 2004).

Benjamin, Walter, 'A Small History of Photography' [1931], tr. Kingsley Shorter, in Walter Benjamin, *One-Way Street and Other Writings* (London: NLB/Verso, 1979), pp. 240–57.

Benjamin, Walter, 'The Paris of the Second Empire in Baudelaire' [1938], tr. Harry Zohn, in Walter Benjamin, *The Writer of Modern Life: Essays on*

Charles Baudelaire, ed. Michael W. Jennngs (Cambridge, MA: Belknap Press of Harvard University Press, 2006), pp. 46–133.

Bennett, Michael, *Democratic Discourses: The Radical Abolition Movement and Antebellum Literature* (Piscataway, NJ: Rutgers University Press, 2005).

Berger, John, 'The Suit and the Photograph', in *About Looking* (London: Writers and Readers Publishing Cooperative, 1980), pp. 27–36.

Bernier, Celeste-Marie, 'A "Typical Negro" or a "Work of Art"? The "Inner" via the "Outer Man" in Frederick Douglass's Manuscripts and Daguerreotypes', *Slavery and Abolition* 33.2 (2012): 287–303.

Bernier, Celeste-Marie, *Characters of Blood: Black Heroism in the Transatlantic Imagination* (Charlottesville: University of Virginia Press, 2012).

Bernier, Celeste-Marie, 'A Visual Call to Arms against the "Caracature [sic] of My Own Face": From Fugitive Slave to Fugitive Image in Frederick Douglass's Theory of Portraiture', *Journal of American Studies* 49.2 (2015): 323–57.

Berthoff, Rowland, 'Under the Kilt: Variations on the Scottish-American Ground', *Journal of American Ethnic History* 1.2 (Spring 1982): 5–34.

Biddis, M. D., 'The Politics of Anatomy: Dr Robert Knox and Victorian Racism', *Proceedings of The Royal Society of Medicine* 69.4 (1976): 245–50.

Billington, Louis, 'British Humanitarians and American Cotton, 1840–1860', *Journal of American Studies* 11.3 (1977): 313–34.

Billington, Louis, and Rosamund Billington, 'A Burning Zeal for Righteousness: Women in the Anti-slavery Movement, 1820–1860', in J. Rendall (ed.), *Equal or Different: Women's Politics, 1800–1914* (Oxford: Oxford University Press, 1987), pp. 82–111.

Birney, James Gillespie, *American Churches the Bulwarks of American Slavery* (London: Johnston and Barrett, 1840).

Black, Aileen, *Gilfillan of Dundee, 1813–1878: Interpreting Religion and Culture in Mid-Victorian Scotland* (Dundee: Dundee University Press, 2006).

Black's Economical Guide through Edinburgh; Including a Description of the Environs (Edinburgh: Adam and Charles Black, 1843).

Black's Economical Guide through Glasgow; Arranged in Three Walks, 2nd edn (Edinburgh: Adam and Charles Black, 1843).

Blackett, Richard J. M., *Building an Antislavery Wall: Black Americans in the Atlantic Abolitionist Movement, 1830–1860* (Ithaca: Cornell University Press, 1983).

Blackett, Richard J. M., 'Cracks in the Antislavery Wall: Frederick Douglass's Second Visit to England (1859–60) and the Coming of the Civil War', in Alan J. Rice and Martin Crawford (eds), *Liberating Sojourn: Frederick Douglass and Transatlantic Reform* (Athens: University of Georgia Press, 1999), pp. 187–206.

Blackwood, Sarah, 'Fugitive Obscura: Runaway Slave Portraiture and Early Photographic Technology', *American Literature* 81.1 (2009): 99–125.

Blanckaert, Claude, 'On the Origins of French Ethnology: William Edwards and the Doctrine of Race', in George W. Stocking (ed.), *Bones, Bodies and Behavior: Essays on Biological Anthropology* (Madison: University of Wisconsin Press, 1988), pp. 18–55.

Blassingame, John W., *The Slave Community: Plantation Life in the Antebellum South* (New York: Oxford University Press, 1979).

Bowen, Frank C., *A Century of Atlantic Travel, 1830–1930* (London: Sampson Low, Marston and Co., 1932[?]).

Bradbury, Richard, 'Frederick Douglass and the Chartists', in Alan J. Rice and Martin Crawford (eds), *Liberating Sojourn: Frederick Douglass and Transatlantic Reform* (Athens: University of Georgia Press, 1999), pp. 169–86.

Bratton, J. S., 'English Ethiopians: British Audiences and Black-Face Acts, 1835–1865', *Yearbook of English Studies* 11 (1981): 127–42.

Breeden, James O. (ed.), *Advice Among the Masters: The Ideal of Slave Management in the Old South* (Westport, CT: Greenwood Press, 1980).

Bremner, David, *The Industries of Scotland: Their Rise, Progress and Present Condition* (Edinburgh: Adam and Charles Black, 1869).

Brontë, Charlotte, *Jane Eyre* [1847], ed. Q. D. Leavis (London: Penguin, 1966).

Brown, David, *Walter Scott and the Historical Imagination* (London: Routledge and Kegan Paul, 1979).

Brown, Michael, *The Black Douglases: War and Lordship in Late Medieval Scotland, 1300–1455* (East Linton: Tuckwell Press, 1998).

Brown, Stewart J., *Thomas Chalmers and the Godly Commonwealth in Scotland* (Oxford: Oxford University Press, 1982).

Brown, Stewart J., 'The Ten Years' Conflict and the Disruption of 1843', in Stewart J. Brown and Michael Fry (eds), *Scotland in the Age of Disruption* (Edinburgh: Edinburgh University Press, 1993), pp. 1–27.

Brown, William Wells, *Three Years in Europe; or, Places I have Seen and People I have Met* (London: Charles Gilpin, 1852).

Brown, William Wells, *The American Fugitive in Europe: Sketches of Places and People Abroad* (Boston: John P. Jewett and Company, 1855).

Bruce, David, *Sun Pictures: The Hill-Adamson Calotypes* (London: Studio Vista, 1973).

Bruce, Dickson D., Jr, *Violence and Culture in the Antebellum South* (Austin: University of Texas Press, 1979).

Bruce, Duncan A., *The Mark of the Scots* (New York: Citadel, 1998).

Bueltman, Tajna, Andrew Hinson and Graeme Morton, *The Scottish Diaspora* (Edinburgh: Edinburgh University Press, 2013).

Burbick, Joan, *Healing the Republic: The Language of Health and the Culture of Nationalism in Nineteenth-Century America* (Cambridge: Cambridge University Press, 1994).

Burns, R. F., *The Life and Times of the Rev. Robert Burns, D.D.* (Toronto: James Campbell & Son, 1872).

Burns, Robert, *The Poems and Songs of Robert Burns*, ed. James Kinsley, 3 vols (Oxford: Clarendon Press, 1968).

Burns, Robert, *The Letters of Robert Burns*, ed. G. Ross Roy, 2 vols (Oxford: Clarendon Press, 1985).

Burns, Robert, *The Songs of Robert Burns*, ed. Donald Low (London: Routledge, 1993).

Butler, Daniel Allen, *The Age of Cunard: A Transatlantic History 1839–2003* (Np: ProStar, 2004).

Butt, John, 'The Industries of Glasgow', in W. Hamish Fraser and Irene Maver (eds), *Glasgow. Vol 2: 1830 to 1912* (Manchester: Manchester University Press, 1996), pp. 96–140.

Byron, Lord George Gordon, *Works, Volume III: Letters and Journals*, ed. Rowland E. Prothero (London: John Murray, 1899).

Calder, Jenni, *Scots in the USA* (Edinburgh: Luath, 2006).

Callanan, Laura, *Deciphering Race: White Anxiety, Racial Conflict, and the Turn to Fiction in Mid-Victorian English Prose* (Columbus: Ohio State University Press, 2006).

[Cameron, Andrew], *The Free Church and Her Accusers in the Matter of American Slavery; Being a Letter to Mr. George Thompson, Regarding His Recent Appearances in this City*, 'Third Thousand' (Edinburgh: John Johnstone, 1846).

Campbell, Stanley W., *The Slave Catchers: Enforcement of the Fugitive Slave Law, 1850–1860* (Chapel Hill: University of North Carolina Press, 1970).

Carruthers, Gerard, 'Burns and Slavery', *The Drouth* 26 (2007): 21–6.

Carruthers, Gerard, and Pauline McKay, 'Re-Reading James Currie: Robert Burns's First Editor', *John Clare Society Journal* 32 (July 2013): 73–84.

Casmier-Paz, Lynn A., 'Slave Narratives and the Rhetoric of Author Portraiture', *New Literary History* 34.1 (2003): 91–116.

Chaffin, Tom, *Giant's Causeway: Frederick Douglass's Irish Odyssey and the Making of an American Visionary* (Charlottesville: University of Virginia Press, 2014).

Chambers-Schiller, Lee, '"A Good Work among the People": The Political Culture of the Boston Antislavery Fair', in Jean Fagan Yellin and John C. Van Horne (eds), *The Abolitionist Sisterhood: Women's Political Culture in Antebellum America* (Ithaca: Cornell University Press, 1994), pp. 249–74.

Chase, Malcolm, *Chartism: A New History* (Manchester: Manchester University Press, 2007).

Chaussier, Hector, *Nouveau manuel du physionomiste et du phrénologiste* (Paris: Roret, 1838).

Child, Francis James (ed.), *The English and Scottish Popular Ballads* [1882–98], 5 vols (New York: Folklore Press in association with Pageant Book Company, 1957).

Christianity Versus Slavery, or, A Report, Published in the 'Glasgow Argus' Newspaper, November 8, 1841, of a Lecture, Delivered at an Anti-Slavery Meeting in that city, by George Thompson, Esq. (Dublin: W. Powell, 1841).

Clarkson, Thomas, *The History of the Rise, Progress, & Accomplishment of the Abolition of the African Slave-Trade*, 2 vols (London: Longman, Hurst, Rees, and Orme, 1808).

Clarkson, Thomas, *A Letter to the Clergy of Various Denominations, and to the Slave-Holding Planters, in the Southern Parts of the United States of America* (London: 1841).

Clarkson, Thomas, *Letter to Such Professing Christians in the Northern States of America* (London: Alexander Macintosh, 1844).

Cockrell, Dale (ed.), *Excelsior: Journals of the Hutchinson Family Singers, 1842–1846* (Stuyvesant, NY: Pendragon Press, 1989).

Cockrell, Dale, *Demons of Disorder: Early Blackface Minstrels and their World* (Cambridge: Cambridge University Press, 1997).

Colbert, Charles, *A Measure of Perfection: Phrenology and the Fine Arts in America* (Chapel Hill: University of North Carolina Press, 1997).

Combe, George, *System of Phrenology*, 3rd edn (Edinburgh: John Anderson, 1830).

Combe, George, 'Observations on the Skull of Robert Burns', *Phrenological Journal*, 8.40 (May 1834): 657–62.

Combe, George, *Lectures on Phrenology* (London: Simpkin, Marshall & Co., 1839).

Combe, George, *Notes on the United States of North America During a Phrenological Visit in 1838-9–40*, 2 vols (Philadelphia: Carey & Hart, 1841).

Combe, George, *The Constitution of Man Considered in Relation to External Objects*, 8th edn (Edinburgh: Maclachlan, Stewart & Co, 1847).

Combe, George, *Phrenology Applied to Painting and* Sculpture (London : Simpkin, Marshall, & Co., 1855).

Cooke, Anthony, 'The Scottish Cotton Masters, 1780–1914', *Textile History* 40.1 (2009): pp. 29–50.

Cooter, Roger, *The Cultural Meaning of Popular Science: Phrenology and the Organization of Consent in Nineteenth-Century Britain* (Cambridge: Cambridge University Press, 1984).

Cornelius, Janet Duisman, *Slave Missions and the Black Church in the Antebellum South* (Columbia: University of South Carolina Press, 1999).

Coughlan, Ann, 'Frederick Douglass and Ireland, 1845: The "Vertiginous Twist(s) of an Irish Encounter"' (PhD diss., University College Cork, 2015).

Cowan, Edward J., 'Tartan Day in America', in Celeste Ray (ed.), *Transatlantic Scots* (Tuscaloosa: University of Alabama Press, 2005), pp. 318–38.

Cowling, Mary, *The Artist as Anthropologist: The Representation of Type and Character in Victorian Art* (Cambridge: Cambridge University Press, 1989).

Cox, Robert, 'Observations on Combativeness: Being an Attempt to Determine the Cerebral Development of Robert Burns', *Phrenological Journal* 9.41 (September 1834): 52–74.

Craft, William, *Running a Thousand Miles for Freedom* (London: William Tweedie, 1860).

Crane, Diana, *Fashion and its Social Agendas: Class, Gender, and Identity in Clothing* (Chicago: University of Chicago Press, 2000).

Crawford, Robert, *The Bard: Robert Burns, A Biography* (London: Jonathan Cape, 2009).

Crawford, Robert, *The Beginning and the End of the World: St Andrews, Scandal and the Birth of Photography* (Edinburgh: Birlinn, 2011).

Crawford, Robert, 'America's Bard', in Sharon Alker, Leith Davis and Holly Faith Nelson (eds), *Robert Burns and Transatlantic Culture* (Farnham: Ashgate, 2012), pp. 99–116.

Cunliffe, Marcus, *Chattel Slavery and Wage Slavery: The Anglo-American Context, 1830–1860* (Athens: University of Georgia Press, 1979).

Currie, James (ed.), *The Works of Robert Burns, with an Account of His Life and Criticism on his Writings, to which are prefixed, Some Observations on the Character and Condition of the Scottish Peasantry*, 2 vols (Philadelphia: J. Crissy, 1841).

Currie, James (ed.), *The Complete Works of Robert Burns, with an Account of His Life and Criticism on his Writings, to which are prefixed, Some Observations on the Character and Condition of the Scottish Peasantry* (Halifax: William Milner, 1844).

Currie, William Wallace (ed.), *Memoir of the Life, Writings, and Correspondence of James Currie, M.D. F.R.S. of Liverpool*, 2 vols (London: Longman, Rees, Orme, Brown, and Green, 1831).

Curtin, Michael, *Propriety and Position: A Study of Victorian Manners* (New York: Garland, 1987).

Daiches, David, *Robert Burns*, revised edn (London: Deutsch, 1966).

Dain, Bruce, *A Hideous Monster of the Mind: American Race Theory in the Early Republic* (Cambridge, MA: Harvard University Press, 2002).

Dallenbach, Karl M., 'Phrenology versus Psychoanalysis', *American Journal of Psychology* 68.4 (1955): 511–25.

Daut, Marlene, *Tropics of Haiti: Race and the Literary History of the Haitian Revolution in the Atlantic World, 1789–1865* (Liverpool: Liverpool University Press, 2015).

Davis, F. James, *Who is Black? One Nation's Definition* (University Park: Pennsylvania State University Press, 1991).

Davis, Leith, 'James Currie's *Works of Robert Burns*: The Politics of Hypochondriasis', *Studies in Romanticism* 36.1 (1997): 43–60.

Davis, Leith, 'Burns and Transnational Culture', in Gerard Carruthers (ed.), *The Edinburgh Companion to Robert Burns* (Edinburgh: Edinburgh University Press, 2009), pp. 150–63.

Davis, Leith, 'Negotiating Cultural Memory: James Currie's *Works of Robert Burns*', *International Journal of Scottish Literature* 6 (2010), available at <http://www.ijsl.stir.ac.uk/issue6/> (last accessed 18 February 2018).

Davis, Tracy C., 'Acting Black, 1824: Charles Mathews's "Trip to America"', *Theatre Journal* (May 2011) 63.2: 163–89.

Day, Charles W. M., *Hints on Etiquette and the Usages of Society* (Boston: William Ticknor, 1844).

Delany, Martin R., *Martin R. Delany: A Documentary Reader*, ed. Robert S. Levine (Chapel Hill: University of North Carolina Press, 2003).

DeLombard, Jeannine Marie, *Slavery on Trial: Law, Abolitionism, and Print Culture* (Chapel Hill: University of North Carolina Press, 2007).

Devine, T. M., *To the Ends of the Earth: Scotland's Global Diaspora, 1750–2010* (London: Allen Lane, 2011).

Devine, T. M., 'Lost to History', in T. M. Devine (ed.), *Recovering Scotland's Slavery Past: The Caribbean Connection* (Edinburgh: Edinburgh University Press, 2015), pp. 21–40.

Devine, T. M. (ed.), *Recovering Scotland's Slavery Past: The Caribbean Connection* (Edinburgh: Edinburgh University Press, 2015).

Dickens, Charles, *American Notes for General Circulation* [1842], ed. John S. Whitley and Arnold Goldman (London: Penguin, 1972).

Dickens, Charles, *The Letters of Charles Dickens, Volume 5: 1847–1849*, ed. Graham Storey and K. J. Fielding (Oxford: Clarendon Press, 1981).

Dickens, Charles, *The Letters of Charles Dickens, Volume 6: 1850–1852*, ed. Graham Storey, Kathleen Tillotson and Nina Burgis (Oxford: Clarendon Press, 1988).

Dinius, Marcy J., *The Camera and the Press: American Visual and Print Culture in the Age of the Dageurreotype* (Philadelphia: University of Pennsylvania Press, 2012).

Disraeli, Benjamin, *Sybil, or the Two Nations* [1845] (Oxford: Oxford University Press, 1981).

[Dodd, William], *The Laboring Classes of England, Especially Those Engaged in Agriculture and Manufactures; in a Series of Letters. By an Englishman* (Boston: John Putnam, 1847).

Dodd, William E., 'The Social Philosophy of the Old South', *American Journal of Sociology* 23 (1918): 735–46.

Dorsey, Peter A., 'Becoming the Other: The Mimesis of Metaphor in Douglass's *My Bondage and My Freedom*', *Publications of the Modern Language Association of America* (1996): 435–50.

Durbach, Nadja, *Spectacle of Deformity: Freak Shows and Modern British Culture* (Berkeley: University of California Press, 2010).

Eckenrode, H. J., 'Sir Walter Scott and the South', *North American Review* 106 (1917): 595–603.

Egan, Gerald, 'Radical Moral Authority and Desire: The Image of the Male Romantic Poet in Frontispiece Portraits of Byron and Shelley', *The Eighteenth Century* 50.2–3 (2010): 185–205.

Ellison, Thomas, *The Cotton Trade of Great Britain* (London: Effingham Wilson, 1886).

Evangelical Alliance, *Report of the Proceedings of the Conference, Held at Freemasons' Hall, London, From August 19th to September 2nd Inclusive, 1846* (London: Partridge and Oakey, 1847).

Evans, Nicholas M., 'Ira Aldridge: Shakespeare and Minstrelsy', *American Transcendental Quarterly* 16.33 (2002): 165–87.

Ewing, Elizabeth, *Everyday Dress 1650–1900* (London: Batsford, 1984).

Fabian, Ann, *The Skull Collectors: Race, Science and America's Unburied Dead* (Chicago: University of Chicago Press, 2010).

Fagan, Benjamin, 'The *North Star* and the Atlantic 1848', *African American Review* 47.1 (2014): 51–67.

Falkoff, Marc D., 'Heads and Tales: American Letters in the Age of Phrenology' (PhD diss., Brandeis University, 1997).

Farrison, William Edward, *William Wells Brown: Author and Reformer* (Chicago and London: University of Chicago Press, 1969).

Faulkner, Carol, 'The Root of the Evil: Free Produce and Radical Antislavery, 1820–1860', *Journal of the Early Republic* 27.3 (2007): 377–405.

Fenton, Laurence, *Frederick Douglass in Ireland: 'The Black O'Connell'* (Cork: The Collins Press, 2014).

Ferguson, Adam, *An Essay on the History of Civil Society* [1767] (Edinburgh: Edinburgh University Press, 1966).

Ferreira, Patricia J., 'Frederick Douglass and the 1846 Dublin Edition of His Narrative', *New Hibernia Review* 5.1 (2001): 53–67.

Fett, Sharla M., *Working Cures: Healing, Health, and Power on Southern Slave Plantations* (Chapel Hill: University of North Carolina Press, 2002).

Fisher, Michael, *Counterflows to Colonialism: Indian Travellers and Settlers in Britain 1600–1857* (Delhi: Permanent Black, 2004).

Fladeland, Betty, *Men and Brothers: Anglo-American Anti-Slavery Co-Operation* (Urbana: University of Illinois Press, 1972).

Folsom, Ed, 'Appearing in Print: Illustrations of the Self in *Leaves of Grass*', in Ezra Greenspan (ed.), *The Cambridge Companion to Walt Whitman* (Cambridge: Cambridge University Press, 1995), pp. 135–65.

Folsom, Ed, 'Portrait of the Artist as a Young Slave: Douglass's Frontispiece Engravings', in James C. Hall (ed.), *Approaches to Teaching 'The Narrative of the Life of Frederick Douglass'* (New York: MLA, 1999), pp. 55–65.

Foner, Philip S., *Frederick Douglass* (New York: Citadel Press, 1964).

Fought, Leigh, *Women in the World of Frederick Douglass* (New York: Oxford University Press, 2017).

Fowler, John, *Mr Hill's Big Picture: The Day that Changed Scotland Forever – Captured on Canvas* (Edinburgh: St Andrew Press, 2006).

Fox, Stephen, *The Ocean Railway: Isambard Kingdom Brunel, Samuel Cunard and the Revolutionary World of the Great Atlantic Steamships* (London: Harper Perennial, 2004).

Fox-Genovese, Elizabeth, *Within the Plantation Household: Black and White Women of the Old South* (Chapel Hill: University of South Carolina Press, 1988).

Fraser, W. Hamish, *Chartism in Scotland* (Pontypool: Merlin Press, 2010).

Fredrickson, George M., *The Black Image in the White Mind: The Debate on Afro-American Character and Destiny, 1817–1914* (New York: Harper and Row, 1971).

Free Church of Scotland, *Proceedings of the General Assembly of the Free Church of Scotland held at Glasgow, October 17–24, 1843* (Edinburgh: Balfour and Jack,1843).

Free Church of Scotland, *Proceedings of the General Assembly of the Free Church of Scotland held in Edinburgh May 1844* (Edinburgh: W. P. Kennedy, 1844).

Free Church of Scotland, *Proceedings of the General Assembly of the Free Church of Scotland Held at Edinburgh, May 1845* (Edinburgh: W. P. Kennedy, 1845).

Free Church of Scotland, *Report of the Proceedings of the General Assembly on Saturday, May 30, and Monday, June 1, 1846, regarding the Relations of the Free Church of Scotland and the Presbyterian Churches of America* (Edinburgh: John Johnstone, 1846).

Free Church of Scotland, *Proceedings of the General Assembly of the Free Church of Scotland Held at Edinburgh, May 1847* (Edinburgh: W. P. Kennedy, 1847).

The Free Church and her Accusers: The Question at Issue. A Letter from George Thompson, Esq. To Henry C. Wright; and One from Henry C. Wright to Ministers and Members of the Free Church of Scotland (Glasgow: George Gallie, 1846).

The Free Church of Scotland and American Slavery: Substance of Speeches Delivered in the Music Hall, Edinburgh, During May and June 1846 by George Thompson, Esq. and the Rev. Henry C. Wright. With an Appendix, Containing the Deliverances of the Free Church on the Subject of Slavery, 1844, 1845 and 1846, and other Valuable Documents (Edinburgh: Scottish Anti-Slavery Society, 1846).

Fried, Gregory, 'True Pictures', *Common-Place* 2.2 (2002), available at <http://www.common-place-archives.org/vol-02/no-02/fried/> (last accessed 18 February 2018).

Frothingham, Paul Revere, *Edward Everett, Orator and Statesman* (Boston: Houghton Mifflin, 1925).

Fry, Michael, *'Bold, Independent, Unconquer'd and Free': How the Scots Made America Safe for Liberty, Democracy and Captalism* (Ayr: Fort, 2003).

Fulkerson, Gerald, 'Exile as Emergence: Frederick Douglass in Great Britain, 1845–1847', *Quarterly Journal of Speech* 60.1 (1974): pp. 69–82.

Fuller, Margaret, *At Home and Abroad; or Things and Thoughts in America and Europe* (Boston: Brown, Taggard and Chase, 1860).

Gac, Scott, *Singing for Freedom: The Hutchinson Family Singers and the Nineteenth-Century Culture of Reform* (New Haven: Yale University Press, 2007).

G.A.S., *Notes of Travel at Home: During a Month's Tour in Scotland and England* (London: Simpkin, Marshall, & Co., 1846).

Genovese, Eugene, *Roll, Jordan, Roll: The World the Slaves Made* (London: Deutsch, 1965).

Gibbon, Charles, *The Life of George Combe, Author of 'The Constitution of Man'*, 2 vols (London: Macmillan & Co., 1878).

Gibbs, Jenna M., *Performing the Temple of Liberty: Slavery, Theater, and Popular Culture in London and Philadelphia, 1760–1850* (Baltimore: Johns Hopkins University Press, 2014).

Gilfillan, George, *The Debasing and Demoralizing Influence of Slavery, On All and On Everything Connected With it: A Lecture . . . Delivered at the Request of the Free Church Anti-Slavery Society* (Edinburgh: Charles Ziegler, 1847).

Gilmore, Paul, *The Genuine Article: Race, Mass Culture, and American Literary Manhood* (Durham, NC: Duke University Press, 2001).

Ginsberg, Madeleine, *Victorian Dress in Photographs* (London: Batsford, 1982).

Girouard, Mark, *The Return to Camelot: Chivalry and the English Gentleman* (New Haven: Yale University Press, 1981).

Glasgow Emancipation Society, *First Annual Report* (Glasgow: John Young, 1835).

Glasgow Emancipation Society, *Second Annual Report* (Glasgow: Aird & Russell, 1836).

Glasgow Emancipation Society, *Britain and America United in the Cause of Universal Freedeom: Being the Third Annual Report of the Glasgow Emancipation Society* (Glasgow, Aird & Russell, 1837).

Glasgow Emancipation Society, *Report of the Annual Meeting of the Glasgow Emancipation Society, Held August 8, 1840* (Glasgow: John Clark, 1840).

Glasgow Emancipation Society, *Eighth Annual Report* (Glasgow: David Russell, 1842).

Glasgow Emancipation Society, *Tenth Annual Report* (Glasgow: David Russell, 1844).

Godwin, William, 'On Phrenology', in *Thoughts on Man* (London: Effingham Wilson, 1831), pp. 357–75.

Godwin, William, 'On the Systems of Lavater and Gall', *London Medical Gazette*, 21 May 1831: 232–7.

Goodman, Paul, *Of One Blood: Abolitionism and the Origins of Racial Equality* (Berkeley: University of California Press, 1998).

Gordon, Robert C., 'Scott, Racine, and the Future of Honor', in J. H. Alexander and David Hewitt (eds), *Scott and his Influence: The Papers of the Aberdeen Scott Conference, 1982* (Aberdeen: Association for Scottish Literary Studies, 1983), pp. 255–65.

Goyder, David George, *My Battle for Life: The Autobiography of a Phrenologist* (London: Simpkin, Marshall & Co., 1857).

Graham, Eric J., *Burns and the Sugar Plantocracy of Ayrshire* (Ayr: Ayrshire Archaeological and Natural History Society, 2009).

Graham, Eric J., 'The "Black Minstrelsy" in Scotland', *Scottish Local History* 80 (2011): 21–30.

Greenberg, Kenneth S., *Honor and Slavery* (Princeton: Princeton University Press, 1996).

Greenspan, Ezra, *William Wells Brown: An African American Life* (New York: W. W. Norton, 2014).

Gross, Ariela J., *What Blood Won't Tell: A History of Race on Trial in America* (Cambridge, MA: Harvard University Press, 2008).

Guide to the Glasgow & Ayrshire Railway (Ayr: McCormick & Gemmell, 1841).

Hague, Euan, 'National Tartan Day: Rewriting History in the United States', *Scottish Affairs* 38.1 (2002): 94–124.

Hague, Euan, 'The Scottish Diaspora: Tartan Day and the Appropriation of Scottish Identities in the United States', in David C. Harvey, Rhys Jones, Neil McInroy and Christine Milligan (eds), *Celtic Geographies: Old Culture, New Times* (London: Routledge, 2002), pp. 139–56.

Haley, Alex, and David Stevens, *Queen: The Story of an American Family* (London: Pan, 1993).

Hall, Lee, *Common Threads: A Parade of American Clothing* (Boston: Little, Brown, 1992).

Hamilton, Cynthia S., '"Am I Not a Man and a Brother": Phrenology and Anti-slavery', *Slavery & Abolition* 29:2 (2008): 173–87.

Hamilton, Douglas, *Scotland, the Caribbean and the Atlantic World, 1750–1820* (Manchester: Manchester University Press, 2005).

Hammond, James Henry, *Two Letters on Slavery in the United States, Addressed to Thomas Clarkson, Esq.* (Columbia: Allen, McCarter, & Co, The South-Carolinian Press, 1845).

Hanna, William, *Memoirs of the Life and Writings of Thomas Chalmers, DD, LLD*, 4 vols (Edinburgh: Thomas Constable, 1852).

Harling, Philip, 'Sugar Wars: The Culture of Free Trade versus the Culture of Anti-slavery in Britain and the British Caribbean, 1840–50', in Barry Crosbie and Mark Hampton (eds), *The Cultural Construction of the British World* (Manchester: Manchester University Press, 2015), pp. 59–72.

Harvey, John, *Men in Black* (London: Reaktion, 1995).

Heads of the People; or, Portraits of the English (London: Robert Tyas, 1840).

Heier, Edmund, *Literary Portraiture in Nineteenth-Century Russian Prose* (Köln: Böhlau, 1993).

Hendrick, George, and Willene Hendrick, *The Creole Mutiny: A Tale of Revolt Aboard a Slave Ship* (Chicago: Ivan R. Dee, 2003).

Hesse, David, *Warrior Dreams: Playing Scotsmen in Mainland Europe* (Manchester: Manchester University Press, 2014).

Hewitson, Jim, *Tam Blake & Co: The Story of the Scots in America* (Edinburgh: Canongate, 1993).

Hill, Ginger, '"Rightly Viewed": Theorizations of Self in Frederick Douglass's Lectures on Pictures', in Maurice O. Wallace and Shawn Michelle Smith (eds), *Pictures and Progress: Early Photography and the Making of African American Identity* (Durham, NC: Duke University Press, 2012), pp. 41–82.

Hill, Matthew Davenport (ed.), *Our Exemplars Poor and Rich; or, Biographical Sketches of Men and Women Who Have, By an Extraordinary Use of their Opportunities, Benefited their Fellow Creatures* (London: Cassell, Petter and Galpin, 1861).

History of the Bosjesmans, or Bush People (London: Chapman, Elcoate, and Company, 1847).

Holcomb, Julie L., *Moral Commerce: Quakers and the Transatlantic Boycott of the Slave Labor Economy* (Ithaca: Cornell University Press, 2016).

Holland, Richard, *The Buke of the Howlat* [1448], ed. Ralph Hanna (Woodbridge: Boydell Press for Scottish Text Society, 2014).

Home, John, *Douglas: A Tragedy* [1757], ed. Gerald D. Parker (Edinburgh: Oliver and Boyd, 1972).

Honeycutt, Michael W., 'William Cunningham: His Life, Thought, and Controversies' (PhD diss., University of Edinburgh, 2002).

Hook, Andrew, *From Goosecreek to Gandercleugh: Studies in Scottish-American Literary and Cultural History* (East Linton: Tuckwell Press, 1999).

Hook, Andrew, 'Troubling Times in the Scottish-American Relationship', in Celeste Ray (ed.), *Transatlantic Scots* (Tuscaloosa: University of Alabama Press, 2005), pp. 215–31.

Horsman, Reginald, *Josiah Nott of Mobile: Southerner, Physician and Racial Theorist* (Baton Rouge: Louisiana State University Press, 1987).

House, John, 'Toward a "Modern" Lavater? Degas and Monet', in Melissa Percival and Graeme Tytler (eds), *Physiognomy in Profile* (Newark: University of Delaware Press, 2005), pp. 180–97.

Huggins, Nathan Irvin, *Slave and Citizen: The Life of Frederick Douglass* (New York: Harper Collins, 1980).

Hughes, Langston, *I Wonder as I Wander* [1956] (New York: Hill and Wang, 1993).

Hume, David, of Godscroft, *The History of the House of Douglas* [1644], ed. David Reid, 2 vols (Edinburgh: Scottish Text Society, 1996).

Hume, David, of Godscroft, *The History of the House of Angus* [1644], ed. David Reid, 2 vols (Edinburgh: Scottish Text Society, 2005).

Hunnisett, Basil, *Steel-Engraved Book Illustration in England* (London: Scolar Press, 1980).

Hunter, James, *Scottish Exodus: Travels Among a Worldwide Clan* (Edinburgh: Mainsteam, 2005).

Hutchinson, John Wallace, *Story of the Hutchinsons (Tribe of Jesse)*, 2 vols, ed. Charles E. Mann, with an introduction by Frederick Douglass (Boston: Lee and Shepard, 1896).

Huzzey, Richard, *Freedom Burning: Anti-Slavery and Empire in Victorian Britain* (Ithaca: Cornell University Press, 2012).

Hyde, Francis, *Cunard and the North Atlantic, 1840–1973: A History of Shipping and Financial Management* (London: Macmillan, 1975).

Irving, Washington, *Abbotsford and Newstead Abbey* (London: John Murray, 1835).

James, Henry, *The American Scene* [1907] (New York: Scribner's, 1946).

Jarvie, Grant, *Highland Games: The Making of the Myth* (Edinburgh: Edinburgh University Press, 1991).

Jenkins, Lee, 'Beyond the Pale: Frederick Douglass in Cork', *The Irish Review* 24 (1999): 80–95.

Jenkins, Lee, '"The Black O'Connell": Frederick Douglass and Ireland', *Nineteenth-Century Studies* 13 (1999): 22–47.

Jezierski, Rachael A., 'The Glasgow Emancipation Society and the American Anti-Slavery Movement' (PhD diss., University of Glasgow, 2010).

Johnson, Stephen, 'Death and the Minstrel', in Stephen Johnson (ed.), *Burnt Cork: Traditions and Legacies of Blackface Minstrelsy* (Amherst: University of Massachusetts Press, 2012), pp. 73–103.

Jones, Anne Goodwyn, 'Engendered in the South: Blood and Irony in Douglass and Jacobs', in Alan J. Rice and Martin Crawford (eds), *Liberating Sojourn: Frederick Douglass and Transatlantic Reform* (Athens: University of Georgia Press, 1999), pp. 93–111.

Jones, Charles Colcock, *The Religious Instruction of the Negroes in the United States* (Savannah: Thomas Purse, 1842).

Jones, Charles K., *Francis Johnson (1792–1844): Chronicle of a Black Musician in Early Nineteenth-Century Philadelphia* (Bethlehem, PA: Lehigh University Press, 2006).

Karcher, Carolyn L., *The First Woman in the Republic: A Cultural Biography of Lydia Maria Child* (Durham, NC: Duke University Press, 1994).

Kaufman, Matthew H., *Medical Teaching in Edinburgh During the 18th and 19th Centuries* (Edinburgh: Royal College of Surgeons, 2003).

Kaufman, Matthew H., *Edinburgh Phrenological Society: A History* (Edinburgh: William Ramsay Henderson Trust, 2005).

Kay, Billy, *The Scottish World: A Journey into the Scottish Diaspora* (Edinburgh: Mainstream, 2006).

Kerr, James, *Fiction Against History: Scott as Storyteller* (Cambridge: Cambridge University Press, 1989).

Kerr-Ritchie, Jeffrey R., *Rites of August: Emancipation Day in the Black Atlantic World.* (Baton Rouge: Louisiana State University Press, 2007).

Killick, John, 'Transatlantic Steerage Fares, British and Irish Migration, and Return Migration, 1815–60', *Economic History Review* 67.1 (2014): 170–91.

Kinealy, Christine, *Daniel O'Connell and the Anti-Slavery Movement: 'The Saddest People the Sun Sees'* (London: Pickering & Chatto, 2011).

Kling, Blair B., *Partner in Empire: Dwarkanath Tagore and the Age of Enterprise in Eastern India* (Berkeley: University of California Press, 1976).

Knox, Robert, 'Lectures on Physiological Anatomy: Lecture IV', *Medical Times* 12.292 (26 April 1845): 55–7.

Knox, Robert, *The Races of Men: A Philosophical Enquiry into the Influence of Race over the Destinies of Man*, 2nd edn (London: Henry Renshaw, 1862).

Koivunen, Leila, *Visualizing Africa in Nineteenth-Century British Travel Accounts* (London: Routledge, 2008).

Kronshage, Eike, *Vision and Character: Physiognomics and the English Realist Novel* (New York: Routledge, 2018).

Kuchta, David, *The Three-Piece Suit and Modern Masculinity: England, 1550–1850* (Berkeley: University of California Press, 2002).

Laidlaw, Zoë, '"Justice to India – Prosperity to England – Freedom to the Slave!": Humanitarian and Moral Reform Campaigns on India, Aborigines and American slavery', *Journal of the Royal Asiatic Society of Great Britain & Ireland* 22.2 (2012): 299–324.

The Land We Live In: A Pictorial and Literary Sketch-Book of the British Empire, 4 vols (London: Charles Knight, 1847–50).

Landrum, Grace Warren, 'Sir Walter Scott and his Literary Rivals in the Old South', *American Literature* 2.3 (1930): 256–76.

Landrum, Grace Warren, 'Notes on the Reading of the Old South', *American Literature* 3.1 (1931): 60–71.

Leask, Nigel, '"The Shadow Line": James Currie's "Life of Burns" and British Romanticism', in Claire Lamont and Michael Rossington (eds), *Romanticism's Debatable Lands* (Basingstoke: Palgrave Macmillan, 2007), pp. 64–79.

Leask, Nigel, 'Burns and the Poetics of Abolition', in Gerard Carruthers (ed.), *The Edinburgh Companion to Robert Burns* (Edinburgh: Edinburgh University Press, 2009), pp. 47–60.

Leask, Nigel, '"Their Groves o' Sweet Myrtles": Robert Burns and the Scottish Colonial Experience', in Murray Pittock (ed.), *Robert Burns in Global Culture* (Lewisburg, PA: Bucknell University Press, 2011), pp. 172–88.

Lee, Julia Sun-Joo, *The American Slave Narrative and the Victorian Novel* (Oxford: Oxford University Press, 2010).

Lehman, Eric D., *Becoming Tom Thumb: Charles Stratton, P. T. Barnum, and the Dawn of American Celebrity* (Middletown, CT: Wesleyan University Press, 2013).

Leith, Murray Stewart, and Duncan Sim (eds), *The Modern Scottish Diaspora: Contemporary Debates and Perspectives* (Edinburgh: Edinburgh University Press, 2014).

Levine, Lawrence W., *Black Culture and Black Consciousness: Afro-American Folk Thought from Slavery to Freedom* (New York: Oxford University Press, 1977).

Levine, Lawrence, W., *Highbrow/Lowbrow: The Emergence of Cultural Hierarchy in America* (Cambridge, MA: Harvard University Press, 1988).

Levine, Robert S., *The Lives of Frederick Douglass* (Cambridge, MA: Harvard University Press, 2016).

Lewis, George, *Impressions of America and the American Churches: From the Journal of the Rev. G. Lewis* (Edinburgh: W. P. Kennedy, 1845).

Lewis, Samuel, *A Topographical Dictionary of Scotland*, 2 vols (London: S. Lewis, 1846).

Lhamon, W. T., Jr, *Raising Cain: Blackface Performance from Jim Crow to Hip Hop* (Cambridge, MA: Harvard University Press, 1998).

Lincoln, Andrew, *Walter Scott and Modernity* (Edinburgh: Edinburgh University Press, 2007).

Lindfors, Bernth, 'Hottentot, Bushman, Kaffir: Taxonomic Tendencies in Nineteenth-Century Racial Iconography', *Nordic Journal of African Studies* 5 (1996): 1–18.

Lindfors, Bernth, *Ira Aldridge: The Early Years, 1807–33* (Rochester, NY: University of Rochester Press, 2011).

Lindfors, Bernth, *Ira Aldridge: The Vagabond Years, 1833–1852* (Rochester, NY: University of Rochester Press, 2011).

Lindsay, Andrew O., *Illustrious Exile: Journal of my Sojourn in the West Indies by Robert Burns* (Leeds: Peepal Tree Press, 2006).

Lorimer, Douglas A., *Colour, Class and the Victorians* (Leicester: Leicester University Press, 1978).

Lott, Eric, *Love and Theft: Blackface Minstrelsy and the American Working Class* (New York: Oxford University Press, 1995).

Loveland, Anne C., *Southern Evangelicals and the Social Order, 1800–1860* (Baton Rouge: Louisiana State University Press, 1980).

Lovett, William, *Life and Struggles of William Lovett* [1876] (London: MacGibbon & Kee, 1967).

Lumpkin, Katharine Du Pre, *The Emancipation of Angelina Grimké* (Chapel Hill: University of North Carolina Press, 1974).

McAllister, Marvin, *Whiting Up: Whiteface Minstrels and Stage Europeans in African American Performance* (Chapel Hill: University of North Carolina Press, 2011).

McCann, Colum, *Transatlantic* (London: Bloomsbury, 2013).

McCarthy, Angela, and John M. Mackenzie (eds), *Global Migrations: The Scottish Diaspora since 1600* (Edinburgh: Edinburgh University Press, 2016).

McDaniel, W. Caleb, 'Saltwater Anti-slavery: American Abolitionists on the Atlantic Ocean in the Age of Steam', *Atlantic Studies* 8.2 (2011): 141–63.

McDaniel, W. Caleb, *The Problem of Democracy in the Age of Slavery: Garrisonian Abolitionists and Transatlantic Reform* (Baton Rouge: Louisiana State University Press, 2013).

McFeeley, William, *Frederick Douglass* (New York: Simon and Schuster, 1991).

McGuirk, Carol, 'Haunted by Authority: Nineteenth-century Constructions of Robert Burns and Scotland', in Robert Crawford (ed.), *Robert Burns and Cultural Authority* (Iowa City: University of Iowa Press, 1997), pp. 136–58.

McKivigan, John R., *The War against Proslavery Religion: Abolitionism and the Northern Churches, 1830–1865* (Ithaca: Cornell University Press, 1984).

Maclear, J. F., 'Thomas Smyth, Frederick Douglass, and the Belfast Anti-slavery Campaign', *South Carolina Historical Magazine* 80.4 (1979): 286–97.

Mann, James A., *The Cotton Trade of Great Britain: Its Rise, Progress, & Present Extent* (London: Simpkin, Marshall & Co., 1860).

Manning, Susan, 'Did Mark Twain Bring Down the Temple on Scott's Shoulders?', in Janet Beer and Bridget Bennett (eds), *Special Relationships: Anglo-American Antagonisms and Affinities, 1854–1936* (Manchester: Manchester University Press, 2002), pp. 8–27.

Marable, Manning, *Malcolm X: A Life of Reinvention* (London: Allen Lane, 2011).

Marjoribanks, Captain [John], *Slavery: An Essay in Verse* (Edinburgh: J Robertson, 1792).

Martineau, Harriet, *The Hour and the Man*, 3 vols (London: Edward Moxon,1841).

Mathews, Donald G., 'Charles Colcock Jones and the Southern Evangelical Crusade to Form a Biracial Community', *Journal of Southern History* 41.3 (1975): 299–320.

Mathews, Donald G., *Religion in the Old South* (Chicago and London: University of Chicago Press, 1977).

Maynard, Douglas H., 'The World's Anti-Slavery Convention of 1840', *Mississippi Valley Historical Review* 47.3 (1960): 452–71.

Meehan, Ross, *Mediating American Autobiography: Photography in Emerson, Thoreau, Douglass and Whitman* (Columbia: University of Missouri Press, 2008).

Meer, Sarah, *Uncle Tom Mania: Slavery, Minstrelsy, and Transatlantic Culture in the 1850s* (Athens: University of Georgia Press, 2005).

Merrill, Lisa, '"Most Fitting Companions": Making Mixed-Race Bodies Visible in Antebellum Public Spaces', *Theatre Survey* 56.2 (2015): 138–65.

Miller, David Prince, *The Life of a Showman*, 2nd edn (London: Thomas Hailes Lacy, [1866]).

Miskell, Louise, and C. A. Whatley, '"Juteopolis" in the Making: Linen and the Industrial Transformation of Dundee, c.1820–1850', *Textile History* 30.2 (1999): 176–98.

Montgomery, James, *An Essay on the Phrenology of the Hindoos and Negroes. Together with Strictures Thereon by Corden Thompson* (London: E. Lloyd & Co, 1829).

Morgan, Simon, 'The Anti-Corn Law League and British Anti-Slavery in Transatlantic Perspective', *The Historical Journal* 52.1 (2009): 87–107.

Morgan, Simon, 'The Politics As Personal: Transatlantic Abolitionism, c. 1833–67', in William Mulligan and Maurice Bric (eds), *A Global History of Anti-Slavery Politics in the Nineteenth Century* (Houndmills: Palgrave Macmillan, 2013), pp. 78–96.

Morris, Michael, *Scotland and the Caribbean, c.1740–1833: Atlantic Archipelagos* (New York: Routledge, 2015).

Morris, Michael, 'Yonder Awa: Slavery and Distancing Strategies in Scottish Literature', in T. M. Devine (ed.), *Recovering Scotland's Slavery Past: The Caribbean Connection* (Edinburgh: Edinburgh University Press, 2015), pp. 41–61.

Morton, Samuel G., *Crania Americana: A Comparative View of the Skulls of Various Aboriginal Nations of North and South America to Which Is Prefixed an Essay on the Varieties of the Human Species* (Philadelphia: J. Dobson, 1839).

Moser, Barry, *Wood Engraving: Notes on the Craft* (Northampton, MA: Pennyroyal Press, 1979).

Mott, James, *Three Months in Great Britain* (Philadelphia: J. Miller M'Kim, 1841).

Mott, Lucretia, *Slavery and 'The Woman Question': Lucretia Mott's Diary of Her Visit to Great Britain to Attend the World's Anti-Slavery Convention of 1840*, ed. Frederick B. Tolles (Haverford, PA: Friends' Historical Association, 1952).

Mullan, Don, 'Introduction' to Frederick Douglass, *Narrative of the Life of Frederick Douglass, an American Slave*, ed. Don Mullan (Dublin: A Little Book Company, 2011), pp. 5–15.

Mullen, Stephen, *It Wisnae Us: The Truth about Glasgow and Slavery* (Edinburgh: Royal Incorporation of Architects in Scotland, 2009).

Murray, Hannah-Rose, 'A "Negro Hercules": Frederick Douglass' Celebrity in Britain', *Celebrity Studies* 7.2 (2016): 264–79.

Nathan, Hans, *Dan Emmett and the Rise of Early Negro Minstrelsy* (Norman: University of Oklahoma Press, 1962).

Neilson, Peter, *Recollections of a Six Years' Residence in the United States of America* (Glasgow: David Robertson, 1830).

Nichols, Thomas L., *Forty Years of American Life*, 2 vols (London: John Maxwell, 1864).

Nelson, Alondra, *The Social Life of DNA: Race, Reparations, and Reconciliation after the Genome* (Boston: Beacon Press, 2016).

Nogee, Joseph, 'The Prigg Case and Fugitive Slavery, 1842–1850: Part I', *Journal of Negro History* 39.3 (1954): 185–205.

Nott, Josiah C., and George R. Gliddon, *Types of Mankind: or, Ethnological Researches Based on the Ancient Monuments, Paintings, Sculptures, and Crania of Races, and upon their Natural, Geographical, Philological, and Biblical History* (Philadelphia: Lippincott, Grambo & Co, 1854).

Nowatzki, Robert, *Representing African Americans in Transatlantic Abolitionism and Blackface Minstrelsy* (Baton Rouge: Louisiana State University Press, 2010).

Numbers, Ronald L., and Todd L. Savitt (eds), *Science and Medicine in the Old South* (Baton Rouge: Louisiana State University Press, 1989).

Nyong'o, Tavia, *The Amalgamation Waltz: Race, Performance, and the Ruses of Memory* (Minneapolis, University of Minnesota Press, 2009).

O'Brien, Michael, *Rethinking the South: Essays in Intellectual History* (Athens, GA: Brown, Thrasher, 1993).

O'Kelly, Donal, *The Cambria* (2005), script available from Playography Ireland, <http://www.irishplayography.com> (last accessed 18 February 2018).

Orians, G. Harrison, 'Walter Scott, Mark Twain and the Civil War', *South Atlantic Quarterly* 40.4 (1941): 342–59.

Osterweis, Rollin G., *Romanticism and Nationalism in the Old South* (New Haven: Yale University Press, 1949).

Parssinen, T. M., 'Popular Science and Society: The Phrenology Movement in Early Victorian Britain', *Journal of Social History* 8.1 (Autumn 1974): 1–20.

Partridge, Eric, *A Dictionary of Catch Phrases: British and American, from the Sixteenth Century to the Present Day*, ed. Paul Beale (London: Routledge & Kegan Paul, 1986).

Patterson, Orlando, *The Sociology of Slavery: An Analysis of the Origins, Development and Structure of Negro Slave Society in Jamaica* (London: MacGibbon & Kee, 1967).

Pearl, Sharrona, *About Faces: Physiognomy in Nineteenth-Century Britain* (Cambridge, MA: Harvard University Press, 2010).

Penn, I. Garland, *The Afro-American Press and its Editors* (Springfield, MA: Willey & Co., 1891).

Petrie, William L., and Douglas E. Stover, *Bibliography of the Frederick Douglass Library at Cedar Hill* (Fort Washington, MD: Silesia Companies, 1995).

Pettinger, Alasdair, 'Send Back the Money: Douglass and the Free Church of Scotland', in Alan J. Rice and Martin Crawford (eds), *Liberating Sojourn: Frederick Douglass and Transatlantic Reform* (Athens: University of Georgia Press, 1999), pp. 31–55.

Pettinger, Alasdair, '"At Sea – Coloured Passenger"', in Bernhard Klein and Gesa Mackenthun (eds), *Sea Changes: Historicizing the Ocean* (New York: Routledge, 2004), pp. 149–66.

Pettinger, Alasdair, 'George Lewis and the American Churches', in Tim Youngs (ed.), *Travel Writing in the Nineteenth Century: Filling in the Blank Spaces* (London: Anthem, 2006), pp. 145–62.

Pettinger, Alasdair, '"The Greatest Genius That I Had Met in Europe": The Strange Case of Joseph Jenkins', in Sebastian Jobs and Gesa Mackenthun (eds), *Agents of Transculturation: Border-Crossers, Mediators, Go-Betweens* (Münster: Waxmann, 2013), pp. 139–55.

Phillippo, James M., *Jamaica: Its Past and Present State* (London: John Snow, 1843).

Pickering, Michael, 'White Skin, Black Masks: "Nigger" Minstrelsy in Victorian England', in J. S. Bratton (ed.), *Music Hall: Performance and Style* (Milton Keynes: Open University Press, 1986), pp. 70–91.

Pickering, Michael, *Blackface Minstrelsy in Britain* (Aldershot: Ashgate, 2008).

Pickering, Paul, and Alex Tyrrell, *The People's Bread: A History of the Anti-Corn Law League* (London: Leicester University Press, 2000).

Pittock, Murray, 'Slavery as a Political Metaphor in Scotland and Ireland in the Age of Burns', in Sharon Alker, Leith Davis and Holly Faith Nelson (eds), *Robert Burns and Transatlantic Culture* (Farnham: Ashgate, 2012), pp. 19–30.

Pope, Alexander, 'Peri Bathous, Or the Art of Sinking in Poetry' [1727], in Pat Rogers (ed.), *Alexander Pope* (Oxford: Oxford University Press, 1993), pp. 195–239.

Porter, Jane, *The Scottish Chiefs: A Romance* [1809] (New York: Derby and Jackson, 1856).

Postlethwaite, Diana, 'George Eliot and Science', in George Levine (ed.), *The Cambridge Companion to George Eliot* (Cambridge: Cambridge University Press, 2001), pp. 98–118.

Post-Office Edinburgh and Leith Directory 1846–7 (Edinburgh: Ballantyne and Hughes, 1846).

Post-Office Glasgow Annual Directory for 1841–42 (Glasgow: John Graham, 1841).

Powell, Richard J., *Cutting a Figure: Fashioning Black Portraiture* (Chicago: University of Chicago Press, 2008).

Preston, Dickson J., *Young Frederick Douglass: The Maryland Years* (Baltimore: Johns Hopkins University Press, 1980).

Proceedings of the General Anti-Slavery Convention [. . .] Held in London, 2 vols (London: British and Foreign Anti-Slavery Society, 1841).

Prochaska, Frank, *The Voluntary Impulse: Philanthropy in Modern Britain* (London: Faber and Faber, 1988).

Pryor, Elizabeth Stordeur, *Colored Travelers: Mobility and the Fight for Citizenship before the Civil War* (Chapel Hill: University of North Carolina Press, 2016).

Q.Q.Q. [Samuel Warren], 'Dickens's American Notes for General Circulation', *Blackwood's Edinburgh Magazine* (December 1842): 783–801.

Quarles, Benjamin, *Frederick Douglass* [1947] (New York: Da Capo Press, 1997).

Quinn, John F., 'Safe in Old Ireland': Frederick Douglass's Tour, 1845–1846', *The Historian* 64.3/4 (2002): 535–50.

Raboteau, Albert J., *Slave Religion: The 'Invisible Institution' in the Antebellum South* (New York: Oxford University Press, 1980).

Rainsford, Marcus, *An Historical Account of the Black Empire of Hayti* (London: James Cundee, 1805).

Ray, Celeste, *Highland Heritage: Scottish Americans in the American South* (Chapel Hill: University of North Carolina Press, 2001).

Redmond, Gerald, *The Caledonian Games in Nineteenth-Century America* (Rutherford, NJ: Fairleigh Dickinson University Press, 1971).

Rehin, George F., 'Harlequin Jim Crow: Continuity and Convergence in Blackface Clowning', *Journal of Popular Culture* 9.3 (1975): 682–701.

Rehin, George F., 'Blackface Street Minstrels in Victorian London and its Resorts: Popular Culture and its Racial Connotations as Revealed in Polite Opinion', *Journal of Popular Culture* 15.1 (1981): 19–38.

Report of the Proceedings at the Soiree given to Frederick Douglass, London Tavern, March 30, 1847 (London: R. Yorke Clarke & Co, 1847).

Rezek, Joseph, *London and the Making of Provincial Literature: Aesthetics and the Transatlantic Book Trade, 1800–1850* (Philadelphia: University of Pennsylvania Press, 2015).

Riach, Douglas C., 'Daniel O'Connell and American Anti-Slavery', *Irish Historical Studies* 20.77 (1976): 3–25.

Ribeiro, Aileen, *Dress and Morality* [1986] (Oxford: Berg, 2003).

Rice, Alan, *Radical Narratives of the Black Atlantic* (London: Continuum, 2003).

Rice, Alan, *Creating Memorials, Building Identities: The Politics of Memory in the Black Atlantic* (Liverpool: Liverpool University Press, 2010).

Rice, C. Duncan., 'Controversies over Slavery in Eighteenth- and Nineteenth-century Scotland', in Lewis Perry and Michael Fellman (eds), *Antislavery Reconsidered* (Baton Rouge: Louisiana State University Press, 1979), pp. 24–48.

Rice, C. Duncan, *The Scots Abolitionists, 1833–1861* (Baton Rouge: Louisiana State University Press, 1981).

Richards, Evelleen, 'The "Moral Anatomy" of Robert Knox: The Interplay between Biological and Social Thought in Victorian Scientific Naturalism', *Journal of the History of Biology* 22 (1989): 373–436.

Richardson, Alan (ed.), *Slavery, Abolition and Emancipation: Writings in the British Romantic Period, Volume 4: Verse* (London: Pickering & Chatto, 1999).

Rigney, Ann, *The Afterlives of Walter Scott: Memory on the* Move (Oxford: Oxford University Press, 2012).

Rogers, Nathaniel P., *A Collection from the Newspaper Writings of Nathaniel Peabody Rogers* (Concord, MA: John R. French, 1847).

Ross, Larry, 'European Lecture-Circuit (1845–47)', in Julius E. Thompson, James L. Conyers, Jr and Nancy J. Dawson (eds), *The Frederick Douglass Encyclopedia* (Santa Barbara: Greenwood Press, 2010), pp. 60–1.

Ross, Peter, *The Scot in America* (New York: Raeburn Book Company, 1896).

Rusert, Britt, *Fugitive Science: Empiricism and Freedom in Early African American Culture* (New York: New York University Press, 2017).

Salenius, Sirpa, *An Abolitionist Abroad: Sarah Parker Remond in Cosmopolitan Europe* (Amherst: University of Massachusetts Press, 2016).

Savitt, Todd L., *Medicine and Slavery: The Diseases and Health Care of Blacks in Antebellum Virginia* (Urbana: University of Illinois Press, 1978).

Saxon, A. H., *P. T. Barnum: The Legend and the Man* (New York: Columbia University Press, 1989).

Schermerhorn, Calvin, *The Business of Slavery and the Rise of American Capitalism, 1815–1860* (New Haven: Yale University Press, 2015).

Schermerhorn, Calvin, 'The Coastwise Slave Trade and a Mercantile Community of Interest', in Sven Beckert and Seth Rothman (eds), *Slavery's Capitalism: A New History of American Economic Development* (Philadelphia: University of Pennsylvania Press, 2016), pp. 209–24.

Schwarz, Suzanne, 'Scottish Surgeons in the Liverpool Slave Trade in the Late Eighteenth and Early Nineteenth Centuries', in T. M. Devine (ed.), *Recovering Scotland's Slavery Past: The Caribbean Connection* (Edinburgh: Edinburgh University Press, 2015), pp. 145–65.

Scott, Derek B., *The Singing Bourgeois: Songs of the Victorian Drawing Room and Parlour* (Aldershot: Ashgate, 2001).

Scott, Derek B., *Sounds of the Metropolis: The 19th Century Popular Music Revolution in London, New York, Paris and Vienna* (Oxford: Oxford University Press, 2008).

[Scott, Walter] (ed.), *Minstrelsy of the Scottish Border*, 2nd edn, 3 vols (Edinburgh: James Ballantyne, 1803).

Scott, Walter, *Waverley* [1814], ed. Andrew Hook (London: Penguin, 1972).

Scott, Walter, *Old Mortality* [1816], ed. Angus Calder (London: Penguin, 1975).

Scott, Walter, *The History of Scotland*, 2 vols (London: Longman, Rees, Orme, Brown, & Green, 1830).

Scott, Walter, *Tales of a Grandfather*, 6 vols (Edinburgh: Robert Cadell, 1836).

Scott, Walter, *The Journal of Sir Walter Scott*, 2 vols (New York: Harper & Brothers, 1891).

Scott, Walter, *The Poetical Works of Sir Walter Scott*, ed. J. Logie Robertson (London: Oxford University Press, 1904).

Secord, James A., *Victorian Sensation: The Extraordinary Publication, Reception, and Secret Authorship of Vestiges of the Natural History of Creation* (Chicago: University of Chicago Press, 2000).

Sennett, Richard, *The Fall of Public Man* (Cambridge: Cambridge University Press, 1977).

Sernett, Milton, *Black Religion and American Evangelicalism: White Protestants, Plantation Missions, and the Flowering of Negro Christianity, 1787–1865* (Methuchen, NJ: Scarecrow Press, 1975).

Severa, Joan L., *Dressed for the Photographer: Ordinary Americans and Fashion, 1840–1900* (Kent, OH: Kent State University Press, 1995).

Shell, Marc, *Children of the Earth: Literature, Politics and Nationhood* (New York: Oxford University Press, 1993).

Shepperson, George, 'The Free Church and American Slavery', *Scottish Historical Review* 30.110 (1951): 126–43.

Shepperson, George, 'Thomas Chalmers, the Free Church of Scotland, and the South', *Journal of Southern History* 17.4 (1951): 517–37.

Shepperson, George, 'Frederick Douglass and Scotland', *Journal of Negro History* 38.3 (July 1953): 307–21.

Sim, Duncan, *American Scots: The Scottish Diaspora and the USA* (Edinburgh: Dunedin, 2011).

Simmons, Charles A., *The African American Press: A History of News Coverage During National Crises, with Special Reference to Four Black Newspapers, 1827–1965* (Jefferson, NC: McFarland, 1998).

Sinha, Manisha, *The Slave's Cause: A History of Abolition* (New Haven: Yale University Press, 2016).

Sklar, Kathryn Kish, '"Women Who Speak for an Entire Nation": American and British Women at the World Anti-Slavery Convention, London, 1840', in Jean Fagan Yellin and John C. Van Horne (eds), *The Abolitionist Sisterhood: Women's Political Culture in Antebellum America* (Ithaca: Cornell University Press, 1994), pp. 301–32.

Smith, Hilrie Shelton, *In His Image, But . . .: Racism in Southern Religion, 1780–1910* (Durham, NC: Duke University Press, 1972).

Smith, James McCune, *The Works of James McCune Smith: Black Intellectual and Abolitionist*, ed. John Stauffer (New York: Oxford University Press, 2006).

Smyth, Thomas, *Autobiographical Notes, Letters and Reflections*, ed. Louisa Cleves Stoney (Charleston: Walker, Evans & Cogswell Co., 1914).

Stack, David, *Queen Victoria's Skull: George Combe and the Mid-Victorian Mind* (London: Continuum, 2008).

Stadler, Gustavus, *Troubling Minds: The Cultural Politics of Genius in the United States, 1840–1890* (Minneapolis: University of Minnesota Press, 2006).

Stanton, William Ragan, *The Leopard's Spots: Scientific Attitudes toward Race in America, 1815–59* (Chicago: University of Chicago Press, 1960).

Stauffer, John, 'Creating an Image in Black: The Power of Abolition Pictures', in W. Fitzhugh Brundage (ed.), *Beyond Blackface: African Americans and the Creation of American Popular Culture, 1890–1930* (Chapel Hill: University of North Carolina Press, 2011), pp. 66–94.

Stauffer, John, Zoë Trodd and Celeste-Marie Bernier, *Picturing Frederick Douglass: An Illustrated Biography of the Nineteenth-Century's Most Photographed American* (New York: Liveright, 2015).

Stern, Madeleine, *Heads and Headlines: The Phrenological Fowlers* (Norman: University of Oklahoma Press, 1971).

Stevenson, Sara, *Facing the Light: The Photography of Hill and Adamson* (Edinburgh: Scottish National Gallery, 2002).

Stocking, George W., Jr, *Victorian Anthropology* (New York: The Free Press, 1987).

Stoever, Jennifer Lynn, *The Sonic Color Line: Race and the Cultural Politics of Listening* (New York: New York University Press, 2016).

Stowe, Harriet Beecher, *Sunny Memories of Foreign Lands*, 2 vols (Boston: Phillips, Sampson & Co., 1854).

Stowe, Steven M., *Intimacy and Power in the Old South: Ritual in the Lives of Planters* (Baltimore: Johns Hopkins University Press, 1987).

Stowe, Steven M., 'Seeing Themselves at Work: Physicians and the Case Narrative in the Mid-Nineteenth Century American South', *American Historical Review* 101 (1996): 41–79.

Stowe, Steven M., *Doctoring the South: Southern Physicians and Everyday Medicine in the Mid-Nineteenth Century* (Chapel Hill: University of North Carolina Press, 2004).

Sundquist, Eric J. (ed.), *New Essays on Uncle Tom's Cabin* (Cambridge: Cambridge University Press, 1986).

Sweeney, Fionnghuala, *Frederick Douglass and the Atlantic World* (Liverpool: Liverpool University Press, 2007).

Sweeney, Fionnghuala, 'Other People's History: Slavery, Refuge and Irish Citizenship in Dónal O Kelly's *The Cambria*', *Slavery & Abolition* 29.2 (2008): 279–91.

Takanashi, Kyoko, 'Circulation, Monuments, and the Politics of Transmission in Sir Walter Scott's *Tales of My Landlord*', *ELH* 79.2 (Summer 2012): 289–314.

Tamagni, Daniele, *Gentlemen of Bacongo* (London: Trolley, 2009).

Tamarkin, Elisa, 'Black Anglophilia; or, the Sociability of Antislavery', *American Literary History* 14.3 (2002): 444–78.

Taylor, Yuval (ed.), *I Was Born a Slave: An Anthology of Classic Slave Narratives*, 2 vols (Edinburgh: Payback Press, 1999).

Temperley, Howard, *British Antislavery 1833–1870* (London: Longman, 1972).

Thompson, George A., Jr, *A Documentary History of the African Theatre* (Evanston: Northwestern University Press, 1998).

Thornton, Robert Donald, *James Currie: The Entire Stranger and Robert Burns* (Edinburgh: Oliver & Boyd, 1963).

Todd, Emily Bishop, 'The Transatlantic Context: Walter Scott and Nineteenth-Century American Literary History' (PhD diss., University of Minnesota, 1999).

Todd, Emily Bishop, 'Antebellum Libraries in Richmond and New Orleans and the Search for the Practices and Preferences of "Real" Readers', *American Studies* 42.3 (2001): 195–209.

Todd, Emily Bishop, 'Establishing Routes for Fiction in the United States: Walter Scott's Novels and the Early Nineteenth-century American Publishing Industry', *Book History* 12.1 (2009): 100–28.

Toll, Robert C., *Blacking Up: The Minstrel Show in Nineteenth-Century America* (New York: Oxford University Press, 1974).

Tomlinson, Stephen, *Head Masters: Phrenology, Secular Education, and Nineteenth-Century Social Thought* (Tuscaloosa: University of Alabama Press, 2005).

The Topographical, Statistical, and Historical Gazetteer of Scotland, 2 vols (Glasgow: A. Fullarton, 1843).

Torrance, David (ed.), *Great Scottish Speeches*, new edn (Edinburgh: Luath, 2011).

Tosh, John, 'Gentlemanly Politeness and Manly Simplicity in Victorian England', *Transactions of the Royal Historical Society* 12 (2002): 455–72.

Touchstone, Blake, 'Planters and Slave Religion in the Deep South', in John B. Boles (ed.), *Masters and Slaves in the House of the Lord: Race and Religion in the American South, 1740–1870* (Lexington: University Press of Kentucky, 1988), pp. 99–126.

Truth, Sojourner, *The Narrative of Sojourner Truth: A Bondswoman of Olden Time* (Boston: For the Author, 1875).

Twain, Mark, *Life on the Mississippi* (Boston: James B. Osgood, 1883).

Tyrrell, Alex, '"Woman's Mission" and Pressure Group Politics in Britain (1825–1860)', *Bulletin of the John Rylands Library* 63 (1980–81): 194–230.

Tyrrell, Alex, 'Paternalism, Public Memory and National Identity in Early Victorian Scotland: The Robert Burns Festival at Ayr in 1844', *History* 90.297 (January 2005): pp. 42–61.

Tytler, Graeme, *Physiognomy in the European Novel: Faces and Fortunes* (Princeton: Princeton University Press, 1982).

Van Wyhe, John, *Phrenology and the Origins of Victorian Scientific Naturalism* (Aldershot: Ashgate, 2004).

Walker, Alexander, *Intermarriage; or, The Mode in Which, and the Causes Why, Beauty, Health, and Intellect Result from Certain Unions, and Deformity, Disease and Insanity from Others* (London: Churchill, 1838).

[Warburton, George], *Hochelaga; or, England in the New World*, ed. Eliot Warburton, 2 vols (London: Henry Colburn, 1846).

Ward, Samuel Ringgold, *Autobiography of a Fugitive Negro* (London: John Snow, 1855).

Waters, Hazel, *Racism on the Victorian Stage: Representation of Slavery and the Black Character* (Cambridge: Cambridge University Press, 2007).

Waters, Mary C., *Ethnic Options: Choosing Identities in America* (Berkeley: University of California Press, 1990).

Watkins, James, *Struggles for Freedom; or The Life of James Watkins, Formerly a Slave in Maryland, US*, 19th edn (Manchester: James Watkins, 1860).

Watson, Hewett C., *Statistics of Phrenology: Being a Sketch of the Progress and Present State of that Science in the British Islands* (London: Longman, Rees, Orme, Brown, Green, and Longman, 1836).

Watson, Ritchie Devon, *Normans and Saxons: Southern Race Mythology and the Intellectual History of the American Civil War* (Baton Rouge: Louisiana State University Press, 2008).

Watson, Robert A., and Elizabeth S. Watson, *George Gilfillan: Letters and Journals, with Memoir* (London: Hodder and Stoughton, 1892).

Wechsler, Judith, *A Human Comedy: Physiognomy and Caricature in 19th-Century Paris* (London: Thames and Hudson, 1982).

Weidman, Bette S., 'The Pinto Letters of Charles Frederick Briggs', *Studies in the American Renaissance* (1979): 93–157.

Weiner, Marli F., with Mazie Hough, *Sex, Sickness and Slavery: Illness in the Antebellum South* (Urbana: University of Illinois Press, 2012).

Wells, Ida B., 'Newcastle Notes' [1894], in *Crusade for Justice: The Autobiography of Ida B. Wells*, ed. Alfreda M. Duster (Chicago: University of Chicago Press, 1970), pp. 161–9.

Welsh, Louise (ed.), *Yonder Awa: Poetry from the Empire Cafe* ([Glasgow]: Empire Cafe, 2014).

Westerbeck, Colin L., 'Frederick Douglass Chooses His Moment', *Art Institute of Chicago Museum Studies* 24.2 (1999): 144–61, 260–2.

Whatley, Christopher A., 'The Political and Cultural Legacy of Robert Burns in Scotland and Ulster, c.1796–1859', in John Kirk, Michael Brown and Andrew Noble (eds), *Cultures of Radicalism in Britain and Ireland* (London: Pickering and Chatto, 2013), pp. 79–84.

White, Charles, 'Negro Minstrelsy: Its Starting Place Traced Back over Sixty Years, Arranged and Compiled from the Best Authorities' [1860], in William L. Slout (ed.), *Burnt Cork and Tambourines: A Source Book of Negro Minstrelsy* (San Bernadino, CA: Borgo Press, 2007), pp. 193–8.

White, Shane, and Graham White, *Stylin': African American Expressive Culture, from Its Beginnings to the Zoot Suit* (Ithaca: Cornell University Press, 1998).

Whyte, Iain, *Scotland and the Abolition of Black Slavery, 1756–1838* (Edinburgh: Edinburgh University Press, 2006).

Whyte, Iain, *Zachary Macaulay 1768–1838: The Steadfast Scot in the British Anti-Slavery Movement* (Liverpool: Liverpool University Press, 2011).

Whyte, Iain, *'Send Back the Money!': The Free Church of Scotland and American Slavery* (Cambridge: James Clarke, 2012).

Williamson, Karina, 'The Antislavery Poems of John Marjoribanks', *EnterText* 7:1 (2007): 60–79.

Willox, John, *Guide to the Edinburgh and Glasgow Railway* (Edinburgh: John Johnstone and W. & A. K. Johnston, 1842).

Wilson, Alexander, *The Chartist Movement in Scotland* (Manchester: Manchester University Press, 1970).

Winter, Marian Hannah, 'Juba and American Minstrelsy' [1947], in Annemarie Bean, James V. Hatch and Brooks McNamara (eds), *Inside the Minstrel Mask: Readings in Nineteenth-Century Blackface Minstrelsy* (Middletown, CT: Wesleyan University Press, 1996), pp. 223–41.

Wood, Marcus, *Blind Memory: Visual Representations of Slavery in England and America, 1780–1865* (Manchester: Manchester University Press, 2000).

Wood, Marcus, 'Popular Graphic Images of Slavery and Emancipation in Nineteenth-century England', in Douglas Hamilton and Robert J. Blyth (eds), *Representing Slavery: Art, Artefacts and Archives in the Collections of the National Maritime Museum* (Aldershot: Lund Humphries, in association with the National Maritime Museum, 2007), pp. 136–52.

W.R.G. [William Rathbone Greg], 'Review of Benjamin D'Israeli, *Sybil*', *Westminster Review* (American edn) 53.76 (1845): 71–6.

Wright, Tom F., *Lecturing the Atlantic: Speech, Print, and an Anglo-American Commons 1830–1870* (New York: Oxford University Press, 2017).

Wyatt-Brown, Bertram, *Southern Honor: Ethics and Behavior in the Old South* (New York and Oxford: Oxford University Press, 1982).

Wyatt-Brown, Bertram, *The Shaping of Southern Culture: Honor, Grace, and War, 1760s–1880s* (Chapel Hill: University of North Carolina Press, 2001).

X, Malcolm, with the assistance of Alex Haley, *The Autobiography of Malcolm X* [1965] (London: Penguin, 1968).

Yellin, Jean Fagan, *Harriet Jacobs: A Life* (New York: Basic Civitas, 2004).

Young, Jeffrey Robert, *Domesticating Slavery: The Master Class in Georgia and South Carolina, 1670–1837* (Chapel Hill: University of North Carolina Press, 1999).

Young, Robert J. C., *Colonial Desire: Hybridity in Theory, Culture and Race* (London: Routledge, 1995).

Ysabeau, A., *Lavater et Gall: Physiognomie et phrénologie rendues intelligibles pour tout le monde* (Paris: Garnier, 1862).

Index

Page numbers in **bold** refer to illustrations